St. Agnes, Virgin and Martyr.

FABIOLA;

OR,

THE CHURCH OF THE CATACOMBS.

BY HIS EMINENCE CARDINAL WISEMAN.

A Historical Picture

OF THE

SUFFERINGS OF THE EARLY CHURCH

IN PAGAN ROME,

ILLUSTRATING THE

Glories of the Christian Martyrs

AS EXEMPLIFIED IN THE LIVES OF

The fair young Virgin, St. Agnes; the heroic Soldier, St. Sebastian;
the devoted Youth, St. Pancratius; etc., etc.

ILLUSTRATED EDITION.

WITH A PREFACE BY

REV. RICHARD BRENNAN, LL.D.,

Pastor of SS. Peter and Paul's Church, New York.

NEW YORK, CINCINNATI, AND ST. LOUIS:

BENZIGER BROTHERS,

PRINTERS TO THE HOLY APOSTOLIC SEE.

1886.

PREFACE

TO THE ILLUSTRATED EDITION.

THE late Cardinal Wiseman's admirable story, "Fabiola," has been read for the last thirty years in many lands and many tongues. At this late day, to say that it has been everywhere productive of inestimable good to Christian souls, would be the utterance of the merest truism. But while its salutary influence has been felt far and wide, it seems to have been fraught with special blessings most peculiarly adapted to the religious circumstances of our own land; where, thirty years ago, when the work made its first appearance among us, the condition of the Church was not altogether dissimilar from that of the early Church in pagan Rome at the date of the story.

Although the sun of divine faith had long before begun to warm with its vivifying and sanctifying rays the virgin soil of this western land of ours, yet it had hardly risen above the horizon when dark and threatening clouds of persecution seemed about to obscure its light, promising, instead of a bright and cheerful day for the Church, a night of disappointment and suffering. The good already accomplished by the early missionaries seemed imperilled by the coming storm, and the work at that time in progress was meeting with fierce and even cruel opposition. Then it was that men asked themselves, was it necessary that the founding of Christ's Church in America should undergo a process similar to that which it had undergone in pagan Rome. Although the Catholics of America thirty years ago had little cause to fear the torch or the axe of the executioner, though they could hardly hope for the blood-stained crown of martyrdom in the public arena, though they heard not the cry, "to the wild beasts with the Christians," yet they dwelt amid much religious privation, underwent keen mental persecution, and were made the victims of rampant bigotry, furious political partisanship, and humiliating social ostracism. Like the heroic characters so graphically portrayed by the Cardinal's graceful pen in the history of Fabiola, the Catholics in America professed a faith imperfectly known in the land, or known only to be despised and hated by the great majority of the American people, just as that self-same faith had been misrepresented, detested and persecuted in the early ages, by the misguided citizens of pagan Rome.

In such times, Catholics sorely needed the help of bright examples of courage, zeal and perseverance, to beckon them on in the steady pursuit of their arduous and sometimes perilous task of preserving, practising, and declaring their faith. Such examples they found in Cardinal Wiseman's beautiful work, models of fidelity to faith, heroes and heroines who in their patient lives and cruel deaths gave testimony unto Christ Jesus, producing such fruits of virtue, and showing forth so beautifully and so powerfully the effects of the true faith, that that faith itself finally triumphed over all opposition; and verifying the words of the Apostle, became a victory that conquered the world: "Hæc est victoria, quæ vincit mundum, fides nostra." "This is the victory which overcometh the world, our faith."

By the study of these models, as presented in the story of Fabiola, the struggling Catholics of this country learned how to possess their souls in patience. While admiring the heroic fortitude of those martyrs, though not presuming always to imitate their extraordinary ways, our predecessors in the faith felt themselves encouraged to follow in their footsteps, bearing patiently all religious privations and adhering to their faith amid hatred and contempt, and giving bold testimony of it before unbelieving men.

Inspired by the example of these primitive Christians, the priests and people alike of the past generation were strengthened in the conviction that in their poor despised Church, at that time remarkable for its poverty and obscurity, there dwelt the eternal truth brought down to earth from heaven by the Son of the living God, the truth which He had confirmed by miracles and sealed with His precious life's blood; the truth in whose defence millions of the holiest and greatest men sacrificed their very lives; the truth in whose possession the noblest and most enlightened among the children of Adam had found peace in life and consolation in death. For this truth, they were willing to die.

How opportune, at that time, was the appearance in our midst of a work from a master-hand, presenting to view in a most vivid and realistic light the trials and triumphs of those heroes in the Church who raised the cross of Christ, bedewed with martyr-blood, upon the dome of the Roman Capitol! Like the cheering flambeau borne in the hands of the acolyte of the Catacombs, the story of Fabiola served to brighten and cheer the arduous path of many a despised if not persecuted Catholic, amid the religious wilderness then to a great extent prevailing over our broad land.

But as the primitive Church emerged from her hiding-places, so, thank God, has that same Church in our own country bounded forth from obscurity and contempt into the broad light of day, where she stands confessed in all her truth and beauty, at once the envy and admiration of her recent opponents.

While to-day, protestantism is an enemy that no Catholic need fear, a new and more formidable foe confronts us in the shape of materialism. The contest between truth and error is as fierce as ever, though the tactics are changed. We should arm ourselves for the battle against materialism as our fathers did against protestantism. We can win no laurels in a war against protestantism, for it has been subdued by those ahead of us in the ranks. Such laurels have been gathered by earlier and worthier hands than ours. Nor are there places for us by the side of the martyrs Pancratius, Sebastian, and other heroes of primitive Christianity. Yet a great trust has descended to our hands, and sacred obligations have devolved on the present generation of Catholics. There remains to us a great duty of defence and preservation, and there lies open before us a grand and glorious pursuit to which the religious needs of the times loudly call us. We live in an age of sordid materialism, when it is of vital importance to turn the thoughts of all Christians to the really heroic ages of the Church, and to the lives of men and women who have done honor to principle, glorified God and benefited their fellow-beings by their holy and self-sacrificing lives.

As the story of Fabiola taught our immediate predecessors in the faith to admire and imitate the virtues of the primitive Christians, so should we learn to cherish the names and memories of the devoted ones who, amid hardships, privations and contempt, laid the solid foundations in this land, of that stately and magnificent structure beneath whose hallowed roof it is our happy lot to dwell unmolested in peace and prosperity.

Therefore we gladly welcome this first illustrated edition of Cardinal Wiseman's "Fabiola." Viewed in its improved mechanical aspect, it is emblematic of the wondrous development of our Catholic literature, and when contrasted with the simpler and humbler editions which we received thirty years ago, seems like the stately cathedral that has taken the place of the lowly wooden chapel of that period. Its many beautiful engravings will bring more vividly before the reader the scenes of cruel persecution already graphically described, and with its bright examples of constancy and self-sacrifice serve to stimulate and fortify Catholics of the present and future generations in their contest with worldliness, materialism, and, we may say, unmitigated paganism.

R. B.

St. Rose's Rectory, All Saints' Day, 1885.

PREFACE.

WHEN the plan of the *Popular Catholic Library* was formed, the author of the following little work was consulted upon it. He not only approved of the design, but ventured to suggest, among others, a series of tales illustrative of the condition of the Church in different periods of her past existence. One, for instance, might be called "The Church of the Catacombs;" a second, "The Church of the Basilicas;" each comprising three hundred years; a third would be on "The Church of the Cloister;" and then, perhaps, a fourth might be added, called "The Church of the Schools."

In proposing this sketch, he added,—perhaps the reader will find indiscreetly,—that he felt half inclined to undertake the first, by way of illustrating the proposed plan. He was taken at his word, and urged strongly to begin the work. After some reflection, he consented; but with an understanding, that it was not to be an occupation, but only the recreation of leisure hours. With this condition, the work was commenced early in this year; and it has been carried on entirely on that principle.

It has, therefore, been written at all sorts of times and in all sorts of places; early and late, when no duty urged, in scraps and fragments of time, when the body was too fatigued or the mind too worn for heavier occupation; in the road-side inn, in the halt of travel, in strange houses, in every variety of situation and circumstances—sometimes trying ones. It has thus been composed bit by bit, in portions varying from ten lines to half-a-dozen pages at most, and generally with few books or resources at hand. But once begun, it has proved what it was taken for,—a recreation, and often a solace and a sedative; from the memories it has revived, the associations it has renewed, the scattered and broken remnants of old studies and early readings which it has combined, and by the familiarity which it has cherished with better times and better things than surround us in our age.

Why need the reader be told all this? For two reasons:

First, this method of composition may possibly be reflected on the work; and he may find it patchy and ill-assorted, or not well connected in its parts. If so, this account will explain the cause.

Secondly, he will thus be led not to expect a treatise or a learned work even upon ecclesiastical antiquities. Nothing would have been easier than to cast an air of erudition over this little book, and fill half of each page with notes and references. But this was never the writer's idea. His desire was rather to make his reader familiar with the usages, habits, condition, ideas, feeling, and spirit of the early ages of Christianity. This required a certain acquaintance with places and objects connected with the period, and some familiarity, more habitual than learned, with the records of the time. For instance, such writings as the Acts of primitive Martyrs should have been frequently read, so as to leave impressions on the author's mind, rather than have been examined scientifically and critically for mere antiquarian purposes. And so, such places or monuments as have to be explained should seem to stand before the eye of the describer, from frequently and almost casually seeing them, rather than have to be drawn from books.

Another source of instruction has been freely used. Any one acquainted with the Roman Breviary must have observed, that in the offices of certain saints a peculiar style prevails, which presents the holy persons commemorated in a distinct and characteristic form. This is not the result so much of any continuous narrative, as of expressions put into their mouths, or brief descriptions of events in their lives, repeated often again and again, in antiphons, responsories to lessons, and even versicles; till they put before us an individuality, a portrait clear and definite of singular excellence. To this class belong the offices of SS. Agnes, Agatha, Cæcilia, and Lucia; and those of St. Clement and St. Martin. Each of these saints stands out before our minds with distinct features; almost as if we had seen and known them.

If, for instance, we take the first that we have named, we clearly draw out the following circumstances. She is evidently pursued by some heathen admirer, whose suit for her hand she repeatedly rejects. Sometimes she tells him that he is forestalled by another, to whom she is betrothed; sometimes she describes this object of her choice under various images, representing him even as the object of homage to sun and moon. On another occasion she describes the rich gifts, or the beautiful garlands with which he has adorned her, and the chaste caresses by which he has endeared himself to her. Then at last, as if more importunately pressed, she rejects the love of perishable man, "the food of death," and triumphantly proclaims herself the spouse of Christ. Threats are used; but she declares herself under the protection of an angel who will shield her.

This history is as plainly written by the fragments of her office, as a word is by scattered letters brought, and joined together. But throughout, one discerns another peculiarity, and a truly beautiful one in her character. It is clearly represented to us, that the saint had ever before her the unseen Object of her love, saw Him, heard Him, felt Him, and entertained, and had returned, a real affection, such as hearts on earth have for one another. She seems to walk in perpetual vision, almost in ecstatic fruition, of her Spouse's presence. He has actually put a ring upon her finger, has transferred the blood from His own cheek to hers, has crowned her with budding roses. Her eye is really upon him, with unerring gaze, and returned looks of gracious love.

What writer that introduced the person would venture to alter the character? Who would presume to attempt one at variance with it? Or who would hope to draw a portrait more life-like and more exquisite than the Church has done? For, putting aside all inquiry as to the genuineness of the acts by which those passages are suggested; and still more waving the question whether the hard critical spirit of a former age too lightly rejected such ecclesiastical documents, as Guéranger thinks; it is clear that the Church, in her office, intends to place before us a certain type of high virtue embodied in the character of that saint. The writer of the following pages considered himself therefore bound to adhere to this view.

Whether these objects have been attained, it is for the reader to judge. At any rate, even looking at the amount of information to be expected from a work in this form, and one intended for general reading, a comparison between the subjects introduced, either formally or casually, and those given in any elementary work, such as Fleury's *Manners of the Christians*, which embraces several centuries more, will show that as much positive knowledge on the practices and belief of that early period is here imparted, as it is usual to communicate in a more didactic form.

At the same time, the reader must remember that this book is not historical. It takes in but a period of a few months, extended in some concluding chapters. It consists rather of a series of pictures than of a narrative of events. Occurrences, therefore, of different epochs and different countries have been condensed into a small space. Chronology has been sacrificed to this purpose. The date of Diocletian's edict has been anticipated by two months; the martyrdom of St. Agnes by a year; the period of St. Sebastian, though uncertain, has been brought down later. All that relates to Christian topography has been kept as accurate as possible. A martyrdom has been transferred from Imola to Fondi.

It was necessary to introduce some view of the morals and opinions of the Pagan world, as a contrast to those of Christians. But their worst aspect has been carefully suppressed, as nothing could be admitted here which the most sensitive Catholic eye would shrink from contemplating. It is indeed earnestly desired that this little work, written solely for recreation, be read also as a relaxation from graver pursuits; but that, at the same time, the reader may rise from its perusal with a feeling that his time has not been lost, nor his mind occupied with frivolous ideas. Rather let it be hoped, that some admiration and love may be inspired by it of those primitive times, which an over-excited interest in later and more brilliant epochs of the Church is too apt to diminish or obscure.

The Bark of Peter, as found in the Catacombs.

CONTENTS.

Preface to the Illustrated Edition	iii
Author's Preface	vii
List of Illustrations	xiii

PART I.

Peace.

CHAP.	
I. The Christian House	19
II. The Martyr's Boy	26
III. The Dedication	32
IV. The Heathen Household	42
V. The Visit	56
VI. The Banquet	64
VII. Poor and Rich	72
VIII. The First Day's Conclusion	82
IX. Meetings	88
X. Other Meetings	100
XI. A Talk with the Reader	110
XII. The Wolf and the Fox	129
XIII. Charity	135
XIV. Extremes Meet	139
XV. Charity Returns	140
XVI. The Month of October	154
XVII. The Christian Community	170
XVIII. Temptation	183
XIX. The Fall	190

PART II.

Conflict.

I. Diogenes	205
II. The Cemeteries	219
III. What Diogenes could not tell about the Catacombs	239

		PAGE
IV.	What Diogenes did tell about the Catacombs	248
V.	Above Ground	261
VI.	Deliberations	265
VII.	Dark Death	275
VIII.	Darker Still	280
IX.	The False Brother	285
X.	The Ordination in December	291
XI.	The Virgins	300
XII.	The Nomentan Villa	308
XIII.	The Envoy	315
XIV.	The Discovery	325
XV.	Explanations	330
XVI.	The Wolf in the Fold	335
XVII.	The First Flower	356
XVIII.	Retribution	368
XIX.	Twofold Revenge	381
XX.	The Public Works	390
XXI.	The Prison	396
XXII.	The Viaticum	403
XXIII.	The Fight	419
XXIV.	The Christian Soldier	431
XXV.	The Rescue	437
XXVI.	The Revival	448
XXVII.	The Second Crown	457
XXVIII.	The Critical Day: its First Part	464
XXIX.	The same Day: its Second Part	473
XXX.	The same Day: its Third Part	491
XXXI.	Dionysius, Priest and Physician	507
XXXII.	The Sacrifice Accepted	513
XXXIII.	Miriam's History	523
XXXIV.	Bright Death	532

PART III

Victory.

I.	The Stranger from the East	549
II.	The Stranger in Rome	556
III.	And Last	564

LIST OF ILLUSTRATIONS.

FULL-PAGE ILLUSTRATIONS.

CHROMOLITHOGRAPH OF ST. AGNES, VIRGIN AND MARTYR.   FRONTISPIECE.

FROM ORIGINAL DRAWINGS BY VAN DARGENT.

	PAGE
ORDINATION, IN THE EARLY AGES OF THE CHURCH	33
THE SACRAMENT OF PENANCE, IN THE EARLY AGES OF THE CHURCH	125
THE BLESSED EUCHARIST, IN THE EARLY AGES OF THE CHURCH	237
CONFIRMATION, IN THE EARLY AGES OF THE CHURCH	343
BAPTISM, IN THE EARLY AGES OF THE CHURCH	339
ADMINISTERING THE SACRAMENT OF EXTREME UNCTION, IN THE EARLY AGES OF THE CHURCH	545
A MARRIAGE, IN THE EARLY AGES OF THE CHURCH	553

FROM ORIGINAL DRAWINGS BY JOSEPH BLANC.

"WITH TREMBLING HANDS SHE DREW FROM HER NECK THE GOLDEN CHAIN"	29
"FABIOLA GRASPED THE STYLE IN HER RIGHT HAND, AND MADE AN ALMOST BLIND THRUST AT THE UNFLINCHING HANDMAID"	51
"HE WHO WATCHED WITH BEAMING EYE THE ALMS-COFFERS OF JERUSALEM, AND NOTED THE WIDOW'S MITE, ALONE SAW DROPPED INTO THE CHEST, BY THE BANDAGED ARM OF A FOREIGN FEMALE SLAVE, A VALUABLE EMERALD RING"	55
"'HARK!' SAID PANCRATIUS, 'THESE ARE THE TRUMPET-NOTES THAT SUMMON US'"	95
"'HERE IT GOES!' AND HE THRUST IT INTO THE BLAZING PYRE"	331
"'IS IT POSSIBLE?' SHE EXCLAIMED WITH HORROR, 'IS THAT TARCISIUS WHOM I MET A FEW MOMENTS AGO, SO FAIR AND LOVELY?'"	439

"EACH ONE, APPROACHING DEVOUTLY, AND WITH TEARS OF GRATITUDE,
RECEIVED FROM HIS CONSECRATED HAND HIS SHARE—THAT IS, THE
WHOLE OF THE MYSTICAL FOOD" 415
"PANCRATIUS WAS STILL STANDING IN THE SAME PLACE, FACING THE
EMPEROR, APPARENTLY SO ABSORBED IN HIGHER THOUGHTS AS NOT
TO HEED THE MOVEMENTS OF HIS ENEMY" 437
"THE JUDGE ANGRILY REPROVED THE EXECUTIONER FOR HIS HESITA-
TION, AND BID HIM AT ONCE DO HIS DUTY" 461
"FABIOLA WENT DOWN HERSELF, WITH A FEW SERVANTS, AND WHAT WAS
HER DISTRESS AT FINDING POOR EMERENTIANA LYING WELTERING IN
HER BLOOD, AND PERFECTLY DEAD" 525

THE RUINS OF THE COLISEUM, AS SEEN FROM THE PALATINE OF ST.
   BONAVENTURE 89
ST. LAWRENCE DISPLAYING HIS TREASURES 151
INTERIOR OF THE TEMPLE OF JUPITER 163
THE RUINS OF THE ROMAN FORUM, AS THEY ARE TO-DAY . . 190
THE MARTYR'S WIDOW 215
THE TOMB OF ST. CECILIA 227
A COLUMBARIUM, OR UNDERGROUND SEPULCHRE, IN WHICH THE ROMANS
   DEPOSITED THE URNS CONTAINING THE ASHES OF THE DEAD . 233
THE CLAUDIAN AQUEDUCT 267
INSTRUMENTS OF TORTURE USED AGAINST THE CHRISTIANS, FROM BOLLEY'S
   "CATACOMBES DE ROME" 287
AN ATTACK IN THE CATACOMBS 349
THE MARTYR CECILIA 363
THE MARTYR'S BURIAL 377
THE NORTH-WEST SIDE OF THE FORUM 453
THE CHRISTIAN MARTYR 485

ILLUSTRATIONS IN THE TEXT.

EXCLUSIVE OF ORNAMENTAL INITIALS.

THE BARK OF PETER, AS FOUND IN THE CATACOMBS 12
INTERIOR OF A ROMAN DWELLING AT POMPEII 19
PLAN OF PANSA'S HOUSE AT POMPEII 20
DOOR OF PANSA'S HOUSE, WITH THE GREETING SALVE OR WELCOME 22

	Page
ATRIUM OF A POMPEIAN HOUSE	21
ATRIUM OF A HOUSE IN POMPEII	23
CLEPSYDRA, OR WATER-CLOCK, FROM A BAS-RELIEF IN THE MATTEI PALACE, ROME	30
A PORTRAIT OF CHRIST, FROM THE CATACOMB OF ST. PONTIANUS	35
A PIECE OF A "GOLD GLASS" FOUND IN THE CATACOMBS	41
POMPEIAN COUCH	44
TABLE, AFTER A PAINTING IN HERCULANEUM	44
COUCH FROM HERCULANEUM	45
ELEGANT SEAT FROM HERCULANEUM	46
A SEAT, FROM A PAINTING IN HERCULANEUM	46
A LAMP FOUND IN THE CATACOMBS	51
SAINT AGNES, FROM AN OLD VASE	53
SAINT AGNES, FROM AN OLD VASE PRESERVED IN THE VATICAN MUSEUM	54
BANQUET TABLE, FROM A POMPEIAN PAINTING	67
DAVID WITH HIS SLING, FROM THE CATACOMB OF ST. PETRONILLA	71
A DOVE, AS A SYMBOL OF THE SOUL, FOUND IN THE CATACOMBS	81
VOLUMNA, FROM A PAINTING OF POMPEII	84
SCRIPTOR, FROM A PICTURE IN THE CEMETERY OF ST. CALLISTUS	84
OUR SAVIOUR, FROM A REPRESENTATION FOUND IN THE CATACOMBS	87
META SUDANS, AFTER A BRONZE OF VESPASIAN	91
THE ARCH OF TITUS	96
THE APPIAN WAY, AS IT WAS	102
EMBLEMATIC REPRESENTATION OF PARADISE, FOUND IN THE CATACOMBS	105
SAINT SEBASTIAN, FROM THE "ROMA SOTTERANEA" OF DE ROSSI	107
MILITARY TRIBUNES, AFTER A BAS-RELIEF ON TRAJAN'S COLUMN	109
THE ROMAN FORUM	114
A LAMB WITH A MILK CAN, FOUND IN THE CATACOMB OF SS. PETER AND MARCELLUS	118
ST. IGNATIUS, BISHOP OF ANTIOCH	122
MONOGRAMS OF CHRIST, FOUND IN THE CATACOMBS, 126, 159, 264, 274, 275, 276, 294, 395, 436, 472.	
ROMAN GARDENS, FROM AN OLD PAINTING	130
A LAMP, WITH THE MONOGRAM OF CHRIST	134
A DRAGON, FROM DE ROSSI'S "ROMA SOTTERANEA"	137
A FISH CARRYING BREAD AND WINE, FROM THE CEMETERY OF ST. LUCINA	138
A WALL PAINTING, FROM THE CEMETERY OF ST. PRISCILLA	140

	PAGE
CHRIST IN THE MIDST OF HIS APOSTLES, FROM A PAINTING IN THE CATACOMBS	182
INTERIOR OF A ROMAN THEATRE	183
HALLS IN THE BATHS OF CARACALLA	186
THE PEACOCK, AS AN EMBLEM OF THE RESURRECTION	189
A DOVE, AS AN EMBLEM OF THE SOUL	203
DIOGENES, THE EXCAVATOR, FROM A PAINTING IN THE CEMETERY OF DOMITILLA	205
JONAS, AFTER A PAINTING IN THE CEMETERY OF CALLISTUS	206
LAZARUS RAISED FROM THE DEAD	207
TWO FOSSORES, OR EXCAVATORS, FROM A PICTURE AT THE CEMETERY OF CALLISTUS	208
A GALLERY IN THE CEMETERY OF ST. AGNES, ON THE NOMENTAN WAY	211
INSCRIPTION OF THE CEMETERY OF ST. AGNES	212
AN ARCOSOLIUM	213
OUR SAVIOUR BLESSING THE BREAD, FROM A PICTURE IN THE CATACOMBS	218
A STAIRCASE IN THE CATACOMBS	220
A CHAPEL OF THE BLESSED SACRAMENT	224
UNDERGROUND GALLERY IN THE CATACOMBS, FROM TH. ROLLER'S "CATACOMBES DE ROME"	225
A LOCULUS, CLOSED	231
" " OPEN	235
A LAMB WITH A MILK PAIL, EMBLEMATIC OF THE BLESSED EUCHARIST, FOUND IN THE CATACOMBS	238
ST. CORNELIUS AND ST. CYPRIAN, FROM DE ROSSI'S "ROMA SOTTERANEA"	244
THE TOMB OF CORNELIUS	247
A LAMP WITH A REPRESENTATION OF THE GOOD SHEPHERD, FOUND AT OSTIUM, PRIOR TO THE THIRD CENTURY, FROM ROLLER'S "CATACOMBES"	249
CUBICULUM, OR CRYPT, AS FOUND IN THE CATACOMBS	250
THE LAST SUPPER, FROM A PAINTING IN THE CEMETERY OF ST. CALLISTUS	251
A CEILING IN THE CATACOMBS, FROM DE ROSSI'S "ROMA SOTTERANEA"	252
OUR LORD UNDER THE SYMBOL OF ORPHEUS, FROM A PICTURE IN THE CEMETERY OF DOMITILLA	253
THE GOOD SHEPHERD, A WOMAN PRAYING, FROM THE ARCOSOLIUM OF THE CEMETERY OF SS. NEREUS AND ACHILLEUS	254
A CEILING IN THE CATACOMBS, IN THE CEMETERY OF DOMITILLA, THIRD CENTURY	255

	PAGE
THE FISHES AND ANCHOR, THE FISHES AND DOVES	256
THE BLESSED VIRGIN AND THE MAGI, FROM A PICTURE IN THE CEMETERY OF CALLISTUS	258
MOSES STRIKING THE ROCK, FROM THE CEMETERY OF "INTER DUOS LAUROS"	260
MAXIMILIAN HERCULEUS, FROM A BRONZE MEDAL IN THE COLLECTION OF FRANCE	266
THE PEACOCK, AS AN EMBLEM OF THE RESURRECTION, FOUND IN THE CATACOMBS	284
CHRIST AND HIS APOSTLES, FROM A PICTURE IN THE CATACOMBS	290
ST. PUDENTIANA, ST. PRISCILLA, AND ST. PRAXEDES	292
OUR SAVIOUR REPRESENTED AS THE GOOD SHEPHERD, WITH A MILK CAN AT HIS SIDE, AS FOUND IN THE CATACOMBS	299
CHAIR OF ST. PETER	304
THE ANCHOR AND FISHES, AN EMBLEM OF CHRISTIANITY, FOUND IN THE CATACOMBS	307
"HAUGHTY ROMAN DAME! THOU SHALT BITTERLY RUE THIS DAY AND HOUR"	312
A LAMB BETWEEN WOLVES, EMBLEMATIC OF THE CHURCH, FROM A PICTURE IN THE CEMETERY OF ST. PRÆTEXTATUS	324
AN EMBLEM OF PARADISE, FOUND IN THE CATACOMBS	329
RUINS OF THE BASILICA OF ST. ALEXANDER, ON THE NOMENTAN WAY, FROM BOLLER'S "CATACOMBES DE ROME"	342
PLAN OF SUBTERRANEAN CHURCH, IN THE CEMETERY OF ST. AGNES	345
A CATHEDRA, OR EPISCOPAL CHAIR, IN CATACOMB OF ST. AGNES	346
AN ALTAR WITH ITS EPISCOPAL CHAIR, IN THE CEMETERY OF ST. AGNES	348
AN ALTAR IN THE CEMETERY OF ST. SIXTUS	352
THE CURE OF THE MAN BORN BLIND, FROM A PICTURE IN THE CATACOMBS	355
THE WOMAN OF SAMARIA, FROM A PICTURE IN THE CEMETERY OF ST. DOMITILLA	367
JESUS CURES THE BLIND MAN, FROM A PICTURE IN THE CEMETERY OF ST. DOMITILLA	380
THE ANCHOR AND FISH, EMBLEMATIC OF CHRISTIANITY, FOUND IN THE CATACOMBS	388
THE MAMERTINE PRISON	398
THE BLESSED VIRGIN, FROM A PORTRAIT FOUND IN THE CEMETERY OF ST. AGNES	402
THE COLISEUM	420

	PAGE
A Lamp bearing a Monogram of Christ, found in the Catacombs	436
Elias carried to Heaven, from a Picture found in the Catacombs	447
Moses receiving the Law, from a Picture in the Cemetery of "Inter Duos Lauros"	454
Christ Blessing a Child, from a Picture in the Cemetery of the Latin Way	463
Chairs for the Martyrs, after a Picture found in 1841, in a Crypt at Milan	480
A Blood Urn, used as a Mark for a Martyr's Grave	489
The Resurrection of Lazarus, from the Cemetery of St. Domitilla	490
Cemetery of Callistus	508
Ordination, from a Picture in the Catacombs	531
Portrait of Our Saviour, from the Catacomb of St. Callistus	548
Constantine, the First Christian Emperor, after a Medal of the Time	549
Diocletian, after a Medal in the Cabinet of France	550
Licinius, Maxentius, Galerius-Maximinus, from Gold and Silver Medals in the French Collection	550
The Labarum, or Christian Standard, from a Coin of Constantine	552
Noe and the Ark, as a Symbol of the Church, from a Picture in the Catacombs	557
The Sacrifice of Abraham, from a Picture in the Catacombs	563

Interior of a Roman dwelling at Pompeii.

Part First.—Peace.

CHAPTER I.

THE CHRISTIAN HOUSE.

IT is on an afternoon in September of the year 302, that we invite our reader to accompany us through the streets of Rome. The sun has declined, and is about two hours from his setting; the day is cloudless, and its heat has cooled, so that multitudes are issuing from their houses, and making their way towards Cæsar's gardens on one side, or Sallust's on the other, to enjoy their evening walk, and learn the news of the day.

But the part of the city to which we wish to conduct our friendly reader is that known by the name of the Campus Martius. It comprised the flat alluvial plain between the seven hills of older Rome and the Tiber. Before the close of the republican period, this field, once left bare for the athletic and war-

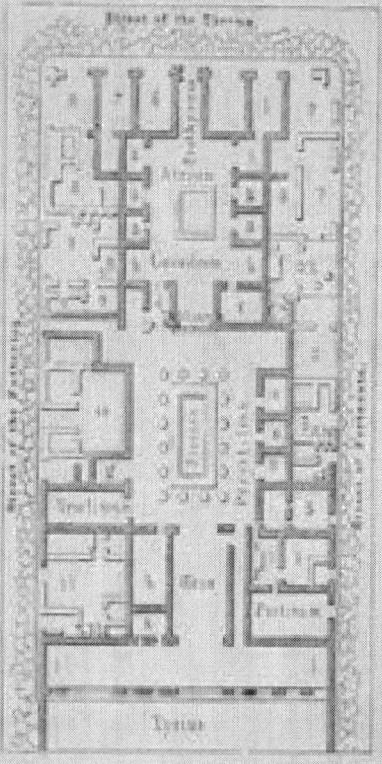

Plan of Pansa's house, at Pompeii.

like exercises of the people, had begun to be encroached upon by public buildings. Pompey had erected in it his theatre; soon after, Agrippa raised the Pantheon and its adjoining baths. But gradually it became occupied by private dwellings; while the hills, in the early empire the aristocratic portion of the city, were seized upon for greater edifices. Thus the Palatine, after Nero's fire, became almost too small for the Imperial residence and its adjoining Circus Maximus. The Esquiline was usurped by Titus's baths, built on the ruins of the Golden House, the Aventine by Caracalla's; and at the period of which we write, the Emperor Diocletian was covering the space sufficient for many lordly dwellings by the erection of his Thermæ* on the Quirinal, not far from Sallust's garden, just alluded to.

The particular spot in the Campus Martius to which we will direct our steps, is one whose situation is so definite, that we can accurately describe it to any one acquainted with the topography of ancient or modern Rome. In republican times there was a large square space in the Campus Martius, surrounded by hoarding, and divided into pens, in which the *Comitia*, or meetings of the tribes of the people, were held, for giving their votes. This was called the *Septa*, or *Ovile*, from its resemblance to a sheepfold. Augustus carried out a plan, described by Cicero in a letter to Atticus,† of transforming this homely contrivance into a magnificent and solid structure. The *Septa Julia*, as it was thenceforth called, was a splendid portico of 1000 by 500 feet, supported by columns, and adorned with paintings. Its ruins are clearly traceable; and it occupied the space now covered by the Doria and Verospi palaces (running thus along the present Corso), the Roman College, the Church of St. Ignatius, and the Oratory of the Caravita.

The house to which we invite our reader is exactly opposite, and on the east side of this edifice, including in its area the present church of St. Marcellus, whence it extended back towards the foot of the Quirinal hill. It is thus found to cover, as noble Roman houses did, a considerable extent of ground. From the outside it presents but a blank and dead appear-

* Hot-baths.   † Lib. iv. ep. 16.

ance. The walls are plain, without architectural ornament, not high, and scarcely broken by windows. In the middle of one side of this quadrangle is a door, *in ostio*, that is, merely relieved by a tympanum or triangular cornice, resting on two half columns. Using our privilege as "artists of fiction," of invisible ubiquity, we will enter in with our friend, or "shadow," as he would have been anciently called. Passing through the porch, on the pavement of which we read with pleasure, in mosaic, the greeting SALVE, or WELCOME, we find ourselves in the *atrium*, or first court of the house, surrounded by a portico or colonnade.*

Door of Pansa's house, with the greeting SALVE or WELCOME.

In the centre of the marble pavement a softly warbling jet of pure water, brought by the Claudian aqueduct from the Tusculan hills, springs into the air, now higher, now lower, and falls into an elevated basin of red marble, over the sides of which it flows in downy waves; and before reaching its lower and wider recipient, scatters a gentle shower on the rare and brilliant flowers placed in elegant vases around. Under the portico we see furniture disposed, of a rich and sometimes rare character; couches inlaid with ivory, and even silver; tables of oriental woods, bearing candelabra, lamps, and other household implements of bronze or silver; delicately chased busts, vases, tripods, and objects of mere art. On the walls are paintings evidently of a former period, still, however, retaining all their brightness of color and freshness of execution. These are separated by niches with stat-

* The Pompeian Court in the Crystal Palace, London, will have familiarized many readers with the forms of an ancient house.

nes, representing indeed, like the pictures, mythological or historical subjects; but we cannot help observing that nothing meets the eye which could offend the most delicate mind. Here and there an empty niche, or a covered painting, proves that this is not the result of accident.

Atrium of a Pompeian house.

As outside the columns, the coving roof leaves a large square opening in its centre, called the *impluvium*, there is drawn across it a curtain, or veil of dark canvas, which keeps out the sun and rain. An artificial twilight therefore alone

Atrium of a house in Pompeii.

enables us to see all that we have described; but it gives greater effect to what is beyond. Through an arch, opposite to the one whereby we have entered, we catch a glimpse of an inner and still richer court, paved with variegated marbles, and adorned with bright gilding. The veil of the opening above, which, however, here is closed with thick glass or talc (*lapis specularis*), has been partly withdrawn, and admits a bright but softened ray from the evening sun on to the place, where we see, for the first time, that we are in no enchanted hall, but in an inhabited house.

Beside a table, just outside the columns of Phrygian marble, sits a matron not beyond the middle of life, whose features, noble yet mild, show traces of having passed through sorrow at some earlier period. But a powerful influence has subdued the recollection of it, or blended it with a sweeter thought; and the two always come together, and have long dwelt united in her heart. The simplicity of her appearance strangely contrasts with the richness of all around her; her hair, streaked with silver, is left uncovered, and unconcealed by any artifice; her robes are of the plainest color and texture, without embroidery, except the purple ribbon sewed on, and called the *segmentum*, which denotes the state of widowhood; and not a jewel or precious ornament, of which the Roman ladies were so lavish, is to be seen upon her person. The only thing approaching to this is a slight gold cord or chain round her neck, from which apparently hangs some object, carefully concealed within the upper hem of her dress.

At the time that we discover her she is busily engaged over a piece of work, which evidently has no personal use. Upon a long rich strip of gold cloth she is embroidering with still richer gold thread; and occasionally she has recourse to one or another of several elegant caskets upon the table, from which she takes out a pearl, or a gem set in gold, and introduces it into the design. It looks as if the precious ornaments of earlier days were being devoted to some higher purpose.

But as time goes on, some little uneasiness may be observed to come over her calm thoughts, hitherto absorbed, to all appearance, in her work. She now occasionally raises her eyes from it towards the entrance; sometimes she listens for footsteps, and seems disappointed. She looks up towards the sun; then perhaps turns her glance towards a *clepsydra* or water-clock, on a bracket near her, but just as a feeling of more serious anxiety begins to
make an impression on her countenance, a cheerful rap strikes the house-door, and she bends forward with a radiant look to meet the welcome visitor.

A Portrait of Christ, from the Catacomb of St. Pontianus.

CHAPTER II.

THE MARTYR'S BOY.

IT is a youth full of grace, and sprightliness, and candor, that comes forward with light and buoyant steps across the atrium, towards the inner-hall; and we shall hardly find time to sketch him before he reaches it. He is about fourteen years old, but tall for that age, with elegance of form and manliness of bearing. His bare neck and limbs are well developed by healthy exercise; his features display an open and warm heart, while his lofty forehead, round which his brown hair naturally curls, beams with a bright intelligence. He wears the usual youth's garment, the short *prætexta*, reaching below the knee, and a golden *bulla*, or hollow spheroid of gold suspended round his neck. A bundle of papers and vellum rolls fastened together, and carried by an old servant behind him, shows us that he is just returning home from school.*

While we have been thus noting him, he has received his mother's embrace, and has sat himself low by her feet. She gazes upon him for some time in silence, as if to discover in his countenance the cause of his unusual delay, for he is an hour late in his return. But he meets her glance with so

---

* This custom suggests to St. Augustine the beautiful idea, that the Jews were the *pedagogi* of Christianity,—carrying for it the books which they themselves could not understand.

frank a look, and with such a smile of innocence, that every cloud of doubt is in a moment dispelled, and she addresses him as follows:

"What has detained you to-day, my dearest boy? No accident, I trust, has happened to you on the way?"

"Oh, none, I assure you, sweetest* mother; on the contrary, all has been delightful,—so much so, that I can scarcely venture to tell you."

A look of smiling expostulation drew from the openhearted boy a delicious laugh, as he continued:

"Well, I suppose I must. You know I am never happy, and cannot sleep, if I have failed to tell you all the bad and the good of the day about myself." (The mother smiled again, wondering what the bad was.) "I was reading the other day that the Scythians each evening cast into an urn a white or a black stone, according as the day had been happy or unhappy; if I had to do so, it would serve to mark, in white or black, the days on which I have, or have not, an opportunity of relating to you all that I have done. But to-day, for the first time, I have a doubt, a fear of conscience, whether I ought to tell you all."

Did the mother's heart flutter more than usual, as from a first anxiety, or was there a softer solicitude dimming her eye, that the youth should seize her hand and put it tenderly to his lips, while he thus replied?

"Fear nothing, mother most beloved, your son has done nothing that may give you pain. Only say, do you wish to hear all that has befallen me to-day, or only the cause of my late return home?"

"Tell me all, dear Pancratius," she answered; "nothing that concerns you can be indifferent to me."

"Well, then," he began, "this last day of my frequenting school appears to me to have been singularly blessed, and yet

* The peculiar epithet of the Catacombs.

full of strange occurrences. First, I was crowned as the successful competitor in a declamation, which our good master Cassianus set us for our work during the morning hours; and this led, as you will hear, to some singular discoveries. The subject was, 'That the real philosopher should be ever ready to die for truth.' I never heard anything so cold or insipid (I hope it is not wrong to say so) as the compositions read by my companions. It was not their fault, poor fellows! what truth can they possess, and what inducements can they have, to die for any of their vain opinions? But to a Christian, what charming suggestions such a theme naturally makes! And so I felt it. My heart glowed, and all my thoughts seemed to burn, as I wrote my essay, full of the lessons you have taught me, and of the domestic examples that are before me. The son of a martyr could not feel otherwise. But when my turn came to read my declamation, I found that my feelings had nearly fatally betrayed me. In the warmth of my recitation the word 'Christian' escaped my lips instead of 'philosopher,' and 'faith' instead of 'truth.' At the first mistake I saw Cassianus start; at the second, I saw a tear glisten in his eye, as bending affectionately towards me, he said, in a whisper, 'Beware, my child; there are sharp ears listening.'"

"What, then," interrupted the mother, "is Cassianus a Christian? I chose his school for you because it was in the highest repute for learning and for morality; and now indeed I thank God that I did so. But in these days of danger and apprehension we are obliged to live as strangers in our own land, scarcely knowing the faces of our brethren. Certainly, had Cassianus proclaimed his faith, his school would soon have been deserted. But go on, my dear boy. Were his apprehensions well grounded?"

"I fear so; for while the great body of my school-fellows, not noticing these slips, vehemently applauded my hearty declamation, I saw the dark eyes of Corvinus bent scowlingly upon me, as he bit his lip in manifest anger."

"And who is he, my child, that was so displeased, and wherefore?"

"He is the oldest and strongest, but, unfortunately, the dullest boy in the school. But this, you know, is not his fault. Only, I know not why, he seems ever to have had an ill-will and grudge against me, the cause of which I cannot understand."

"Did he say aught to you, or do?"

"Yes, and was the cause of my delay. For when we went forth from school into the field by the river, he addressed me insultingly in the presence of our companions, and said, 'Come, Pancratius, this, I understand, is the last time we meet here' (he laid a particular emphasis on the word); 'but I have a long score to demand payment of from you. You have loved to show your superiority in school over me and others older and better than yourself; I saw your supercilious looks at me as you spouted your high-flown declamation to-day; ay, and I caught expressions in it which you may live to rue, and that very soon; for my father, you well know, is Prefect of the city' (the mother slightly started); 'and something is preparing which may nearly concern you. Before you leave us I must have my revenge. If you are worthy of your name, and it be not an empty word,* let us fairly contend in more manly strife than that of the style and tables.† Wrestle with me, or try the cestus‡ against me. I burn to humble you as you deserve, before these witnesses of your insolent triumphs.'"

* The pancratium was the exercise which combined all other personal contests,—wrestling, boxing, etc.

† The implements of writing in schools, the tablets being covered with wax, on which the letters were traced by the sharp point, and effaced by the flat top, of the style.

‡ The hand-bandages worn in pugilistic combats.

The anxious mother bent eagerly forward as she listened, and scarcely breathed. "And what," she exclaimed, "did you answer, my dear son?"

"I told him gently that he was quite mistaken; for never had I consciously done anything that could give pain to him or any of my school-fellows; nor did I ever dream of claiming superiority over them. 'And as to what you propose,' I added, 'you know, Corvinus, that I have always refused to indulge in personal combats, which, beginning in a cool trial of skill, end in an angry strife, hatred, and wish for revenge. How much less could I think of entering on them now, when you avow that you are anxious to begin them with those evil feelings which are usually their bad end?' Our school-mates had now formed a circle round us; and I clearly saw that they were all against me, for they had hoped to enjoy some of the delights of their cruel games; I therefore cheerfully added, 'And now, my comrades, good-bye, and may all happiness attend you. I part from you, as I have lived with you, in peace.' 'Not so,' replied Corvinus, now purple in the face with fury; 'but'"—

The boy's countenance became crimsoned, his voice quivered, his body trembled, and, half choked, he sobbed out, "I cannot go on; I dare not tell the rest!"

"I entreat you, for God's sake, and for the love you bear your father's memory," said the mother, placing her hand upon her son's head, "conceal nothing from me. I shall never again have rest if you tell me not all. What further said or did Corvinus?"

The boy recovered himself by a moment's pause and a silent prayer, and then proceeded:

"'Not so!' exclaimed Corvinus, 'not so do you depart, cowardly worshipper of an ass's head!'* You have concealed your abode from us, but I will find you out; till then bear

* One of the many calumnies popular among the heathens.

this token of my determined purpose to be revenged!' So saying he dealt me a furious blow upon the face, which made me reel and stagger, while a shout of savage delight broke forth from the boys around us."

He burst into tears, which relieved him, and then went on:

"Oh, how I felt my blood boil at that moment! how my heart seemed bursting within me; and a voice appeared to whisper in my ear scornfully the name of 'coward!' It surely was an evil spirit. I felt that I was strong enough— my rising anger made me so—to seize my unjust assailant by the throat, and cast him gasping on the ground. I heard already the shout of applause that would have hailed my victory and turned the tables against him. It was the hardest struggle of my life; never were flesh and blood so strong within me. O God! may they never be again so tremendously powerful!"

"And what did you do, then, my darling boy?" gasped forth the trembling matron.

He replied, "My good angel conquered the demon at my side. I thought of my blessed Lord in the house of Caiphas, surrounded by scoffing enemies, and struck ignominiously on the cheek, yet meek and forgiving. Could I wish to be otherwise?" I stretched forth my hand to Corvinus, and said, 'May God forgive you, as I freely and fully do; and may He bless you abundantly.' Cassianus came up at that moment, having seen all from a distance, and the youthful crowd quickly dispersed. I entreated him, by our common faith, now acknowledged between us, not to pursue Corvinus for what he had done; and I obtained his promise. And now, sweet mother," murmured the boy, in soft, gentle accents, into his parent's bosom, "do you not think I may call this a happy day?"

* This scene is taken from a real occurrence.

CHAPTER III.

THE DEDICATION.

WHILE the foregoing conversation was held, the day had fast declined. An aged female servant now entered unnoticed, and lighted the lamps placed on marble and bronze candelabra, and quietly retired. A bright light beamed upon the unconscious group of mother and son, as they remained silent, after the holy matron Lucina had answered Pancratius's last question only by kissing his glowing brow. It was not merely a maternal emotion that was agitating her bosom; it was not even the happy feeling of a mother who, having trained her child to certain high and difficult principles, sees them put to the hardest test, and nobly stand it. Neither was it the joy of having for her son one, in her estimation, so heroically virtuous at such an age; for surely, with much greater justice than the mother of the Gracchi showed her boys to the astonished matrons of republican Rome as her only jewels, could that Christian mother have boasted to the Church of the son she had brought up.

But to her this was an hour of still deeper, or, shall we say, sublimer feeling. It was a period looked forward to anxiously for years; a moment prayed for with all the fervor of a mother's supplication. Many a pious parent has devoted her infant son from the cradle to the holiest and noblest state

Ordination in the Early Ages of the Church.

that earth possesses; has prayed and longed to see him grow up to be, first a spotless Levite, and then a holy priest at the altar; and has watched eagerly each growing inclination, and tried gently to bend the tender thought towards the sanctuary of the Lord of Hosts. And if this was an only child, as Samuel was to Anna, that dedication of all that is dear to her keenest affection, may justly be considered as an act of maternal heroism. What then must be said of ancient matrons,—Felicitas, Symphorosa, or the unnamed mother of the Maccabees,—who gave up or offered their children, not one, but many, yea all, to be victims whole-burnt, rather than priests, to God?

It was some such thought as this which filled the heart of Lucina in that hour; while, with closed eyes, she raised it high to heaven, and prayed for strength. She felt as though called to make a generous sacrifice of what was dearest to her on earth; and though she had long foreseen it and desired it, it was not without a maternal throe that its merit could be gained. And what was passing in that boy's mind, as he too remained silent and abstracted? Not any thought of a high destiny awaiting him. No vision of a venerable Basilica, eagerly visited 1000 years later by the sacred antiquary and the devout pilgrim, and giving his name, which it shall bear, to the neighboring gate of Rome.* No anticipation of a church in his honor to rise in faithful ages on the banks of the distant Thames, which, even after desecration, should be loved and eagerly sought as their last resting-place, by hearts faithful still to his dear Rome.† No forethought of a silver canopy or *ciborium*, weighing 287 lbs., to be placed over the porphyry urn that should contain his ashes, by Pope Honorius I.‡

---

* Church and gate of San Pancrazio.

† Old St. Pancras's Church, London, the favorite burial-place of Catholics, till they had cemeteries of their own.

‡ Anastasius, Biblioth. in vita *Honorii*.

No idea that his name would be enrolled in every martyrology, his picture, crowned with rays, hung over many altars, as the boy-martyr of the early Church. He was only the simple-hearted Christian youth, who looked upon it as a matter of course that he must always obey God's law and His Gospel; and only felt happy that he had that day performed his duty, when it came under circumstances of more than usual trial. There was no pride, no self-admiration in the reflection; otherwise there would have been no heroism in his act.

When he raised again his eyes, after his calm reverie of peaceful thoughts, in the new light which brightly filled the hall, they met his mother's countenance gazing anew upon him, radiant with a majesty and tenderness such as he never recollected to have seen before. It was a look almost of inspiration; her face was as that of a vision; her eyes what he would have imagined an angel's to be. Silently, and almost unknowingly, he had changed his position, and was kneeling before her; and well he might; for was she not to him as a guardian spirit, who had shielded him ever from evil; or might he not well see in her the living saint whose virtues had been his model from childhood? Lucina broke the silence, in a tone full of grave emotion.

"The time is at length come, my dear child," she said, "which has long been the subject of my earnest prayer, which I have yearned for in the exuberance of maternal love. Eagerly have I watched in thee the opening germ of each Christian virtue, and thanked God as it appeared. I have noted thy docility, thy gentleness, thy diligence, thy piety, and thy love of God and man. I have seen with joy thy lively faith, and thy indifference to worldly things, and thy tenderness to the poor. But I have been waiting with anxiety for the hour which should decisively show me whether thou wouldst be content with the poor legacy of thy mother's weakly virtue, or art the true inheritor of thy martyred father's nobler gifts. That hour, thank God, has come to-day!"

"What have I done, then, that should thus have changed or raised thy opinion of me?" asked Pancratius.

"Listen to me, my son. This day, which was to be the last of thy school education, methinks that our merciful Lord has been pleased to give thee a lesson worth it all; and to prove that thou hast put off the things of a child, and must be treated henceforth as a man; for thou canst think and speak, yea, and act as one."

"How dost thou mean, dear mother?"

"What thou hast told me of thy declamation this morning," she replied, "proves to me how full thy heart must have been of noble and generous thoughts; thou art too sincere and honest to have written, and fervently expressed, that it was a glorious duty to die for the faith, if thou hadst not believed it and felt it."

"And truly I do believe and feel it," interrupted the boy. "What greater happiness can a Christian desire on earth?"

"Yes, my child, thou sayest most truly," continued Lucina. "But I should not have been satisfied with words. What followed afterwards has proved to me that thou canst bear intrepidly and patiently, not merely pain, but what I know it must have been harder for thy young patrician blood to stand; the stinging ignominy of a disgraceful blow, and the scornful words and glances of an unpitying multitude. Nay more; thou hast proved thyself strong enough to forgive and to pray for thine enemy. This day thou hast trodden the higher paths of the mountain, with the cross upon thy shoulders; one step more, and thou wilt plant it on its summit. Thou hast proved thyself the genuine son of the martyr Quintinus. Dost thou wish to be like him?"

"Mother, mother! dearest, sweetest mother!" broke out the panting youth; "could I be his genuine son, and not wish to resemble him? Though I never enjoyed the happiness of knowing him, has not his image been ever before my mind? Has he not been the very pride of my thoughts? When each year the solemn commemoration has been made of him, as of one of the white-robed army that surrounds the Lamb, in whose blood he washed his garments, how have my heart and my flesh exulted in his glory; and how have I prayed to him, in the warmth of filial piety, that he would obtain for me, not fame, not distinction, not wealth, not earthly joy, but what he valued more than all these; nay, that the only thing which he has left on earth may be applied, as I know he now considers it would most usefully and most nobly be."

"What is that, my son?"

"It is his blood," replied the youth, "which yet remains flowing in my veins, and in these only. I know he must wish that it too, like what he held in his own, may be poured out in love of his Redeemer, and in testimony of his faith."

"Enough, enough, my child!" exclaimed the mother, thrilling with a holy emotion; "take from thy neck the badge of childhood, I have a better token to give thee."

He obeyed, and put away the golden bulla.

"Thou hast inherited from thy father," spoke the mother, with still deeper solemnity of tone, "a noble name, a high station, ample riches, every worldly advantage. But there is one treasure which I have reserved for thee from his inheritance, till thou shouldst prove thyself worthy of it. I have concealed it from thee till now, though I valued it more than gold and jewels. It is now time that I make it over to thee."

With trembling hands she drew from her neck the golden chain which hung round it, and for the first time her son saw that it supported a small bag or purse richly embroidered and set with gems. She opened it, and drew from it a sponge, dry indeed, but deeply stained.

"With trembling hands she drew from her neck the golden chain."

"This, too, is thy father's blood, Pancratius," she said, with faltering voice and streaming eyes. "I gathered it myself from his death-wound, as, disguised, I stood by his side, and saw him die from the wounds he had received for Christ."

She gazed upon it fondly, and kissed it fervently; and her gushing tears fell on it, and moistened it once more. And thus liquefied again, its color glowed bright and warm, as if it had only just left the martyr's heart.

The holy matron put it to her son's quivering lips, and they were empurpled with its sanctifying touch. He venerated the sacred relic with the deepest emotions of a Christian and a son; and felt as if his father's spirit had descended into him, and stirred to its depths the full vessel of his heart, that its waters might be ready freely to flow. The whole family thus seemed to him once more united. Lucina replaced her treasure in its shrine, and hung it round the neck of her son, saying: "When next it is moistened, may it be from a nobler stream than that which gushes from a weak woman's eyes!" But heaven thought not so; and the future combatant was anointed, and the future martyr was consecrated, by the blood of his father mingled with his mother's tears.

A piece of a "Gold glass" found in the Catacombs.

CHAPTER IV.

THE HEATHEN HOUSEHOLD.

WHILE the scenes described in the three last chapters were taking place, a very different one presented itself in another house, situated in the valley between the Quirinal and Esquiline hills. It was that of Fabius, a man of the equestrian order, whose family, by farming the revenues of Asiatic provinces, had amassed immense wealth. His house was larger and more splendid than the one we have already visited. It contained a third large peristyle, or court, surrounded by immense apartments; and besides possessing many treasures of European art, it abounded with the rarest productions of the East. Carpets from Persia were laid on the ground, silks from China, many-colored stuffs from Babylon, and gold embroidery from India and Phrygia covered the furniture; while curious works in ivory and in metals, scattered about, were attributed to the inhabitants of islands beyond the Indian ocean, of monstrous form and fabulous descent.

Fabius himself, the owner of all this treasure and of large estates, was a true specimen of an easy-going Roman, who was determined thoroughly to enjoy this life. In fact, he never dreamt of any other. Believing in nothing, yet worshipping, as a matter of course, on all proper occasions, whatever deity happened to have its turn, he passed for a man as good as his neighbors; and no one had a right to exact more. The greater part of his day was passed at one or other of the great baths, which, besides the purposes implied in their name, comprised in their many adjuncts the equivalents of clubs, reading-rooms, gambling-houses, tennis-courts, and gymnasiums. There he took his bath, gossiped, read, and whiled away his hours; or sauntered for a time into the Forum to hear some orator speaking, or some advocate pleading, or into one of the many public gardens, whither the fashionable world of Rome repaired. He returned home to an elegant supper, not later than our dinner; where he had daily guests, either previously invited, or picked up during the day, among the many parasites on the look-out for good fare.

At home he was a kind and indulgent master. His house was well kept for him by an abundance of slaves; and, as trouble was what most he dreaded, so long as every thing was comfortable, handsome, and well-served about him, he let things go on quietly, under the direction of his freedmen.

It is not, however, so much to him that we wish to introduce our reader, as to another inmate of his house, the sharer of its splendid luxury, and the sole heiress of his wealth. This is his daughter, who, according to Roman usage, bears the father's name, softened, however, into the diminutive Fabiola.* As we have done before, we will conduct the reader at once into her apartment. A marble staircase leads to it from the second court, over the sides of which extends a suite of rooms, opening upon a terrace, refreshed and adorned by a graceful fountain, and covered with a profusion of the rarest exotic plants. In these chambers is concentrated whatever is most exquisite and curious, in native and foreign art. A refined taste directing ample means, and peculiar opportunities, has evidently presided over the collection and arrangement of all around. At this moment, the hour of the evening repast is approaching; and we discover the mistress

* Pronounced with the accent on the i.

of this dainty abode engaged in preparing herself, to appear with becoming splendor.

Pompeian Couch.

She is reclining on a couch of Athenian workmanship, inlaid with silver, in a room of Cyzicene form; that is, having glass windows to the ground, and so opening on to the flowery terrace. Against the wall opposite to her hangs a

Table, after a painting at Herculaneum.

mirror of polished silver, sufficient to reflect a whole standing figure; on a porphyry-table beside it is a collection of the innumerable rare cosmetics and perfumes, of which the Roman ladies had become so fond, and on which they lavished immense sums.* On another, of Indian sandal-wood, was a rich display of jewels and trinkets in their precious caskets, from which to select for the day's use.

It is by no means our intention, nor our gift, to describe persons or features; we wish more to deal with minds. We will, therefore, content ourselves with saying, that Fabiola, now at the age of twenty, was not considered inferior in appearance to other ladies of her rank, age, and fortune, and had many aspirants for her hand. But she was a contrast to her father in temper and in character. Proud, haughty, imperious, and irritable, she ruled like an empress all that

Couch from Herculaneum.

surrounded her, with one or two exceptions, and exacted humble homage from all that approached her. An only child, whose mother had died in giving her birth, she had been nursed and brought up in indulgence by her careless, good-natured father; she had been provided with the best masters, had been adorned with every accomplishment, and allowed to gratify every extravagant wish. She had never known what it was to deny herself a desire.

Having been left so much to herself, she had read much, and especially in profounder books. She had thus become a complete philosopher of the refined, that is, the infidel and intellectual, epicureanism, which had been long fashionable in Rome. Of Christianity she knew nothing, except that she

* The milk of 500 asses per day was required to furnish Poppæa, Nero's wife, with one cosmetic.

understood it to be something very low, material, and vulgar. She despised it, in fact, too much to think of inquiring into it. And as to paganism, with its gods, its vices, its fables, and its idolatry, she merely scorned it, though outwardly she followed it. In fact, she believed in nothing beyond the present life, and thought of nothing except its refined enjoyment. But her very pride threw a shield over her virtue; she loathed the wickedness of heathen society, as she despised the frivolous

youths who paid her jealously exacted attention, for she found amusement in their follies. She was considered cold and selfish, but she was morally irreproachable.

If at the beginning we seem to indulge in long descriptions, we trust that our reader will believe that they are requisite, to put him in possession of the state of material and social Rome at the period of our narrative; and will make this the more intelligible. And should he be tempted to think that we describe things as over splendid and refined for an age of decline in arts and good taste, we beg to remind him, that the year we are supposed to visit Rome is not as remote from the better periods of Roman art, for example, that of the Antonines, as our age is from that of Cellini, Raffaele, or Donatello. Yet in how many Italian palaces are still preserved works by these great artists, fully prized, though no longer imitated? So, no doubt, it was with the houses belonging to the old and wealthy families of Rome.

We find, then, Fabiola reclining on her couch, holding in her left hand a silver mirror with a handle, and in the other a strange instrument for so fair a hand. It is a sharp-pointed stiletto, with a delicately carved ivory handle, and a gold ring, to hold it by. This was the favorite weapon with which Roman ladies punished their slaves, or vented their passion on them, upon suffering the least annoyance, or when irritated by pettish anger. Three female slaves are now engaged about their mistress. They belong to different races, and have been purchased at high prices, not merely on account of their appearance, but for some rare accomplishment they are supposed to possess. One is a black; not of the degraded negro stock, but from one of those races, such as the Abyssinians and Numidians, in whom the features are as regular as in the Asiatic people. She is supposed to have great skill in herbs, and their cosmetic and healing properties, perhaps also in more dangerous uses—in compounding philtres, charms, and possibly poisons. She is merely known by her national designation as Afra. A Greek comes next, selected for her taste in dress, and for the elegance and purity of her accent; she is therefore called Graia. The name which the third bears, Syra, tells us that she comes from Asia; and she is distinguished for her exquisite embroidering, and for her assiduous diligence. She is quiet, silent, but completely engaged with the duties which now devolve upon her. The other two are garrulous, light, and make great pretence about any little thing they do. Every moment they address the most extravagant flattery to their young mistress, or try to promote the suit of one or other of the profligate candidates for her hand, who has best or last bribed them.

"How delighted I should be, most noble mistress," said the black slave, "if I could only be in the triclinium* this evening as you enter in, to observe the brilliant effect of this new stibium† on your guests! It has cost me many trials

A Slave. From a painting in Herculaneum.   A Slave. From a painting in Pompeii.

before I could obtain it so perfect: I am sure nothing like it has been ever seen in Rome."

"As for me," interrupted the wily Greek, "I should not presume to aspire to so high an honor. I should be satisfied to look from outside the door, and see the magnificent effect of this wonderful silk tunic, which came with the last remit

* The dining-hall.   † Black antimony applied on the eyelids.

tance of gold from Asia. Nothing can equal its beauty; nor, I may add, is its arrangement, the result of my study, unworthy of the materials."

"And you, Syra," interposed the mistress, with a contemptuous smile, "what would you desire? and what have you to praise of your own doing?"

"Nothing to desire, noble lady, but that you may be ever happy; nothing to praise of my own doing, for I am not conscious of having done more than my duty," was the modest and sincere reply.

It did not please the haughty lady, who said, "Methinks, slave, that you are not over given to praise. One seldom hears a soft word from your mouth."

"And what worth would it be from me," answered Syra; "from a poor servant to a noble dame, accustomed to hear it all day long from eloquent and polished lips? Do you believe it when you hear it from *them?* Do you not despise it when you receive it from *us?*"

A look of spite was darted at her from her two companions. Fabiola, too, was angry at what she thought a reproof. A lofty sentiment in a slave!

"Have you yet to learn, then," she answered haughtily, "that you are mine, and have been bought by me at a high price, that you might serve me as *I* please? I have as good a right to the service of your tongue as of your arms; and if it please me to be praised, and flattered, and sung to, by you, do it you shall, whether *you* like it or not. A new idea, indeed, that a slave has to have any will but that of her mistress, when her very life belongs to her!"

"True," replied the handmaid, calmly but with dignity, "my life belongs to you, and so does all else that ends with life,—time, health, vigor, body, and breath. All this you have bought with your gold, and it has become your property. But I still hold as my own what no emperor's wealth can purchase, no chains of slavery fetter, no limit of life contain."

"And pray what is that?"

"A soul."

"A soul!" re-echoed the astonished Fabiola, who had never before heard a slave claim ownership of such a property. "And pray, let me ask you, what you mean by the word?"

"I cannot speak philosophical sentences," answered the servant, "but I mean that inward living consciousness within me, which makes me feel to have an existence with, and among, better things than surround me, which shrinks sensitively from destruction, and instinctively from what is allied to it, as disease is to death. And therefore it abhors all flattery, and it detests a lie. While I possess that unseen gift, and die it cannot, either is impossible to me."

The other two could understand but little of all this; so they stood in stupid amazement at the presumption of their companion. Fabiola too was startled; but her pride soon rose again, and she spoke with visible impatience.

"Where did you learn all this folly? Who has taught you to prate in this manner? For my part, I have studied for many years, and have come to the conclusion, that all ideas of spiritual existences are the dreams of poets, or sophists; and as such I despise them. Do you, an ignorant, uneducated slave, pretend to know better than your mistress? Or do you really fancy, that when, after death, your corpse will be thrown on the heap of slaves who have drunk themselves, or have been scourged, to death, to be burnt in one ignominious pile, and when the mingled ashes have been buried in a common pit, you will survive as a conscious being, and have still a life of joy and freedom to be lived?"

"'*Non omnis moriar*,'* as one of your poets says," replied

* Not all of me will die.

"Fulvia grasped the style in her right hand, and made an almost blind thrust at the unoffending handiwork."

modestly, but with a fervent look that astonished her mistress, the foreign slave; "yes, I hope, nay, I *intend* to survive all this. And more yet; I believe, and know, that out of that charnel-pit which you have so vividly described, there is a hand that will pick out each charred fragment of my frame. And there is a power that will call to reckoning the four winds of heaven, and make each give back every grain of my dust that it has scattered; and I shall be built up once more in this my body, not as yours, or any one's, bondwoman, but free, and joyful, and glorious, loving for ever, and beloved. This certain hope is laid up in my bosom."*

"What wild visions of an eastern fancy are these, unfitting you for every duty? You must be cured of them. In what school did you learn all this nonsense? I never read of it in any Greek or Latin author."

"In one belonging to my own land; a school in which there is no distinction known, or admitted, between Greek or barbarian, freeman or slave."

"What!" exclaimed, with strong excitement, the haughty lady, "without waiting even for that future ideal existence after death; already, even now, you presume to claim equality with me? Nay, who knows, perhaps superiority over me. Come, tell me at once, and without daring to equivocate or disguise, if you do so or not?" And she sat up in an attitude of eager expectation. At every word of the calm reply her agitation increased; and violent passions seemed to contend within her, as Syra said:

"Most noble mistress, far superior are you to me in place, and power, and learning, and genius, and in all that enriches and embellishes life; and in every grace of form and lineament, and in every charm of act and speech, high are you raised above all rivalry, and far removed from envious thought, from one so lowly and so insignificant as I. But if I

* Job xix. 27.

must answer simple truth to your authoritative question"—she paused, as faltering; but an imperious gesture from her mistress bade her continue—"then I put it to your own judgment, whether a poor slave, who holds an unquenchable consciousness of possessing within her a spiritual and living intelligence, whose measure of existence is immortality, whose only true place of dwelling is above the skies, whose only rightful prototype is the Deity, can hold herself inferior in moral dignity, or lower in greatness of thought, than one who, however gifted, owns that she claims no higher destiny, recognizes in herself no sublimer end, than what awaits the pretty irrational songsters that beat, without hope of liberty, against the gilded bars of that cage."*

Fabiola's eyes flashed with fury; she felt herself, for the first time in her life, rebuked, humbled by a slave. She grasped the style in her right hand, and made an almost blind thrust at the unflinching handmaid. Syra instinctively put forward her arm to save her person, and received the point, which, aimed upwards from the couch, inflicted a deeper gash than she had ever before suffered. The tears started into her eyes through the smart of the wound, from which the blood gushed in a stream. Fabiola was in a moment ashamed of her cruel, though unintentional, act, and felt still more humbled before her servants.

"Go, go," she said to Syra, who was stanching the blood with her handkerchief, "go to Euphrosyne, and have the wound dressed. I did not mean to hurt you so grievously. But stay a moment, I must make you some compensation." Then, after turning over her trinkets on the table, she continued, "Take this ring; and you need not return here again this evening."

Fabiola's conscience was quite satisfied; she had made

* See the noble answer of Evalpistus, an imperial slave, to the judge, in the Acts of St. Justin, ap. Ruinart, tom. i.

"He who watched with knowing eye, the alms-action of Jerusalem, and found the widow's mite, since now dropped into the chest, by the bandaged arm of a foreign female slave, a valuable recipient ring."

what she considered ample atonement for the injury she had inflicted, in the shape of a costly present to a menial dependant. And on the following Sunday, in the title* of St. Pastor, not far from her house, among the alms collected for the poor was found a valuable emerald ring, which the good priest Polycarp thought must have been the offering of some very rich Roman lady; but which He who watched, with beaming eye, the alms-coffers of Jerusalem, and noted the widow's mite, alone saw dropped into the chest by the bandaged arm of a foreign female slave.

* Church.

A Lamp, found in the Catacombs.

CHAPTER V.

THE VISIT.

URING the latter part of the dialogue just recorded, and the catastrophe which closed it, there took place an apparition in Fabiola's room, which, if seen by her, would probably have cut short the one and prevented the other. The interior chambers in a Roman house were more frequently divided by curtains across their entrances than by doors; and thus it was easy, especially during such an excited scene as had just taken place, to enter unobserved. This was the case now; and when Syra turned to leave the room she was almost startled at seeing standing, in bright relief before the deep crimson door-curtain, a figure which she immediately recognized, but which we must briefly describe.

It was that of a lady, or rather a child not more than twelve or thirteen years old, dressed in pure and spotless white, without a single ornament about her person. In her countenance might be seen united the simplicity of childhood with the intelligence of a maturer age. There not merely dwelt in her eyes that dove-like innocence which the sacred poet describes,[*] but often there beamed from them rather an intensity of pure affection, as though they were looking beyond all surrounding objects, and rested upon one, unseen by all else, but to her really present and exquisitely dear. Her

[*] "Thy eyes are as those of doves.—*Cantic.* i. 14.

forehead was the very seat of candor, open and bright with undisguising truthfulness; a kindly smile played about the lips, and the fresh, youthful features varied their sensitive expression with guileless earnestness, passing rapidly from one feeling to the other, as her warm and tender heart received it. Those who knew her believed that she never thought of herself, but was divided entirely between kindness to those about her, and affection for her unseen love.

When Syra saw this beautiful vision, like that of an angel, before her, she paused for a moment. But the child took her hand and reverently kissed it, saying, "I have seen all; meet me in the small chamber near the entrance, when I go out."

She then advanced; and as Fabiola saw her, a crimson blush mantled in her cheek; for she feared the child had been witness of her undignified burst of passion. With a cold wave of her hand she dismissed her slaves, and then greeted her kinswoman, for such she was, with cordial affection. We have said that Fabiola's temper made a few exceptions in its haughty exercise. One of these was her old nurse and freedwoman Euphrosyne, who directed all her private household, and whose only creed was, that Fabiola was the most perfect of beings, the wisest, most accomplished, most admirable lady in Rome. Another was her young visitor, whom she loved, and ever treated with gentlest affection, and whose society she always coveted.

"This is really kind of you, dear Agnes," said the softened Fabiola, "to come at my sudden request, to join our table to-day. But the fact is, my father has called in one or two new people to dine, and I was anxious to have some one with whom I could have the excuse of a duty to converse. Yet I own I have some curiosity about one of our new guests. It is Fulvius, of whose grace, wealth, and accomplishments I hear so much; though nobody seems to know who or what he is, or whence he has sprung up."

"My dear Fabiola," replied Agnes, "you know I am always happy to visit you, and my kind parents willingly allow me; therefore, make no apologies about that."

"And so you have come to me as usual," said the other playfully, "in your own snow-white dress, without jewel or ornament, as if you were every day a bride. You always seem to me to be celebrating one eternal espousal. But, good heavens! what is this? Are you hurt? Or are you

Saint Agnes. From an old vase.

aware that there is, right on the bosom of your tunic, a large red spot—it looks like blood. If so, let me change your dress at once."

"Not for the world, Fabiola; it is the jewel, the only ornament I mean to wear this evening. It is blood, and that of a slave; but nobler, in my eyes, and more generous, than flows in your veins or mine."

The whole truth flashed upon Fabiola's mind. Agnes had seen all; and humbled almost to sickening, she said somewhat pettishly, "Do you then wish to exhibit proof to all the world of my hastiness of temper, in over-chastising a forward slave?"

"No, dear cousin, far from it. I only wish to preserve

for myself a lesson of fortitude, and of elevation of mind, learnt from a slave, such as few patrician philosophers can teach us."

"What a strange idea! Indeed, Agnes, I have often thought that you make too much of that class of people. After all, what are they?"

"Human beings as much as ourselves, endowed with the same reason, the same feelings, the same organization. Thus

Saint Agnes. From an old vase preserved in the Vatican Museum.

far you will admit, at any rate, to go no higher. Then they form part of the same family; and if God, from whom comes our life, is thereby our Father, He is theirs as much, and consequently they are our brethren."

"A slave my brother or sister, Agnes? The gods forbid it! They are our property and our goods; and I have no notion of their being allowed to move, to act, to think, or to feel, except as it suits their masters, or is for their advantage."

"Come, come," said Agnes, with her sweetest tones, "do not let us get into a warm discussion. You are too candid and honorable not to feel, and to be ready to acknowledge, that to-day you have been outdone by a slave in all that you most admire,—in mind, in reasoning, in truthfulness, and in heroic fortitude. Do not answer me; I see it in that tear. But, dearest cousin, I will save you from a repetition of your pain. Will you grant me my request?"

"Any in my power."

"Then it is, that you will allow me to purchase Syra—I think that is her name. You will not like to see her about you."

"You are mistaken, Agnes. I will master pride for once, and own, that I shall now esteem her, perhaps almost admire her. It is a new feeling in me towards one in her station."

"But I think, Fabiola, I could make her happier than she is."

"No doubt, dear Agnes; you have the power of making every body happy about you. I never saw such a household as yours. You seem to carry out in practice that strange philosophy which Syra alluded to, in which there is no distinction of freeman and slave. Every body in your house is always smiling, and cheerfully anxious to discharge his duty. And there seems to be no one who thinks of commanding. Come, tell me your secret." (Agnes smiled.) "I suspect, you little magician, that in that mysterious chamber, which you will never open for me, you keep your charms and potions by which you make every body and every thing love you. If you were a Christian, and were exposed in the amphitheatre, I am sure the very leopards would crouch and nestle at your feet. But why do you look so serious, child? You know I am only joking."

Agnes seemed absorbed; and bent forward that keen and tender look which we have mentioned, as though she saw before her, nay, as if she heard speaking to her, some one delicately beloved. It passed away, and she gaily said, "Well, well, Fabiola, stranger things have come to pass; and at any rate, if aught so dreadful had to happen, Syra would just be the sort of person one would like to see near one; so you really must let me have her."

"For heaven's sake, Agnes, do not take my words so seriously. I assure you they were spoken in jest. I have too high an opinion of your good sense to believe such a calamity possible. But as to Syra's devotedness, you are right. When last summer you were away, and I was so dangerously ill of contagious fever, it required the lash to make the other slaves approach me; while that poor thing would hardly leave me, but watched by me, and nursed me day and night, and I really believe greatly promoted my recovery."

"And did you not love her for this?"

"Love her! Love a slave, child! Of course, I took care to reward her generously; though I cannot make out what she does with what I give her. The others tell me she has nothing put by, and she certainly spends nothing on herself. Nay, I have even heard that she foolishly shares her daily allowance of food with a blind beggar-girl. What a strange fancy, to be sure!"

"Dearest Fabiola," exclaimed Agnes, "she must be mine! You promised me my request. Name your price, and let me take her home this evening."

"Well, be it so, you most irresistible of petitioners. But we will not bargain together. Send some one to-morrow, to see my father's steward, and all will be right. And now this great piece of business being settled between us, let us go down to our guests."

"But you have forgotten to put on your jewels."

"Never mind them; I will do without them for once; I feel no taste for them to-day."

CHAPTER VI.

THE BANQUET.

THEY found, on descending, all the guests assembled in a hall below. It was not a state banquet which they were going to share, but the usual meal of a rich house, where preparation for a tableful of friends was always made. We will therefore content ourselves with saying that every thing was elegant and exquisite in arrangement and material; and we will confine ourselves entirely to such incidents as may throw a light upon our story.

When the two ladies entered the exedra or hall, Fabius, after saluting his daughter, exclaimed, "Why, my child, you have come down, though late, still scarcely fittingly arranged! You have forgotten your usual trinkets."

Fabiola was confused. She knew not what answer to make; she was ashamed of her weakness about her angry display; and still more of what she now thought a silly way of punishing herself for it. Agnes stepped in to the rescue, and blushingly said: "It is my fault, cousin Fabius, both that she is late and that she is so plainly dressed. I detained her with my gossip, and no doubt she wishes to keep me in countenance by the simplicity of her attire."

"You, dear Agnes," replied the father, "are privileged to do as you please. But, seriously speaking, I must say that, even with you, this may have answered while you were a mere child; now that you are marriageable,* you must begin to make a little more display, and try to win the affections of some handsome and eligible youth. A beautiful necklace, for instance, such as you have plenty of at home, would not make you less attractive. But you are not attending to me. Come, come, I dare say you have some one already in view."

During most of this address, which was meant to be thoroughly good-natured, as it was perfectly worldly, Agnes appeared in one of her abstracted moods, her bewitched looks, as Fabiola called them, transfixed, in a smiling ecstasy, as if attending to some one else, but never losing the thread of the discourse, nor saying any thing out of place. She therefore at once answered Fabius: "Oh, yes, most certainly, one who has already pledged me to him by his betrothal-ring, and has adorned me with immense jewels."†

"Really!" asked Fabius, "with what?"

"Why," answered Agnes, with a look of glowing earnestness, and in tones of artless simplicity, "he has girded my hand and neck with precious gems, and has set in my ears rings of peerless pearls."‡

"Goodness! who can it be? Come, Agnes, some day you must tell me your secret. Your first love, no doubt; may it last long and make you happy!"

"For ever!" was her reply, as she turned to join Fabiola, and enter with her into the dining-room. It was well she had not overheard this dialogue, or she would have been hurt to the quick, as thinking that Agnes had concealed the most important thought of her age, as she would have considered it, from her most loving friend. But while Agnes was defend-

---

* Twelve was the age for marriage according to the Roman law.

† "Annulo fidei suæ subarrhavit me, et immensis monilibus ornavit me."— *Office of St. Agnes.*

‡ "Dexteram meam et collum meum cinxit lapidibus pretiosis, tradidit auribus meis inæstimabiles margaritas."

ing her, she had turned away from her father, and had been attending to the other guests. One was a heavy, thick-necked Roman sophist, or dealer in universal knowledge, named Calpurnius; another, Proculus, a mere lover of good fare, often at the house. Two more remain, deserving further notice. The first of them, evidently a favorite both with Fabiola and Agnes, was a tribune, a high officer of the imperial or prætorian guard. Though not above thirty years of age, he had already distinguished himself by his valor, and enjoyed the highest favor with the emperors Dioclesian in the East, and Maximian Herculius in Rome. He was free from all affectation in manner or dress, though handsome in person; and though most engaging in conversation, he manifestly scorned the foolish topics which generally occupied society. In short, he was a perfect specimen of a noble-hearted youth, full of honor and generous thoughts; strong and brave, without a particle of pride or display in him.

Quite a contrast to him was the last guest, already alluded to by Fabiola, the new star of society, Fulvius. Young, and almost effeminate in look, dressed with most elaborate elegance, with brilliant rings on every finger and jewels in his dress, affected in his speech, which had a slightly foreign accent, overstrained in his courtesy of manners, but apparently good-natured and obliging, he had in a short time quietly pushed his way into the highest society of Rome. This was, indeed, owing partly to his having been seen at the imperial court, and partly to the fascination of his manner. He had arrived in Rome accompanied by a single elderly attendant, evidently deeply attached to him; whether slave, freedman, or friend, nobody well knew. They spoke together always in a strange tongue, and the swarthy features, keen fiery eye, and unamiable expression of the domestic, inspired a certain degree of fear in his dependants; for Fulvius had taken an apartment in what was called an *insula*, or house let out in parts, had furnished it luxuriously, and had peopled it with a sufficient bachelor's establishment of slaves. Profusion rather than abundance distinguished all his domestic arrangements; and, in the corrupted and degraded circle of pagan Rome, the obscurity of his history, and the suddenness of his apparition, were soon forgotten in the evidence of his riches, and the charm of his loose conversation. A shrewd observer of character, however, would soon notice a wandering restlessness of eye, and an eagerness of listening attention for all sights and sounds around him, which betrayed an insatiable curiosity; and in moments of forgetfulness, a dark scowl under his knit brows, from his flashing eyes, and a curling of the upper lip, which inspired a feeling of mistrust, and gave an idea that his exterior softness only clothed a character of feline malignity.

The guests were soon at table; and as ladies sat, while men reclined on couches during the repast, Fabiola and Agnes were together on one side, the two younger guests last

Banquet Table, from a Pompeian painting.

described were opposite, and the master, with his two elder friends, in the middle—if these terms can be used to describe their position about three parts of a round table; one side being left unencumbered by the *sigma*,* or semi-circular couch, for the convenience of serving. And we may observe, in passing, that a table-cloth, a luxury unknown in the times of Horace, was now in ordinary use.

* So called from its resemblance to the letter C, the old form of Σ.

When the first claims of hunger, or the palate, had been satisfied, conversation grew more general.

"What news to-day at the baths?" asked Calpurnius; "I have no leisure myself to look after such trifles."

"Very interesting news indeed," answered Proculus. "It seems quite certain that orders have been received from the divine Diocletian, to finish his Thermæ in three years."

"Impossible!" exclaimed Fabius. "I looked in at the works the other day, on my way to Sallust's gardens, and found them very little advanced in the last year. There is an immense deal of heavy work to be done, such as carving marbles and shaping columns."

"True," interposed Fulvius; "but I know that orders have been sent to all parts, to forward hither all prisoners, and all persons condemned to the mines in Spain, Sardinia, and even Chersonesus, who can possibly be spared, to come and labor at the Thermæ. A few thousand Christians, thus set to the work, will soon finish it."

"And why Christians better than other criminals?" asked, with some curiosity, Fabiola.

"Why, really," said Fulvius, with his most winning smile, "I can hardly give a reason for it; but the fact is so. Among fifty workmen so condemned, I would engage to pick out a single Christian."

"Indeed!" exclaimed several at once; "pray how?"

"Ordinary convicts," answered he, "naturally do not love their work, and they require the lash at every step to compel them to perform it; and when the overseer's eye is off them, no work is done. And, moreover, they are, of course, rude, sottish, quarrelsome, and querulous. But the Christians, when condemned to these public works, seem, on the contrary, to be glad, and are always cheerful and obedient. I have seen young patricians so occupied in Asia, whose hands had never before handled a pickaxe, and whose weak shoulders had never borne a weight, yet working hard, and as happy, to all appearance, as when at home. Of course, for all that, the overseers apply the lash and the stick very freely to them; and most justly; because it is the will of the divine emperors that their lot should be made as hard as possible; but still they never complain."

"I cannot say that I admire this sort of justice," replied Fabiola; "but what a strange race they must be! I am most curious to know what can be the motive or cause of this stupidity, or unnatural insensibility, in these Christians?"

Proculus replied, with a facetious look: "Calpurnius here no doubt can tell us; for he is a philosopher, and I hear could declaim for an hour on any topic, from the Alps to an ant-hill."

Calpurnius, thus challenged, and thinking himself highly complimented, solemnly gave mouth: "The Christians," said he, "are a foreign sect, the founder of which flourished many ages ago in Chaldea. His doctrines were brought to Rome at the time of Vespasian by two brothers named Peter and Paul. Some maintain that these were the same twin brothers as the Jews call Moses and Aaron, the second of whom sold his birthright to his brother for a kid, the skin of which he wanted to make *chirotheca** of. But this identity I do not admit; as it is recorded in the mystical books of the Jews, that the second of these brothers, seeing the other's victims give better omens of birds than his own, slew him, as our Romulus did Remus, but with the jaw-bone of an ass; for which he was hung by King Mardocheus of Macedon, upon a gibbet fifty cubits high, at the suit of their sister Judith. However, Peter and Paul coming, as I said, to Rome, the former was discovered to be a fugitive slave of Pontius Pilate, and was crucified by his master's orders on the Janiculum. Their followers, of whom they had many, made the cross their

* Gloves.

symbol, and adore it; and they think it the greatest honor to suffer stripes, and even ignominious death, as the best means of being like their teachers, and, as they fancy, of going to them in a place somewhere among the clouds." *

This lucid explanation of the origin of Christianity was listened to with admiration by all except two. The young officer gave a piteous look towards Agnes, which seemed to say, "Shall I answer the goose, or shall I laugh outright?" But she put her finger on her lips, and smiled imploringly for silence.

"Well, then, the upshot of it is," observed Proculus, "that the Thermæ will be finished soon, and we shall have glorious sport. Is it not said, Fulvius, that the divine Dioclesian will himself come to the dedication?"

"It is quite certain; and so will there be splendid festivals and glorious games. But we shall not have to wait so long; already, for other purposes, have orders been sent to Numidia for an unlimited supply of lions and leopards to be ready before winter." Then turning round sharp to his neighbor, he said, bending a keen eye upon his countenance: "A brave soldier like you, Sebastian, must be delighted with the noble spectacles of the amphitheatre, especially when directed against the enemies of the august emperors, and of the republic."

The officer raised himself upon his couch, looked on his interrogator with an unmoved, majestic countenance, and answered calmly:

"Fulvius, I should not deserve the title which you give me, could I contemplate with pleasure, in cold blood, the struggle, if it deserve the name, between a brute beast and a helpless child or woman, for such are the spectacles which you call noble. No, I will draw my sword willingly against any enemy of the princes or the state; but I would as readily draw it against the lion or the leopard that should rush, even by

* Lucian: De Morte Peregrini.

imperial order, against the innocent and defenceless." Fulvius was starting up; but Sebastian placed his strong hand upon his arm, and continued: "Hear me out. I am not the first Roman, nor the noblest, who has thought thus before me. Remember the words of Cicero: 'Magnificent are these games, no doubt; but what delight can it be to a refined mind to see either a feeble man torn by a most powerful beast, or a noble animal pierced through by a javelin?'* I am not ashamed of agreeing with the greatest of Roman orators."

"Then shall we never see you in the amphitheatre, Sebastian?" asked Fulvius, with a bland but taunting tone.

"If you do," the soldier replied, "depend upon it, it will be on the side of the defenceless, not on that of the brutes that would destroy them."

"Sebastian is right," exclaimed Fabiola, clapping her hands, "and I close the discussion by my applause. I have never heard Sebastian speak, except on the side of generous and high-minded sentiments."

Fulvius bit his lip in silence, and all rose to depart.

* "Magnificos nemo negat; sed quæ potest esse homini polito delectatio, cuum aut homo imbecillus a valentissima bestia laniatur, aut præclara bestia venabulo transverberatur?"—*Ep. ad Fam.* lib. vii. ep. 1.

David with his Sling, from the Catacomb of St. Priscilla.

CHAPTER VII.

POOR AND RICH.

URING the latter part of the conversation just recorded, Fabius had been quite abstracted, speculating upon his conversation with Agnes. How quietly she had kept her secret to herself! But who could this favored person be, who had already won her heart? He thought over many, but could find no answer. The gift of rich jewels particularly perplexed him. He knew no young Roman nobleman likely to possess them; and sauntering, as he did, every day into the great shops, he was sure to have heard if any such costly order had been given. Suddenly the bright idea flashed through his mind, that Fulvius, who daily exhibited new and splendid gems, brought from abroad, could be the only person able to make her such presents. He moreover noticed such occasional looks darted towards his cousin by the handsome foreigner, as left him no doubt that he was deeply enamored of her; and if Agnes did not seem conscious of the admiration, this of course was part of her plan. Once convinced of this important conclusion, he determined to favor the wishes of the two, and astonish his daughter one day by the sagacity he had displayed.

But we must leave our nobler guests for more humble

scenes, and follow Syra from the time that she left her young mistress's apartment. When she presented herself to Euphrosyne, the good-natured nurse was shocked at the cruel wound, and uttered an exclamation of pity. But immediately recognizing in it the work of Fabiola, she was divided between two contending feelings. "Poor thing!" she said, as she went on first washing, then closing and dressing the gash; "it is a dreadful cut! What did you do to deserve it? How it must have hurt you, my poor girl! But how wicked you must have been to bring it upon yourself! It is a savage wound, yet inflicted by the gentlest of creatures! (You must be faint from loss of blood; take this cordial to support you); and no doubt she found herself obliged to strike."

"No doubt," said Syra, amused, "it was all my fault; I had no business to argue with my mistress."

"*Argue* with her!—argue!—O ye gods! who ever heard before of a slave arguing with a noble mistress, and such a learned one! Why, Calpurnius himself would be afraid of disputing with her. No wonder, indeed, she was so—so agitated as not to know that she was hurting you. But this must be concealed; it must not be known that you have been so wrong. Have you no scarf or nice veil that we could throw round the arm, as if for ornament? All the others I know have plenty, given or bought; but you never seem to care for these pretty things. Let us look."

She went into the maid-slave's dormitory, which was within her room, opened Syra's *capsa* or box, and after turning over in vain its scanty contents, she drew forth from the bottom a square kerchief of richest stuff, magnificently embroidered, and even adorned with pearls. Syra blushed deeply, and entreated not to be obliged to wear this most disproportioned piece of dress, especially as it was a token of better days, long and painfully preserved. But Euphrosyne, anxious to hide her mistress's fault, was inexorable; and the rich scarf was gracefully fastened round the wounded arm.

This operation performed, Syra proceeded to the little parlor opposite the porter's room, where the higher slaves could see their friends. She held in her hand a basket covered with a napkin. The moment she entered the door a light step came bounding across the room to meet her. It was that of a girl of about sixteen or seventeen, dressed in the poorest attire, but clean and neat, who threw her arms round Syra's neck with such a bright countenance and such hearty glee, that a bystander would hardly have supposed that her sightless eyes had never communed with the outer world.

"Sit down, dear Cæcilia," said Syra, with a most affectionate tone, and leading her to a seat; "to-day I have brought you a famous feast; you will fare sumptuously."

"How so? I think I do every day."

"No, but to-day my mistress has kindly sent me out a dainty dish from her table, and I have brought it here for you."

"How kind of her; yet how much kinder of you, my sister! But why have you not partaken of it yourself? It was meant for you and not for me."

"Why, to tell the truth, it is a greater treat to me, to see you enjoy any thing, than to enjoy it myself."

"No, dear Syra, no; it must not be. God has wished me to be poor, and I must try to do His will. I could no more think of eating the food, than I could of wearing the dress, of the rich, so long as I can obtain that of the poor. I love to share with you your *pulmentum*,* which I know is given me in charity by one poor like myself. I procure for you the merit of alms-deeds; you give me the consolation of feeling that I am, before God, still only a poor blind thing. I think He will love me better thus, than if feeding on luxurious fare. I

* Porridge.

would rather be with Lazarus at the gate, than with Dives at the table."

"How much better and wiser you are than I, my good child! It shall be as you wish. I will give the dish to my companions, and, in the meantime, here I set before you your usual humble fare."

"Thanks, thanks, dear sister; I will await your return."

Syra went to the maids' apartment, and put before her jealous but greedy companions the silver dish. As their mistress occasionally showed them this little kindness, it did not much surprise them. But the poor servant was weak enough to feel ashamed of appearing before her comrades with the rich scarf round her arm. She took it off before she entered; then, not wishing to displease Euphrosyne, replaced it as well as she could with one hand, on coming out. She was in the court below, returning to her blind friend, when she saw one of the noble guests of her mistress's table alone, and, with a mortified look, crossing towards the door, and she stepped behind a column to avoid any possible, and not uncommon, rudeness. It was Fulvius; and no sooner did she, unseen, catch a glimpse of him, than she stood for a moment as one nailed to the spot. Her heart beat against her bosom, then quivered as if about to cease its action; her knees struck against one another, a shiver ran through her frame, while perspiration started on her brow. Her eyes, wide open, were fascinated, like the bird's before the snake. She raised her hand to her breast, made upon it the sign of life, and the spell was broken. She fled in an instant, still unnoticed, and had hardly stepped noiselessly behind a curtain that closed the stairs, when Fulvius, with downcast eyes, reached the spot on which she had stood. He started back a step, as if scared by something lying before him. He trembled violently; but recovering himself by a sudden effort, he looked around him and saw that he was alone.

There was no eye upon him—except One which he did not heed, but which read his evil heart in that hour. He gazed again upon the object, and stooped to pick it up, but drew back his hand, and that more than once. At last he heard footsteps approaching, he recognized the martial tread of Sebastian, and hastily he snatched up from the ground the rich scarf which had dropped from Syra's arm. He shook as he folded it up; and when, to his horror, he found upon it spots of fresh blood, which had oozed through the bandages, he reeled like a drunken man to the door, and rushed to his lodgings.

Pale, sick, and staggering, he went into his chamber, repulsing roughly the officious advances of his slaves; and only beckoned to his faithful domestic to follow him, and then signed to him to bar the door. A lamp was burning brightly by the table, on which Fulvius threw the embroidered scarf in silence, and pointed to the stains of blood. That dark man said nothing; but his swarthy countenance was blanched, while his master's was ashy and livid.

"It is the same, no doubt," at length spoke the attendant in their foreign tongue; "but she is certainly dead."

"Art thou quite sure, Eurotas?" asked the master, with the keenest of his hawk's looks.

"As sure as man can be of what he has not seen himself. Where didst thou find this? And whence this blood?"

"I will tell thee all to-morrow; I am too sick to-night. As to those stains, which were liquid when I found it, I know not whence they came, unless they are warnings of vengeance—nay, a vengeance themselves, deep as the Furies could meditate, fierce as they could launch. That blood has not been shed *now*."

"Tut, tut! this is no time for dreams or fancies. Did any one see thee pick the—the thing up?"

"No one, I am sure."

"Then we are safe; better in our hands than in others'. A good night's rest will give us better counsel."

"True, Eurotus; but do thou sleep this night in my chamber."

Both threw themselves on their couches; Fulvius on a rich bed, Eurotus on a lowly pallet, from which, raised upon his elbow, with dark but earnest eye, he long watched, by the lamp's light, the troubled slumbers of the youth—at once his devoted guardian and his evil genius. Fulvius tossed about and moaned in his sleep, for his dreams were gloomy and heavy. First he sees before him a beautiful city in a distant land, with a river of crystal brightness flowing through it. Upon it is a galley weighing anchor, with a figure on deck, waving towards him, in farewell, an embroidered scarf. The scene changes; the ship is in the midst of the sea, battling with a furious storm, while on the summit of the mast the same scarf streams out, like a pennant, unruffled and uncrumpled by the breeze. The vessel is now dashed upon a rock, and all with a dreadful shriek are buried in the deep. But the topmast stands above the billows, with its calm and brilliant flag; till, amidst the sea-birds that shriek around, a form with a torch in her hand, and black flapping wings, flies by, snatches it from the staff, and with a look of stern anger displays it, as in her flight she pauses before him. He reads upon it, written in fiery letters, NEMESIS.*

But it is time to return to our other acquaintances in the house of Fabius.

After Syra had heard the door close on Fulvius she paused to compose herself, offered up a secret prayer, and returned to her blind friend. She had finished her frugal meal, and was waiting patiently the slave's return. Syra then commenced her daily duties of kindness and hospitality; she brought water, washed her hands and feet in obedience to Christian

* Vengeance.

practice, and combed and dressed her hair, as if the poor creature had been her own child. Indeed, though not much older, her look was so tender, as she hung over her poor friend, her tones were so soft, her whole action so motherly, that one would have thought it was a parent ministering to her daughter, rather than a slave serving a beggar. And this beggar, too, looked so happy, spoke so cheerily, and said such beautiful things, that Syra lingered over her work to listen to her, and gaze on her.

It was at this moment that Agnes came for her appointed interview, and Fabiola insisted on accompanying her to the door. But when Agnes softly raised the curtain, and caught a sight of the scene before her, she beckoned to Fabiola to look in, enjoining silence by her gesture. The blind girl was opposite, and her voluntary servant on one side, unconscious of witnesses. The heart of Fabiola was touched; she had never imagined that there was such a thing as disinterested love on earth between strangers; as to charity, it was a word unknown to Greece or Rome. She retreated quietly, with a tear in her eye, and said to Agnes, as she took leave:

"I must retire; that girl, as you know, proved to me this afternoon that a slave may have a head; she has now shown me that she may have a heart. I was amazed, when, a few hours ago, you asked me if I did not love a slave. I think, now, I could almost love Syra. I half regret that I have agreed to part with her."

As she went back into the court, Agnes entered the room, and laughing, said:

"So, Cæcilia, I have found out your secret at last. This is the friend whose food you have always said was so much better than mine, that you would never eat at my house. Well, if the dinner is not better, at any rate I agree that you have fallen in with a better hostess."

"Oh, don't say so, sweet Lady Agnes," answered the

blind girl: "it is the dinner indeed that is better. You have plenty of opportunities for exercising charity; but a poor slave can only do so by finding some one still poorer, and helpless, like me. That thought makes her food by far the sweetest."

"Well, you are right," said Agnes, "and I am not sorry to have you present, to hear the good news I bring to Syra. It will make you happy too. Fabiola has allowed me to become your mistress, Syra, and to take you with me. Tomorrow you shall be free, and a dear sister to me."

Cæcilia clapped her hands with joy, and throwing her arms round Syra's neck, exclaimed: "Oh, how good! How happy you will now be, dear Syra!"

But Syra was deeply troubled, and replied with faltering voice, "O good and gentle lady, you have been kind indeed, to think so much about one like me. But pardon me if I entreat you to remain as I am; I assure you, dear Cæcilia, I am quite happy here."

"But why wish to stay?" asked Agnes.

"Because," rejoined Syra, "it is most perfect to abide with God, in the state wherein we have been called.* I own this is not the one in which I was born; I have been brought to it by others." A burst of tears interrupted her for a moment, and then she went on. "But so much the more clear is it to me, that God has willed me to serve Him in this condition. How can I wish to leave it?"

"Well then," said Agnes, still more eagerly, "we can easily manage it. I will not free you, and you shall be my bondwoman. That will be just the same."

"No, no," said Syra, smiling, "that will never do. Our great Apostle's instructions to us are: 'Servants be subject to your masters with all fear, not only to the good and gentle, but also to the froward.'† I am far from saying that my mistress

* 1 Cor. vii. 24.   † 1 Pet. ii. 14.

is one of these; but you, noble Lady Agnes, are too good and gentle for me. Where would be my cross, if I lived with you? You do not know how proud and headstrong I am by nature; and I should fear for myself, if I had not some pain and humiliation."

Agnes was almost overcome; but she was more eager than ever to possess such a treasure of virtue, and said, "I see, Syra, that no motive addressed to your own interest can move you, I must therefore use a more selfish plea. I want to have you with me, that I may improve by your advice and example. Come, you will not refuse such a request."

"Selfish," replied the slave, "you can never be. And therefore I will appeal to yourself from your request. You know Fabiola, and you love her. What a noble soul, and what a splendid intellect she possesses! What great qualities and high accomplishments, if they only reflected the light of truth! And how jealously does she guard in herself that pearl of virtues, which only we know how to prize! What a truly great Christian she would make!"

"Go on, for God's sake, dear Syra," broke out Agnes, all eagerness. "And do you hope for it?"

"It is my prayer day and night; it is my chief thought and aim; it is the occupation of my life. I will try to win her by patience, by assiduity, even by such unusual discussions as we have held to-day. And when all is exhausted, I have one resource more."

"What is that?" both asked.

"To give my life for her conversion. I know that a poor slave like me has few chances of martyrdom. Still, a fiercer persecution is said to be approaching, and perhaps it will not disdain such humble victims. But be that as God pleases, my life for her soul is placed in His hands. And oh, dearest, best of ladies," she exclaimed, falling on her knees and bedewing Agnes's hand with tears, "do not come in thus between me and my prize."

"You have conquered, sister Syra (oh! never again call me lady)," said Agnes. "Remain at your post; such single-hearted, generous virtue must triumph. It is too sublime for so homely a sphere as my household."

"And I, for my part," subjoined Cæcilia, with a look of arch gravity, "say that she has said one very wicked thing, and told a great story, this evening."

"What is that, my pet?" asked Syra, laughing.

"Why, you said that I was wiser and better than you, because I declined eating some trumpery delicacy, which would have gratified my palate for a few minutes, at the expense of an act of greediness; while you have given up liberty, happiness, the free exercise of your religion, and have offered to give up life itself, for the salvation of one who is your tyrant and tormentor. Oh, fie! how could you tell me such a thing!"

The servant now announced that Agnes's litter was waiting at the door; and any one who could have seen the affectionate farewell of the three,—the noble lady, the slave, and the beggar, would have justly exclaimed, as people had often done before, "See how these Christians love one another!"

A Dove, as a Symbol of the Soul, Found in the Catacombs.

CHAPTER VIII.

THE FIRST DAY'S CONCLUSION.

IF we linger a little time about the door, and see Agnes fairly off, and listen to the merry conversation between her and Cæcilia, in which Agnes asks her to allow herself to be accompanied home by one of her attendants, as it has grown dark, and the girl is amused at the lady's forgetfulness that day and night are the same to her, and that on this very account she is the appointed guide to thread the mazes of the catacombs, familiar to her as the streets of Rome, which she walks in safety at all hours; if thus we pass a little time before re-entering, to inquire how the mistress within fares after the day's adventures, we shall find the house turned topsy-turvy. Slaves, with lamps and torches, are running about in every direction, looking for something or other that is lost, in every possible and impossible place. Euphrosyne insists it must be found; till at last the search is given up in despair. The reader will probably have anticipated the solution of the mystery. Syra had presented herself to have her wound re-dressed, according to orders, and the scarf which had bound it was no longer there. She could give no account of it, further than that she had taken it off, and put it on, certainly not so well as Euphrosyne had done it, and she gave the reason, for she scorned to tell a lie. Indeed she had never missed it till now. The kind-hearted old nurse was much grieved at the loss, which she considered must be heavy to a poor slave-girl, as she probably reserved that object for the purchase of her liberty. And Syra too was sorry, but for reasons which she could not have made the good housekeeper comprehend.

Euphrosyne had all the servants interrogated, and many even searched, to Syra's great pain and confusion; and then ordered a grand general battue through every part of the house where Syra had been. Who for a moment could have dreamt of suspecting a noble guest at the master's table of purloining any article, valuable or not? The old lady therefore came to the conclusion, that the scarf had been spirited away by some magical process; and greatly suspected that the black slave Afra, who she knew could not bear Syra, had been using some spell to annoy the poor girl. For she believed the Moor to be a very Canidia,* being often obliged to let her go out alone at night, under pretence of gathering herbs at full moon for her cosmetics, as if plucked at any other time, they would not possess the same virtues; to procure deadly poisons Euphrosyne suspected, but in reality to join in the hideous orgies of Fetichism† with others of her race, or to hold interviews with such as consulted her imaginary art. It was not till all was given up, and Syra found herself alone, that on more coolly recollecting the incidents of the day, she remembered the pause in Fulvius's walk across the court, at the very spot where she had stood, and his hurried steps after this, to the door. The conviction then flashed on her mind, that she must have there dropped her kerchief, and that he must have picked it up. That he should have passed it with indifference she believed impossible. She was confident, therefore, that it was now in his possession. After attempting to speculate on the possible consequences of this misadventure, and coming to no satisfactory conclusion, she

---

* A famous sorceress in Augustus's age.
† The worship of interior Africa.

determined to commit the matter entirely to God, and sought that repose which a good conscience was sure to render balmy and sweet.

Fabiola, on parting with Agnes, retired to her apartment; and after the usual services had been rendered to her by her other two servants and Euphrosyne, she dismissed them with a gentler manner than ever she had shown before. As soon as they had retired, she went to recline upon the couch where first we found her; when, to her disgust, she discovered lying on it the style with which she had wounded Syra. She opened a chest, and threw it in with horror; nor did she ever again use any such weapon.

She took up the volume which she had last laid down, and which had greatly amused her; but it was quite insipid, and seemed most frivolous to her. She laid it down again, and gave free course to her thoughts on all that had happened. It struck her first what a wonderful child her cousin Agnes was,—how unselfish, how pure, how simple; how sensible, too, and even wise! She determined to be her protector, her elder sister in all things. She had observed, too, as well as her father, the frequent looks which Fulvius had fixed upon her; not, indeed, those libertine looks which she herself had often borne with scorn, but designing, cunning glances, such as she thought betrayed some scheme or art, of which Agnes might become the victim. She resolved to frustrate it, whatever it might be, and arrived at exactly the opposite conclusion to her father's about him. She made up her mind to prevent Fulvius having any access to Agnes, at least at her house; and even blamed herself for having brought one so young into the strange company which often met at her father's table, especially as she now found that her motives for doing so had been decidedly selfish. It was nearly at the same moment that Fulvius, tossing on his couch, had come to the determination never again, if possible, to go inside Fabius's door, and to resist or elude every invitation from him.

Fabiola had measured his character; had caught, with her penetrating eye, the affectation of his manner, and the cunning of his looks; and could not help contrasting him with the frank and generous Sebastian. "What a noble fellow that Sebastian is!" she said to herself. "How different from all the other youths that come here. Never a foolish word escapes his lips, never an unkind look darts from his bright and cheerful eye. How abstemious, as becomes a soldier, at the table; how modest, as befits a hero, about his own strength and bold actions in war, which others speak so much about. Oh, if he only felt towards me as others pretend to do—" She did not finish the sentence, but a deep melancholy seemed to steal over her whole soul.

Then Syra's conversation, and all that had resulted from it, passed again through her mind; it was painful to her, yet she could not help dwelling on it; and she felt as if that day were a crisis in her life. Her pride had been humbled by a slave, and her mind softened, she knew not how. Had her eyes been opened in that hour; and had she been able to look up above this world, she would have seen a soft cloud like incense, but tinged with a rich carnation, rising from the bed-side of a kneeling slave (prayer and willing sacrifice of life breathed upwards together), which, when it struck the crystal footstool of a mercy-seat in heaven, fell down again as a dew of gentlest grace upon her arid heart.

She could not indeed see this; yet it was no less true; and wearied, at length she sought repose. But she too had a distressing dream. She saw a bright spot as in a delicious garden, richly illuminated by a light like noonday, but inexpressibly soft; while all around was dark. Beautiful flowers formed the sward, plants covered with richest bloom grew festooned from tree to tree, on each of which glowed golden fruit. In the midst of this space she saw the poor blind girl, with her look of happiness on her cheerful countenance, seated on the ground; while on one side, Agnes, with her sweetest simple looks, and on the other, Syra, with her quiet patient smile, hung over her and caressed her. Fabiola felt an irresistible desire to be with them; it seemed to her that they were enjoying some felicity which she had never known or witnessed; and she thought they even beckoned her to join them. She ran forward to do so, when to her horror she found a wide, and black, and deep ravine, at the bottom of which roared a torrent between herself and them. By degrees its waters rose, till they reached the upper margin of the dyke, and there flowed, though so deep, yet sparkling and brilliant, and most refreshing. Oh, for courage to plunge into this stream, through which alone the gorge could be crossed, and land in safety on the other side! And still they beckoned, urging her on to try it. But as she was standing on the brink, clasping her hands in despair, Calpurnius seemed to emerge from the dark air around, with a thick heavy curtain stretched out, on which were worked all sorts of monstrous and hideous chimeras, most curiously running into, and interwoven with, each other; and this dark veil grew and grew, till it shut out the beautiful vision from her sight. She felt disconsolate, till she seemed to see a bright genius (as she called him), in whose features she fancied she traced a spiritualized resemblance to Sebastian, and whom she had noticed standing sorrowful at a distance, now approach her, and, smiling on her, fan her fevered face with his gold and purple wing; when she lost her vision in a calm and refreshing sleep.

Our Saviour, from a representation found in the Catacombs.

CHAPTER IX.

MEETINGS.

OF all the Roman hills, the most distinctly traceable on every side is undoubtedly the Palatine. Augustus having chosen it for his residence, successive emperors followed his example; but gradually transformed his modest residence into a *palace*, which covered the entire hill. Nero, not satisfied with its dimensions, destroyed the neighborhood by fire, and then extended the imperial residence to the neighboring Esquiline; taking in the whole space now occupied between the two hills by the Coliseum. Vespasian threw down that "golden house," of which the magnificent vaults remain, covered with beautiful paintings; and built the amphitheatre just mentioned, and other edifices, with its materials. The entrance to the palace was made, soon after this period, from the *Via Sacra*, or Sacred Way, close to the arch of Titus. After passing through a vestibule, the visitor found himself in a magnificent court, the plan of which can be distinctly traced. Turning from this on the left side, he entered into an immense square space, arranged and consecrated to Adonis by Domitian, and planted with trees, shrubs, and flowers.

Still keeping to the left, you would enter into sets of chambers, constructed by Alexander Severus in honor of his

mother Mammæa, whose name they bore. They looked out opposite to the Cœlian hill, just at the angle of it, which abuts upon the later triumphal arch of Constantine, and the fountain called the *Meta Sudans*.* Here was the apartment occupied by Sebastian as a tribune, or superior officer, of the imperial guard. It consisted of a few rooms, most modestly furnished, as became a soldier and a Christian. His household was limited to a couple of freedmen, and a venerable matron, who had been his nurse, and loved him as a  child. They were Christians, as were all the men in his cohort; partly by conversion, but chiefly by care in recruiting new soldiers.

It was a few evenings after the scenes described in the last chapter, that Sebastian, a couple of hours after dark, ascended the steps of the vestibule just described, in company with another youth, of whom we have already spoken. Pancratius admired and loved Sebastian with the sort of affection that an ardent young officer may be supposed to bear towards an older and gallant soldier, who receives him into his friendship. But it was not as to a soldier of Cæsar, but as to a champion of Christ, that the civilian boy looked up to the young tribune, whose generosity, noble-mindedness, and valor, were enshrouded in such a gentle, simple bearing, and were accompanied by such prudence and considerateness, as gave confidence and encouragement to all that dealt with him. And Sebastian loved Pancratius no less, on account of his single-hearted ardor, and the innocence and candor of his mind. But he well saw the dangers to which his youthful warmth and impetuosity might lead him; and he encouraged

* "The sweating goal." It was an obelisk of brick (which yet remains), cased with marble, from the top of which issued water, and flowed down like a sheet of glass, all round it, into a basin on the ground.

him to keep close to himself, that he might guide, and perhaps sometimes restrain him.

As they were entering the palace, that part of which Sebastian's cohort guarded, he said to his companion: "Every time that I enter here, it strikes me how kind an act of Divine Providence it was, to plant almost at the very gate of Cæsar's palace, the arch which commemorates at once the downfall of the first great system that was antagonistic to

The Arch of Titus.

Christianity, and the completion of the greatest prophecy of the Gospel,—the destruction of Jerusalem by the Roman power.* I cannot but believe that another arch will one day

* The triumphal arch of Titus, on which are represented the spoils of the Temple.

arise to commemorate no less a victory, over the second enemy of our religion, the heathen Roman empire itself."

"What! do you contemplate the overthrow of this vast empire, as the means of establishing Christianity?"

"God forbid! I would shed the last drop of my blood, as I shed my first, to maintain it. And depend upon it, when the empire is converted, it will not be by such gradual growth as we now witness, but by some means, so unhuman, so divine, as we shall never, in our most sanguine longings, forecast; but all will exclaim, 'This is the change of the right hand of the Most High!'"

"No doubt; but your idea of a Christian triumphal arch supposes an earthly instrument; where do you imagine this to lie?"

"Why, Pancratius, my thoughts, I own, turn towards the family of one of the Augusti, as showing a slight germ of better thoughts: I mean, Constantius Chlorus."

"But, Sebastian, how many of even our learned and good men will say, nay, do say, if you speak thus to them, that similar hopes were entertained in the reigns of Alexander, Gordian, or Aurelian; yet ended in disappointment. Why, they ask, should we not expect the same results now?"

"I know it too well, my dear Pancratius, and bitterly have I often deplored those dark views which damp our energies; that lurking thought that vengeance is perpetual, and mercy temporary, that martyr's blood, and virgin's prayer have no power even to shorten times of visitation, and hasten hours of grace."

By this time they had reached Sebastian's apartment, the principal room of which was lighted, and evidently prepared for some assembly. But opposite the door was a window open to the ground, and leading to a terrace that ran along that side of the building. The night looked so bright through it, that they both instinctively walked across the room, and stood upon the terrace. A lovely and splendid view presented itself to them. The moon was high in the heavens, swimming in them, as an Italian moon does; a round, full globe, not a flat surface, bathed all round in its own refulgent atmosphere. It dimmed, indeed, the stars near itself; but they seemed to have retired, in thicker and more brilliant clusters, into the distant corners of the azure sky. It was just such an evening as, years after, Monica and Augustine enjoyed from a window at Ostia, as they discoursed of heavenly things.

It is true that, below and around, all was beautiful and grand. The Coliseum, or Flavian amphitheatre, rose at one side, in all its completeness; and the gentle murmur of the fountain, while its waters glistened in a silvery column, like the refluent sea-wave gliding down a slanting rock, came soothingly on the ear. On the other side, the lofty building called the Septizonium of Severus, in front, towering above the Coelian, the sumptuous baths of Caracalla, reflected from their marble walls and stately pillars the radiance of the autumn moon. But all these massive monuments of earthly glory rose unheeded before the two Christian youths, as they stood silent; the elder with his right arm round his youthful companion's neck, and resting on his shoulder. After a long pause, he took up the thread of his last discourse, and said, in a softer tone: "I was going to show you, when we stepped out here, the very spot just below our feet, where I have often fancied the triumphal arch, to which I have alluded, would stand.* But who can think of such paltry things below, with the splendid vault above us, lighted up so brilliantly, as if on purpose to draw upwards our eyes and hearts?"

"True, Sebastian; and I have sometimes thought, that, if

* The arch of Constantine stands exactly under the spot where this scene is described.

"Hail!" said Prudentius, "these are the trumpet-tones that announce us."

the under-side of that firmament up to which the eye of man, however wretched and sinful, may look, be so beautiful and bright, what must that upper-side be, down upon which the eye of boundless Glory deigns to glance! I imagine it to be like a richly-embroidered veil, through the texture of which a few points of golden thread may be allowed to pass; and these only reach us. How transcendently royal must be that upper surface, on which tread the lightsome feet of angels, and of the just made perfect!"

"A graceful thought, Pancratius, and no less true. It makes the veil, between us laboring here and the triumphal church above, thin and easily to be passed."

"And pardon me, Sebastian," said the youth, with the same look up to his friend, as a few evenings before had met his mother's inspired gaze, "pardon me if, while you wisely speculate upon a future arch to record the triumph of Christianity, I see already before me, built and open, the arch through which we, feeble as we are, may lead the Church speedily to the triumph of glory, and ourselves to that of bliss."

"Where, my dear boy, where do you mean?"

Pancratius pointed steadily with his hand towards the left,* and said: "There, my noble Sebastian; any of these open arches of the Flavian amphitheatre, which lead to its arena; over which, not denser than the outstretched canvas which shades our spectators, is that veil of which you spoke just now. But hark!"

"That was a lion's roar from beneath the Cœlian!" exclaimed Sebastian, surprised. "Wild beasts must have arrived at the *vivarium** of the amphitheatre; for I know there were none there yesterday."

"Yes, hark!" continued Pancratius, not noticing the interruption. "These are the trumpet-notes that summon

_{* The place where live beasts were kept for the shows.}

us; that is the music that must accompany us to our triumph!"

Both paused for a time, when Pancratius again broke the silence, saying: "This puts me in mind of a matter on which I want to take your advice, my faithful counsellor; will your company be soon arriving?"

"Not immediately; and they will drop in one by one; till they assemble, come into my chamber, where none will interrupt us."

They walked along the terrace, and entered the last room of the suite. It was at the corner of the hill, exactly opposite the fountain; and was lighted only by the rays of the moon, streaming through the open window on that side. The soldier stood near this, and Pancratius sat upon his small military couch.

"What is this great affair, Pancratius," said the officer, smiling, "upon which you wish to have my sage opinion?"

"Quite a trifle, I dare say," replied the youth, bashfully, "for a bold and generous man like you; but an important one to an unskilful and weak boy like me."

"A good and virtuous one, I doubt not; do let me hear it; and I promise you every assistance."

"Well, then, Sebastian—now don't think me foolish," proceeded Pancratius, hesitating and blushing at every word. "You are aware I have a quantity of useless plate at home— mere lumber, you know, in our plain way of living; and my dear mother, for any thing I can say, won't wear the lots of old-fashioned trinkets, which are lying locked up, and of no use to any body. I have no one to whom all this should descend. I am, and shall be, the last of my race. You have often told me, who in that case are a Christian's natural heirs, —the widow and the fatherless, the helpless and the indigent. Why should these wait my death, to have what by reversion is theirs? And if a persecution is coming, why run the risk of confiscation seizing them, or of plundering lictors stealing them, whenever our lives are wanted, to the utter loss of our rightful heirs?"

"Pancratius," said Sebastian, "I have listened without offering a remark to your noble suggestion. I wished you to have all the merit of uttering it yourself. Now, just tell me, what makes you doubt or hesitate about what I know you wish to do?"

"Why, to tell the truth, I feared it might be highly presumptuous and impertinent in one of my age to offer to do what people would be sure to imagine was something grand or generous; while I assure you, dear Sebastian, it is no such thing. For I shall not miss these things a bit; they are of no value to me whatever. But they will be to the poor, especially in the hard times coming."

"Of course Lucina consents?"

"Oh, no fear about that! I would not touch a grain of gold-dust without her even wishing it. But why I require your assistance is principally this. I should never be able to stand its being known that I presumed to do any thing considered out of the way, especially in a boy. You understand me? So I want you, and beg of you, to get the distribution made at some other house; and as from a—say from one who needs much the prayers of the faithful, especially the poor, and desires to remain unknown."

"I will serve you with delight, my good and truly noble boy! Hush! did you not hear the Lady Fabiola's name just mentioned? There again, and with an epithet expressive of no good will."

Pancratius approached the window; two voices were conversing together so close under them that the cornice between prevented their seeing the speakers, evidently a woman and a man. After a few minutes they walked out into the moonlight, almost as bright as day.

"I know that Moorish woman," said Sebastian; "it is Fabiola's black slave, Afra."

"And the man," added Pancratius, "is my late school-fellow, Corvinus."

They considered it their duty to catch, if possible, the thread of what seemed a plot; but, as the speakers walked up and down, they could only make out a sentence here and there. We will not, however, confine ourselves to these parts, but give the entire dialogue. Only, a word first about the interlocutors.

Of the slave we know enough for the present. Corvinus was son, as we have said, to Tertullus, originally prefect of the Prætorium. This office, unknown in the republic, and of imperial creation, had, from the reign of Tiberius, gradually absorbed almost all civil as well as military power; and he who held it often discharged the duties of chief criminal judge in Rome. It required no little strength of nerve to occupy this post to the satisfaction of despotic and unsparing masters. To sit all day in a tribunal, surrounded with hideous implements of torture, unmoved by the moans or the shrieks of old men, youths, or women, on whom they were tried; to direct a cool interrogatory to one stretched upon the rack, and quivering in agony on one side, while the last sentence of beating to death with bullet-laden scourges was being executed on the other; to sleep calmly after such scenes, and rise with appetite for their repetition, was not an occupation to which every member of the bar could be supposed to aspire. Tertullus had been brought from Sicily to fill the office, not because he was a cruel, but because he was a cold-hearted, man, not susceptible of pity or partiality. His tribunal, however, was Corvinus's early school; he could sit, while quite a boy, for hours at his father's feet, thoroughly enjoying the cruel spectacles before him, and angry when any one got off. He grew up sottish, coarse, and brutal; and not yet arrived at man's estate, his bloated and freckled countenance and bleary eyes, one of which was half closed, announced him to be already a dissolute and dissipated character. Without taste for any thing refined, or ability for any learning, he united in himself a certain amount of animal courage and strength, and a considerable measure of low cunning. He had never experienced in himself a generous feeling, and he had never curbed an evil passion. No one had ever offended him, whom he did not hate, and pursue with vengeance. Two, above all, he had sworn never to forgive—the school-master who had often chastised him for his sulky idleness, and the school-fellow who had blessed him for his brutal contumely. Justice and mercy, good and evil done to him, were equally odious to him.

Tertullus had no fortune to give him, and he seemed to have little genius to make one. To become possessed of one, however, was all-important to his mind; for wealth, as the means of gratifying his desires, was synonymous with him to supreme felicity. A rich heiress, or rather her dower, seemed the simplest object at which to aim. Too awkward, shy, and stupid to make himself a way in society, he sought other means, more kindred to his mind, for the attainment of his ambitious or avaricious desires. What these means were, his conversation with the black slave will best explain.

"I have come to meet you at the Meta Sudans again, for the fourth time, at this inconvenient hour. What news have you for me?"

"None, except that after to-morrow my mistress starts for her villa at Cajeta,* and of course I go with her. I shall want more money to carry on my operations in your favor."

"More still? You have had all I have received from my father for months."

"Why, do you know what Fabiola is?"

* Gaeta.

"Yes, to be sure, the richest match in Rome."

"The haughty and cold-hearted Fabiola is not so easily to be won."

"But yet you promised me that your charms and potions would secure me her acceptance, or at any rate her fortune. What expense can these things cause?"

"Very great indeed. The most precious ingredients are requisite, and must be paid for. And do you think I will go

The Appian Way, as it was.

out at such an hour as this amidst the tombs of the Appian way, to gather my simples, without being properly rewarded? But how do you mean to second my efforts? I have told you this would hasten their success."

"And how can I? You know I am not cut out by nature, or fitted by accomplishments, to make much impression on any one's affections. I would rather trust to the power of your black art."

"Then let me give you one piece of advice; if you have no grace or gift by which you can gain Fabiola's heart——"

"Fortune, you mean."

"They cannot be separated;—depend upon it, there is one thing which you may bring with you that is irresistible."

"What is that?"

"Gold."

"And where am I to get it? it is that I seek."

The black slave smiled maliciously, and said:

"Why cannot you get it as Fulvius does?"

"How does he get it?"

"By blood!"

"How do you know it?"

"I have made acquaintance with an old attendant that he has, who, if not as dark as I am in skin, fully makes up for it in his heart. His language and mine are sufficiently allied for us to be able to converse. He has asked me many questions about poisons, and pretended he would purchase my liberty, and take me back home as his wife; but I have something better than that in prospect, I trust. However, I got all that I wanted out from him."

"And what was that?"

"Why, that Fulvius had discovered a great conspiracy against Dioclesian; and from the wink of the old man's awful eye, I understood he had hatched it first; and he has been sent with strong recommendations to Rome to be employed in the same line."

"But I have no ability either to make or to discover conspiracies, though I may have to punish them."

"One way, however, is easy."

"What is that?"

"In my country there are large birds, which you may attempt in vain to run down with the fleetest horses; but which, if you look about for them quietly, are the first to betray themselves, for they only hide their heads."

"What do you wish to represent by this?"

"The Christians. Is there not going to be a persecution of them soon?"

"Yes, and a most fierce one; such as has never been before."

"Then follow my advice. Do not tire yourself with hunting them down, and catching, after all, but mean prey; keep your eyes open and look about for one or two good fat ones, half trying to conceal themselves; pounce upon them, get a good share of their confiscation, and come with one good handful to get two in return."

"Thank you, thank you; I understand you. You are not fond of these Christians, then?"

"Fond of them? I hate the entire race. The spirits which I worship are the deadly enemies of their very name." And she grinned horrible a ghastly smile as she proceeded: "I suspect one of my fellow-servants is one. Oh, how I detest her!"

"What makes you think it?"

"In the first place, she would not tell a lie for anything, and gets us all into dreadful scrapes by her absurd truthfulness."

"Good! what next?"

"Then she cares not for money or gifts; and so prevents our having them offered."

"Better!"

"And moreover she is—" the last word died in the ear of Corvinus, who replied:

"Well, indeed, I have to-day been out of the gate to meet a caravan of your countryfolk coming in; but you beat them all!"

"Indeed!" exclaimed Afra with delight, "who were they?"

"Simply Africans,"* replied Corvinus, with a laugh: "lions, panthers, leopards."

---

* The generic name for the wild beasts of that continent, as opposed to bears and others from the north.

"Wretch! do you insult me thus?"

"Come, come, be pacified. They are brought expressly to rid you of your hateful Christians. Let us part friends. Here is your money. But let it be the last; and let me know when the philtres begin to work. I will not forget your hint about Christian money. It is quite to my taste."

As he departed by the Sacred Way, she pretended to go along the Carinæ, the street between the Palatine and the Cœlian mounts; then turned back, and looking after him, exclaimed: "Fool! to think that I am going to try experiments for you on a person of Fabiola's character!"

She followed him at a distance; but as Sebastian, to his amazement, thought, turned into the vestibule of the palace. He determined at once to put Fabiola on her guard against this new plot; but this could not be done till her return from the country.

CHAPTER X.

OTHER MEETINGS.

WHEN the two youths returned to the room by which they had entered the apartment, they found the expected company assembled. A frugal repast was laid upon the table, principally as a blind to any intruder who might happen unexpectedly to enter. The assembly was large and varied, containing clergy and laity, men and women. The purpose of the meeting was to concert proper measures, in consequence of something which had lately occurred in the palace. This we must briefly explain.

Sebastian, enjoying the unbounded confidence of the emperor, employed all his influence in propagating the Christian faith within the palace. Numerous conversions had gradually been made; but shortly before this period there had been a wholesale one effected, the particulars of which are recorded in the genuine Acts of this glorious soldier. In virtue of former laws, many Christians were seized and brought to trial, which often ended in death. Two brothers, Marcus and Marcellianus, had been so accused, and were expecting execution; when their friends, admitted to see them, implored them with tears to save their lives by apostasy. They seemed to waver; they promised to deliberate. Sebastian heard of this, and rushed to save them. He was too well known to be refused admittance, and he entered into their gloomy prison like an angel of light. It consisted of a strong room in the house of the magistrate to whose care they had been intrusted. The place of confinement was generally left to that officer; and here Tranquillinus, the father of the two youths, had obtained a respite for them of thirty days to try to shake their constancy; and, to second his efforts, Nicostratus, the magistrate, had placed them in custody in his own house. Sebastian's was a bold and perilous office. Besides the two Christian captives, there were gathered in the place sixteen heathen prisoners; there were the parents of the unfortunate youths weeping over them, and caressing them, to allure them from their threatened doom; there was the gaoler, Claudius, and there was the magistrate, Nicostratus, with his wife, Zoë, drawn thither by the compassionate wish of seeing the youths snatched from their fate. Could Sebastian hope, that of this crowd not one would be found, whom a sense of official duty, or a hope of pardon, or hatred of Christianity, might impel to betray him, if he avowed himself a Christian? And did he not know that such a betrayal involved his death?

He knew it well; but what cared he? If three victims would thus be offered to God instead of two, so much the better; all that he dreaded was, that there should be none. The room was a banqueting-hall but seldom opened in the day, and consequently requiring very little light; what it had, entered only, as in the Pantheon, by an opening in the roof; and Sebastian, anxious to be seen by all, stood in the ray which now darted through it, strong and brilliant where it beat, but leaving the rest of the apartment almost dark. It broke against the gold and jewels of his rich tribune's armor, and, as he moved, scattered itself in sparks of brilliant hues into the darkest recesses of that gloom; while it beamed with serene steadiness upon his uncovered head, and displayed his noble features, softened by an emotion of tender grief, as he looked upon the two vacillating confessors. It was some

Military Tribune, after a bas-relief on Trajan's Column.

moments before he could give vent in words to the violence of his grief, till at length it broke forth in impassioned tones.

"Holy and venerable brothers," he exclaimed, "who have borne witness to Christ; who are imprisoned for Him; whose limbs are marked by chains worn for His sake; who have tasted torments with Him, —I ought to fall at your feet and do you homage, and ask your prayers; instead of standing before you as your exhorter, still less as your reprover. Can this be true which I have heard, that while angels were putting the last flower to your crowns, you have bid them pause, and even thought of telling them to unweave them, and scatter their blossoms to the winds? Can I believe that you who have already your feet on the threshold of Paradise, are thinking of drawing them back, to tread once more the valley of exile and of tears?"

The two youths hung down their heads and wept in humble confession of their weakness. Sebastian proceeded:

"You cannot meet the eye of a poor soldier like me, the least of Christ's servants; how then will you stand the angry glance of the Lord whom you are about to deny before men (but cannot in your hearts deny), on that terrible day, when He, in return, will deny you before His angels? When, instead of standing manfully before Him, like good and faithful servants, as to-morrow ye might have done, you shall have to come into His presence after having crawled through a few more years of infamy, disowned by the Church, despised by its enemies, and, what is worse, gnawed by an undying worm, and victims of a sleepless remorse?"

"Cease; oh, in pity cease, young man, whoever thou art," exclaimed Tranquillinus, the father of the youths. "Speak not thus severely to my sons; it was, I assure thee, to their mother's tears and to my entreaties that they had begun to yield, and not to the tortures which they have endured with such fortitude. Why should they leave their wretched parents to misery and sorrow? does thy religion command this, and dost thou call it holy?"

"Wait in patience, my good old man," said Sebastian, with the kindest look and accent, "and let me speak first with thy sons. They know what I mean, which thou canst not yet; but with God's grace thou too shalt soon. Your father, indeed, is right in saying, that for his sake and your mother's you have been deliberating whether you should not prefer them to Him who told you, 'He that loveth father or mother more than Me, is not worthy of Me.' You cannot hope to purchase for these your aged parents, eternal life by your own loss of it. Will you make them Christians by abandoning Christianity? will you make them soldiers of the Cross by deserting its standard? will you teach them that its doctrines are more precious than life, by preferring life to them? Do you want to gain for them, not the mortal life of the perishable body, but the eternal life of the soul? then hasten yourselves to its acquisition; throw down at the feet of your Saviour the crowns you will receive, and entreat for your parents' salvation."

"Enough, enough, Sebastian, we are resolved," cried out together both the brothers.

"Claudius," said one, "put on me again the chains you have taken off."

"Nicostratus," added the other, "give orders for the sentence to be carried out."

Yet neither Claudius nor Nicostratus moved.

"Farewell, dear father; adieu, dearest mother," they in turn said, embracing their parents.

"No," replied the father, "we part no more. Nicostratus, go tell Chromatius that I am from this moment a Christian with my sons; I will die with them for a religion which can make heroes thus of boys." "And I," continued the mother, "will not be separated from my husband and children."

The scene which followed baffles description. All were moved; all wept; the prisoners joined in the tumult of these new affections; and Sebastian saw himself surrounded by a group of men and women smitten by grace, softened by its influences, and subdued by its power; yet all was lost if one remained behind. He saw the danger, not to himself, but to the Church, if a sudden discovery were made, and to those souls fluttering upon the confines of life. Some hung upon his arms; some clasped his knees; some kissed his feet, as though he had been a spirit of peace, such as visited Peter in his dungeon at Jerusalem.

Two alone had expressed no thought. Nicostratus was indeed moved, but by no means conquered. His feelings were agitated, but his convictions unshaken. His wife, Zoë, knelt before Sebastian with a beseeching look and outstretched arms, but she spoke not a word.

"Come, Sebastian," said the keeper of the records, for

such was Nicostratus's office; "it is time for thee to depart. I cannot but admire the sincerity of belief, and the generosity of heart, which can make thee act as thou hast done, and which impel these young men to death; but my duty is imperative, and must overweigh my private feelings."

"And dost not thou believe with the rest?"

"No, Sebastian, I yield not so easily; I must have stronger evidences than even thy virtue."

"Oh, speak to him then, thou!" said Sebastian to Zoë; "speak, faithful wife; speak to thy husband's heart; for I am mistaken indeed, if those looks of thine tell me not that *thou* at least believest."

Zoë covered her face with her hands, and burst into a passion of tears.

"Thou hast touched her to the quick, Sebastian," said her husband; "knowest thou not that she is dumb?"

"I knew it not, noble Nicostratus; for when last I saw her in Asia she could speak."

"For six years," replied the other, with a faltering voice, "her once eloquent tongue has been paralyzed, and she has not uttered a single word."

Sebastian was silent for a moment; then suddenly he threw out his arms, and stretched them forth, as the Christians always did in prayer, and raised his eyes to heaven; then burst forth in these words:

"O God! Father of our Lord Jesus Christ, the beginning of this work is Thine; let its accomplishment be Thine alone. Put forth Thy power, for it is needed; intrust it for once to the weakest and poorest of instruments. Let me, though most unworthy, so wield the sword of Thy victorious Cross, as that the spirits of darkness may fly before it, and Thy salvation may embrace us all! Zoë, look up once more to me."

All were hushed in silence, when Sebastian, after a

moment's silent prayer, with his right hand made over her mouth the sign of the cross, saying: "Zoë, speak; dost thou believe?"

"I believe in the Lord Jesus Christ," she replied, in a clear and firm voice, and fell upon Sebastian's feet.

It was almost a shriek that Nicostratus uttered, as he threw himself on his knees, and bathed Sebastian's right hand with tears.

The victory was complete. Every one was gained; and immediate steps were taken to prevent discovery. The person responsible for the prisoners could take them where he wished; and Nicostratus transferred them all, with Tranquillinus and his wife, to the full liberty of his house. Sebastian lost no time in putting them under the care of the holy priest Polycarp, of the title of St. Pastor. It was a case so peculiar, and requiring such concealment, and the times were so threatening, and all new irritations had so much to be avoided, that the instruction was hurried, and continued night and day: so that baptism was quickly administered.

The new Christian flock was encouraged and consoled by a fresh wonder. Tranquillinus, who was suffering severely from the gout, was restored to instant and complete health by baptism. Chromatius was the prefect of the city, to whom Nicostratus was liable for his prisoners; and this officer could not long conceal from him what had happened. It was indeed a matter of life or death to them all; but, strengthened now by faith, they were prepared for either. Chromatius was a man of upright character, and not fond of persecution; and listened with interest to the account of what had occurred. But when he heard of Tranquillinus's cure, he was greatly struck. He was himself a victim to the same disease, and suffered agonies of pain. "If," he said, "what you relate be true, and if I can have personal experience of this healing power, I certainly will not resist its evidence."

Sebastian was sent for. To have administered baptism without faith preceding, as an experiment of its healing virtue, would have been a superstition. Sebastian took another course, which will be later described, and Chromatius completely recovered. He received baptism soon after, with his son Tibertius.

It was clearly impossible for him to continue in his office, and he had accordingly resigned it to the emperor. Tertullus, the father of the hopeful Corvinus, and prefect of the Prætorium, had been named his successor; so the reader will perceive that the events just related from the Acts of St. Sebastian, had occurred a little before our narrative begins; for in an early chapter we spoke of Corvinus's father as already prefect of the city.

Let us now come down again to the evening in which Sebastian and Pancratius met most of the persons above enumerated in the officer's chamber. Many of them resided in, or about, the palace; and besides them were present Castulus, who held a high situation at court,* and his wife Irene. Several previous meetings had been held, to decide upon some plan for securing the completer instruction of the converts, and for withdrawing from observation so many persons, whose change of life and retirement from office would excite wonder and inquiry. Sebastian had obtained permission from the emperor for Chromatius to retire to a country-house in Campania; and it had been arranged that a considerable number of the neophytes should join him there, and, forming one household, should go on with religious instruction, and unite in common offices of piety. The season was come when every body retired to the country, and the emperor himself was going to the coast of Naples, and thence would take a journey to southern Italy. It was therefore a favorable moment for carrying out the preconcerted plan. Indeed the Pope, we are

* It is not mentioned what it precisely was.

told, on the Sunday following this conversion, celebrated the divine mysteries in the house of Nicostratus, and proposed this withdrawal from the city.

At this meeting all details were arranged; different parties were to start, in the course of the following days, by various roads—some direct by the Appian, some along the Latin, others round by Tibur and a mountain road, through Arpinum; but all were to meet at the villa, not far from Capua.

The Roman Forum.

Through the whole discussion of these somewhat tedious arrangements, Torquatus, one of the former prisoners, converted by Sebastian's visit, showed himself forward, impatient, and impetuous. He found fault with every plan, seemed discontented with the directions given him, spoke almost contemptuously of this flight from danger, as he called it; and boasted that, for his part, he was ready to go into the Forum on the morrow, and overthrow any altar, or confront any judge, as a Christian. Every thing was said and done to soothe, and even to cool him; and it was felt to be most important that he should be taken with the rest into the country. He insisted, however, upon going his own way.

Only one more point remained to be decided: it was, who should head the little colony, and direct its operations. Here was renewed a contest of love between the holy priest Polycarp and Sebastian; each wishing to remain in Rome, and have the first chance of martyrdom. But now the difference was cut short by a letter brought in, from the Pope, addressed to his "Beloved son Polycarp, priest of the title of St. Pastor," in which he commanded him to accompany the converts, and leave Sebastian to the arduous duty of encouraging confessors, and protecting Christians in Rome. To hear was to obey; and the meeting broke up with a prayer of thanksgiving.

Sebastian, after bidding affectionate farewell to his friends, insisted upon accompanying Pancratius home. As they were leaving the room, the latter remarked, "Sebastian, I do not like that Torquatus. I fear he will give us trouble."

"To tell the truth," answered the soldier, "I would rather he were different; but we must remember that he is a neophyte, and will improve in time, and by grace."

As they passed into the entrance-court of the palace, they heard a Babel of uncouth sounds, with coarse laughter and occasional yells, proceeding from the adjoining yard, in which were the quarters of the Mauritanian archers. A fire seemed to be blazing in the midst of it, for the smoke and sparks rose above the surrounding porticoes.

Sebastian accosted the sentinel in the court where they were, and asked: "Friend, what is going on there among our neighbors?"

"The black slave," he replied, "who is their priestess, and who is betrothed to their captain, if she can purchase her freedom, has come in for some midnight rites, and this horrid turmoil takes place every time she comes."

"Indeed!" said Pancratius, "and can you tell me what is the religion these Africans follow?"

"I do not know, sir," replied the legionary, "unless they be what are called Christians."

"What makes you think so?"

"Why, I have heard that the Christians meet by night, and sing detestable songs, and commit all sorts of crimes; and cook and eat the flesh of a child murdered for the purpose*—just what might seem to be going on here."

"Good night, comrade," said Sebastian; and then exclaimed, as they were issuing from the vestibule, "Is it not strange, Pancratius, that, in spite of all our efforts, we who are conscious that we worship only the One living God in spirit and truth, who know what care we take to keep ourselves undefiled by sin, and who would die rather than speak an unclean word, should yet, after 300 years, be confounded by the people with the followers of the most degraded superstitions, and have our worship ranked with the very idolatry, which above all things we abhor? 'How long, O Lord! how long?'"

"So long," said Pancratius, pausing on the steps outside the vestibule, and looking at the now declining moon, "so long as we shall continue to walk in this pale light, and until the Sun of Justice shall rise upon our country in His beauty, and enrich it with His splendor. Sebastian, tell me, whence do you best like to see the sun rise?"

"The most lovely sunrise I have ever seen," replied the soldier, as if humoring his companion's fanciful question, "was from the top of the Latial mountain,† by the temple of Jupiter. The sun rose behind the mountain, and projected its huge shadow like a pyramid over the plain, and far upon the sea; then, as it rose higher, this lessened and withdrew;

* These were the popular ideas of Christian worship.
† Now Monte Cavo, above Albano.

and every moment some new object caught the light, first the galleys and skiffs upon the water, then the shore with its dancing waves; and by degrees one white edifice after the other sparkled in the fresh beams, till at last majestic Rome itself, with its towering pinnacles, basked in the effulgence of day. It was a glorious sight, indeed; such as could not have been witnessed or imagined by those below."

"Just what I should have expected, Sebastian," observed Pancratius; "and so it will be when that more brilliant sun rises fully upon this benighted country. How beautiful will it then be to behold the shades retiring, and each moment one and another of the charms, as yet concealed, of our holy faith and worship starting into light, till the imperial city itself shines forth a holy type of the city of God. Will they who live in those times see these beauties, and worthily value them? Or, will they look only at the narrow space around them, and hold their hands before their eyes, to shade them from the sudden glare? I know not, dear Sebastian, but I hope that you and I will look down upon that grand spectacle, from where alone it can be duly appreciated, from a mountain higher than Jupiter's, be he Alban or be he Olympian,—dwelling on that holy mount, whereon stands the Lamb, from whose feet flow the streams of life." *

They continued their walk in silence through the brilliantly-lighted streets; † and when they had reached Lucina's house, and had affectionately bid one another good-night, Pancratius seemed to hesitate a moment, and then said:

"Sebastian, you said something this evening, which I should much like to have explained."

* "Vidi supra montem Agnum stantem, de sub cujus pede fons vivus emanat."—*Office of St. Clement.*

† Ammianus Marcellinus tells us that, at the decline of the empire, the streets at night were lighted so as to rival day. "Et hoc confidenter agebat (Gallus) ubi pernoctantium luminum claritudo dierum nitet imitari fulgorem." Lib. xiv. c. 1.

"What was it?"

"When you were contending with Polycarp, about going into Campania, or remaining in Rome, you promised that if you stayed you would be most cautious, and not expose yourself to unnecessary risks; then you added, that there was one purpose in your mind which would effectually restrain you; but that when that was accomplished, you would find it difficult to check your longing ardor to give your life for Christ."

"And why, Pancratius, do you desire so much to know this foolish thought of mine?"

"Because I own I am really curious to learn what can be the object high enough to check in you the aspiration, after what I know you consider to be the very highest of a Christian's aim."

"I am sorry, my dear boy, that it is not in my power to tell you now. But you shall know it sometime."

"Do you promise me?"

"Yes, most solemnly. God bless you!"

A Lamp with a Milk can, found in the Catacomb of SS. Peter and Marcellin.

CHAPTER XI.

A TALK WITH THE READER.

WE will take advantage of the holiday which Rome is enjoying, sending out its inhabitants to the neighboring hills, or to the whole line of sea-coast from Genoa to Pæstum, for amusement on land and water; and, in a merely didactic way, endeavor to communicate to our reader some information, which may throw light on what we have already written, and prepare him for what will follow.

From the very compressed form in which the early history of the Church is generally studied, and from the unchronological arrangement of the saints' biographies, as we usually read them, we may easily be led to an erroneous idea of the state of our first Christian ancestors. This may happen in two different ways.

We may come to imagine, that during the first three centuries the Church was suffering unrespited, under active persecution; that the faithful worshipped in fear and trembling, and almost lived in the catacombs; that bare existence, with scarcely an opportunity for outward development or inward organization, none for splendor, was all that religion could enjoy; that, in fine, it was a period of conflict and of tribulation, without an interval of peace or consolation. On the other hand, we may suppose, that those three centuries were divided into epochs by ten distinct persecutions, some of longer and some of shorter duration, but definitely separated from one another by breathing times of complete rest.

Either of these views is erroneous; and we desire to state more accurately the real condition of the Christian Church, under the various circumstances of that most pregnant portion of her history.

When once persecution had broken loose upon the Church, it may be said never entirely to have relaxed its hold, till her final pacification under Constantine. An edict of persecution once issued by an emperor was seldom recalled; and though the rigor of its enforcement might gradually relax or cease, through the accession of a milder ruler, still it never became completely a dead letter, but was a dangerous weapon in the hands of a cruel or bigoted governor of a city or province. Hence, in the intervals between the greater general persecutions, ordered by a new decree, we find many martyrs, who owed their crowns either to popular fury, or to the hatred of Christianity in local rulers. Hence also we read of a bitter persecution being carried on in one part of the empire, while other portions enjoyed complete peace.

Perhaps a few examples of the various phases of persecution will illustrate the real relations of the primitive Church with the State, better than mere description; and the more learned reader can pass over this digression, or must have the patience to hear repeated, what he is so familiar with, that it will seem commonplace.

Trajan was by no means one of the cruel emperors; on the contrary, he was habitually just and merciful. Yet, though he published no new edicts against the Christians, many noble martyrs—amongst them St. Ignatius, bishop of Antioch, at Rome, and St. Simeon at Jerusalem—glorified their Lord in his reign. Indeed, when Pliny the younger consulted him on the manner in which he should deal with

Christians, who might be brought before him as governor of Bithynia, the emperor gave him a rule which exhibits the lowest standard of justice: that they were not to be sought out; but if accused, they were to be punished. Adrian, who

S. Ignatius, Bishop of Antioch.

issued no decree of persecution, gave a similar reply to a similar question from Serenius Granianus, pro-consul of Asia. And under him, too, and even by his own orders, cruel martyrdom was suffered by the intrepid Symphorosa and her seven sons at Tibur, or Tivoli. A beautiful inscription found in the catacombs mentions Marius, a young officer, who shed his blood for Christ under this emperor." Indeed, St. Justin Martyr, the great apologist of Christianity, informs us that he owed his conversion to the constancy of the martyrs under this emperor.

In like manner, before the Emperor Septimus Severus had published his persecuting edicts, many Christians had suffered torments and death. Such were the celebrated martyrs of Scillita in Africa, and SS. Perpetua and Felicitas, with their companions; the Acts of whose martyrdom, containing the diary of the first noble lady, twenty years of age, brought down by herself to the eve of her death, form one of the most touching, and exquisitely beautiful, documents preserved to us from the ancient Church.

From these historical facts it will be evident, that while there was from time to time a more active, severe, and general persecution of the Christian name all through the empire, there were partial and local cessations, and sometimes even a general suspension, of its rigor. An occurrence of this sort has secured for us most interesting information, connected with our subject. When the persecution of Severus had relaxed in other parts, it happened that Scapula, pro-consul of Africa, prolonged it in his province with unrelenting cruelty. He had condemned, among others, Mavilus of Adrumetum to be devoured by beasts, when he was seized with a severe illness. Tertullian, the oldest Christian Latin writer, addressed a letter to him, in which he bids him take warning from this visitation, and repent of his crimes: reminding him of many judgments which had befallen cruel judges of the Christians, in various parts of the world. Yet such was the charity of those holy men, that he tells him they were offering up earnest prayers for their enemy's recovery!

He then goes on to inform him, that he may very well fulfil his duties without practising cruelty, by acting as other

* Euseb. Sebterr. l. iii. c. 22.

magistrates had done. For instance, Cincius Severus suggested to the accused the answers they should make, to be acquitted. Vespronius Candidus dismissed a Christian, on the ground that his condemnation would encourage tumults. Asper, seeing one ready to yield upon the application of slight torments, would not press him further; and expressed regret that such a case should have been brought before him. Pudens, on reading an act of accusation, declared the title informal, because calumnious, and tore it up.

We thus see how much might depend upon the temper, and perhaps the tendencies, of governors and judges, in the enforcing even of imperial edicts of persecution. And St. Ambrose tells us that some governors boasted that they had brought back from their provinces their swords unstained with blood (*incruentos enses*).

We can also easily understand how, at any particular time, a savage persecution might rage in Gaul, or Africa, or Asia, while the main part of the Church was enjoying peace. But Rome was undoubtedly the place most subject to frequent outbreaks of the hostile spirit; so that it might be considered as the privilege of its pontiffs, during the first three centuries, to bear the witness of blood to the faith, which they taught. To be elected Pope was equivalent to being promoted to martyrdom.

At the period of our narrative, the Church was in one of those longer intervals of comparative peace, which gave opportunity for great development. From the death of Valerian, in 268, there had been no new formal persecution, though the interval is glorified by many noble martyrdoms. During such periods, the Christians were able to carry out their religious system with completeness, and even with splendor. The city was divided into districts or parishes, each having its title, or church, served by priests, deacons, and inferior ministers. The poor were supported, the sick visited, catechumens instructed; the Sacraments were administered, daily worship was practised, and the penitential canons were enforced by the clergy of each title; and collections were made for these purposes, and others connected with religious charity, and its consequence, hospitality. It is recorded, that in 250, during the pontificate of Cornelius, there were in Rome forty-six priests, a hundred and fifty-four inferior ministers, who were supported by the alms of the faithful, together with fifteen hundred poor.* This number of the priests pretty nearly corresponds to that of the titles, which St. Optatus tells us there were in Rome.

Although the tombs of the martyrs in the catacombs continued to be objects of devotion during these more peaceful intervals, and these asylums of the persecuted were kept in order and repair, they did not then serve for the ordinary places of worship. The churches to which we have already alluded were often public, large, and even splendid; and heathens used to be present at the sermons delivered in them, and such portions of the liturgy as were open to catechumens. But generally they were in private houses, probably made out of the large halls, or *triclinia*, which the nobler mansions contained. Thus we know that many of the titles in Rome were originally of that character. Tertullian mentions Christian cemeteries under a name, and with circumstances, which show that they were above ground, for he compares them to "threshing-floors," which were necessarily exposed to the air.

A custom of ancient Roman life will remove an objection which may arise, as to how considerable multitudes could assemble in these places without attracting attention, and consequently persecution. It was usual for what may be called a levée to be held every morning by the rich, attended by dependents, or clients, and messengers from their friends, either slaves or freedmen, some of whom were admitted into

* Euseb. E. H. l. vi. c. 43.

The Sacrament of Penance, in the Early Ages of the Church.

the inner court, to the master's presence, while others only presented themselves, and were dismissed. Hundreds might thus go in and out of a great house, in addition to the crowd of domestic slaves, tradespeople and others who had access to it, through the principal or the back entrance, and little or no notice would be taken of the circumstance.

There is another important phenomenon in the social life of the early Christians, which one would hardly know how to believe, were not evidence of it brought before us in the most authentic Acts of the martyrs, and in ecclesiastical history. It is, the concealment which they contrived to practise. No doubt can be entertained, that persons were moving in the highest society, were occupying conspicuous public situations, were near the persons of the emperors, who were Christians; and yet were not suspected to be such by their most intimate heathen friends. Nay, cases occurred where the nearest relations were kept in total ignorance on this subject. No lie, no dissembling, no action especially, inconsistent with Christian morality or Christian truth, was ever permitted to ensure such secrecy. But every precaution compatible with complete uprightness was taken to conceal Christianity from the public eye.*

However necessary this prudential course might be, to prevent any wanton persecution, its consequences fell often heavily upon those who held it. The heathen world, the world of power, of influence, and of state, the world which made laws as best suited it, and executed them, the world that loved earthly prosperity and hated faith, felt itself sur-

* No domestic concealment surely could be more difficult than that of a wife's religion from her husband. Yet Tertullian supposes this to have been not uncommon. For, speaking of a married woman communicating herself at home, according to practice in those ages of persecution, he says, "Let not your husband know what you taste secretly, before every other food; and if he shall know of the bread, may he not know it to be what it is called." *Ad Uxor.* lib. ii. c. 5. Whereas, in another place, he writes of a Catholic husband and wife giving communion to one another. *De Monogamia*, c. 11.

rounded, filled, compenetrated by a mysterious system, which spread, no one could see how, and exercised an influence derived no one knew whence. Families were startled at finding a son or daughter to have embraced this new law, with which they were not aware that they had been in contact, and which, in their heated fancies and popular views, they considered stupid, grovelling, and anti-social. Hence the hatred of Christianity was political as well as religious; the system was considered as un-Roman, as having an interest opposed to the extension and prosperity of the empire, and as obeying an unseen and spiritual power. The Christians were pronounced *irreligiosi in Cæsares*, "disloyal to the emperors," and that was enough. Hence their security and peace depended much upon the state of popular feeling; when any demagogue or fanatic could succeed in rousing this, neither their denial of the charges brought against them, nor their peaceful demeanor, nor the claims of civilized life, could suffice to screen them from such measure of persecution as could be safely urged against them.

After these digressive remarks, we will resume, and unite again the broken thread of our narrative.

A Monogram of Christ.

CHAPTER XII.

THE WOLF AND THE FOX.

THE hints of the African slave had not been thrown away upon the sordid mind of Corvinus. Her own hatred of Christianity arose from the circumstance, that a former mistress of hers had become a Christian and had manumitted all her other slaves; but, feeling it wrong to turn so dangerous a character as Afra, or rather Jubala (her proper name), upon the world, had transferred her to another proprietor.

Corvinus had often seen Fulvius at the baths and other places of public resort, had admired and envied him, for his appearance, his dress, his conversation. But with his untoward shyness, or moroseness, he could never have found courage to address him, had he not now discovered, that though a more refined, he was not a less profound, villain than himself. Fulvius's wit and cleverness might supply the want of these qualities in his own sottish composition, while his own brute force, and unfeeling recklessness, might be valuable auxiliaries to those higher gifts. He had the young stranger in his power, by the discovery which he had made of his real character. He determined, therefore, to make an effort, and enter into alliance with one who otherwise might prove a dangerous rival.

It was about ten days after the meeting last described, that Corvinus went to stroll in Pompey's gardens. These covered the space round his theatre, in the neighborhood of the present Piazza Farnese. A conflagration in the reign of Carinus had lately destroyed the scene, as it was called, of the edifice, and Dioclesian had repaired it with great magnificence. The gardens were distinguished from others by rows of plane-trees, which formed a delicious shade. Statues of wild beasts, fountains, and artificial brooks, profusely adorned them.

Roman Gardens, from an old painting.

While sauntering about, Corvinus caught a sight of Fulvius, and made up to him.

"What do you want with me?" asked the foreigner, with a look of surprise and scorn at the slovenly dress of Corvinus.

"To have a talk with you, which may turn out to your advantage—and mine."

"What can you propose to me, with the first of these recommendations? No doubt at all as to the second."

"Fulvius, I am a plain-spoken man, and have no pretensions to your cleverness and elegance; but we are both of one trade, and both consequently of one mind."

Fulvius started, and deeply colored; then said, with a contemptuous air, "What do you mean, sirrah?"

"If you double your fist," rejoined Corvinus, "to show me the fine rings on your delicate fingers, it is very well. But if you mean to threaten by it, you may as well put your hand again into the folds of your toga. It is more graceful."

"Cut this matter short, sir. Again I ask, what do you mean?"

"This, Fulvius," and he whispered into his ear, "that you are a spy and an informer."

Fulvius was staggered; then rallying, said, "What right have you to make such an odious charge against me?"

"You *discovered*" (with a strong emphasis) "a conspiracy in the East, and Dioclesian—"

Fulvius stopped him, and asked, "What is your name, and who are you?"

"I am Corvinus, the son of Tertullus, prefect of the city."

This seemed to account for all; and Fulvius said, in subdued tones, "No more here; I see friends coming. Meet me disguised at daybreak to-morrow in the Patrician Street,* under the portico of the Baths of Novatus. We will talk more at leisure."

Corvinus returned home, not ill-satisfied with his first attempt at diplomacy; he procured a garment shabbier than his own from one of his father's slaves, and was at the appointed spot by the first dawn of day. He had to wait a long time, and had almost lost patience, when he saw his new friend approach.

Fulvius was well wrapped up in a large overcoat, and wore its hood over his face. He thus saluted Corvinus:

"Good morning, comrade; I fear I have kept you waiting in the cold morning air, especially as you are thinly clad."

"I own," replied Corvinus, "that I should have been tired, had I not been immensely amused and yet puzzled, by what I have been observing."

"What is that?"

"Why, from an early hour, long, I suspect, before my coming, there have been arriving here from every side, and entering into that house, by the back door in the narrow

* The Vicus Patricius.

street, the rarest collection of miserable objects that you ever saw; the blind, the lame, the maimed, the decrepit, the deformed of every possible shape; while by the front door several persons have entered, evidently of a different class."

"Whose dwelling is it, do you know? It looks a large old house, but rather out of condition."

"It belongs to a very rich, and, it is said, very miserly old patrician. But look! there come some more."

At that moment a very feeble man, bent down by age, was approaching, supported by a young and cheerful girl, who chatted most kindly to him as she supported him.

"We are just there," she said to him; "a few more steps, and you shall sit down and rest."

"Thank you, my child," replied the poor old man, "how kind of you to come for me so early!"

"I knew," she said, "you would want help; and as I am the most useless person about, I thought I would go and fetch you."

"I have always heard that blind people are selfish, and it seems but natural; but you, Cecilia, are certainly an exception."

"Not at all; this is only my way of showing selfishness."

"How do you mean?"

"Why, first, I get the advantage of your eyes, and then I get the satisfaction of supporting you. 'I was an eye to the blind,' that is you; and 'a foot to the lame,' that is myself."*

They reached the door as she spoke these words.

"That girl is blind," said Fulvius to Corvinus. "Do you not see how straight she walks, without looking right or left?"

"So she is," answered the other. "Surely this is not the place so often spoken of, where beggars meet, and the blind

* Job xxix. 15.

see, and the lame walk, and all feast together? But yet I observed these people were so different from the mendicants on the Arician bridge.* They appeared respectable and even cheerful; and not one asked me for alms as he passed."

"It is very strange; and I should like to discover the mystery. A good job might, perhaps, be got out of it. The old patrician, you say, is very rich?"

"Immensely!"

"Humph! How could one manage to get in?"

"I have it! I will take off my shoes, screw up one leg like a cripple, and join the next group of queer ones that come, and go boldly in, doing as they do."

"That will hardly succeed; depend upon it every one of these people is known at the house."

"I am sure not, for several of them asked me if this was the house of the Lady Agnes."

"Of whom?" asked Fulvius, with a start.

"Why do you look so?" said Corvinus. "It is the house of her parents; but she is better known than they, as being a young heiress, nearly as rich as her cousin Fabiola."

Fulvius paused for a moment; a strong suspicion, too subtle and important to be communicated to his rude companion, flashed through his mind. He said, therefore, to Corvinus:

"If you are sure that these people are not familiar at the house, try your plan. I have met the lady before, and will venture by the front door. Thus we shall have a double chance."

"Do you know what I am thinking, Fulvius?"

"Something very bright, no doubt."

"That when you and I join in any enterprise, we shall *always* have two chances."

---

* The place most noted in the neighborhood of Rome for whining and importunate beggars.

"What are they?"

"The fox's and the wolf's, when they conspire to rob a fold."

Fulvius cast on him a look of disdain, which Corvinus returned by a hideous leer; and they separated for their respective posts.

A Lamp, with the Monogram of Christ.

CHAPTER XIII.

CHARITY.

AS we do not choose to enter the house of Agnes, either with the wolf or with the fox, we will take a more spiritual mode of doing so, and find ourselves at once inside.

The parents of Agnes represented noble lines of ancestry, and her family was not one of recent conversion, but had for several generations professed the faith. As in heathen families was cherished the memory of ancestors who had won a triumph, or held high offices in the state, so in this, and other Christian houses, was preserved with pious reverence and affectionate pride, the remembrance of those relations who had, in the last hundred and fifty years or more, borne the palm of martyrdom, or occupied the sublimer dignities of the Church. But, though ennobled thus, and with a constant stream of blood poured forth for Christ, accompanying the waving branches of the family-tree, the stem had never been hewn down, but had survived repeated storms. This may appear surprising; but when we reflect how many a soldier goes through a whole campaign of frequent actions and does not receive a wound; or how many a family remains untainted through a plague, we cannot be surprised if Providence watched over the well-being of the Church, by preserving in it, through old family successions, long unbroken chains of tradition, and so enabling the faithful to say: "Unless the Lord of Hosts had left us seed, we had been as Sodom, and we should have been like to Gomorrha."*

All the honors and the hopes of this family centred now in one, whose name is already known to our readers, Agnes, the only child of that ancient house. Given to her parents as they had reached the very verge of hope that their line could be continued, she had been from infancy blest with such a sweetness of disposition, such a docility and intelligence of mind, and such simplicity and innocence of character, that she had grown up the common object of love, and almost of reverence, to the entire house, from her parents down to the lowest servant. Yet nothing seemed to spoil, or warp, the compact virtuousness of her nature; but her good qualities expanded, with a well-balanced adjustment, which at the early age in which we find her, had ripened into combined grace and wisdom. She shared all her parents' virtuous thoughts, and cared as little for the world as they. She lived with them in a small portion of the mansion, which was fitted up with elegance, though not with luxury; and their establishment was adequate to all their wants. Here they received the few friends with whom they preserved familiar relations; though, as they did not entertain, nor go out, these were few. Fabiola was an occasional visitor, though Agnes preferred going to see her at her house; and she often expressed to her young friend her longing for the day, when, meeting with a suitable match, she would re-embellish and open all the splendid dwelling. For, notwithstanding the Voconian law "on the inheritance of women,"† now quite obsolete, Agnes had received, from collateral sources, large personal additions to the family property.

* Is. i. 9.
† "Ne quis heredem virginem neque mulierem faceret," that no one should have a virgin or a woman his heiress.—Cicero in Verrem, i.

In general, of course, the heathen world, who visited, attributed appearances to avarice, and calculated what immense accumulations of wealth the miserly parents must be putting by; and concluded that all beyond the solid screen which shut up the second court, was left to fall into decay and ruin.

It was not so, however. The inner part of the house, consisting of a large court, and the garden, with a detached dining-hall, or triclinium, turned into a church, and the upper portion of the house, accessible from those parts, were devoted to the administration of that copious charity, which the Church carried on as a *business* of its life. It was under the care and direction of the deacon Reparatus, and his exorcist Secundus, officially appointed by the supreme Pontiff to take care of the sick, poor, and strangers, in one of the seven regions into which Pope Cajus, about five years before, had divided the city for this purpose; committing each region to one of the seven deacons of the Roman Church.

Rooms were set apart for lodging strangers who came from a distance, recommended by other churches; and a frugal table was provided for them. Upstairs were apartments for an hospital for the bed-ridden, the decrepit, and the sick, under the care of the deaconesses, and such of the faithful as loved to assist in this work of charity. It was here that the blind girl had her cell, though she refused to take her food, as we have seen, in the house. The *tablinum*, or muniment-room, which generally stood detached in the middle of the passage between the inner courts, served as the office and archives for transacting the business of this charitable establishment, and preserving all local documents, such as the acts of martyrs, procured or compiled by the one of the seven notaries kept for that purpose, by institution of St. Clement I., who was attached to that region.

A door of communication allowed the household to assist in these works of charity; and Agnes had been accustomed from childhood to run in and out, many times a day, and to pass hours there; always beaming, like an angel of light, consolation and joy on the suffering and distressed. This house, then, might be called the almonry of the region, or district, of charity and hospitality in which it was situated, and it was accessible for these purposes through the *posticum* or back door, situated in a narrow lane little frequented. No wonder that with such an establishment, the fortune of the inmates should find an easy application.

We heard Pancratius request Sebastian, to arrange for the distribution of his plate and jewels among the poor, without its being known to whom they belonged. He had not lost sight of the commission, and had fixed on the house of Agnes as the fittest for this purpose. On the morning which we have described the distribution had to take place; other regions had sent their poor, accompanied by their deacons; while Sebastian, Pancratius, and other persons of higher rank had come in through the front door, to assist in the division. Some of these had been seen to enter by Corvinus,

A Fish carrying Bread and Wine, from the Cemetery of St. Lucina.

CHAPTER XIV.

EXTREMES MEET.

A GROUP of poor coming opportunely towards the door, enabled Corvinus to tack himself to them,—an admirable counterfeit, in all but the modesty of their deportment. He kept sufficiently close to them to hear that each of them, as he entered in, pronounced the words, "*Deo gratias,*" "Thanks be to God." This was not merely a Christian, but a Catholic pass-word; for St. Augustine tells us that heretics ridiculed Catholics for using it, on the ground that it was not a salutation but rather a reply; but that Catholics employed it, because consecrated by pious usage. It is yet heard in Italy on similar occasions.

Corvinus pronounced the mystic words, and was allowed to pass. Following the others closely, and copying their manners and gestures, he found himself in the inner court of the house, which was already filled with the poor and infirm. The men were ranged on one side, the women on the other. Under the portico at the end were tables piled with costly plate, and near them was another covered with brilliant jewelry. Two silver and goldsmiths were weighing and valuing most conscientiously this property; and beside them was the money which they would give, to be distributed amongst the poor, in just proportion.

Corvinus eyed all this with a gluttonous heart. He would

have given anything to get it all, and almost thought of making a dash at something, and running out. But he saw at once the folly or madness of such a course, and resolved to wait for a share, and in the meantime take note for Fulvius of all he saw. He soon, however, became aware of the awkwardness of his present position. While the poor were all mixed up together and moving about, he remained unnoticed. But he soon saw several young men of peculiarly gentle manners, but active, and evidently in authority, dressed in the garment known to him by the name of Dalmatic, from its Dalmatian origin; that is, having over the tunic, instead of the toga, a close-fitting shorter tunicle, with ample, but not over long or wide sleeves; the dress adopted and worn by the deacons, not only at their more solemn ministrations in church, but also when engaged in the discharge of their secondary duties about the sick and poor.

These officers went on marshalling the attendants, each evidently knowing those of his own district, and conducting them to a peculiar spot within the porticoes. But as no one recognized or claimed Corvinus for one of his poor, he was at length left alone in the middle of the court. Even his dull mind could feel the anomalous situation into which he had thrust himself. Here he was, the son of the prefect of the city, whose duty it was to punish such violators of domestic rights, an intruder into the innermost parts of a nobleman's house, having entered by a cheat, dressed like a beggar, and associating himself with such people, of course for some sinister, or at least unlawful, purpose. He looked towards the door, meditating an escape; but he saw it guarded by an old man named Diogenes and his two stout sons, who could hardly restrain their hot blood at this insolence, though they only showed it by scowling looks, and repressive biting of their lips. He saw that he was a subject of consultation among the young deacons, who cast occasional glances towards him;

he imagined that even the blind were staring at him, and the decrepit ready to wield their crutches like battle-axes against him. He had only one consolation; it was evident he was not known, and he hoped to frame some excuse for getting out of the scrape.

At length the Deacon Reparatus came up to him, and thus courteously accosted him:

"Friend, you probably do not belong to one of the regions invited here to-day. Where do you live?"

"In the region of the Alta Semita."*

This answer gave the civil, not the ecclesiastical, division of Rome; still Reparatus went on: "The Alta Semita is in my region, yet I do not remember to have seen you."

While he spoke these words, he was astonished to see the stranger turn deadly pale, and totter as if about to fall, while his eyes were fixed upon the door of communication with the dwelling-house. Reparatus looked in the same direction, and saw Pancratius, just entered, and gathering some hasty information from Secundus. Corvinus's last hope was gone. He stood the next moment confronted with the youth (who asked Reparatus to retire), much in the same position as they had last met in, only that, instead of a circle round him of applauders and backers, he was here hemmed in on all sides by a multitude who evidently looked with preference upon his rival. Nor could Corvinus help observing the graceful development and manly bearing, which a few weeks had given his late school-mate. He expected a volley of keen reproach, and, perhaps, such chastisement as he would himself have inflicted in similar circumstances. What was his amazement when Pancratius thus addressed him in the mildest tone:

"Corvinus, are you really reduced to distress and lamed by some accident? Or how have you left your father's house?"

* The upper part of the Quirinal, leading to the Nomentan gate, *Porta Pia*.

"Not quite come to that yet, I hope," replied the bully, encouraged to insolence by the gentle address, "though, no doubt, you would be heartily glad to see it."

"By no means, I assure you; I hold you no grudge. If, therefore, you require relief, tell me; and though it is not right that you should be here, I can take you into a private chamber where you can receive it unknown."

"Then I will tell you the truth: I came in here merely for a freak; and I should be glad if you could get me quietly out."

"Corvinus," said the youth, with some sternness, "this is a serious offence. What would your father say, if I desired these young men, who would instantly obey, to take you as you are, barefoot, clothed as a slave, counterfeiting a cripple, into the Forum before his tribunal, and publicly charge you with what every Roman would resent, forcing your way into the heart of a patrician's house?"

"For the gods' sakes, good Pancratius, do not inflict such frightful punishment."

"You know, Corvinus, that your own father would be obliged to act towards you the part of Junius Brutus, or forfeit his office."

"I entreat you by all that you love, by all that you hold sacred, not to dishonor me and name so cruelly. My father and his house, not I, would be crushed and ruined for ever. I will go on my knees and beg your pardon for my former injuries, if you will only be merciful."

"Hold, hold, Corvinus, I have told you that was long forgotten. But hear me now. Every one but the blind around you is a witness to this outrage. There will be a hundred evidences to prove it. If ever, then, you speak of this assembly, still more if you attempt to molest any one for it, we shall have it in our power to bring you to trial at your own father's judgment-seat. Do you understand me, Corvinus?"

"I do, indeed," replied the captive in a whining tone. "Never, as long as I live, will I breathe to mortal soul that I came into this dreadful place. I swear it by the—"

"Hush, hush! we want no such oaths here. Take my arm, and walk with me." Then turning to the others, he continued: "I know this person; his coming here is quite a mistake."

The spectators, who had taken the wretch's supplicating gestures and tone for accompaniments to a tale of woe, and strong application for relief, joined in crying out, "Pancratius, you will not send him away fasting and unsuccored?"

"Leave that to me," was the reply. The self-appointed porters gave way before Pancratius, who led Corvinus, still pretending to limp, into the street, and dismissed him, saying: "Corvinus, we are now quits; only, take care of your promise."

Fulvius, as we have seen, went to try his fortune by the front door. He found it, according to Roman custom, unlocked; and, indeed, no one could have suspected the possibility of a stranger entering at such an hour. Instead of a porter, he found, guarding the door, only a simple-looking girl about twelve or thirteen years of age, clad in a peasant's garment. No one else was near; and he thought it an excellent opportunity to verify the strong suspicion which had crossed his mind. Accordingly, he thus addressed the little portress:

"What is your name, child, and who are you?"

"I am," she replied, "Emerentiana, the Lady Agnes's foster-sister."

"Are you a Christian?" he asked her sharply.

The poor little peasant opened her eyes in the amazement of ignorance, and replied: "No, sir." It was impossible to resist the evidence of her simplicity; and Fulvius was satisfied that he was mistaken. The fact was, that she was the daughter of a peasant who had been Agnes's nurse. The mother had just died, and her kind sister had sent for the orphan daughter, intending to have her instructed and baptized. She had only arrived a day or two before, and was yet totally ignorant of Christianity.

Fulvius stood embarrassed what to do next. Solitude made him feel as awkwardly situated, as a crowd was making Corvinus. He thought of retreating, but this would have destroyed all his hopes; he was going to advance, when he reflected that he might commit himself unpleasantly. At this critical juncture, whom should he see coming lightly across the court, but the youthful mistress of the house, all joy, all spring, all brightness and sunshine. As soon as she saw him, she stood, as if to receive his errand, and he approached with his blandest smile and most courtly gesture, and thus addressed her:

"I have anticipated the usual hour at which visitors come, and, I fear, must appear an intruder, Lady Agnes; but I was impatient to inscribe myself as an humble client of your noble house."

"Our house," she replied, smiling, "boasts of no clients, nor do we seek them; for we have no pretensions to influence or power."

"Pardon me; with such a ruler, it possesses the highest of influences and the mightiest of powers, those which reign, without effort, over the heart as a most willing subject."

Incapable of imagining that such words could allude to herself, she replied, with artless simplicity:

"Oh, how true are your words! the Lord of this house is indeed the sovereign over the affections of all within it."

"But I," interposed Fulvius, "allude to that softer and benigner dominion, which graceful charms alone can exercise on those who from near behold them."

Agnes looked as one entranced; her eyes beheld a very

different image before them from that of her wretched flatterer; and with an impassioned glance towards heaven, she exclaimed:

"Yes, He whose beauty sun and moon in their lofty firmament gaze on and admire, to Him is pledged my service and my love."*

Fulvius was confounded and perplexed. The inspired look, the rapturous attitude, the music of the thrilling tones in which she uttered these words, their mysterious import, the strangeness of the whole scene, fastened him to the spot, and sealed his lips; till, feeling that he was losing the most favorable opportunity he could ever expect of opening his mind (affection it could not be called) to her, he boldly said, "It is of you I am speaking; and I entreat you to believe my expression of sincerest admiration of you, and of unbounded attachment to you." As he uttered these words, he dropt on his knee, and attempted to take her hand; but the maiden bounded back with a shudder, and turned away her burning countenance.

Fulvius started in an instant to his feet; for he saw Sebastian, who was come to summon Agnes to the poor, impatient of her absence, striding forward towards him, with an air of indignation.

"Sebastian," said Agnes to him, as he approached, "be not angry; this gentleman has probably entered here by some unintentional mistake, and no doubt will quietly retire." Saying this, she withdrew.

Sebastian, with his calm but energetic manner, now addressed the intruder, who quailed beneath his look. "Fulvius, what do you here? what business has brought you?"

"I suppose," answered he, regaining courage, "that hav-

* "Cujus pulchritudinem sol et luna mirantur, ipsi soli servo fidem."—*Office of St. Agnes.*

ing met the lady of the house at the same place with you, her noble cousin's table, I have a right to wait upon her, in common with other voluntary clients."

"But not at so unreasonable an hour as this, I presume?"

"The hour that is not unreasonable for a young officer," retorted Fulvius insolently, "is not, I trust, so for a civilian."

Sebastian had to use all his power of self-control to check his indignation, as he replied:

"Fulvius, be not rash in what you say; but remember that two persons may be on a very different footing in a house. Yet not even the longest familiarity, still less a one dinner's acquaintance, can authorize or justify the audacity of your bearing towards the young mistress of this house, a few moments ago."

"Oh, you are jealous, I suppose, brave captain!" replied Fulvius, with his most refined sarcastic tone. "Report says that you are the acceptable, if not accepted, candidate for Fabiola's hand. She is now in the country; and, no doubt, you wish to make sure for yourself of the fortune of one or the other of Rome's richest heiresses. There is nothing like having two strings to one's bow."

This coarse and bitter sarcasm wounded the noble officer's best feelings to the quick; and had he not long before disciplined himself to Christian meekness, his blood would have proved too powerful for his reason.

"It is not good for either of us, Fulvius, that you remain longer here. The courteous dismissal of the noble lady whom you have insulted has not sufficed; I must be the ruder executor of her command." Saying this, he took the unbidden guest's arm in his powerful grasp, and conducted him to the door. When he had put him outside, still holding him fast, he added: "Go now, Fulvius, in peace; and remember that you have this day made yourself amenable to the laws of the state by this unworthy conduct. I will spare you, if you know how to keep your own counsel; but it is well that you should know, that I am acquainted with your occupation in Rome; and that I hold this morning's insolence over your head, as a security that you will follow it discreetly. Now, again I say, go in peace."

But he had no sooner let go his grasp, than he felt himself seized from behind by an unseen, but evidently an athletic, assailant. It was Eurotas, from whom Fulvius durst conceal nothing, and to whom he had confided the intended interview with Corvinus, that had followed and watched him. From the black slave he had before learnt the mean and coarse character of this client of her magical arts; and he feared some trap. When he saw the seeming struggle at the door, he ran stealthily behind Sebastian, who, he fancied, must be his pupil's new ally, and pounced upon him with a bear's rude assault. But he had no common rival to deal with. He attempted in vain, though now helped by Fulvius, to throw the soldier heavily down; till, despairing of success in this way, he detached from his girdle a small but deadly weapon, a steel mace of finished Syrian make, and was raising it over the back of Sebastian's head, when he felt it wrenched in a trice from his hand, and himself twirled two or three times round, in an iron gripe, and flung flat in the middle of the street.

"I am afraid you have hurt the poor fellow, Quadratus," said Sebastian to his centurion, who was coming up at that moment to join his fellow-Christians, and was of most Herculean make and strength.

"He well deserves it, tribune, for his cowardly assault," replied the other, as they re-entered the house.

The two foreigners, crest-fallen, slunk away from the scene of their defeat; and as they turned the corner, caught a glimpse of Corvinus, no longer limping, but running as fast as his legs would carry him, from his discomfiture at the back-door. However often they may have met afterwards, neither ever alluded to their feats of that morning. Each knew that the other had incurred only failure and shame; and they came both to the conclusion, that there was one fold at least in Rome, which either fox or wolf would assail in vain.

A wall painting from the Cemetery of St. Priscilla.

CHAPTER XV.

CHARITY RETURNS.

WHEN calm had been restored, after this twofold disturbance, the work of the day went quietly on. Besides the distribution of greater alms, such as was made by St. Laurence, from the Church, it was by no means so uncommon in early ages, for fortunes to be given away at once, by those who wished to retire from the world.* Indeed we should naturally expect to find that the noble charity of the Apostolic Church at Jerusalem would not be a barren example to that of Rome. But this extraordinary charity would be most naturally suggested at periods when the Church was threatened with persecution; and when Christians, who from position and circumstances might look forward to martyrdom, would, to use a homely phrase, clear their hearts and houses for action, by removing from both whatever could attach themselves to earth, and become the spoil of the iniquous soldier, instead of having been made the inheritance of the poor.[†]

Nor would the great principles be forgotten, of making the

---

* We have it recorded of Nepotian, that on his conversion he distributed all his property to the poor. St. Paulinus of Nola did the same.

† "Dabis imputo militi quod non vis dare sacerdoti, et hoc tollit fiscus, quod non accipit Christus."—St. Aug.

light of good works to shine before men, while the hand which filled the lamp, poured in its oil in the secret, which only He who seeth in secret can penetrate. The plate and jewels of a noble family publicly valued, sold, and, in their price, distributed to the poor, must have been a bright example of charity, which consoled the Church, animated the generous, shamed the avaricious, touched the heart of the catechumen, and drew blessings and prayers from the lips of the poor. And yet the individual right hand that gave them remained closely shrouded from the scrutiny or consciousness of the left; and the humility and modesty of the noble giver remained concealed in His bosom, into which these earthly treasures were laid up, to be returned with boundless and eternal usury.

And such was the case in the instance before us. When all was prepared, Dionysius the priest, who at the same time was the physician to whom the care of the sick was committed, and who had succeeded Polycarp in the title of St. Pastor, made his appearance, and seated in a chair at one end of the court, thus addressed the assembly:

"Dear brethren, our merciful God has touched the heart of some charitable brother, to have compassion on his poorer brethren, and strip himself of much worldly possession, for Christ's sake. Who he is I know not; nor would I seek to know. He is some one who loves not to have his treasures where rust consumes, and thieves break in and steal, but prefers, like the blessed Laurence, that they should be borne up, by the hands of Christ's poor, into the heavenly treasury.

"Accept then, as a gift from God, who has inspired this charity, the distribution which is about to be made, and which may be a useful help in the days of tribulation which are preparing for us. And as the only return which is desired from you, join all in that familiar prayer which we daily recite for those who give, or do us good."

During this brief address poor Pancratius knew not which

St. Laurence displaying his Treasures.

way to look. He had shrunk into a corner behind the assistants, and Sebastian had compassionately stood before him, making himself as large as possible. And his emotion did all but betray him, when the whole of that assembly knelt down, and with outstretched hands, uplifted eyes, and fervent tone, cried out, as if with one voice:

"*Retribuere dignare, Domine, omnibus nobis bona facientibus, propter Nomen tuum, vitam æternam. Amen.*"*

The alms were then distributed, and they proved unexpectedly large. Abundant food was also served out to all, and a cheerful banquet closed the edifying scene. It was yet early; indeed many partook not of food, as a still more delicious, and spiritual, feast was about to be prepared for them in the neighboring titular church.

When all was over, Cæcilia insisted upon seeing her poor old cripple safe home, and upon carrying for him his heavy canvas purse; and chatted so cheerfully to him that he was surprised when he found they had reached the door of his poor but clean lodging. His blind guide then thrust his purse into his hand, and giving him a hurried good day, tripped away most lightly, and was soon lost to his sight. The bag seemed uncommonly full; so he counted carefully its contents, and found, to his amazement, that he had a double portion. He tried again, and still it was so. At the first opportunity, he made inquiries from Reparatus, but could get no explanation. If he had seen Cæcilia, when she had turned the corner, laugh outright, as if she had been playing some one a good trick, and running as lightly as if she had nothing heavy about her, he might have discovered a solution of the problem of his wealth.

* "Be pleased to render, O Lord, eternal life to all who for Thy Name's sake do unto us good things."

CHAPTER XVI.

THE MONTH OF OCTOBER.

HE month of October in Italy is certainly a glorious season. The sun has contracted his heat, but not his splendor; he is less scorching, but not less bright. As he rises in the morning, he dashes sparks of radiance over awakening nature, as an Indian prince, upon entering his presence chamber, flings handfuls of gems and gold into the crowd; and the mountains seem to stretch forth their rocky heads, and the woods to wave their lofty arms, in eagerness to catch his royal largess. And after careering through a cloudless sky, when he reaches his goal and finds his bed spread with molten gold on the western sea, and canopied above with purple clouds, edged with burnished yet airy fringes, more brilliant than Ophir supplied to the couch of Solomon, he expands himself into a huge disk of most benignant effulgence, as if to bid farewell to his past course; but soon sends back, after disappearing, radiant messengers from the world he is visiting and cheering, to remind us he will soon come back, and gladden us again. If less powerful, his ray is certainly richer and more active. It has taken months to draw out of the sapless, shrivelled vine-stem, first green leaves, then crisp slender tendrils, and last little clusters of hard sour berries; and the growth has been provokingly slow. But now the leaves are large and mantling, and worthy in vine-countries to have a name of their own;* and the separated little knots have swelled up into luxurious bunches of grapes. And of these some are already assuming their bright amber tint, while those which are to glow in rich imperial purple, are passing rapidly to it, through a changing opal hue, scarcely less beautiful.

It is pleasant then to sit in a shady spot, on a hill-side, and look ever and anon, from one's book, over the varied and varying landscape. For, as the breeze sweeps over the olives on the hill-side, and turns over their leaves, it brings out from them light and shade, for their two sides vary in sober tint; and as the sun shines, or the cloud darkens, on the vineyards, in the rounded hollows between, the brilliant web of unstirring vine-leaves displays a yellower or browner shade of its delicious green. Then, mingle with these the innumerable other colors that tinge the picture, from the dark cypress, the duller ilex, the rich chestnut, the reddening orchard, the adust stubble, the melancholy pine—to Italy what the palm-tree is to the East—towering above the box, and the arbutus, and laurels of villas, and these scattered all over the mountain, hill, and plain, with fountains leaping up, and cascades gliding down, porticoes of glittering marble, statues of bronze and stone, painted fronts of rustic dwellings, with flowers innumerable, and patches of greensward; and you have a faint idea of the attractions which, for this month, as in our days, used to draw out the Roman patrician and knight, from what Horace calls the clatter and smoke of Rome, to feast his eyes upon the calmer beauties of the country.

And so, as the happy month approached, villas were seen open to let in air; and innumerable slaves were busy, dusting and scouring, trimming the hedges into fantastic shapes, clearing the canals for the artificial brooklets, and plucking

* *Pampinus, pampino.*

up the weeds from the gravel-walks. The *villicus* or country
steward superintends all; and with sharp word, or sharper
lash, makes many suffer, that perhaps one only may enjoy.

At last the dusty roads become encumbered with every
species of vehicle, from the huge wain carrying furniture, and
slowly drawn by oxen, to the light chariot or gig, dashing
on behind spirited barbs; and as the best roads were narrow,
and the drivers of other days were not more smooth-tongued
than those of ours, we may imagine what confusion and noise
and squabbling filled the public ways. Nor was there a
favored one among these. Sabine, Tusculan, and Alban hills
were all studded over with splendid villas, or humbler cottages, such as a Mæcenas or a Horace might respectively
occupy; even the flat Campagna of Rome is covered with the
ruins of immense country residences; while from the mouth
of the Tiber, along the coast of Laurentum, Lanuvium, and
Antium, and so on to Cajeta, Bajæ, and other fashionable
watering-places round Vesuvius, a street of noble residences
may be said to have run. Nor were these limits sufficient to
satisfy the periodical fever for rustication in Rome. The
borders of Benacus (now the Lago Maggiore, north of Milan),
Como, and the beautiful banks of the Brenta, received their
visitors not from neighboring cities only, still less from wan-
derers of Germanic origin, but rather from the inhabitants of
the imperial capital.

It was to one of these "tender eyes of Italy," as Pliny
calls its villas,* because forming its truest beauty, that Fabiola
had hastened, before the rush on the road, the day after her
black slave's interview with Corvinus. It was situated on
the slope of the hill which descends to the bay of Gaeta, and
was remarkable, like her house, for the good taste which
arranged the most costly, though not luxurious, elements of
comfort. From the terrace in front of the elegant villa could

* *Ocelli Italiæ.*

be seen the calm azure bay, embowered in the richest of shores, like a mirror in an embossed and enamelled frame, relieved by the white sun-lit sails of yachts, galleys, pleasure-boats, and fishing-skiffs; from some of which rose the roaring laugh of excursionists, from others the song or harp-notes of family parties, or the loud, sharp, and not over-refined ditties of the various ploughmen of the deep. A gallery of lattice, covered with creepers, led to the baths on the shore; and half way down was an opening on a favorite spot of green, kept ever fresh by the gush, from an out-cropping rock, of a crystal spring, confined for a moment in a natural basin, in which it bubbled and fretted, till, rushing over its ledge, it went down murmuring and chattering, in the most good-natured way imaginable, along the side of the trellis, into the sea. Two enormous plane-trees cast their shade over this classic ground, as did Plato's and Cicero's over their choice scenes of philosophical disquisition. The most beautiful flowers and plants from distant climates had been taught to make this spot their home, sheltered, as it was, equally from sultriness and from frost.

Fabius, for reasons which will be explained later, seldom paid more than a flying visit for a couple of days to this villa; and even then it was generally on his way to some gayer resort of Roman fashion, where he had, or pretended to have, business. His daughter was, therefore, mostly alone, and enjoyed a delicious solitude. Besides a well-furnished library always kept at the villa, chiefly containing works on agriculture, or of a local interest, a stock of books, some old favorites, other lighter productions of the season (of which she generally procured an early copy at a high price), was brought every year from Rome, together with a quantity of smaller familiar works of art, such as, distributed through new apartments, make them become a home. Most of her morning hours were spent in the cherished retreat just described, with a book-casket at her side, from which she selected first one volume, and then another. But any visitor calling upon her this year, would have been surprised to find her almost always with a companion—and that a slave!

We may imagine how amazed she was when, the day following the dinner at her house, Agnes informed her that Syra had declined leaving her service, though tempted by a bribe of liberty. Still more astonished was she at learning, that the reason was attachment to herself. She could feel no pleasurable consciousness of having earned this affection by any acts of kindness, nor even by any decent gratitude for her servant's care of her in illness. She was therefore at first inclined to think Syra a fool for her pains. But it would not do in her mind. It was true she had often read or heard of instances of fidelity and devotedness in slaves, even towards oppressive masters;* but these were always accounted as exceptions to the general rule; and what were a few dozen cases, in as many centuries, of love, compared with the daily ten thousand ones of hatred around her? Yet here was a clear and palpable one at hand, and it struck her forcibly. She waited a time, and watched her maid eagerly, to see if she could discover in her conduct any airs, any symptom of thinking she had done a grand thing, and that her mistress must feel it. Not in the least. Syra pursued all her duties with the same simple diligence, and never betrayed any signs of believing herself less a slave than before. Fabiola's heart softened more and more; and she now began to think that not quite so difficult, which, in her conversation with Agnes, she had pronounced impossible—to love a slave. And she had also discovered a second evidence, that there was such a thing in the world as disinterested love, affection that asked for no return.

* Such as are given by Macrobius in his *Saturnalia*, lib. i., and by Valerius Maximus.

Her conversations with her slave, after the memorable one which we have recounted, had satisfied her that she had received a superior education. She was too delicate to question her on her early history; especially as masters often had young slaves highly educated, to enhance their value. But she soon discovered that she read Greek and Latin authors with ease and elegance, and wrote well in both languages. By degrees she raised her position, to the great annoyance of her companions: she ordered Euphrosyne to give her a separate room, the greatest of comforts to the poor maid; and she employed her near herself as a secretary and reader. Still she could perceive no change in her conduct, no pride, no pretensions; for the moment any work presented itself of the menial character formerly allotted to her, she never seemed to think of turning it over to any one else, but at once naturally and cheerfully set herself about it.

The reading generally pursued by Fabiola was, as has been previously observed, of rather an abstruse and refined character, consisting of philosophical literature. She was surprised, however, to find how her slave, by a simple remark, would often confute an apparently solid maxim, bring down a grand flight of virtuous declamation, or suggest a higher view of moral truth, or a more practical course of action, than authors whom she had long admired proposed in their writings. Nor was this done by any apparent shrewdness of judgment or pungency of wit; nor did it seem to come from much reading, or deep thought, or superiority of education. For though she saw traces of this in Syra's words, ideas, and behavior, yet the books and doctrines which she was reading now, were evidently new to her. But there seemed to be in her maid's mind some latent but infallible standard of truth, some master-key, which opened equally every closed deposit of moral knowledge, some well-attuned chord, which vibrated in unfailing unison with what was just and right, but jangled in dissonance with whatever was wrong, vicious, or even inaccurate. What this secret was, she wanted to discover; it was more like an intuition than any thing she had before witnessed. She was not yet in a condition to learn, that the meanest and least in the Kingdom of Heaven (and what lower than a slave?) was greater in spiritual wisdom, intellectual light, and heavenly privileges, than even the Baptist Precursor.*

It was on a delicious morning in October, that, reclining by the spring, the mistress and slave were occupied in reading; when the former, wearied with the heaviness of the volume, looked for something lighter and newer; and, drawing out a manuscript from her casket, said:

"Syra, put that stupid book down. Here is something, I am told, very amusing, and only just come out. It will be new to both of us."

The handmaid did as she was told, looked at the title of the proposed volume, and blushed. She glanced over the few first lines, and her fears were confirmed. She saw that is was one of those trashy works, which were freely allowed to circulate, as St. Justin complained, though grossly immoral, and making light of all virtue; while every Christian writing was suppressed, or as much as possible discountenanced. She put down the book with a calm resolution, and said:

"Do not, my good mistress, ask me to read to you from that book. It is fit neither for me to recite, nor for you to hear."

Fabiola was astonished. She had never heard, or even thought, of such a thing as restraint put upon her studies. What in our days would be looked upon as unfit for common perusal, formed part of current and fashionable literature. From Horace to Ausonius all classical writers demonstrate

* Matt. xii. 11.

this. And what rule of virtue could have made that reading seem indelicate, which only described by the pen a system of morals, which the pencil and the chisel made hourly familiar to every eye? Fabiola had no higher standard of right and wrong than the system under which she had been educated could give her.

"What possible harm can it do either of us?" she asked, smiling. "I have no doubt there are plenty of foul crimes and wicked actions described in the book; but it will not induce us to commit them. And, in the meantime, it is amusing to read them of others."

"Would you yourself, for any consideration, do them?"

"Not for the world."

"Yet, as you hear them read, their image must occupy your mind; as they amuse you, your thoughts must dwell upon them with pleasure."

"Certainly. What then?"

"That image is foulness, that thought is wickedness."

"How is that possible? Does not wickedness require an action, to have any existence?"

"True, my mistress; and what is the action of the mind, or as I call it the soul, but thought? A passion which *wishes* death, is the action of this invisible power, like it, unseen; the blow which inflicts it is but the mechanical action of the body, discernible like its origin. But which power commands, and which obeys? In which resides the responsibility of the final effect?"

"I understand you," said Fabiola, after a pause of some little mortification. "But one difficulty remains. There is responsibility, you maintain, for the inward, as well as the outward act. To whom? If the second follow, there is joint responsibility for both, to society, to the laws, to principles of justice, to self; for painful results will ensue. But if only the inward action exist, to whom can there be responsibility?

Who sees it? Who can presume to judge it? Who to control it?"

"God," answered Syra, with simple earnestness.

Fabiola was disappointed. She expected some new theory, some striking principle, to come out. Instead, they had sunk down into what she feared was mere superstition, though not so much as she once had deemed it. "What, Syra, do you then really believe in Jupiter, and Juno, or perhaps Minerva, who is about the most respectable of the Olympian family? Do you think they have any thing to do with our affairs?"

"Far indeed from it; I loathe their very names, and I detest the wickedness which their histories or fables symbolize on earth. No, I spoke not of gods and goddesses, but of one only God."

"And what do you call Him, Syra, in your system?"

"He has no name but God; and that only men have given Him, that they may speak of Him. It describes not His nature, His origin, His attributes."

"And what are these?" asked the mistress, with awakened curiosity.

"Simple as light is His nature, one and the same every where, indivisible, undefilable, penetrating yet diffusive, ubiquitous and unlimited. He existed before there was any beginning; He will exist after all ending has ceased. Power, wisdom, goodness, love, justice too, and unerring judgment belong to Him by His nature, and are as unlimited and unrestrained as it. He alone can create, He alone preserve, and He alone destroy."

Fabiola had often read of the inspired looks which animated a sibyl, or the priestess of an oracle; but she had never witnessed them till now. The slave's countenance glowed, her eyes shone with a calm brilliancy, her frame was immovable, the words flowed from her lips, as if these were but the opening of a musical reed, made vocal by another's breath.

Interior of the Temple of Isis

Her expression and manner forcibly reminded Fabiola of that abstracted and mysterious look, which she had so often noticed in Agnes; and though in the child it was more tender and graceful, in the maid it seemed more earnest and oracular. "How enthusiastic and excitable an Eastern temperament is, to be sure!" thought Fabiola, as she gazed upon her slave. "No wonder the East should be thought the land of poetry and inspiration." When she saw Syra relaxed from the evident tension of her mind, she said, in as light a tone as she could assume: "But, Syra, can you think that a Being such as you have described, far beyond all the conception of ancient fable, can occupy Himself with constantly watching the actions, still more the paltry thoughts, of millions of creatures?"

"It is no occupation, lady, it is not even choice. I called Him light. Is it occupation or labor to the sun to send his rays through the crystal of this fountain, to the very pebbles in its bed? See how, of themselves they disclose, not only the beautiful, but the foul that harbors there; not only the sparkles that the falling drops strike from its rough sides; not only the pearly bubbles that merely rise, glisten for a moment, then break against the surface; not only the golden fish that bask in their light, but black and loathsome creeping things, which seek to hide and bury themselves in dark nooks below, and cannot; for the light pursues them. Is there toil or occupation in all this, to the sun that thus visits them? Far more would it appear so, were he to restrain his beams at the surface of the transparent element, and hold them back from throwing it into light. And what he does here he does in the next stream, and in that which is a thousand miles off, with equal ease; nor can any imaginable increase of their number, or bulk, lead us to fancy, or believe, that rays would be wanting, or light would fail, to scrutinize them all."

"Your theories are beautiful always, Syra, and, if true, most wonderful," observed Fabiola, after a pause, during which her eyes were fixedly contemplating the fountain, as though she were testing the truth of Syra's words.

"And they sound like truth," she added; "for could falsehood be more beautiful than truth? But what an awful idea, that one has never been alone, has never had a wish to oneself, has never held a single thought in secret, has never hidden the most foolish fancy of a proud or childish brain, from the observation of One that knows no imperfection. Terrible thought, that one is living, if you say true, under the steady gaze of an Eye, of which the sun is but a shadow, for he enters not the soul! It is enough to make one any evening commit self-destruction, to get rid of the torturing watchfulness! Yet it sounds so true!"

Fabiola looked almost wild as she spoke these words. The pride of her pagan heart rose strong within her, and she rebelled against the supposition that she could never again feel alone with her own thoughts, or that any power should exist which could control her inmost desires, imaginings, or caprices. Still the thought came back: "Yet it seems so true!" Her generous intellect struggled against the writhing passion, like an eagle with a serpent; more with eye, than with beak and talons, subduing the quailing foe. After a struggle, visible in her countenance and gestures, a calm came over her. She seemed for the first time to feel the presence of One greater than herself, some one whom she feared, yet whom she would wish to love. She bowed down her mind, she bent her intelligence to His feet; and her heart too owned, for the first time, that it had a Master, and a Lord.

Syra, with calm intensity of feeling, silently watched the workings of her mistress's mind. She knew how much depended on their issue, what a mighty step in her unconscious pupil's religious progress was involved in the recognition of the truth before her; and she fervently prayed for this grace.

At length Fabiola raised her head, which seemed to have been bowed down in accompaniment to her mind, and with graceful kindness said:

"Syra, I am sure I have not yet reached the depths of your knowledge; you must have much more to teach me." (A tear and a blush came to the poor handmaid's relief.) "But to-day you have opened a new world, and a new life, to my thoughts. A sphere of virtue beyond the opinions and the judgments of men, a consciousness of a controlling, an approving, and a *rewarding* Power too; am I right?" (Syra expressed approbation.) "standing by us when no other eye can see, or restrain, or encourage us; a feeling that, were we shut up forever in solitude, we should be ever the same, because that influence on us must be so superior to that of any amount of human principles, in guiding us, and could not leave us; such, if I understand your theory, is the position of moral elevation, in which it would place each individual. To fall below it, even with an outwardly virtuous life, is mere deceit, and positive wickedness. Is this so?"

"O my dear mistress," exclaimed Syra, "how much better you can express all this than I!"

"You have never flattered me yet, Syra," replied Fabiola, smilingly; "do not begin now. But you have thrown a new light upon other subjects, till to-day obscure to me. Tell me, now, was it not this you meant, when you once told me that in your view there was no distinction between mistress and slave; that is, that as the distinction is only outward, bodily and social, it is not to be put in comparison with that equality which exists before your Supreme Being, and that possible moral superiority which He might see of the one over the other, inversely of their visible rank?"

"It was in a great measure so, my noble lady; though there are other considerations involved in the idea, which would hardly interest you at present."

"And yet, when you stated that proposition, it seemed to me so monstrous, so absurd, that pride and anger overcame me. Do you remember that, Syra?"

"Oh, no, no!" replied the gentle servant; "do not allude to it, I pray!"

"Have you forgiven me that day, Syra?" said the mistress, with an emotion quite new to her.

The poor maid was overpowered. She rose and threw herself on her knees before her mistress, and tried to seize her hand; but she prevented her, and, for the first time in her life, Fabiola threw herself upon a slave's neck, and wept.

Her passion of tears was long and tender. Her heart was getting above her intellect; and this can only be by its increasing softness. At length she grew calm; and as she withdrew her embrace she said:

"One thing more, Syra: dare one address, by worship, this Being whom you have described to me? Is He not too great, too lofty, too distant for this?"

"Oh, no! far from it, noble lady," answered the servant. "He is not distant from any of us; for as much as in the light of the sun, so in the very splendor of His might, His kindness, and His wisdom, we live and move and have our being. Hence, one may address Him, not as far off, but as around us and within us, while we are in Him; and He hears us not with ears, but our words drop at once into His very bosom, and the desires of our hearts pass directly into the divine abyss of His."

"But," pursued Fabiola, somewhat timidly, "is there no great act of acknowledgment, such as sacrifice is supposed to be, whereby He may be formally recognized and adored?"

Syra hesitated, for the conversation seemed to be trenching upon mysterious and sacred ground, never opened by the Church to profane foot. She, however, answered in a simple and general affirmative.

"And could not I," still more humbly asked her mistress, "be so far instructed in your school as to be able to perform this sublimer act of homage?"

"I fear not, noble Fabiola; one must needs obtain a Victim worthy of the Deity."

"Ah, yes! to be sure," answered Fabiola. "A bull may be good enough for Jupiter, or a goat for Bacchus; but where can be found a sacrifice worthy of Him whom you have brought me to know?"

"It must indeed be one every way worthy of Him, spotless in purity, matchless in greatness, unbounded in acceptableness."

"And what can that be, Syra?"

"Only Himself."

Fabiola shrouded her face with her hands, and then looking up earnestly into Syra's face, said to her:

"I am sure that, after having so clearly described to me the deep sense of responsibility under which you must habitually speak, as well as act, you have a real meaning in this awful saying, though I understand you not."

"As surely as every word of mine is heard, as every thought of mine is seen, it is a truth which I have spoken."

"I have not strength to carry the subject further at present; my mind has need of rest."

A Monogram of Christ, found in the Catacombs.

CHAPTER XVII.

THE CHRISTIAN COMMUNITY.

AFTER this conversation Fabiola retired; and during the rest of the day her mind was alternately agitated and calm. When she looked steadily on the grand view of moral life which her mind had grasped, she found an unusual tranquillity in its contemplation; she felt as if she had made discovery of a great phenomenon, the knowledge of which guided her into a new and lofty region, whence she could smile on the errors and follies of mankind. But when she considered the responsibility which this light imposed, the watchfulness which it demanded, the unseen and unrequited struggles which it required, the desolateness, almost, of a virtue without admiration or even sympathy, she again shrunk from the life that was before her, as about to be passed without any stay or help, from the only sources of it which she knew. Unconscious of the real cause, she saw that she possessed not instruments or means, to carry out the beautiful theory. This seemed to stand like a brilliant lamp in the midst of a huge, bare, unfurnished hall, lighting up only a wilderness. What was the use of so much wasted splendor?

The next morning had been fixed for one of those visits which used to be annually paid in the country,—that to the now ex-prefect of the city, Chromatius. Our reader will remember, that after his conversion and resignation of office, this magistrate had retired to his villa in Campania, taking with him a number of the converts made by Sebastian, with the holy priest Polycarp, to complete their instruction. Of these circumstances, of course, Fabiola had never been informed; but she heard all sorts of curious reports about Chromatius's villa. It was said that he had a number of visitors never before seen at his house; that he gave no entertainments; that he had freed all his country slaves, but that many of them had preferred remaining with him; that if numerous, the whole establishment seemed very happy, though no boisterous sports or frolicsome meetings seemed to be indulged in. All this stimulated Fabiola's curiosity, in addition to her wish to discharge a pleasing duty of courtesy to a most kind friend of hers from childhood; and she longed to see, with her own eyes, what appeared to her to be a very Platonic, or, as we should say, Utopian, experiment.

In a light country carriage, with good horses, Fabiola started early, and dashed gaily along the level road across the "happy Campania." An autumnal shower had laid the dust, and studded with glistening gems the garlands of vine which bordered the way, festooned, instead of hedges, from tree to tree. It was not long before she reached the gentle acclivity, for hill it could scarce be called, covered with box, arbutus, and laurels, relieved by tall tapering cypresses, amidst which shone the white walls of the large villa on the summit. A change, she perceived, had taken place, which at first she could not exactly define; but when she had passed through the gate, the number of empty pedestals and niches reminded her that the villa had entirely lost one of its most characteristic ornaments,—the number of beautiful statues which stood gracefully against the clipped evergreen hedges, and gave it the name, now become quite an empty one, of *Ad Statuas.*

* "The Villa of Statues," or "at the Statues."

Chromatius, whom she had last seen limping with gout, now a hale old man, courteously received her, and inquired kindly after her father, asking if the report were true that he was going shortly to Asia. At this Fabiola seemed grieved and mortified; for he had not mentioned his intention to her. Chromatius hoped it might be a false alarm, and asked her to take a stroll about the grounds. She found them kept with the same care as ever, full of beautiful plants; but still much missed the old statues. At last they reached a grotto with a fountain, in which formerly nymphs and sea-deities disported, but which now presented a black unbroken surface. She could contain herself no longer, and turning to Chromatius, she said:

"Why, what on earth have you been doing, Chromatius, to send away all your statues, and destroy the peculiar feature of your handsome villa? What induced you to do this?"

"My dear young lady," answered the good-humored old gentleman, "do not be so angry. Of what use were those figures to any one?"

"If you thought so," replied she, "others might not. But tell me, what have you done with them all?"

"Why, to tell you the truth, I have had them brought under the hammer."

"What! and never let me know any thing about it? You know there were several pieces I would most gladly have purchased."

Chromatius laughed outright, and said, with that familiar tone, which acquaintance with Fabiola from a child authorized him always to assume with her:

"Dear me! how your young imagination runs away, far too fast for my poor old tongue to keep pace with; I meant not the auctioneer's hammer, but the sledge-hammer. The gods and goddesses have been all smashed, pulverized! If you happen to want a stray leg, or a hand minus a few fingers, perhaps I may pick up such a thing for you. But I cannot promise you a face with a nose, or a skull without a fracture."

Fabiola was utterly amazed, as she exclaimed: "What an utter barbarian you have become, my wise old judge! What shadow of reason can you give to justify so outrageous a proceeding?"

"Why, you see, as I have grown older, I have grown wiser! and I have come to the conclusion that Mr. Jupiter and Mrs. Juno are no more gods than you or I; so I summarily got rid of them."

"Yes, that may be very well; and I, though neither old nor wise, have been long of the same opinion. But why not retain them as mere works of art?"

"Because they had been set up here, not in that capacity, but as divinities. They were here as impostors, under false pretences; and as you would turn out of your house, for an intruder, any bust or image found among those of your ancestors, but belonging to quite another family, so did I these pretenders to a higher connection with me, when I found it false. Neither could I run a risk of their being bought for the continuance of the same imposture."

"And pray, my most righteous old friend, is it not an imposture to continue calling your villa *Ad Statuas*, after not a single statue is left standing in it?"

"Certainly," replied Chromatius, amused at her sharpness, "and you will see that I have planted palm-trees all about; and, as soon as they show their heads above the evergreens, the villa will take the title of *Ad Palmas** instead."

"That will be a pretty name," said Fabiola, who little thought of the higher sense of appropriateness which it would contain. She, of course, was not aware that the villa was now

* "At" or "to the palms"

a training-school, in which many were being prepared, as wrestlers or gladiators used to be, in separate institutions, for the great combat of faith, martyrdom to death. They who had entered in, and they who would go out, might equally say they were on their way to pluck the conqueror's palm, to be borne by them before God's judgment-seat, in token of their victory over the world. Many were the palm-branches shortly to be gathered in that early Christian retreat.

But we must here give the history of the demolition of Chromatius's statues, which forms a peculiar episode in the "Acts of St. Sebastian."

When Nicostratus informed him, as prefect of Rome, of the release of his prisoners, and of the recovery of Tranquillinus from gout by baptism, Chromatius, after making every inquiry into the truth of the fact, sent for Sebastian, and proposed to become a Christian, as a means of obtaining a cure of the same complaint. This of course could not be; and another course was proposed, which would give him new and personal evidence of Christianity, without risking an insincere baptism. Chromatius was celebrated for the immense number of idolatrous images which he possessed; and was assured by Sebastian that, if he would have them all broken in pieces, he would at once recover. This was a hard condition, but he consented. His son Tiburtius, however, was furious, and protested that if the promised result did not follow, he would have Sebastian and Polycarp thrown into a blazing furnace: not perhaps so difficult a matter for the prefect's son.

In one day two hundred pagan statues were broken in pieces, including, of course, those in the villa, as well as those in the house at Rome. The images indeed were broken; but Chromatius was not cured. Sebastian was sent for and sharply rebuked. But he was calm and inflexible. "I am sure," he said, "that all have not been destroyed. Something has been withheld from demolition." He proved right. Some small objects had been treated as works of art rather than religious things, and, like Achan's coveted spoil," concealed. They were brought forth and broken up; and Chromatius instantly recovered. Not only was he converted, but his son Tiburtius became also one of the most fervent of Christians; and, dying in glorious martyrdom, gave his name to a catacomb. He had begged to stay in Rome, to encourage and assist his fellow-believers, in the coming persecution, which his connection with the palace, his great courage and activity, would enable him to do. He had become, naturally, the great friend and frequent companion of Sebastian and Pancratius.

After this little digression, we resume the conversation between Chromatius and Fabiola, who continued her last sentence by adding:

"But do you know, Chromatius—let us sit down in this lovely spot, where I remember there was a beautiful Bacchus—that all sorts of strange reports are going round the country, about your doings here?"

"Dear me! What are they? Do tell me."

"Why, that you have a quantity of people living with you whom nobody knows; that you see no company, go out nowhere, and lead quite a philosophical sort of life, forming a most Platonic republic."

"Highly flattered!" interrupted Chromatius, with a smile and bow.

"But that is not all," continued Fabiola. "They say you keep most unfashionable hours, have no amusements, and live most abstemiously; in fact, almost starve yourselves."

"But I hope they do us the justice to add, that we pay our way?" observed Chromatius. "They don't say, do they, that we have a long score run up at the baker's or grocer's?"

"Oh, no!" replied Fabiola, laughing.

"How kind of them!" rejoined the good-humored old judge. "They—the whole public I mean—seem to take a wonderful interest in our concerns. But is it not strange, my dear young lady, that so long as my villa was on the free-and-easy system, with as much loose talk, deep drinking, occasional sallies of youthful mirth, and troublesome freaks in the neighborhood, as others,—I beg your pardon for alluding to such things; but, in fact, so long as I and my friends were neither temperate nor irreproachable, nobody gave himself the least trouble about us? But let a few people retire to live in quiet, be frugal, industrious, entirely removed from public affairs, and never even talk about politics or society, and at once there springs up a vulgar curiosity to know all about them, and a mean *pruritus* in third-rate statesmen to meddle with them; and there must needs fly about flocks of false reports and foul suspicions about their motives and manner of living. Is not this a phenomenon?"

"It is, indeed; but how do you account for it?"

"I can only do so by that faculty of little minds which makes them always jealous of any aims higher than their own; so that, almost unconsciously, they depreciate whatever they feel to be better than they dare aspire to."

"But what is really your object and your mode of life here, my good friend?"

"We spend our time in the cultivation of our higher faculties. We rise frightfully early—I hardly dare tell you how early; we then devote some hours to religious worship; after which we occupy ourselves in a variety of ways; some read, some write, some labor in the gardens; and I assure you no hired workmen ever toiled harder and better than these spontaneous agriculturists. We meet at different times, and sing beautiful songs together, all breathing virtue and purity, and read most improving books, and receive oral instruction from eloquent teachers. Our meals are indeed very temperate;

we live entirely on vegetables; but I have already found out that laughing is quite compatible with lentils, and that good cheer does not necessarily mean good fare."

"Why, you are turned complete Pythagoreans. I thought that was quite out of date. But it must be a most economical system," remarked Fabiola, with a knowing look.

"Ha! you cunning thing!" answered the judge; "so you really think that this may be a saving plan after all? But it won't be, for we have taken a most desperate resolution."

"And what on earth is that?" asked the young lady.

"Nothing less than this. We are determined that there shall not be such a thing as a poor person within our reach; this winter we will endeavor to clothe all the naked, and feed the hungry, and attend to all the sick about. All our economy will go for this."

"It is indeed a very generous, though very new, idea in our times; and no doubt you will be well laughed at for your pains, and abused on all sides. They will even say worse of you than they do now, if it were possible; but it is not."

"How so?"

"Do not be offended if I tell you; but already they have gone so far as to hint, that possibly you are Christians. But this, I assure you, I have every where indignantly contradicted."

Chromatius smiled, and said: "Why an *indignant* contradiction, my dear child?"

"Because, to be sure, I know you and Tiburtius, and Nicostratus, and that dear dumb Zoë, too well to admit, for a moment, that you had adopted the compound of stupidity and knavery called by that name."

"Let me ask you one question. Have you taken the trouble of reading any Christian writings, by which you might know what is really held and done by that despised body?"

"Oh, not I indeed; I would not waste my time over them; I could not have patience to learn any thing about them. I scorn them too much, as enemies of all intellectual progress, as doubtful citizens, as credulous to the last degree, and as sanctioning every abominable crime, ever to give myself a chance of a nearer acquaintance with them."

"Well, dear Fabiola, I thought just the same about them once, but I have much altered my opinion of late."

"This is indeed strange; since, as prefect of the city, you must have had to punish many of these wretched people, for their constant transgression of the laws."

A cloud came over the cheerful countenance of the old man, and a tear stood in his eye. He thought of St. Paul, who had once persecuted the Church of God. Fabiola saw the change, and was distressed. In the most affectionate manner she said to him, "I have said something very thoughtless, I fear, or stirred up recollections of what must be painful to your kind heart. Forgive me, dear Chromatius, and let us talk of something else. One purpose of my visit to you was, to ask you if you knew of any one going immediately to Rome. I have heard, from several quarters, of my father's projected journey, and I am anxious to write to him,* lest he repeat what he did before,—go without taking leave of me, to spare me pain."

"Yes," replied Chromatius, "there is a young man starting early to-morrow morning. Come into the library, and write your letter; the bearer is probably there."

They returned to the house, and entered an apartment on the ground-floor, full of book-chests. At a table in the middle of the room a young man was seated, transcribing a large volume; which, on seeing a stranger enter, he closed and put aside.

* There was no post in those days, and persons wishing to send letters had to dispatch an express, or find some opportunity.

"Torquatus," said Chromatius, addressing him, "this lady desires to send a letter to her father in Rome."

"It will always give me great pleasure," replied the young man, "to serve the noble Fabiola, or her illustrious father."

"What, do you know them?" asked the judge, rather surprised.

"I had the honor, when very young, as my father had had before me, to be employed by the noble Fabius in Asia. Ill-health compelled me to leave his service."

Several sheets of fine vellum, cut to a size, evidently for transcription of some book, lay on the table. One of these the good old man placed before the lady, with ink and a reed, and she wrote a few affectionate lines to her father. She doubled the paper, tied a thread round it, attached some wax to this, and impressed her seal, which she drew from an embroidered bag, upon the wax. Anxious, some time, to reward the messenger, when she could better know how, she took another piece of the vellum, and made on it a memorandum of his name and residence, and carefully put this into her bosom. After partaking of some slight refreshment, she mounted her car, and bid Chromatius an affectionate farewell. There was something touchingly paternal in his look, as though he felt he should never see her again. So she thought; but it was a very different feeling which softened his heart. Should she always remain thus? Must he leave her to perish in obstinate ignorance? Were that generous heart, and that noble intellect, to grovel on in the slime of bitter paganism, when every feeling and every thought in them seemed formed of strong yet finest fibres, across which truth might weave the richest web? It could not be; and yet a thousand motives restrained him from an avowal, which he felt would, at present, only repulse her fatally from any nearer approach to the faith. "Farewell, my child," he exclaimed, "may you be blessed a hundredfold in ways which as yet you know not." He turned away his face, as he dropped her hand, and hastily withdrew.

Fabiola too was moved by the mystery, as well as the tenderness, of his words; but was startled, before reaching the gate, to find her chariot stopped by Torquatus. She was, at that moment, painfully struck by the contrast between the easy and rather familiar, though respectful, manner of the youth, and the mild gravity, mixed with cheerfulness, of the old ex-prefect.

"Pardon this interruption, madam," he said, "but are you anxious to have this letter quickly delivered?"

"Certainly, I am *most* anxious that it should reach my father as speedily as possible."

"Then I fear I shall hardly be able to serve you. I can only afford to travel on foot, or by chance and cheap conveyance, and I shall be some days upon the road."

Fabiola, hesitating, said: "Would it be taking too great a liberty, if I should offer to defray the expenses of a more rapid journey?"

"By no means," answered Torquatus, rather eagerly, "if I can thereby better serve your noble house."

Fabiola handed him a purse abundantly supplied, not only for his journey, but for an ample recompense. He received it with smiling readiness, and disappeared by a side alley. There was something in his manner which made a disagreeable impression; she could not think he was fit company for her dear old friend. If Chromatius had witnessed the transaction, he would have seen a likeness to Judas, in that eager clutching of the purse. Fabiola, however, was not sorry to have discharged, by a sum of money, once for all, any obligation she might have contracted by making him her messenger. She therefore drew out her memorandum to destroy it as useless, when she perceived that the other side of the vellum was written on; as the transcriber of the book, which she saw put by, had just commenced its continuation on that sheet. Only a few sentences, however, had been written, and she proceeded to read them. Then for the first time she perused the following words from a book unknown to her:

"I say to you, love your enemies; do good to them that hate you, and pray for them that persecute and calumniate you: that you may be the children of your Father who is in heaven, who maketh his sun to rise on the good and the bad, and raineth upon the just and the unjust."[*]

We may imagine the perplexity of an Indian peasant who has picked up in a torrent's bed a white pellucid pebble, rough and dull outside, but where chipped emitting sparks of light; unable to decide whether he have become possessed of a splendid diamond, or of a worthless stone, a thing to be placed on a royal crown, or trodden under a beggar's feet. Shall he put an end to his embarrassment by at once flinging it away, or shall he take it to a lapidary, ask its value, and perhaps be laughed at to his face? Such were the alternating feelings of Fabiola on her way home. "Whose can these sentences be? No Greek or Roman philosopher's. They are either very false or very true, either sublime morality or base degradation. Does any one practise this doctrine, or is it a splendid paradox? I will trouble myself no more on the subject. Or rather I will ask Syra about it; it sounds very like one of her beautiful, but impracticable, theories. No; it is better not. She overpowers me by her sublime views, so impossible for me, though they seem easy to her. My mind wants rest. The shortest way is to get rid of the cause of my perplexity, and forget such harassing words. So here it goes to the winds, or to puzzle some one else, who may find it on the road-side. Ho! Phormio, stop the chariot, and pick up that piece of parchment which I have dropped."

[*] Matt. v. 44.

The outrider obeyed, though he had thought the sheet deliberately flung out. It was replaced in Fabiola's bosom: it was like a seal upon her heart, for that heart was calm and silent till she reached home.

Christ in the midst of His Apostles, from a painting in the Catacombs.

CHAPTER XVIII.

TEMPTATION.

VERY early next morning a mule and guide came to the door of Chromatius's villa. On it was packed a moderate pair of saddle-bags, the whole known property of Torquatus. Many friends were up to see him off, and receive from him the kiss of peace ere he departed. May it not prove like that of Gethsemani! Some whispered a kind, soft word in his ear, exhorting him to be faithful to the graces he had received; and he earnestly, and probably sincerely, promised that he would. Others, knowing his poverty, put a little present into his hand, and entreated him to avoid his old haunts and acquaintances. Polycarp, however, the director of the community, called him aside; and with fervent words and flowing tears, conjured him to correct the irregularities, slight perhaps, but threatening, which had appeared in his conduct, repress the levity which had manifested itself in his bearing, and cultivate more all Christian virtues. Torquatus, also with tears, promised obedience, knelt down, kissed the good priest's hand, and obtained his blessing; then received from him letters of recommendation for his journey, and a small sum for its moderate expenses.

At length all was ready; the last farewell was spoken, the last good wish expressed; and Torquatus, mounted on his mule, with his guide at its bridle, proceeded slowly along the straight avenue which led to the gate. Long after every one else had re-entered the house, Chromatius was standing at the door, looking wistfully, with a moist eye, after him. It was just such a look as the Prodigal's father kept fixed on his departing son.

As the villa was not on the high road, this modest quadrupedal conveyance had been hired to take him across the country to Fundi (now Fondi), as the nearest point where he could reach it. There he was to find what means he could for prosecuting his journey. Fabiola's purse, however, had set him very much at ease on that score.

The road by which he travelled was varied in its beauties. Sometimes it wound along the banks of the Liris, gay with villas and cottages. Then it plunged into a miniature ravine, in the skirts of the Apennines, walled in by rocks, matted with myrtle, aloes, and the wild vine; amidst which white goats shone like spots of snow; while beside the path, gurgled and wriggled on, a tiny brook, that seemed to have worked itself into the bright conceit that it was a mountain torrent; so great was the bustle and noise with which it pushed on, and pretended to foam, and appeared to congratulate itself loudly on having achieved a waterfall by leaping down two stones at a time, and plunging into an abyss concealed by a wide acanthus-leaf. Then the road emerged, to enjoy a wide prospect of the vast garden of Campania, with the blue bay of Cajeta in the background, speckled by the white sails of its craft, that looked at that distance like flocks of bright-plumed waterfowl, basking and fluttering on a lake.

What were the traveller's thoughts amidst these shifting scenes of a new act in his life's drama? did they amuse him? did they delight him? did they elevate him, or did they depress? His eye scarcely noted them. It had run on far beyond them, to the shady porticoes and noisy streets of the

capital. The dusty garden and the artificial fountain, the
marble bath and the painted vault, were more beautiful in his
eyes than fresh autumn vineyards, pure streams, purple ocean,

Interior of a Roman Theatre.

and azure sky. He did not, of course, for a moment turn his
thoughts towards its foul deeds and impious practices, its
luxury, its debauchery, its profaneness, its dishonesties, its
calumnies, its treacheries, its uncleannesses. Oh, no! what

would be, a Christian, have again to do with these? Sometimes, as his mind became abstracted, it saw, in a dark nook of a hall in the Thermæ, a table, round which moody but eager gamesters were casting their knuckle-bone dice; and he felt a quivering creep over him of an excitement long suppressed; but a pair of mild eyes, like Polycarp's, loomed on him from behind the table, and aroused him. Then he caught himself, in fancy, seated at a maple board, with a ruby gem

Hall in the Baths of Caracalla.

of Falernian wine, set in the rim of a golden goblet, and discourse, ungirded by inebriety, going round with the cup; when the reproving countenance of Chromatius would seem placed opposite, repelling with a scowl the approach of either.

He was, in fact, returning only to the innocent enjoyments of the imperial city, to its walks, its music, its paintings, its magnificence, its beauty. He forgot that all these were but the accessories to a living and panting mass of human beings, whose passions they enkindled, whose evil desires they inflamed, whose ambition they fanned, whose resolutions they melted, and whose minds they enervated. Poor youth! he thought he could walk through that fire and not be scorched! Poor moth! he imagined he could fly through that flame, and have his wings unscathed!

It was in one of his abstracted moods that he journeyed through a narrow overhung defile, when suddenly he found himself at its opening, with an inlet of the sea before him, and in it one solitary and motionless skiff. The sight at once brought to his memory a story of his childhood, true or false, it mattered not; but he almost fancied its scene was before him.

Once upon a time there was a bold young fisherman living on the coast of southern Italy. One night, stormy and dark, he found that his father and brothers would not venture out in their tight and strong smack; so he determined, in spite of every remonstrance, to go alone in the little cockle-shell attached to it. It blew a gale, but he rode it out in his tiny buoyant bark, till the sun rose, warm and bright, upon a placid, glassy sea. Overcome by fatigue and heat, he fell asleep; but, after some time, was awakened by a loud shouting at a distance. He looked round and saw the family-boat, the crew of which were crying aloud, and waving their hands to invite him back; but they made no effort to reach him. What could they want? what could they mean? He seized his oars, and began to pull lustily towards them; but he was soon amazed to find that the fishing-boat, towards which he had turned the prow of his skiff, appeared upon his quarter; and soon, though he righted his craft, it was on the opposite side. Evidently he had been making a circle; but the end came within its beginning, in a spiral curve, and now he was commencing another and a narrower one. A horrible suspicion flashed upon his mind: he threw off his tunic and pulled like a madman at his oars. But though he broke the circle a bit here and a bit there, still round he went, and every time nearer to the centre, in which he could see a downward funnel of hissing and foaming water. Then, in despair, he threw down his oars, and standing he flung up his arms frantically; and a sea-bird screaming near, heard him cry out as loud as itself, "Charibdis!"* And now the circle his boat went spinning round was only a few times longer than itself, and he cast himself flat down, and shut his ears and eyes with his hands, and held his breath, till he felt the waters gurgling above him, and he was whirled down into the abyss.

"I wonder," Torquatus said to himself, "did any one ever perish in this way? or is it a mere allegory?—if so, of what? Can a person be drawn on gradually in this manner to spiritual destruction? are my present thoughts, by any chance, an outer circle, which has caught me, and——"

"Fundi!" exclaimed the muleteer, pointing to a town before them; and presently the mule was sliding along the broad flags of its pavement.

Torquatus looked over his letters, and drew one out for the town. He was taken to a little inn of the poorest class, by his guide, who was paid handsomely, and retired swearing and grumbling at the niggardliness of the traveller. He then inquired the way to the house of Cassianus, the school-master, found it, and delivered his letter. He received as kind a welcome as if he had arrived at home; joined his host in a frugal meal, during which he learned the master's history.

A native of Fundi, he had started the school in Rome, with which we became acquainted at an early period of our history, and had proved eminently successful. But finding a persecution imminent, and his Christianity discovered, he had disposed of his school and retired to his small native town, where he was promised, after the vacation, the children of the principal inhabitants. In a fellow-Christian he saw nothing but a brother; and as such he talked freely with him, of his

* A whirlpool between Italy and Sicily.

past adventures and his future prospects. A strange idea dashed through the mind of Torquatus, that some day that information might be turned into money.

It was still early when Torquatus took his leave, and, pretending to have some business in the town, he would not allow his host to accompany him. He bought himself some more respectable apparel, went to the best inn, and ordered a couple of horses, with a postillion to accompany him; for, to fulfill Fabiola's commission it was necessary to ride forward quick, change his horses at each relay, and travel through the night. He did so till he reached Bovillae, on the skirts of the Alban hills. Here he rested, changed his travelling suit, and rode on gaily between the lines of tombs, which brought him to the gate of that city, within whose walls there was more of good and more of evil contained, than in any province of the empire.

The Peacock, as an Emblem of the Resurrection.

CHAPTER XIX.

THE FALL.

TORQUATUS, now elegantly attired, proceeded at once to the house of Fabius, delivered his letter, answered all inquiries, and accepted, without much pressing, an invitation to supper that evening. He then went to seek a respectable lodging, suited to the present state of his purse; and easily found one.

Fabius, we have said, did not accompany his daughter into the country, and rarely visited her there. The fact was, that he had no love for green fields or running brooks; his tastes were for the gossip and free society of Rome. During the year, his daughter's presence was a restraint on his liberty; but when she was gone, with her establishment, into Campania, his house presented scenes and entertained persons, that he would not have presumed to bring in contact with her. Men of prodigate life surrounded his table; and deep drinking till late hours, with gambling and loose conversation, generally followed his sumptuous entertainments.

Having invited Torquatus to sup with him, he went forth in search of guests to meet him. He soon picked up a batch of sycophants, who were loitering about his known haunts, in readiness for invitations. But as he was sauntering home from the baths of Titus, he saw two men in a small grove round a temple earnestly conversing together. After a moment's look, he advanced towards them; but waited, at a small distance, for a pause in the dialogue, which was something to this effect.

"There is no doubt, then, about the news?"

"None at all. It is quite certain that the people have risen at Nicomedia and burnt down the church, as they call it, of the Christians, close to, and in sight of, the palace. My father heard it from the emperor's secretary himself this morning."

"What ever possessed the fools to go and build a temple, in one of the most conspicuous places of the metropolis? They must have known that, sooner or later, the religious spirit of the nation would rise against them and destroy the eye-sore, as every exhibition of a foreign religion must be to an empire."

"To be sure, as my father says, these Christians, if they had any wit in them, would hide their heads, and slink into corners, when they are so condescendingly tolerated for a time by the most humane princes. But as they do not choose to do so, but will build temples in public instead of skulking in by-lanes, as they used to do, I for one am not sorry. One may gain some notoriety, and profit too, by hunting these odious people down, and destroying them if possible."

"Well, be it so; but to come to the purpose. It is understood between us, that when we can discover who are Christians among the rich, and not too powerful at first, there shall be a fair division. We will aid one another. You propose bold and rough means; I will keep my counsel as to mine. But each shall reap all the profit from those whom he discovers; and his right proportion from those who are shared between us. Is it not so?"

"Exactly."

Fabius now stepped forward, with a hearty "How are you,

Fulvius? I have not seen you for an age; come and sup with me to-day. I have friends engaged; and your friend too,— Corvinus, I believe" (the gentleman alluded to made an uncouth bow), "will accompany you, I hope."

"Thank you," replied Fulvius; "but I fear I have an engagement already."

"Nonsense, man," said the good-natured knight; "there is nobody left in the city with whom you could sup, except myself. But has my house the plague, that you have never ventured into it, since you dined there with Sebastian, and quarrelled with him? Or did you get struck by some magical charm, which has driven you away?"

Fulvius turned pale, and drew away Fabius to one side, while he said: "To tell the truth, something very like it."

"I hope," answered Fabius, somewhat startled, "that the black witch has been playing no tricks with you; I wish heartily she were out of my house. But, come," he continued in good humor, "I really thought you were struck by a better charm that evening. I have my eyes open; I saw how your heart was fixed on my little cousin Agnes."

Fulvius stared at him, with some amazement; and, after a pause, replied: "And if it was so, I saw that your daughter made up her mind, that no good should ever come out of it."

"Say you so? Then that explains your constant refusal to come to me again. But Fabiola is a philosopher, and understands nothing of such matters. I wish, indeed, she would give up her books, and think of settling herself in life, instead of preventing others. But I can give you better news than that; Agnes is as much attached to you as you can be to her."

"Is it possible? How can you happen to know it?"

"Why, then, to tell you what I should have told you long

since, if you had not fought so shy of me, she confided it to me that very day."

"To you?"

"Yes, to me; those jewels of yours quite won her heart. She told me as much. I knew she could only mean you. Indeed, I am sure she meant you."

Fulvius understood these words of the rich gems which he displayed; while the knight spoke of the jewels which he imagined Agnes had received. She had proved, Fulvius was thinking, an easy prize, in spite of her demureness; and here lay fortune and rank open before him, if he could only manage his game; when Fabius thus broke in upon his dream: "Come now, you have only to press your suit boldly; and I tell you, you will win it, whatever Fabiola may think. But you have nothing to fear from her now. She and all her servants are absent; her part of the house is closed, and we enter by the back-door to the more enjoyable part of the establishment."

"I will wait on you without fail," replied Fulvius. "And Corvinus with you," added Fabius, as he turned away.

We will not describe the banquet farther than to say, that wines of rare excellence flowed so plentifully, that almost all the guests got, more or less, heated and excited. Fulvius, however, for one, kept himself cool.

The news from the East came into discussion. The destruction of the church at Nicomedia had been followed by incendiary fires in the imperial palace. Little doubt could exist that the Emperor Galerius was their author; but he charged them on the Christians; and thus goaded on the reluctant mind of Diocletian to become their fiercest persecutor. Every one began to see that, before many months were over, the imperial edict to commence the work of destruction would reach Rome, and find in Maximian a ready executor.

The guests were generally inclined to gore the stricken deer; for generosity, in favor of those whom popular clamor hunts down, requires an amount of courage too heroic to be common. Even the most liberal found reasons for Christians being excepted from all kind consideration. One could not bear their mysteriousness, another was vexed at their supposed progress; this man thought them opposed to the real glory of the empire, that considered them a foreign element, that ought to be eliminated from it. One thought their doctrine detestable, another their practice infamous. During all this debate, if it could be so called, where both sides came to the same conclusion, Fulvius, after having glanced from one to the other of the guests, had fixed his evil eye upon Torquatus.

The youth was silent; but his countenance, by turns, was pale and flushed. Wine had given him a rash courage, which some strong principle restrained. Now he clenched his hand, and pressed it to his breast; now he bit his lip. At one time he was crumbling the bread between his fingers; at another, he drank off, unconsciously, a cup of wine.

"These Christians hate us, and would destroy us all if they could," said one. Torquatus leaned forward, opened his lips, but remained silent.

"Destroy us, indeed! Did they not burn Rome, under Nero; and have they not just set fire to the palace in Asia, over the emperor's head?" asked a second. Torquatus rose upon his couch, stretched forth his hand, as if about to reply, but drew it back.

"But what is infinitely worse is, their maintaining such anti-social doctrines, conniving at such frightful excesses, and degrading themselves to the disgusting worship of an ass's head," proceeded a third. Torquatus now fairly writhed; and rising, had lifted his arm, when Fulvius, with a cool calculation of time and words, added, in bitter sarcasm: "Ay, and massacre a child, and devour his flesh and blood, at every assembly."*

The arm descended on the table, with a blow that made every goblet and beaker dance and ring, as, in a choked voice, Torquatus exclaimed: "It is a lie! a cursed lie!"

"How can you know that?" asked Fulvius, with his blandest tone and look.

"Because," answered the other, with great excitement, "I am myself a Christian; and ready to die for my faith!"

If the beautiful alabaster statue, with a bronze head, in the niche beside the table, had fallen forward, and been smashed on the marble pavement, it could not have caused a more fearful sensation than this sudden announcement. All were startled for a moment. Next, a long blank pause ensued, after which, each began to show his feelings in his features. Fabius looked exceedingly foolish, as if conscious that he had brought his guests into bad company. Calpurnius puffed himself out, evidently thinking himself ill-used, by having a guest brought in, who might absurdly be supposed to know more about Christians than himself. A young man opened his mouth as he stared at Torquatus; and a testy old gentleman was evidently hesitating, whether he should not knock down somebody or other, no matter whom. Corvinus looked at the poor Christian with the sort of grin of delight, half idiotic, half savage, with which a countryman might gaze upon the vermin that he finds in his trap in a morning. Here was a man ready to hand, to put on the rack, or the gridiron, whenever he pleased. But the look of Fulvius was worth them all. If ever any microscopic observer has had the opportunity of witnessing the expression of the spider's features, when, after a long fast, it sees a fly, plump with others' blood, approach its net, and keenly watches every stroke of its wing, and studies how it can best throw only

* The heathen notion of the Blessed Eucharist.

the first thread round it, sure that then all that gorges it shall be its own; that we fancy would be the best image of his looks, as certainly it is of his feelings. To get hold of a Christian, ready to turn traitor, had long been his desire and study. Here, he was sure, was one, if he could only manage him. How did he know this? Because he knew sufficient of Christians to be convinced, that no genuine one would have allowed himself either to drink to excess, or to boast of his readiness to court martyrdom.

The company broke up; every body slunk away from the discovered Christian, as from one pest-stricken. He felt alone and depressed, when Fulvius, who had whispered a word to Fabius, and to Corvinus, went up to him, and taking him by the hand said, courteously: "I fear, I spoke inconsiderately, in drawing out from you a declaration which may prove dangerous."

"I fear nothing," replied Torquatus, again excited; "I will stand to my colors to the last."

"Hush, hush!" broke in Fulvius, "the slaves may betray you. Come with me to another chamber, where we can talk quietly together."

So saying, he led him into an elegant room, where Fabius had ordered goblets and flagons of the richest Falernian wine to be brought, for such as, according to Roman fashion, liked to enjoy a *commissatio*, or drinking-bout. But only Corvinus, engaged by Fulvius, followed.

On a beautifully inlaid table were dice. Fulvius, after plying Torquatus with more liquor, negligently took them up, and threw them playfully down, talking in the mean time on indifferent subjects. "Dear me!" he kept exclaiming, "what throws! It is well I am not playing with any one, or I should have been ruined. You try, Torquatus."

Gambling, as we learnt before, had been the ruin of Torquatus: for a transaction arising out of it he was in prison when Sebastian converted him. As he took the dice into his hand, with no intention, as he thought, of playing, Fulvius watched him as a lynx might its prey. Torquatus's eye flashed keenly, his lips quivered, his hand trembled. Fulvius at once recognized in all this, coupled with the poising of his hand, the knowing cast of the wrist, and the sharp eye to the value of the throw, the violence of a first temptation to resume a renounced vice.

"I fear you are not a better hand than I am at this stupid occupation," said he indifferently; "but, I dare say, Corvinus here will give you a chance, if you will stake something very low."

"It must be very low indeed,—merely for recreation; for I have renounced gambling. Once, indeed—but no matter."

"Come on," said Corvinus, whom Fulvius had pressed to his work by a look.

They began to throw for the most trifling stakes, and Torquatus generally won. Fulvius made him drink still, from time to time, and he became very talkative.

"Corvinus, Corvinus," he said at length, as if recollecting himself, "was not that the name that Cassianus mentioned?"

"Who?" asked the other, surprised.

"Yes, it was," continued Torquatus to himself,—"the bully, the big brute. Were you the person," he asked, looking up to Corvinus, "who struck that nice Christian boy Pancratius?"

Corvinus was on the point of bursting into a rage; but Fulvius checked him by a gesture, and said, with timely interference:

"That Cassianus whom you mentioned is an eminent school-master; pray, where does he live?"

This he knew his companion wished to ascertain; and thus he quieted him. Torquatus answered:

"He lives, let me see,—no, no; I won't turn traitor. No;

I am ready to be burnt, or tortured, or die for my faith; but I won't betray any one,—that I won't."

"Let me take your place, Corvinus," said Fulvius, who saw Torquatus's interest in the game deepening. He put forth sufficient skill to make his antagonist more careful and more intent. He threw down a somewhat larger stake. Torquatus, after a moment's pause of deliberation, matched it. He won it. Fulvius seemed vexed. Torquatus threw back both sums. Fulvius seemed to hesitate, but put down an equivalent, and lost again. The play was now silent: each won and lost; but Fulvius had steadily the advantage, and he was the more collected of the two.

Once Torquatus looked up and started. He thought he saw the good Polycarp behind his adversary's chair. He rubbed his eyes, and saw it was only Corvinus staring at him. All his skill was now put forth. Conscience had retreated; faith was wavering; grace had already departed. For the demon of covetousness, of rapine, of dishonesty, of recklessness, had come back, and brought with him seven spirits worse than himself, to that cleansed but ill-guarded soul; and as they entered in, all that was holy, all that was good, departed.

At length, worked up, by repeated losses and draughts of wine, into a frenzy, after he had drawn frequently upon the heavy purse which Fabiola had given him, he threw the purse itself upon the table. Fulvius coolly opened it, emptied it, counted the money, and placed opposite an equal heap of gold. Each prepared himself for a final throw. The fatal bones fell; each glanced silently upon their spots. Fulvius drew the money towards himself. Torquatus fell upon the table, his head buried and hidden within his arms. Fulvius motioned Corvinus out of the room.

Torquatus beat the ground with his foot; then moaned, next gnashed his teeth and growled; then put his fingers in

The Ruins of the Roman Forum, as they are To-day

his hair, and begun to pull and tear it. A voice whispered in his ear, "Are you a Christian?" Which of the seven spirits was it? surely the worst.

"It is hopeless," continued the voice; "you have disgraced your religion, and you have betrayed it too."

"No, no," groaned the despairing wretch.

"Yes; in your drunkenness you have told us all; quite enough to make it impossible for you ever to return to those you have betrayed."

"Begone, begone," exclaimed piteously the tortured sinner. "They will forgive me still. God——"

"Silence; utter not His name; you are degraded, perjured, hopelessly lost. You are a beggar; to-morrow you must beg your bread. You are an outcast, a ruined prodigal and gamester. Who will look at you? will your Christian friends? And nevertheless you *are* a Christian; you will be torn to pieces by some cruel death for it; yet you will not be worshipped by them as one of their martyrs. You are a hypocrite, Torquatus, and nothing more."

"Who is it that is tormenting me?" he exclaimed, and looked up. Fulvius was standing with folded arms at his side. "And if all this be true, what is it to you? What have you to say more to me?" he continued.

"Much more than you think. You have betrayed yourself into my power completely. I am master of your money" —(and he showed him Fabiola's purse)—"of your character, of your peace, of your life. I have only to let your fellow-Christians know what you have done, what you have said, what you have been to-night, and you dare not face them. I have only to let that 'bully—that big brute,' as you called him, but who is son of the prefect of the city, loose upon you, (and no one else can now restrain him after such provocation), and to-morrow you will be standing before his father's tribunal to die for that religion which you have betrayed and disgraced. Are you ready now, any longer, to reel and stagger as a drunken gambler, to represent your Christianity before the judgment-seat in the Forum?"

The fallen man had not courage to follow the prodigal in repentance, as he had done in sin. Hope was dead in him; for he had relapsed into his capital sin, and scarcely felt remorse. He remained silent, till Fulvius aroused him by asking, "Well, have you made your choice; either to go at once to the Christians with to-night on your head, or to-morrow to the court? Which do you choose?"

Torquatus raised his eyes to him, with a stolid look, and faintly answered, "Neither."

"Come, then, what will you do?" asked Fulvius, mastering him with one of his falcon glances.

"What you like," said Torquatus, "only neither of those things."

Fulvius sat down beside him, and said, in a soft and soothing voice, "Now, Torquatus, listen to me; do as I tell you, and all is mended. You shall have house, and food, and apparel, ay, and money to play with, if you will only do my bidding."

"And what is that?"

"Rise to-morrow as usual; put on your Christian face; go freely among your friends; act as if nothing had happened; but answer all my questions, tell me every thing."

Torquatus groaned, "A traitor at last!"

"Call it what you will; that or death! Ay, death by inches. I hear Corvinus pacing impatiently up and down the court. Quick! which is it to be?"

"Not death! Oh, no, any thing but that!"

Fulvius went out, and found his friend fuming with rage and wine; he had hard work to pacify him. Corvinus had almost forgotten Cassianus in fresher resentments; but all his former hatred had been rekindled, and he burnt for revenge.

Fulvius promised to find out where he lived, and used this means to secure the suspension of any violent and immediate measure.

Having sent Corvinus sulky and fretting home, he returned to Torquatus, whom he wished to accompany, that he might ascertain his lodgings. As soon as he had left the room, his victim had arisen from his chair, and endeavored, by walking up and down, to steady his senses and regain self-possession. But it was in vain; his head was swimming from his inebriety, and his subsequent excitement. The apartment seemed to turn round and round, and float up and down; he was sick too, and his heart was beating almost audibly. Shame, remorse, self-contempt, hatred of his destroyers and of himself, the desolateness of the outcast, and the black despair of the reprobate, rolled like dark billows through his soul, each coming in turn uppermost. Unable to sustain himself longer on his feet, he threw himself on his face upon a silken couch, and buried his burning brow in his icy hands, and groaned. And still all whirled round and round him, and a constant moaning sounded in his ears.

Fulvius found him in this state, and touched his shoulder to rouse him. Torquatus shuddered, and was convulsed; then exclaimed: "Can this be Charybdis?"

A Dove, as an Emblem of the Soul.

Diogenes the excavator, from a painting in the Cemetery of Domitilla.*

Part Second.—Conflict.

CHAPTER I.

DIOGENES.

THE scenes through which we have hitherto led our reader have been laid in one of those slippery truces, rather than peace, which often intervened between persecution and persecution. Already rumors of war have crossed our path, and its note of preparation has been

* "Diogenes, the excavator, deposited in peace, eight days before the first of October."—From St. Sebastian's. Boldetti, l. 15, p. 60.

distinctly heard. The roar of the lions near the Amphitheatre, which startled but dismayed not Sebastian, the reports from the East, the hints of Fulvius, and the threats of Corvinus, have brought us the same news, that before long the horrors of persecution will re-appear, and Christian blood will have to flow, in a fuller and nobler stream than had hitherto watered the Paradise of the New Law. The Church, ever calmly provident, cannot neglect the many signs of a threatened combat, nor the preparations necessary for meeting it. From the moment she earnestly begins to arm herself, we date the second period of our narrative. It is the commencement of conflict.

It was towards the end of October that a young man, not unknown to us, closely muffled up in his cloak, for it was dark and rather chill, might be seen threading his way through the narrow alleys of the district called the Suburra; a region, the extent and exact position of which is still under dispute, but which lay in the immediate vicinity of the Forum. As vice is unfortunately too often linked with poverty, the two found a common asylum here. Pancratius did not seem much at home in this part of the city, and made several wrong turns, till at length he found the street he was in search of. Still, without numbers on the doors, the house he wanted was an unsolved problem, although not quite insoluble. He looked for the neatest dwelling in the street; and being particularly struck with the cleanliness and good order of one beyond the rest, he boldly knocked at its door. It was opened by an old man, whose name has already appeared in our pages, Diogenes. He was tall and broad-shouldered, as if accustomed to bear burdens, which, however, had given him a stoop in his gait. His hair was a perfect silver, and hung down at the sides of a large massive head; his features were strongly marked in deep melancholy lines, and though the

Lazarus raised from the dead. A similar representation is found in the Catacomb Juxta duos lauros, and in the Cemetery of Saints Nereus and Achilles.

expression of his countenance was calm, it was solemnly sad. He looked like one who had lived much among the dead, and was happiest in their company. His two sons, Majus and Severus, fine athletic youths, were with him. The first was busy carving, or scratching rather, a rude epitaph on an old slab of marble, the reverse of which still bore traces of a heathen sepulchral inscription, rudely effaced by its new possessor.

Pancratius looked over the work in hand and smiled; there was hardly a word rightly spelt, or a part of speech correct; indeed, here it is:

DE BIANOBA
POLLECLA QVE ORDEV BENDET DE BIANOBA*

The other son was making a rough design, in which could be distinguished Jonas devoured by the whale, and Lazarus raised from the dead, both most conventionally drawn with

Two Fossors or excavators, from a picture in the Cemetery of Callistus.

charcoal on a board; a sketch evidently for a more permanent painting elsewhere. Further, it was clear that when the knock came to the door, old Diogenes was busy fitting a new handle to an old pick-axe. These varied occupations in one family might have surprised a modern, but they did not at all the youthful visitor; he well knew that the family belonged to the honorable and religious craft of the Fossores, or exca-

---

* "From New Street. Pollecla, who sells barley in New Street." Found in the cemetery of Callistus.

vators of the Christian cemeteries. Indeed, Diogenes was the head and director of that confraternity. In conformity with the assertion of an anonymous writer, contemporary with St. Jerome, some modern antiquarians have considered the *fosso* as forming a lesser ecclesiastical order in the primitive Church, like the *lector*, or reader. But although this opinion is untenable, it is extremely probable that the duties of this office were in the hands of persons appointed and recognized by ecclesiastical authority. The uniform system pursued in excavating, arranging, and filling up of the numerous cemeteries round Rome, a system too, so complete from the beginning, as not to leave positive signs of improvement or change as time went on, gives us reason to conclude that these wonderful and venerable works were carried on under one direction, and probably by some body associated for that purpose. It was not a cemetery or necropolis company, which made a speculation of burying the dead, but rather a pious and recognized confraternity which was associated for the purpose.

A series of interesting inscriptions, found in the cemetery of St. Agnes, proves that this occupation was continued in particular families; grandfather, father, and sons, having carried it on in the same place.* We can thus easily understand the great skill and uniformity of practice observable in the catacombs. But the *fossores* had evidently a higher office, or even jurisdiction, in that underground world. Though the Church provided space for the burial of all her children, it was natural that some should make compensation for their place of sepulture, if chosen in a favorite spot, such as the vicinity of a martyr's tomb. These sextons had the management of such transactions, which are often recorded in the ancient cemeteries. The following inscription is preserved in the Capitol:

* Given by F. Marchi in his *Architecture of Subterranean Christian Rome*, 1844; a work on which we will freely draw.

EMPTV LOCVM AB ARTEMISIVM VISOMVM HOC EST
ET PRAETIVM DATVM FOSSORI HILARO IDEST
FOL NOOD PRAESENTIA SEVERI FOSS ET LAVRENTI

That is—

"This is the grave for two bodies, bought by Artimisius; and the price was given to the Fossor Hilarus,—that is, purses . . . . . * In the presence of Severus the Fossor and Laurentius."

Possibly the last named was the witness on the purchaser's side, and Severus on the seller's. However this may be, we trust we have laid before our readers all that is known about the profession, as such, of Diogenes and his sons.

We left Pancratius amused at Majus's rude attempts in glyptic art; his next step was to address him.

"Do you always execute these inscriptions yourself?"

"Oh, no," answered the artist, looking up and smiling. "I do them for poor people who cannot afford to pay a better hand. This was a good woman who kept a small shop in the *Vicusow*, and you may suppose did not become rich, especially as she was very honest. And yet a curious thought struck me as I was carving her epitaph."

"Let me hear it, Majus."

"It was, that perhaps some thousand years hence or more, Christians might read with reverence my scratches on the wall, and hear of poor old Pollecla and her barley stall with interest, while the inscription of not a single emperor, who persecuted the Church, would be read or even known."

"Well, I can hardly imagine that the superb mausoleums of sovereigns will fall to utter decay, and yet the memory of a market-wife descend to distant ages. But what is your reason for thinking thus?"

"Simply because I would sooner commit to the keeping of posterity the memory of the pious poor than that of the wicked

* The number, unfortunately, is not intelligible, being in cipher.

rich. And my rude record may possibly be read when triumphal arches have been demolished. It's dreadfully written though, is it not?"

A gallery in the Cemetery of St. Agnes, on the Nomentan Way.

"Never mind that; its simplicity is worth much fine writing. What is that slab leaning against the wall?"

"Ah, that *is* a beautiful inscription brought us to put up; you will see the writer and engraver were different people. It is to go to the cemetery at the Lady Agnes's villa, on the Nomentan way. I believe it is in memory of a most sweet child, whose death is deeply felt by his virtuous parents." Pancratius took a light to it, and read as follows:

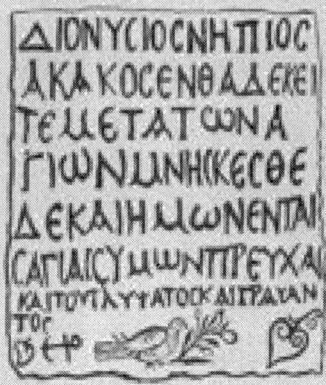

Inscription in the Cemetery of Saint Agnes

"The innocent boy Dionysius lieth here among the saints. Remember us in your holy prayers, the writer and the engraver."

"Dear, happy child!" continued Pancratius, when he had perused the inscription; "add me the reader, to the writer and carver of thine epitaph, in thy holy prayers."

"Amen," answered the pious family.

But Pancratius, attracted by a certain husky sound in Diogenes's voice, turned round, and saw the old man vigorously trying to cut off the end of a little wedge which he had driven into the top of the handle of his pick-axe, to keep it fast in the iron; but every moment baffled by some defect in his vision, which he removed by drawing the back of his brawny hand across his eyes. "What is the matter, my good old friend?" said the youth kindly. "Why does this epitaph of young Dionysius particularly affect you?"

"It does not of itself; but it reminds me of so much that is past, and suggests so much that may be about to come, that I feel almost faint to think of either."

"What are your painful thoughts, Diogenes?"

"Why, do you see, it is all simple enough to take into one's arms a good child like Dionysius, wrapped in his cerecloth, fragrant with spices, and lay him in his grave. His parents may weep, but his passage from sorrow to joy was easy and sweet. It is a very different thing, and requires a heart as hardened as mine by practice" (another stroke of the hand across the eyes) "to gather up hastily the torn flesh and broken limbs of such another youth, to wrap them hurriedly in their winding-sheet, then fold them into another sheet full of lime, instead of balsams, and shove them precipitately into

their tomb.* How differently one would wish to treat a martyr's body!"

"True, Diogenes; but a brave officer prefers the plain soldier's grave, on the field of battle, to the carved sarcophagus on the Via Appia. But are such scenes as you describe common, in times of persecution?"

* In the cemetery of St. Agnes, pieces of lime have been found in tombs forming exact moulds of different parts of the body, with the impression of a finer linen inside, and a coarser outside. As to spices and balsams, Tertullian observes that "the Arabs and Sabæans well know that the Christians annually consume more for their dead than the heathen world did for its gods."

"By no means uncommon, my good young master. I am sure a pious youth like you must have visited, on his anniversary, the tomb of Restitutus in the cemetery of Hermes."

"Indeed I have, and often have I been almost jealous of his early martyrdom. Did you bury him?"

"Yes; and his parents had a beautiful tomb made, the *arcosolium* of his crypt.* My father and I made it of six slabs of marble, hastily collected, and I engraved the inscription now beside it. I think I carved better than Majus there," added the old man, now quite cheerful.

"That is not saying much for yourself, father," rejoined his son, no less smiling; "but here is the copy of the inscription which you wrote," he added, drawing out a parchment from a number of sheets.

"I remember it perfectly," said Pancratius, glancing over it, and reading it as follows, correcting the errors in orthography, but not those in grammar, as he read:

> AELIO FABIO RESTVTO
> FILIO PIISSIMO PARIN
> TES FECERVNT QVIVI
> XIT ANNI. S XVIII MENS
> VII INIRENE.

"To Ælius Fabius Restitutus, their most pious son, his parents erected (this tomb). Who lived eighteen years and seven months. In peace."

He continued: "What a glorious youth, to have confessed Christ at such an age!"

"No doubt," replied the old man; "but I dare say you have always thought that his body reposes alone in his sepulchre. Any one would think so from the inscription."

"Certainly I have always thought so. Is it otherwise?"

---

* These terms will be explained later.

"Yes, noble Pancratius, he has a comrade younger than himself lying in the same bed. As we were closing the tomb of Restitutus, the body of a boy not more than twelve or thirteen years old was brought to us. Oh, I shall never forget the sight! He had been hung over a fire, and his head, trunk, and limbs nearly to the knees, were burnt to the very bone; and so disfigured was he that no feature could be recognized. Poor little fellow, what he must have suffered! But why should I pity him? Well, we were pressed for time, and we thought the youth of eighteen would not grudge room for his fellow-soldier of twelve, but would own him for a younger brother; so we laid him at Ælius Fabius's feet. But we had no second phial of blood to put outside, that a second martyr might be known to lie there; for the fire had dried his blood up in his veins."*

"What a noble boy! If the first was older, the second was younger than I. What say you, Diogenes, don't you think it likely you may have to perform the same office for me one of these days?"

"Oh, no, I hope not," said the old digger, with a return of his husky voice. "Do not, I entreat you, allude to such a possibility. Surely my own time must come sooner. How the old trees are spared, indeed, and the young plants cut down!"

"Come, come, my good friend, I won't afflict you. But I have almost forgotten to deliver the message I come to bring. It is, that to-morrow at dawn you must come to my mother's house, to arrange about preparing the cemeteries for our com-

---

* On the 22d of April, 1833, this tomb was discovered unviolated. On being opened the bones, white, bright, and polished as ivory, were found, corresponding to the framework of a youth of eighteen. At his head was the phial of blood. With the head to his feet was the skeleton of a boy, of twelve or thirteen, black and charred chiefly at the head and upper parts, down to the middle of the thighbones, from which to the feet the bones gradually whitened. The two bodies, richly clothed, repose side by side under the altar of the Jesuits' college at Loreto.

ing troubles. Our holy Pope will be there, with the priests of the titles, the regionary deacons, the notaries, whose number has been filled up, and you, the head *fossor*, that all may act in concert."

"I will not fail, Pancratius," replied Diogenes.

"And now," added the youth, "I have a favor to ask you."

"A favor from me?" asked the old man, surprised.

"Yes; you will have to begin your work immediately, I suppose. Now, often as I have visited, for devotion, our sacred cemeteries, I have never studied or examined them; and this I should like to do with you, who know them so well."

"Nothing would give me greater pleasure," answered Diogenes, somewhat flattered by the compliment, but still more pleased by this love for what he so much loved. "After I have received my instructions, I shall go at once to the cemetery of Callistus. Meet me out of the Porta Capena, half an hour before mid-day, and we will go on together."

"But I shall not be alone," continued Pancratius. "Two youths, recently baptized, desire much to become acquainted with our cemeteries, which they do not yet much know; and have asked me to initiate them there."

"Any friends of yours will be always welcome. What are their names, that we may make no mistake?"

"One is Tiburtius, the son of Chromatius, the late prefect; the other is a young man named Torquatus."

Severus started a little, and said: "Are you quite sure about him, Pancratius?"

Diogenes rebuked him, saying, "That he comes to us in Pancratius's company is security enough."

"I own," interposed the youth, "that I do not know as much about him as about Tiburtius, who is really a gallant, noble fellow. Torquatus is, however, very anxious to obtain all information about our affairs, and seems in earnest. What makes you fear, Severus?"

"Only a trifle, indeed. But as I was going early to the cemetery this morning, I turned into the Baths of Antoninus."*

"What!" interrupted Pancratius, laughing, "do you frequent such fashionable resorts?"

"Not exactly," replied the honest artist; "but you are not perhaps aware that Cucumio the *capsarius*† and his wife are Christians?"

"Is it possible; where shall we find them next?"

"Well, so it is; and moreover they are making a tomb for themselves in the cemetery of Callistus; and I had to show them Majus's inscription for it."

"Here it is," said the latter, exhibiting it, as follows:

**CVCVMIO ET VICTORIA
SE VIVOS FECERVNT
CAPSARARIVS DE ANTONINIANAS.‡**

"Capital!" exclaimed Pancratius, amused at the blunders in the epitaph; "but we are forgetting Torquatus."

"As I entered the building, then," said Severus, "I was not a little surprised to find in one corner, at that early hour, this Torquatus in close conversation with the present prefect's son, Corvinus, the pretended cripple, who thrust himself into Agnes's house, you remember, when some charitable unknown person (God bless him!) gave large alms to the poor there. Not good company I thought, and at such an hour, for a Christian."

---

* Better known as Caracalla's.
† The person who had charge of the bathers' clothes, from *capsa*, a chest.
‡ "Cucumio and Victoria made (the tomb) for themselves while living. Capsarius of the Antonine" (baths). Found in the cemetery of Callistus, first published by F. Marchi, who attributes it, erroneously, to the cemetery of Praetextatus.

"True, Severus," returned Pancratius, blushing deeply; "but he is young as yet in the faith, and probably his old friends do not know of his change. We will hope for the best."

The two young men offered to accompany Pancratius, who rose to leave, and see him safe through the poor and profligate neighborhood. He accepted their courtesy with pleasure, and bade the old excavator a hearty good night.

CHAPTER II.

THE CEMETERIES.

> M. ANTONI
> VS. RESTVTV
> S. FECIT. YPO
> CEVSIBI. ET
> SVIS. FIDENTI
> BVS. IN. DOMINO.*

T seems to us as though we had neglected one, whose character and thoughts opened this little history, the pious Lucina. Her virtues were indeed of that quiet, unobtrusive nature, which affords little scope for appearing on a public scene, or taking part in general affairs. Her house, besides being, or rather containing, a title or parochial church, was now honored by being the residence of the supreme Pontiff. The approach of a violent persecution, in which the rulers of Christ's spiritual kingdom were sure to be the first sought out, as the enemies of Cæsar,

---

* "Marcus Antonius Restitutus made this subterranean for himself and his family, that trust in the Lord." Lately found in the cemetery of SS. Nereus and Achilleus. It is singular that in the inscription of the martyr Restitutus, given in the last chapter, as in this, a syllable should be omitted in the name, one easily slurred in pronouncing it.

A PASSAGE IN THE CATACOMBS.

The Martyr's Widow.

rendered it necessary to transfer the residence of the Ruler of the Church, from his ordinary dwelling, to a securer asylum. For this purpose Lucina's house was chosen; and it continued to be so occupied, to her great delight, in that and the following pontificate, when the wild beasts were ordered to be transferred to it, that Pope Marcellus might feed them at home. This loathsome punishment soon caused his death.

Lucina admitted, at forty,* into the order of deaconesses, found plenty of occupation in the duties of her office. The charge and supervision of the women in church, the care of the sick and poor of her own sex, the making and keeping in order of sacred vestments and linen for the altar, and the instruction of children and female converts preparing for baptism, as well as the attending them at that sacred rite, belonged to the deaconesses, and gave sufficient occupation in addition to domestic offices. In the exercise of both these classes of duties, Lucina quietly passed her life. Its main object seemed to be attained. Her son had offered himself to God; and lived ready to shed his blood for the faith. To watch over him, and pray for him, were her delight, rather than an additional employment.

Early in the morning of the appointed day, the meeting mentioned in our last chapter took place. It will be sufficient to say, that in it full instructions were given for increasing the collection of alms, to be employed in enlarging the cemeteries and burying the dead, in succoring those driven to concealment by persecution, in nourishing prisoners, and obtaining access to them, and finally in ransoming or rescuing the bodies of martyrs. A notary was named for each region, to collect their acts and record interesting events. The cardinals, or titular priests, received instructions about the administration of sacraments, particularly of the Holy Eucharist, during the persecution; and to each was intrusted one cemetery or

* Sixty was the full age, but admission was given sometimes at forty.

more, in whose subterranean church he was to perform the sacred mysteries. The holy Pontiff chose for himself that of Callistus, which made Diogenes, its chief sexton, not a little, but innocently, proud.

The good old excavator seemed rather more cheery than otherwise, under the exciting forebodings of a coming perse-

A Chapel of the Blessed Sacrament.

cution. No commanding officer of engineers could have given his orders more briskly, or more decidedly, for the defence of a fortified city committed to his skill to guard, than he issued his to the subordinate superintendents of the various cemeteries round Rome, who met him by appointment at his own house, to learn the instructions of the superior assembly. The shadow of the sun-dial at the Porta Capena was pointing to mid-day, as he issued from it with his sons, and found already waiting the three young men. They walked in parties of two along the Appian road; and at nearly two miles from the

Underground gallery in the Catacombs, from Th. Roller's "Catacombes de Rome"

gate,* they entered by various ways (slipping round different tombs that lined the road) into the same villa on the right-hand. Here they found all the requisites for a descent into the subterranean cemeteries, such as candles, lanterns, and the instruments for procuring light. Severus proposed that, as the guides and the strangers were in equal number, they should be divided into pairs; and in the division he allotted Torquatus to himself. What his reason was we may easily conjecture.

It would probably weary our readers to follow the whole conversation of the party. Diogenes not only answered all questions put to him, but, from time to time, gave intelligent little lectures, on such objects as he considered peculiarly attractive. But we believe we shall better interest and inform our friends, if we digest the whole matter of these into a more connected narrative. And besides, they will wish to know something of the subsequent history of those wonderful excavations, into which we have conducted our youthful pilgrims.

The history of the early Christian cemeteries, the *Catacombs* as they are commonly called, may be divided into three portions: from their beginning to the period of our narrative, or a few years later; from this term to the eighth century; then down to our own time, when we have reason to hope that a new epoch is being commenced.

We have generally avoided using the name of catacombs, because it might mislead our readers into an idea that this was either the original or a generic name of those early Christian crypts. It is not so, however: Rome might be said to be surrounded by a circumvallation of cemeteries, sixty or thereabouts in number, each of which was generally known by the name of some saint or saints, whose bodies reposed there. Thus we have the cemeteries of SS. Nereus and Achil-

* Now St. Sebastian's. The older *Porta Capena* was nearly a mile within the present.

THE TOMB OF SAINT CECILIA.

On October 20, 1599, Cardinal Sfondrati had her tomb opened, and the body of the saint, in a state of perfect preservation, was found in the position here depicted. The sculptor, Stefano Maderno, made an exact copy of it, and his statue now ornaments her tomb.

lesi, of St. Agnes, of St. Pancratius, of Prætextatus, Priscilla, Hermes, &c. Sometimes these cemeteries were known by the names of the places where they existed.* The cemetery of St. Sebastian, which was called sometimes *Cœmeterium ad Sanctum Cæciliam*,† and by other names, had among them that of *Ad Catacumbas*.‡ The meaning of this word is completely unknown; though it may be attributed to the circumstance of the relics of SS. Peter and Paul having been for a time buried there, in a crypt still existing near the cemetery. This term became the name of that particular cemetery, then was generalized, till we familiarly call the whole system of these underground excavations—the Catacombs.

Their origin was, in the last century, a subject of controversy. Following two or three vague and equivocal passages, some learned writers pronounced the catacombs to have been originally heathen excavations, made to extract sand for the building of the city. These sand-pits were called *arenaria*, and so occasionally are the Christian cemeteries. But a more scientific and minute examination, particularly made by the accurate F. Marchi, has completely confuted this theory. The entrance to the catacombs was often, as can yet be seen, from these sand-pits, which are themselves under ground, and no doubt were a convenient cover for the cemetery; but several circumstances prove that they were never used for Christian burial, nor converted into Christian cemeteries.

The man who wishes to get the sand out of the ground will keep his excavation as near as may be to the surface; will have it of easiest possible access, for drawing out materials; and will make it as ample as is consistent with the safety of the roof, and the supply of what he is seeking. And

---

* As *Ad Nymphas, Ad Ursum pileatum, Inter duas lauros, Ad Statum Philippi*, &c.

† The cemetery at St. Cæcilia's tomb.

‡ Formed apparently of a Greek preposition and a Latin verb.

all this we find in the *arenario* still abounding round Rome. But the catacombs are constructed on principles exactly contrary to all these.

The catacomb dives at once, generally by a steep flight of steps, below the stratum of loose and friable sand,* into that where it is indurated to the hardness of a tender, but consistent rock; on the surface of which every stroke of the pick-axe is yet distinctly traceable. When you have reached this depth you are in the first story of the cemetery, for you descend again by stairs to the second and third below, all constructed on the same principle.

A catacomb may be divided into three parts, its passages or streets, its chambers or squares, and its churches. The passages are long, narrow galleries, cut with tolerable regularity, so that the roof and floor are at right angles with the sides, often so narrow as scarcely to allow two persons to go abreast. They sometimes run quite straight to a great length; but they are crossed by others, and these again by others, so as to form a complete labyrinth, or net-work, of subterranean corridors. To be lost among them would easily be fatal.

But these passages are not constructed, as the name would imply, merely to lead to something else. They are themselves the catacomb or cemetery. Their walls, as well as the sides of the staircases, are honeycombed with graves, that is, with rows of excavations, large and small, of sufficient length to admit a human body, from a child to a full-grown man, laid with its side to the gallery. Sometimes there are as many as fourteen, sometimes as few as three or four, of these rows, one above the other. They are evidently so made to measure, that it is probable the body was lying by the side of the grave, while this was being dug.

* That is, the red volcanic sand called *pozzolana*, so much prized for making Roman cement.

When the corpse, wrapped up, as we heard from Diogenes, was laid in its narrow cell, the front was hermetically closed either by a marble slab, or more frequently by several broad tiles, put edgeways in a groove or mortice, cut for them in the rock, and cemented all round. The inscription was cut upon the marble, or scratched in the wet mortar. Thousands of the former sort have been collected, and may be seen in museums and churches; many of the latter have been

A loculus, closed.

copied and published; but by far the greater number of tombs are anonymous, and have no record upon them. And now the reader may reasonably ask, through what period does the interment in the catacombs range, and how are its limits determined. We will try to content him, as briefly as possible.

There is no evidence of the Christians having ever buried any where, anteriorily to the construction of catacombs. Two principles as old as Christianity regulate this mode of burial. The first is, the manner of Christ's entombment. He was laid in a grave in a cavern, wrapped up in linen, embalmed with spices; and a stone, sealed up, closed His sepulchre,

As St. Paul so often proposes Him for the model of our resurrection, and speaks of our being buried with Him in baptism, it was natural for His disciples to wish to be buried after His example, so as to be ready to rise with Him.

This lying in wait for resurrection was the second thought that guided the formation of these cemeteries. Every expression connected with them alluded to the rising again. The word to *bury* is unknown in Christian inscriptions. "*Deposited* in peace," "the *deposition* of ——," are the expressions used; that is, the dead are but left there for a time, till called for again, as a pledge, or precious thing, intrusted to faithful, but temporary, keeping. The very name of cemetery suggests that it is only a place where many lie, as in a dormitory, slumbering for a while; till dawn come, and the trumpet's sound awake them. Hence the grave is only called "the place," or more technically, "the small home," * of the dead in Christ.

These two ideas, which are combined in the planning of the catacombs, were not later insertions into the Christian system, but must have been more vivid in its earlier times. They inspired abhorrence of the pagan custom of burning the dead; nor have we a hint that this mode was, at any time, adopted by Christians.

But ample proof is to be found in the catacombs themselves, of their early origin. The style of paintings, yet remaining, belongs to a period of still flourishing art. Their symbols, and the symbolical taste itself, are characteristic of a very ancient period. For this peculiar taste declined, as time went on. Although inscriptions with dates are rare, yet out of ten thousand collected, and about to be published, by the learned and sagacious Cavalier De Rossi, about three hundred are found bearing consular dates, through every period, from the early emperors to the middle of the fourth

* Locus, loculus.

A COLUMBARIUM.

Or underground sepulchre in which the Romans deposited the urns containing the ashes of the dead.

century (A.D. 350). Another curious and interesting custom furnishes us with dates on tombs. At the closing of the grave, the relations or friends, to mark it, would press into its wet plaster, and leave there a coin, a cameo, or engraved gem, sometimes even a shell or pebble; probably that they might find the sepulchre again, especially where no inscription was left. Many of these objects continue to be found, many have

been long collected. But it is not uncommon, where the coin, or, to speak scientifically, the medal, has fallen from its place, to find a mould of it left, distinct and clear in the cement, which equally gives its date. This is sometimes of Domitian, or other early emperors.

It may be asked, wherefore this anxiety to rediscover with certainty the tomb? Besides motives of natural piety, there is one constantly recorded on sepulchral inscriptions. In England, if want of space prevented the full date of a person's death being given, we should prefer chronicling the year, to the day of the month, when it occurred. It is more historical.

No one cares about remembering the day on which a person died, without the year; but the year without the day, is an important recollection. Yet while so few ancient Christian inscriptions supply the year of people's deaths, thousands give us the very day of it, on which they died, whether in the hopefulness of believers, or in the assurance of martyrs. This is easily explained. Of both classes annual commemoration had to be made, on the very day of their departure; and accurate knowledge of this was necessary. Therefore it alone was recorded.

In a cemetery close to the one in which we have left our three youths, with Diogenes and his sons,* were lately found inscriptions mingled together, belonging to both orders of the dead. One in Greek, after mentioning the "Deposition of Augenda on the 13th day before the Calends, or 1st of June," adds this simple address:

ΖΗϹΑΙϹ ΕΝΚΩ ΚΑΙ
ΕΡΩΤΑ ΥΠΕΡΗΜΩΝ

"Live in the Lord, and pray for us."

Another fragment is as follows:

. . . . . N. IVN·
. . . . . . IVIBAS·
IN PACE ET PETE
PRO NOBIS

* . . . Nones of June . . . Live in peace, and pray for us."

This is a third:

VICTORIA . REFRIGERER (ET)
ISSPIRITVS . TVS IN BONO

"Victoria, be refreshed, and may thy spirit be in enjoyment" (good).

* That of SS. Nereus and Achilleus.

This last reminds us of a most peculiar inscription found scratched in the mortar beside a grave in the cemetery of Prætextatus, not many yards from that of Callistus. It is remarkable, first, for being in Latin written with Greek letters; then, for containing a testimony of the Divinity of our Lord; lastly, for expressing a prayer for the refreshment of the departed. We fill up the portions of words wanting, from the falling out of part of the plaster.

BENE MERENTI	SORORI BON
	VIII KAL NOB
AG	CTI
OYC	PIT
XPIC	TOY
THC	PEO
ONH	ICPE
ITO	
TEC	IN X

"To the well-deserving sister Bon . . . The eighth day before the calends of Nov. Christ God Almighty refresh thy spirit in Christ."

In spite of this digression on prayers inscribed over tombs, the reader will not, we trust, have forgotten, that we were establishing the fact, that the Christian cemeteries of Rome owe their origin to the earliest ages. We have now to state down to what period they were used. After peace was restored to the Church, the devotion of Christians prompted them to desire burial near the martyrs, and holy people of an earlier age. But, generally speaking, they were satisfied to lie under the pavement. Hence the sepulchral stones which are often found in the rubbish of the catacombs, and sometimes in their places, bearing consular dates of the fourth century, are thicker, larger, better carved, and in a less simple style, than those of an earlier period, placed upon the walls. But before the end of that century, these monuments become rarer; and interment in the catacombs ceased in the following, at latest. Pope Damasus, who died in 384, reverently shrunk, as he tells us, in his own epitaph, from intruding into the company of the saints.

Restitutus, therefore, whose sepulchral tablet we gave for a title to our chapter, may well be considered as speaking in the name of the early Christians, and claiming as their own exclusive work and property, the thousand miles of subterranean city, with their six millions of slumbering inhabitants, who trust in the Lord, and await His resurrection.*

<small>* So P. Marchi calculates them, after diligent examination. We may mention here that, in the construction of these cemeteries, the sand extracted from one gallery was rammed into another already excavated. Hence many are now found completely filled up.</small>

A Lamb with a Milk Pail, emblematic of the Blessed Eucharist, found in the Catacombs

CHAPTER III.

WHAT DIOGENES COULD NOT TELL ABOUT THE CATACOMBS.

DIOGENES lived during the first period in the history of the cemeteries, though near its close. Could he have looked into their future fate, he would have seen, near at hand, an epoch that would have gladdened his heart, to be followed by one that would have deeply afflicted him. Although, therefore, the matter of this chapter have no direct bearing upon our narrative, it will serve essentially to connect it with the present topography of its scene.

When peace and liberty were restored to the Church, these cemeteries became places of devotion, and of great resort. Each of them was associated with the name of one, or the names of several, of the more eminent martyrs buried in it; and, on their anniversaries, crowds of citizens and of pilgrims thronged to their tombs, where the Divine mysteries were offered up, and the homily delivered in their praise. Hence began to be compiled the first martyrologies, or calendars of martyrs' days, which told the faithful whither to go. "At Rome, on the Salarian, or the Appian, or the Ardeatine way," such are the indications almost daily read in the Roman martyrology, now swelled out, by the additions of later ages."

* One or two entries from the old *Kalendarium Romanum* will illustrate this:

An ordinary reader of the book hardly knows the importance of these indications; for they have served to verify several otherwise dubious cemeteries. Another class of valuable writers also comes to our aid; but before mentioning them, we will glance at the changes which this devotion produced in the cemeteries. First, commodious entrances, with easy staircases were made; then walls were built to support the crumbling galleries; and, from time to time, funnel-shaped apertures in the vaults were opened, to admit light and air. Finally, basilicas or churches were erected over their entrances, generally leading immediately to the principal tomb, then called the *confession* of the church. The pilgrim, thus, on arriving at the holy city, visited each of these churches, a custom yet practised; descended below, and without having to grope his way about, went direct, by well-constructed passages, to the principal martyr's shrine, and so on to others, perhaps equally objects of reverence and devotion.

During this period, no tomb was allowed to be opened, no body to be extracted. Through apertures made into the grave, handkerchiefs or scarfs, called *brandia*, were introduced, to touch the martyr's relics; and these were carried to distant countries, to be held in equal reverence. No wonder

"ii. Non. Mart. Lucii in Callisti.
vi. Id. Dec. Eutichiani in Callisti.
xiii. Kal. Feb. Fabiani in Callisti, et Sebastiani ad Catacumbas.
viii. Id. Aug. Systi in Callisti."

We have extracted these entries of depositions in the cemetery of Callistus, because, while actually writing this chapter, we have received news of the discovery of the tombs and lapidary inscriptions of every one of these Popes, together with those of St. Antherus, in one chapel of the newly-ascertained cemetery of Callistus, with an inscription in verse by St. Damasus;

"Prid. Kal. Jan. Sylvestri in Priscilla.
iv. Id. (Aug.) Laurentii in Tiburtina.
iii. Kal. Dec. Saturnini in Thrasonis."

Published by Ruinart,—Acta, tom. iii.

that St. Ambrose, St. Gaudentius, and other bishops, should have found it so difficult to obtain bodies, or large relics of martyrs for their churches. Another sort of relics consisted of what was called familiarly the oil of a martyr, that is, the oil, often mixed with balsam, which burned in a lamp beside his tomb. Often a round stone pillar, three feet or so in height, and scooped out at the top, stands beside a monument; probably to hold the lamp, or serve for the distribution of its contents. St. Gregory the Great wrote to Queen Theodelinda, that he sent her a collection of the oils of the popes who were martyrs. The list which accompanied them was copied by Mabillon in the treasury of Monza, and republished by Ruinart.* It exists there yet, together with the very phials containing them, sealed up in metal tubes.

This jealousy of disturbing the saints, is displayed most beautifully in an incident, related by St. Gregory of Tours. Among the martyrs most honored in the ancient Roman Church were Sts. Chrysanthus and Daria. Their tombs became so celebrated for cures, that their fellow-Christians built (that is excavated) over them a chamber, with a vault of beautiful workmanship, where crowds of worshippers assembled. This was discovered by the heathens, and the emperor closed them in, walled up the entrance, and from above, probably through the *luminare*, or ventilating shaft, showered down earth and stones, and buried the congregation alive, as the two holy martyrs had been before them. The place was unknown at the peace of the Church, till discovered by Divine manifestation. But instead of being permitted to enter again into this hallowed spot, pilgrims were merely allowed to look at it, through a window opened in the wall, so as to see, not only the tombs of the martyrs, but also the bodies of those who had been buried alive at their shrines. And as the cruel massacre had taken place while preparations were being

* Acta Martyr. tom. iii.

made for oblation of the holy Eucharist, there were still to be seen lying about, the silver cruets in which the wine was brought for that spotless sacrifice."

It is clear that pilgrims resorting to Rome would want a hand-book to the cemeteries, that they might know what they had to visit. It is likewise but natural that, on their return home, they may have sought to edify their less fortunate neighbors, by giving an account of what they had seen. Accordingly there exists, no less fortunately for us than for their untravelled neighbors, several records of this character. The first place, among these, is held by catalogues compiled in the fourth century; one, of the places of sepulture of Roman pontiffs, the other of martyrs.† After these come three distinct guides to the catacombs; the more interesting because they take different rounds, yet agree marvellously in their account.

To show the value of these documents, and describe the changes which took place in the catacombs during the second period of their history, we will give a brief account of one discovery, in the cemetery where we have left our little party. Among the rubbish near the entrance of a catacomb, the name of which was yet doubtful, and which had been taken for that of Prætextatus, was found a fragment of a slab of marble which had been broken across obliquely, from left to right, with the following letters:

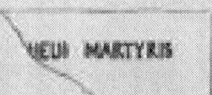

The young Cavalier de Rossi at once declared that this was part of the sepulchral inscription of the holy Pope Corne-

* S. Greg. Turon, de Gloria Mart. lib. i. c. 28, ap. Marchi, p. 81. One would apply St. Damasus's epigram on these martyrs to this occurrence, Carm. xxvii.
† Published by Bucherius in 1634.
‡ (Ori) . . . nelius martyr.

lius; that probably his tomb would be found below, in a distinguished form; and that as all the itineraries above mentioned concurred in placing it in the cemetery of Callistus, this, and not the one at St. Sebastian's, a few hundred yards off, must claim the honor of that name. He went further, and foretold that as these works pronounced St. Cyprian to be buried near Cornelius, there would be found something at the tomb which would account for that idea, for it was known that his body rested in Africa. It was not long before every prediction was verified. The great staircase discovered* was found to lead at once to a wider space, carefully secured by brick-work of the time of peace, and provided with light and air from above. On the left was a tomb, cut like others in the rock, without any exterior arch over it. It was, however, large and ample; and except one, very high above it, there were no other graves below, or over, or at the sides. The remaining portion of the slab was found within it; the first piece was brought from the Kircherian Museum, where it had been deposited, and exactly fitted to it; and both covered the tomb, thus:

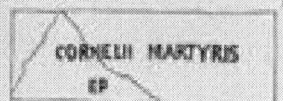

Below, reaching from the lower edge of this stone to the ground was a marble slab covered with an inscription, of which only the left-hand end remains, the rest being broken off and lost. Above the tomb was another slab let into the sand-stone, of which the right-hand end exists, and a few more fragments have been recovered in the rubbish; not enough to make out the lines, but sufficient to show it was an inscription in verse, by Pope Damasus. How is this author-

---

* The crypt, we believe, was discovered below the stairs.
† Of Cornelius Martyr Bishop.

ship traceable? Very easily. Not only do we know that
this holy pope, already mentioned, took pleasure in putting
verses, which he loved to write, on the tombs of martyrs,* but
the number of inscriptions of his yet extant exhibit a particular and very elegant form of letters, known among antiquari-

Saint Cornelius and Saint Cyprian, from De Rossi's "Roma Sotterranea."

ans by the name of "Damasian." The fragments of this
marble bear portions of verses, in this character.

To proceed: on the wall, right of the tomb, and on the
same plane, were painted two full-length figures in sacerdotal
garments, with glories round their heads, evidently of Byzan-

* These form the great bulk of his extant works in verse.

tine work of the seventh century. Down the wall, by the left side of each, letter below letter, were their names; some letters were effaced, which we supply in italics as follow:

SIS CORNELI PP   SCIS PRI*NCI*S

We here see how a foreigner, reading these two inscriptions, with the portraits, and knowing that the Church commemorates the two martyrs on the same day, might easily be led to suppose that they were here deposited together. Finally at the right hand of the tomb stands a truncated column, about three feet high, concave at the top, as before described; and as a confirmation of the use to which we said it might be put, St. Gregory has, in his list of oils sent to the Lombard Queen, "Oleum S. Cornelii," the oil of St. Cornelius.

We see, then, how, during the second period, new ornaments, as well as greater conveniences, were added to the primitively simple forms of the cemeteries. But we must not, on that account, imagine that we are in any danger of mistaking these later embellishments for the productions of the early ages. The difference is so immense that we might as easily blunder by taking a Rubens for a Beato Angelico, as by considering a Byzantine figure to be a production of the two first centuries.

* "(The picture) of St. Cornelius Pope, of St. Cyprian." On the other side, on a narrow wall projecting at a right angle, are two more similar portraits; but only one name can be deciphered, that of St. Sixtus, or, as he is there and elsewhere called, Sistus. On the paintings of the principal saints may still be read, scratched in the mortar, in characters of the seventh century, the names of visitors to the tomb. Those of two priests are thus—

OLEO PRB I ANNIS PRB.

It may be interesting to add the entry in the Roman calendar.

"xviii. Kal. Oct. Cypriani Africæ: Romæ celebratur in Callisti." "Sept. 14. (The deposition) of Cyprian in Africa: at Rome it is kept in (the cemetery) of Callistus."

We come now to the third period of these holy cemeteries, the sad one of their desolation. When the Lombards, and later the Saracens, began to devastate the neighborhood of Rome, and the catacombs were exposed to desecration, the popes extracted the bodies of the most illustrious martyrs, and placed them in the basilicas of the city. This went on till the eighth or ninth century; when we still read of repairs made in the cemeteries by the sovereign pontiffs. The catacombs ceased to be so much places of devotion; and the churches, which stood over their entrances, were destroyed, or fell to decay. Only those remained which were fortified, and could be defended. Such are the extramural basilicas of St. Paul on the Ostian way, of St. Sebastian on the Appian, St. Laurence on the Tiburtine, or in the Ager Veranus, St. Agnes on the Nomentan road, St. Pancratius on the Aurelian, and, greatest of all, St. Peter's on the Vatican. The first and last had separate *burghs* or cities round them; and the traveller can still trace remains of strong walls round some of the others.

Strange it is, however, that the young antiquarian, whom we have frequently named with honor, should have re-discovered two of the basilicas over the entrance to the cemetery of Callistus, almost entire; the one being a stable and bakehouse, the other a wine-store. One is, most probably, that built by Pope Damasus, so often mentioned. The earth washed down, through air-holes, the spoliation practised during ages, by persons entering from vineyards through unguarded entrances, the mere wasting action of time and weather, have left us but a wreck of the ancient catacombs. Still there is much to be thankful for. Enough remains to verify the records left us in better times, and these serve to guide us to the reconstruction of our ruins. The present Pontiff* has done more in a few years for these sacred places,

* Pope Pius IX.—*Pub.*

which he has appointed have done wonders. With very limited means, they are going systematically to work, finishing as they advance. Nothing is taken from the spot where it is found; but every thing is restored, as far as possible, to its original state. Accurate tracings are made of all the paintings, and plans of every part explored. To secure these good results, the Pope has, from his own resources, bought vineyards and fields, especially at Tor Marancia, where the cemetery of SS. Nereus and Achilleus is situated; and we believe also over that of Callistus. The French emperor too has sent to Rome, artists, who have produced a most magnificent work, perhaps somewhat overdone, upon the catacombs: a truly imperial undertaking.

It is time, however, for us to rejoin our party below, and finish our inspection of these marvellous cities of departed saints, under the guidance of our friends the excavators.

The Tomb of Cornelius.

CHAPTER IV.

WHAT DIOGENES DID TELL ABOUT THE CATACOMBS.

ALL that we have told our readers of the first period of the history of subterranean Rome, as ecclesiastical antiquarians love to call the catacombs, has no doubt been better related by Diogenes to his youthful hearers, as, taper in hand, they have been slowly walking through a long straight gallery, crossed, indeed, by many others, but adhered to faithfully; with sundry pauses, and, of course, lectures, embodying what we have put together in our prosaic second chapter.

At length Diogenes turned to the right, and Torquatus looked around him anxiously.

"I wonder," he said, "how many turns we have passed by, before leaving this main gallery?"

"A great many," answered Severus, drily.

"How many do you think, ten or twenty?"

"Full that, I fancy; for I never have counted them."

Torquatus had, however; but wished to make sure. He continued, still pausing:

"How do you distinguish the right turn, then? Oh, what is this?" and he pretended to examine a small niche in the corner. But Severus kept too sharp a look-out, and saw thus he was making a mark in the sand.

"Come, come along," he said, "or we shall lose sight of the rest, and not see which way they turn. That little niche is to hold a lamp; you will find one at each angle. As to ourselves, we know every alley and turn here below, as you do those of the city above."

Torquatus was somewhat reassured by this account of the lamps—those little earthen ones, evidently made on purpose

A Lamp with a representation of the Good Shepherd, found at Ostium prior to the third century. From Bosio's "Catacombs."

for the catacombs, of which so many are there found. But not content, he kept as good count as he could of the turns, as they went; and now with one excuse, and now with another, he constantly stopped, and scrutinized particular spots and corners. But Severus had a lynx's eye upon him, and allowed nothing to escape his attention.

At last they entered a doorway, and found themselves in a square chamber, richly adorned with paintings.

"What do you call this?" asked Tiburtius.

"It is one of the many crypts, or *cubicula*," which abound in our cemeteries," answered Diogenes; "sometimes they are merely family sepultures, but generally they contain the tomb of some martyr, on whose anniversary we meet here. See that tomb opposite us, which, though flush with the wall, is

Cubiculum or Crypt, as found in the Catacombs.

arched over. That becomes, on such an occasion, the altar whereon the Divine mysteries are celebrated. You are of course aware of the custom of so performing them."

"Perhaps my two friends," interposed Pancratius, "so recently baptized, may not have heard it; but I know it well. It is surely one of the glorious privileges of martyrdom, to have the Lord's sacred Body and precious Blood offered upon

* Chambers.

one's ashes, and to repose thus under the very feet of God.* But let us see well the paintings all over this crypt."

"It is on account of them that I brought you into this chamber, in preference to so many others in the cemetery.

The Last Supper. From a picture in the Cemetery of St. Callixtus.

It is one of the most ancient, and contains a most complete series of pictures, from the remotest times down to some of my son's doing."

"Well, then, Diogenes, explain them systematically to my

* "Sic veneratur ossa licet,
   Ossibus altar et impositum;
   Illa Dei sita sub pedibus,
   Prospicit haec, populosque suos
   Carmine propitiata fovet."
                          Prudentius, περι στεφ. iii. 42.

"With her relics gathered here,
The altar o'er them placed rears,
She beneath God's feet reposes,
Nor to us her soft eye closes,
Nor her gracious ear."

The idea that the martyr lies " beneath the feet of God " is an allusion to the Real Presence in the Blessed Eucharist.

friends," said Pancratius. "I think I know most of them, but not all; and I shall be glad to hear you describe them."

"I am no scholar," replied the old man, modestly, "but when one has lived sixty years, man and boy, among things, one gets to know them better than others, because one loves them more. All here have been fully initiated, I suppose?" he added, with a pause.

"All," answered Tiburtius, "though not so fully instructed

A Ceiling in the Catacombs. From Sir Rossi's "Roma Sotteranea."

as converts ordinarily are. Torquatus and myself have received the sacred gift."

"Enough," resumed the excavator. "The ceiling is the oldest part of the painting, as is natural; for that was done when the crypt was excavated, whereas the walls were decorated, as tombs were hollowed out. You see the ceiling has a sort of trellis-work painted over it, with grapes, to represent perhaps our true Vine, of which we are the branches. There you see Orpheus sitting down, and playing sweet music, not only to his own flock, but to the wild beasts of the desert, which stand charmed around him."

"Why, that is a heathen picture altogether," interrupted

Torquatus, with pettishness, and some sarcasm; "what has it to do with Christianity?"

"It is an allegory, Torquatus," replied Pancratius, gently, "and a favorite one. The use of Gentile images, when in themselves harmless, has been permitted. You see masks,

Our Lord under the Symbol of Orpheus. From a picture in the Cemetery of Domitilla.

for instance, and other pagan ornaments in this ceiling, and they belong generally to a very ancient period. And so our Lord was represented under the symbol of Orpheus, to conceal His sacred representation from Gentile blasphemy and sacrilege. Look, now, in that arch; you have a more recent representation of the same subject."

"I see," said Torquatus, "a shepherd with a sheep over his shoulders—the Good Shepherd; that I can understand; I remember the parable."

"But why is this subject such a favorite one?" asked Tiburtius; "I have observed it in other cemeteries."

"If you will look over the *arcosolium*,* answered Severus, "you will see a fuller representation of the scene. But I think we had better first continue what we have begun, and finish the ceiling. You see that figure on the right?"

The Good Shepherd. A woman praying. From the arcosolium of the Cemetery of SS. Nereus and Achilleus.

"Yes," replied Tiburtius; "it is that of a man apparently in a chest, with a dove flying towards him. Is that meant to represent the Deluge?"

"It is," said Severus, "as the emblem of regeneration by water and the Holy Spirit; and of the salvation of the world. Such is our beginning; and here is our end: Jonas thrown out of the boat, and swallowed by the whale; and then sitting in enjoyment under his gourd. The resurrection with our Lord, and eternal rest as its fruit."

"How natural is this representation in such a place!" observed Pancratius, pointing to the other side; "and here we have another type of the same consoling doctrine."

"Where?" asked Torquatus, languidly; "I see nothing but a figure bandaged all round, and standing up, like a huge

* The arched tombs were so called. A homely illustration would be an arched fireplace, walled up to the height of three feet. The paintings would be inside, above the wall.

infant in a small temple; and another person opposite to it."

"Exactly," said Severus; "that is the way we always represent the resurrection of Lazarus. Here look, is a touch-

A Ceiling in the Catacombs. In the Cemetery of Domitilla, third century.

ing expression of the hopes of our fathers in persecution: The three Babylonian children in the fiery furnace."

"Well, now, I think," said Torquatus, "we may come to the *arcosolium*, and finish this room. What are these pictures round it?"

"If you look at the left side, you see the multiplication of the loaves and fishes. The fish* is, you know, the symbol of Christ."

* The word is usually given in Greek, and Christ is familiarly called the ίχθύς, *ichthys*.

"Why so?" asked Torquatus, rather impatiently. Severus turned to Pancratius, as the better scholar, to answer.

"There are two opinions about its origin," said the youth, readily; "one finds the meaning in the word itself; its letters forming the beginning of words, so as to mean 'Jesus Christ, Son of God, Saviour.'* Another puts it in the symbol itself; that as fish are born and live in the water, so is the Christian born of water, and buried with Christ in it, by baptism.† Hence, as we came along, we saw the figure of a fish carved

The fishes and anchor.   The fishes and doves.

on tombs, or its name engraven on them. Now go on, Severus."

"Then the union of the bread and the fish in one multiplication shows us how, in the Eucharist, Christ becomes the food of all.‡ Opposite, is Moses striking the rock, from which all drank, and which is Christ, our drink as well as our food."§

* This is the interpretation of St. Optatus (adv. Parm. lib. iii.) and St. Augustine (de C. D. lib. xviii. c. 23).

† This is Tertullian's explanation (de Baptismo, lib. ii. c. 2).

‡ In the same cemetery is another interesting painting. On a table lie a loaf and a fish; a priest is stretching his hands over them; and opposite is a female figure in adoration. The priest is the same as, in a picture close by, is represented administering baptism. In another chamber just cleared out, are very ancient decorations, such as masks, &c., and fishes bearing baskets of bread and flasks of wine, on their backs as they swim.

§ The type of the figure is that of St. Peter, as he is represented to us in the cemeteries. On a glass, bearing a picture of this scene, the person striking the rock has written over his head PETRVS.

"Now, at last," said Torquatus, "we are come to the Good Shepherd."

"Yes," continued Severus, "you see Him in the centre of the *arcosolium*, in His simple tunic and leggings, with a sheep upon His shoulders, the recovered wanderer from the flock. Two more are standing at His sides; the truant ram on His right, the gentle ewe upon His left; the penitent in the post of honor. On each side too, you see a person evidently sent by Him to preach. Both are leaning forward, and addressing sheep not of the fold. One on either side is apparently giving no heed to their words, but browsing quietly on, while one is turning up its eyes and head, looking and listening with eager attention. Rain is falling copiously on them; that is the grace of God. It is not difficult to interpret this picture."

"But what makes this emblem such a particular favorite?" again pressed Tiburtius.

"We consider this, and similar paintings, to belong chiefly to the time when the Novatian heresy so much plagued the Church," answered Severus.

"And pray what heresy is that?" asked Torquatus, carelessly; for he thought he was losing time.

"It was, and indeed is, the heresy," answered Pancratius, "that teaches, that there are sins which the Church has not power to forgive; which are too great for God to pardon."

Pancratius was not aware of the effect of his words; but Severus, who never took off his eye from Torquatus, saw the blood come and go violently in his countenance.

"Is that a heresy?" asked the traitor, confused.

"Surely a dreadful one," replied Pancratius, "to limit the mercy and forgiveness of Him, who came to call not the just, but sinners to repentance. The Catholic Church has always held, that a sinner, however dark the dye, however huge the mass, of his crimes, on truly repenting, may receive forgiveness, through the penitential remedy left in her hands. And, therefore, she has always so much loved this type of the Good Shepherd, ready to run into the wilderness, to bring back a lost sheep."

"But suppose," said Torquatus, evidently moved, "that one who had become a Christian, and received the sacred Gift, were to fall away, and plunge into vice, and—and"—(his voice faltered)—"almost betray his brethren, would not the Church reject such a one from hope?"

The Blessed Virgin and the Magi. From a picture in the Cemetery of Ostrianus.

"No, no," answered the youth; "these are the very crimes, which the Novatians insult the Catholics for admitting to pardon. The Church is a mother, with her arms ever open to re-embrace her erring children."

There was a tear trembling in Torquatus's eye; his lips quivered with the confession of his guilt, which ascended to them for a moment; but as if a black poisonous drop rose up his throat with it and choked him, he changed in a moment to a hard, obstinate look, bit his lip, and said, with an effort at coolness: "It is certainly a consoling doctrine for those that need it."

Severus alone observed that a moment of grace had been forfeited, and that some despairing thought had quenched a flash of hope, in that man's heart. Diogenes and Majus, who had been absent looking at a new place for opening a gallery near, now returned. Torquatus addressed the old master-digger:

"We have now seen the galleries and the chambers; I am anxious to visit the church in which we shall have to assemble."

The unconscious excavator was going to lead the way, when the inexorable artist interposed.

"I think, father, it is too late for to-day; you know we have got our work to do. These young friends will excuse us, especially as they will see the church in good time, and in better order also, as the holy Pontiff intends to officiate in it."

They assented; and when they arrived at the point where they had turned off from the first straight gallery to visit the ornamented chamber, Diogenes stopped the party, turned a few steps along an opposite passage, and said:

"If you pursue this corridor, and turn to the right, you come to the church. I have merely brought you here to show you an *arcosolium*, with a beautiful painting. You here see* the Virgin Mother holding her Divine Infant in her arms, while the wise Easterns, here represented as four, though generally we only reckon three, are adoring Him."*

All admired the painting; but poor Severus was much chagrined at seeing how his good father had unwittingly supplied the information desired by Torquatus, and had furnished him with a sure clue to the desired turn, by calling his attention to the tomb close round it, distinguishable by so remarkable a picture.

* There are several repetitions of this painting. One has been lately found, if we remember right, in the cemetery of Nereus and Achilleus. It is long anterior to the Council of Chalcedon, whence this mode of representing our Lord is usually dated. It is given in our title-page.

When their company was departed, he told all that he had observed to his brother, remarking, "That man will give us trouble yet: I strongly suspect him."

In a short time they had removed every mark which Torquatus had made at the turnings. But this was no security against his reckonings; and they determined to prepare for changing the road, by blocking up the present one, and turning off at another point. For this purpose they had the sand of new excavations brought to the ends of a gallery which crossed the main avenue, where this was low, and left it heaped up there till the faithful could be instructed of the intended change.

Moses striking the rock, from the Cemetery of "Inter duos Lauros."

CHAPTER V.

ABOVE GROUND.

TO recover our reader from his long subterranean excursion, we must take him with us on another visit, to the "happy Campania," or, "Campany the blest," as an old writer might have called it. There we left Fabiola perplexed by some sentences which she had found. They came to her like a letter from another world; she hardly knew of what character. She wished to learn more about them, but she hardly durst inquire. Many visitors called the next day, and for several days after, and she often thought of putting before some or other of them the mysterious sentences, but she could not bring herself to do it.

A lady, whose life was like her own, philosophically correct, and coldly virtuous, came; and they talked together over the fashionable opinions of the day. She took out her vellum page to puzzle her; but she shrank from submitting it to her: it felt profane to do so. A learned man, well read in all branches of science and literature, paid her a long visit, and spoke very charmingly on the sublimer views of the older schools. She was tempted to consult *him* about her discovery; but it seemed to contain something higher than he could comprehend. It was strange that, after all, when wisdom or consolation was to be sought, the noble and haughty Roman lady should turn instinctively to her Christian slave. And so it was now. The first moment they were alone, after several days of company and visits, Fabiola produced her parchment, and placed it before Syra. There passed over her countenance an emotion not observable to her mistress; but she was perfectly calm, as she looked up from reading.

"That writing," said her mistress, "I got at Chromatius's villa, on the back of a note, probably by mistake. I cannot drive it out of my mind, which is quite perplexed by it."

"Why should it be so, my noble lady? Its sense seems plain enough."

"Yes; and that very plainness gives me trouble. My natural feelings revolt against this sentiment: I fancy I ought to despise a man who does not resent an injury, and return hatred for hatred. To forgive at most would be much; but to do good in return for evil, seems to me an unnatural exaction from human nature. Now, while I feel all this, I am conscious that I have been brought to esteem you, for conduct exactly the reverse of what I am naturally impelled to expect."

"Oh, do not talk of me, my dear mistress; but look at the simple principle; you honor it in others, too. Do you despise, or do you respect, Aristides, for obliging a boorish enemy, by writing, when asked, his own name on the shell that voted his banishment? Do you, as a Roman lady, contemn or honor the name of Coriolanus, for his generous forbearance to your city?"

"I venerate both, most truly, Syra; but then you know those were heroes, and not every-day men."

"And why should we not all be heroes?" asked Syra, laughing.

"Bless me, child! what a world we should live in, if we were. It is very pleasant reading about the feats of such wonderful people; but one would be very sorry to see them performed by common men, every day."

"Why so?" pressed the servant.

"Why so? who would like to find a baby she was nursing, playing with, or strangling, serpents in the cradle? I should be very sorry to have a gentleman, whom I invited to dinner, telling me coolly he had that morning killed a minotaur, or strangled a hydra; or to have a friend offering to send the Tiber through my stables, to cleanse them. Preserve us from a generation of heroes, say I." And Fabiola laughed heartily at the conceit. In the same good humor Syra continued:

"But suppose we had the misfortune to live in a country where such monsters existed, centaurs and minotaurs, hydras and dragons. Would it not be better that common men should be heroes enough to conquer them, than that we should have to send off to the other side of the world for a Theseus, or a Hercules, to destroy them? In fact, in that case, a man would be no more a hero if he fought them, than a lion-slayer is in my country."

"Quite true, Syra; but I do not see the application of your idea."

"It is this: anger, hatred, revenge, ambition, avarice, are to my mind as complete monsters as serpents or dragons; and they attack common men as much as great ones. Why should not I try to be as able to conquer them as Aristides, or Coriolanus, or Cincinnatus? Why leave it to heroes only, to do what we can do as well?"

"And do you really hold this as a common moral principle? If so, I fear you will soar too high."

"No, dear lady. You were startled when I ventured to maintain that inward and unseen virtue was as necessary as the outward and visible: I fear I must surprise you still more."

"Go on, and do not fear to tell me all."

"Well, then, the principle of that system which I profess is this: that we must treat and practise, as every-day and common virtue, nay, as simple duty, whatever any other code, the purest and sublimest that may be, considers heroic, and proof of transcendent virtue."

"That is indeed a sublime standard to form, of moral elevation; but mark the difference between the two cases. The hero is supported by the praises of the world; his act is recorded and transmitted to posterity, when he checks his passions, and performs a sublime action. But who sees, cares for, or shall requite, the poor obscure wretch, who in humble secrecy imitates his conduct?"

Syra, with solemn, reverential look and gesture, raised her eyes and her right hand to heaven, and slowly said: "His Father, who is in heaven, who maketh His sun to rise on the good and the bad, and raineth on the just and the unjust."

Fabiola paused for a time, overawed; then said affectionately and respectfully: "Again, Syra, you have conquered my philosophy. Your wisdom is consistent as it is sublime. A virtue heroic, even when unseen, you propose as the ordinary daily virtue of every one. Men must indeed become more than what gods have been thought to be, to attempt it; but the very idea is worth a whole philosophy. Can you lead me higher than this?"

"Oh, far!—far higher still."

"And where at length would you leave me?"

"Where your heart should tell you that it had found peace."

Monogram of Christ, found in the Catacombs.

CHAPTER VI.

DELIBERATIONS.

THE persecution had now been some time raging in the East under Dioclesian and Galerius; and the decree for enkindling it throughout the West, had reached Maximian. But it had been resolved to make this a work, not of repression, but of extermination, of the Christian name. It had been determined to spare no one; but cutting off the chiefs of the religion first, to descend down to the wholesale butchery of the poorest classes. It was necessary for this purpose to concert measures, that the various engines of destruction might work in cruel harmony; that every possible instrument should be employed to secure completeness to the effort; and also that the majesty of imperial command should add its grandeur and its terror to the crushing blow.

For this purpose the emperor, though impatient to begin his work of blood, had yielded to the opinion of his counsellors, that the edict should be kept concealed till it could be published simultaneously in every province, and government, of the West. The thundercloud, fraught with vengeance, would thus hang for a time, in painful mystery, over its intended victims, and then burst suddenly upon them, discharging upon their heads its mingled elements, and its "fire, hail, snow, ice, and boisterous blast."

It was in the month of November, that Maximian Herculeus convoked the meeting in which his plans had finally to be adjusted. To it were summoned the leading officers of his court, and of the state. The principal one, the prefect of the city, had brought with him his son, Corvinus, whom he had proposed to be captain of a body of armed pursuivants, picked out for their savageness and hatred of Christians; who should hunt them out, or down, with unrelenting assiduity. The chief prefects or governors of Sicily, Italy, Spain, and Gaul, were present, to receive their orders. In addition to these, several learned men, philosophers, and orators, among whom was our old acquaintance Calpurnius, had been invited; and many priests, who had come from different parts, to petition for heavier persecution, were commanded to attend.

The usual residence of the emperors, as we have seen, was the Palatine. There was, however, another much esteemed by them, which Maximian Herculeus in particular preferred. During the reign of Nero, the wealthy senator, Plautius Lateranus, was charged with conspiracy, and of course punished with death. His immense property was seized by the emperor, and part of this was his house, described by Juvenal, and other writers, as of unusual size and magnificence. It was

beautifully situated on the Cœlian hill, and on the southern verge of the city; so that from it was a view unequalled even in the vicinity of Rome. Stretching across the wavy campagna, here bestrided by colossal aqueducts, crossed by lines of roads, with their fringes of marble tombs, and bespangled all over with glittering villas, set like gems in the dark green enamel of laurel and cypress, the eye reached, at evening, the purple slope of hills on which, as on a couch, lay stretched luxuriously Alba and Tusculum, with "their daughters," according to oriental phrase,

The Claudian Aqueduct

basking brightly in the setting sun. The craggy range of Sabine mountains on the left, and the golden expanse of the sea on the right of the beholder, closed in this perfect landscape.

It would be attributing to Maximian a quality which he did not possess, were we to give him credit for loving a residence so admirably situated, through any taste for the beautiful. The splendor of the buildings, which he had still further adorned, or possibly the facility of running out of the city for the chase of boar and wolf, was the motive of this preference. A native of Sirmium, in Sclavonia, a reputed barbarian therefore of the lowest extraction, a mere soldier of fortune, without any education, endowed with little more than a brute strength, which made his surname of Herculeus most appropriate, he had been raised to the purple by his brother-barbarian Diocles, known as the emperor Dioclesian. Like him, covetous to meanness, and spendthrift to recklessness, addicted to the same coarse vices and foul crimes, which a Christian pen refuses to record, without restraint of any passion, without sense of justice, or feeling of humanity, this monster had never ceased to oppress, persecute, and slay whoever stood in his way. To him the coming persecution looked like an approaching feast does to a glutton, who requires the excitement of a surfeit to relieve the monotony of daily excess. Gigantic in frame, with the well-known features of his race, with the hair on his head and face more yellow than red, shaggy and wild, like tufts of straw, with eyes restlessly rolling in a compound expression of suspicion, profligacy, and ferocity, this almost last of Rome's tyrants struck terror into the heart of any beholder, except a Christian. Is it wonderful that he hated the race and its name?

In the large basilica, or hall, then, of the Ædes Lateranæ,* Maximian met his motley council, in which secrecy was

* The Lateran house or palace.

ensured by penalty of death. In the semicircular apse at the upper end of the hall, sat the emperor, on an ivory throne richly adorned, and before him were arranged his obsequious and almost trembling advisers. A chosen body of guards kept the entrance; and the officer in command, Sebastian, was leaning negligently against it on the inside, but carefully noted every word that was spoken.

Little did the emperor think, that the hall in which he sat, and which he afterwards gave, with the contiguous palace, to Constantine, as part of the dowry of his daughter, Fausta, would be transferred by him to the head of the religion he was planning to extirpate, and become, retaining its name of the Lateran Basilica, the cathedral of Rome, "of all the churches of the city and of the world the mother and chief."[*] Little did he imagine, that on the spot whereon rested his throne, would be raised a Chair, whence commands should issue, to reach worlds unknown to Roman sway, from an immortal race of sovereigns, spiritual and temporal.

Precedence was granted, by religious courtesy, to the priests; each of whom had his tale to tell. Here a river had overflowed its banks, and done much mischief to the neighboring plains; there an earthquake had thrown down part of a town; on the northern frontiers the barbarians threatened invasion; at the south, the plague was ravaging the pious population. In every instance, the oracles had declared, that it was all owing to the Christians, whose toleration irritated the gods, and whose evil charms brought calamity on the empire. Nay, some had afflicted their votaries by openly proclaiming, that they would utter no more, till the odious Nazarenes had been exterminated; and the great Delphic oracle had not hesitated to declare, "that *the Just* did not allow the gods to speak."

Next came the philosophers and orators, each of whom

[*] Inscription on the front, and medals, of the Lateran Basilica.

made his own long-winded oration; during which Maximian gave unequivocal signs of weariness. But as the Emperors in the East had held a similar meeting, he considered it his duty to sit out the annoyance. The usual calumnies were repeated, for the ten-thousandth time, to an applauding assembly; the stories of murdering and eating infants, of committing foul crimes, of worshipping martyrs' bodies, of adoring an ass's head, and inconsistently enough of being unbelievers, and serving no God. These tales were all most firmly believed; though probably their reciters knew perfectly well, they were but good sound heathen lies, very useful in keeping up a horror of Christianity.

But, at length, up rose the man, who was considered to have most deeply studied the doctrines of the enemy, and best to know their dangerous tactics. He was supposed to have read their own books, and to be drawing up a confutation of their errors, which would fairly crush them. Indeed, so great was his weight with his own side, that when he asserted that Christians held any monstrous principle, had their supreme pontiff in person contradicted it, every one would have laughed at the very idea of taking his word for his own belief, against the assertion of Calpurnius.

He struck up a different strain, and his learning quite astonished his fellow-sophists. He had read the original books, he said, not only of the Christians themselves, but of their forefathers, the Jews; who, having come into Egypt in the reign of Ptolemy Philadelphus, to escape from a famine in their own country, through the arts of their leader, Josephus, bought up all the corn there, and sent it home. Upon which Ptolemy imprisoned them, telling them, that as they had eaten up all the corn, they should live on the straw, by making bricks with it for building a great city. Then Demetrius-Phalerius, hearing from them of a great many curious histories of their ancestors, shut up Moses and Aaron, their most learned men, in a tower, having shaved half their beards, till they should write in Greek all their records. These rare books Calpurnius had seen, and he would build his argument entirely on them. This race made war upon every king and people that came in their way; and destroyed them all. It was their principle, if they took a city, to put every one to the sword; and this was all because they were under the government of their ambitious priests; so that when a certain king, Saul, called also Paul, spared a poor captive monarch whose name was Agag, the priests ordered him to be brought out and hewed in pieces.

"Now," continued he, "these Christians are still under the domination of the same priesthood, and are quite as ready to-day, under their direction, to overthrow the great Roman empire, burn us all in the Forum, and even sacrilegiously assail the sacred and venerable heads of our divine emperors."

A thrill of horror ran through the assembly, at this recital. It was soon hushed, as the emperor opened his mouth to speak.

"For my part," he said, "I have another and a stronger reason for my abhorrence of these Christians. They have dared to establish in the heart of the empire, and in this very city, a supreme religious authority, unknown here before, independent of the government of the State, and equally powerful over their minds as this. Formerly, all acknowledged the emperor as supreme in religious, as in civil, rule. Hence he bears still the title of Pontifex Maximus. But these men have raised up a divided power, and consequently bear but a divided loyalty. I hate, therefore, as a usurpation in my dominions, this sacerdotal sway over my subjects. For I declare, that I would rather hear of a new rival starting up to my throne, than of the election of one of these priests in Rome."*

* These are the very words of Decius, on the election of St. Cornelius to the

This speech, delivered in a harsh grating voice, and with a vulgar foreign accent, was received with immense applause; and plans were formed for the simultaneous publication of the Edict through the West, and for its complete and exterminating execution.

Then turning sharp upon Tertullus, the emperor said: "Prefect, you said you had some one to propose, for superintending these arrangements, and for merciless dealings with these traitors."

"He is here, sire, my son Corvinus." And Tertullus handed the youthful candidate to the grim tyrant's footstool, where he knelt. Maximian eyed him keenly, burst into a hideous laugh, and said: "Upon my word, I think he'll do. Why, prefect, I had no idea you had such an ugly son. I should think he is just the thing; every quality of a thorough-paced, unconscientious scape-grace is stamped upon his features."

Then turning to Corvinus, who was scarlet with rage, terror, and shame, he said to him: "Mind you, sirrah, I must have clean work of it; no hacking and hewing, no blundering. I pay up well if I am well served; but I pay off well, too, if badly served. So now go; and remember, that if your back can answer for a small fault, your head will for a greater. The lictors' *fasces* contain an axe as well as rods."

The emperor rose to depart, when his eye caught Fulvius, who had been summoned as a paid court-spy, but who kept as much in the back-ground as possible. "Ho, there, my eastern worthy," he called out to him; "draw nearer."

Fulvius obeyed with apparent cheerfulness, but with real reluctance; much the same as if he had been invited to go very

---

See of St. Peter: "Cum medio patentur audiret levari adversum se zonchum principem, quam comitati Roma Dei sacerdotem." *S. Cypr. Ep.* lii. *ad Antonianum*, p. 69, ed. Manr. Could there be a stronger proof, that under the heathen empire, the papal power was sensible and external, even to the extent of exciting imperial jealousy?

near a tiger, the strength of whose chain he was not quite sure about. He had seen, from the beginning, that his coming to Rome had not been acceptable to Maximian, though he knew not fully the cause. It was not merely that the tyrant had plenty of favorites of his own to enrich, and spies to pay, without Dioclesian's sending him more from Asia, though this had its weight; but it was more. He believed in his heart that Fulvius had been sent principally to act the spy upon himself, and to report to Nicomedia the sayings and doings of his court. While, therefore, he was obliged to tolerate him, and employ him, he mistrusted and disliked him, which in him was equivalent to hating him. It was some compensation, therefore, to Corvinus, when he heard his more polished confederate publicly addressed, as rudely as himself, in the following terms:

"None of your smooth, put-on looks for me, fellow. I want deeds, not smirks. You came here as a famous plot-hunter, a sort of stoat, to pull conspirators out of their nests, or suck their eggs for me. I have seen nothing of this so far; and yet you have had plenty of money to set you up in business. These Christians will afford you plenty of game; so make yourself ready, and let us see what you can do. You know my ways; you had better look sharp about you, therefore, or you may have to look at something very sharp before you. The property of the convicted will be divided between the accusers and the treasury; unless I see particular reasons for taking the whole to myself. Now you may go."

Most thought that these particular reasons would turn out to be very general.

CHAPTER VII.

DARK DEATH.

A FEW days after Fabiola's return from the country, Sebastian considered it his duty to wait upon her, to communicate so much of the dialogue between Corvinus and her black slave, as he could without causing unnecessary suffering. We have already observed, that of the many noble youths whom Fabiola had met in her father's house, none had excited her admiration and respect except Sebastian. So frank, so generous, so brave, yet so unboasting; so mild, so kind in act and speech, so unselfish and so careful of others, blending so completely in one character nobleness and simplicity, high wisdom and practical sense, he seemed to her the most finished type of manly virtue, one which would not easily suffer by time, nor weary by familiarity.

When, therefore, it was announced to her that the officer Sebastian wished to speak to her alone, in one of the halls below, her heart beat at the unusual tidings, and conjured up a thousand strange fancies, about the possible topics of his interview. This agitation was not diminished, when, after apologizing for his seeming intrusion, he remarked with a smile, that, well knowing how sufficiently she was already annoyed by the many candidates for her hand, he felt regret at the idea that he was going to add another, yet undeclared,

to her list. If this ambiguous preface surprised, and perhaps
elated her, she was soon depressed again, upon being told it
was the vulgar and stupid Corvinus. For her father, even,
little as he knew how to discriminate characters out of business, had seen enough of him at his late banquet to characterize him to his daughter by those epithets.

Sebastian, fearing rather the physical, than the moral
activity of Afra's drugs, thought it right to inform her of the
compact between the two dabblers in the black art, the principal efficacy of which, however, seemed to consist in drawing
money from the purse of a reluctant dupe. He of course said
nothing of what related to the Christians in that dialogue.
He put her on her guard, and she promised to prevent the
nightly excursions of her necromancer slave. What Afra had
engaged to do, she did not for a moment believe it was ever
her intention to attempt; neither did she fear arts which she
utterly despised. Indeed Afra's last soliloquy seemed satis-
factorily to prove that she was only deceiving her victim.
But she certainly felt indignant at having been bargained
about by two such vile characters, and having been represented as a grasping avaricious woman, whose price was gold.

"I feel," she said at last to Sebastian, "how very kind it
is of you, to come thus to put me on my guard; and I admire
the delicacy with which you have unfolded so disagreeable a
matter, and the tenderness with which you have treated every
one concerned."

"I have only done in this instance," replied the soldier,
"what I should have done for any human being,—save him,
if possible, from pain or danger."

"Your friends, I hope you mean," said Fabiola, smiling;
"otherwise I fear your whole life would go in works of unrequited benevolence."

"And so let it go; it could not be better spent."

"Surely, you are not in earnest, Sebastian. If you saw

one who had ever hated you, and sought your destruction, threatened with a calamity, which would make him harmless, would you stretch out your hand to save, or succor, him?"

"Certainly I would. While God sends His sunshine and His rain equally upon His enemies, as upon His friends, shall weak man frame another rule of justice?"

At these words Fabiola wondered; they were so like those of her mysterious parchment, identical with the moral theories of her slave.

"You have been in the East, I believe, Sebastian," she asked him, rather abruptly; "was it there that you learnt these principles? For I have one near me, who is yet, by her own choice, a servant, a woman of rare moral perceptions, who has propounded to me the same ideas; and she is an Asiatic."

"It is not in any distant country that I learnt them; for here I sucked them in with my mother's milk; though, originally, they doubtless came from the East."

"They are certainly beautiful in the abstract," remarked Fabiola; "but death would overtake us before we could half carry them out, were we to make them our principles of conduct."

"And how better could death find us, though not surprise us, than in thus doing our duty, even if not to its completion?"

"For my part," resumed the lady, "I am of the old Epicurean poet's mind. This world is a banquet, from which I shall be ready to depart when I have had my fill—*ut conviva satur**—and not till then. I wish to read life's book through, and close it calmly, only when I have finished its last page."

Sebastian shook his head, smiling, and said, "The last page of this world's book comes but in the middle of the

* "As a sated guest."

volume, wherever 'death' may happen to be written. But on the next page begins the illuminated book of a new life—without a last page."

"I understand you," replied Fabiola, good-humoredly; "you are a brave soldier, and you speak as such. You must be always prepared for death from a thousand casualties; we seldom see it approach suddenly; it comes more mercifully, and stealthily, upon the weak. You no doubt are musing on a more glorious fate, on receiving in front full sheaves of arrows from the enemy, and falling covered with honor. You look to the soldier's funeral pile, with trophies erected over it. To you, after death, opens its bright page the book of glory."

"No, no, gentle lady," exclaimed Sebastian, emphatically. "I mean not so. I care not for glory, which can only be enjoyed by an anticipating fancy. I speak of vulgar death, as it may come to me in common with the poorest slave; consuming me by slow burning fever, wasting me by long lingering consumption, racking me by slowly eating ulcers; nay, if you please, by the still crueller inflictions of men's wrath. In any form let it come; it comes from a hand that I love."

"And do you really mean that death, so contemplated, would be welcomed by you?"

"As joyful as is the epicure, when the doors of the banqueting-hall are thrown wide open, and he sees beyond them the brilliant lamps, the glittering table, and its delicious viands, with its attendant ministers well girt, and crowned with roses; as blithe as is the bride when the bridegroom is announced, coming with rich gifts, to conduct her to her new home, will my exulting heart be, when death, under whatever form, throws back the gates, iron on this side, but golden on the other, which lead to a new and perennial life. And I care not how grim the messenger may be, that proclaims the approach of Him who is celestially beautiful."

"And who is He?" asked Fabiola, eagerly. "Can He not be seen, save through the fleshless ribs of death?"

"No," replied Sebastian; "for it is He who must reward us, not only for our lives, but for our deaths also. Happy they whose inmost hearts, which He has ever read, have been kept pure and innocent, as well as their deeds have been virtuous! For them is this bright vision of Him, whose true rewards only then begin."

How very like Syra's doctrines! she thought. But before she could speak again, to ask whence they came, a slave entered, stood on the threshold, and respectfully said:

"A courier, madam, is just arrived from Baiæ."*

"Pardon me, Sebastian!" she exclaimed. "Let him enter immediately."

The messenger came in, covered with dust and jaded, having left his tired horse at the gate; and offered her a sealed packet.

Her hand trembled as she took it; and while she was unloosening its bands, she hesitatingly asked:

"From my father?"

"About him, at least," was the ominous reply.

She opened the sheet, glanced over it, shrieked, and fell. Sebastian caught her before she reached the ground, laid her on a couch, and delicately left her in the hands of her handmaids, who had rushed in at the cry.

One glance had told her all. Her father was dead.

* A fashionable watering-place near Naples.

Monogram of Christ, found in the Catacombs.

CHAPTER VIII.

DARKER STILL.

WHEN Sebastian came into the court, he found a little crowd of domestics gathered round the courier, listening to the details of their master's death.

The letter of which Torquatus was the bearer to him, had produced its desired effect. He called at his villa, and spent a few days with his daughter, on his way to Asia. He was more than usually affectionate; and when they parted, both father and daughter seemed to have a melancholy foreboding that they would meet no more. He soon, however, recovered his spirits at Baiæ, where a party of good livers anxiously awaited him; and where he considered himself obliged to stay, while his galley was being fitted up and stored with the best wines and provisions which Campania afforded, for his voyage. He indulged, however, his luxurious tastes to excess; and on coming out of a bath, after a hearty supper, he was seized with a chill, and in four-and-twenty hours was a corpse. He had left his undivided wealth to his only child. In fine, the body was being embalmed when the courier started, and was to be brought by his galley to Ostia.

On hearing this sad tale, Sebastian was almost sorry that he had spoken as he had done of death, and left the house with mournful thoughts.

Fabiola's first plunge into the dark abyss of grief was deep and dismal, down into unconsciousness. Then the buoyancy of youth and mind bore her up again to the surface; and her view of life, to the horizon, was as of a boundless ocean of black seething waves, on which floated no living thing save herself. Her woe seemed utter and unmeasured; and she closed her eyes with a shudder, and suffered herself to sink again into obliviousness, till once more roused to wakefulness of mind. Again and again she was thus tossed up and down, between transient death and life, while her attendants applied remedies to what they deemed a succession of alarming fits and convulsions. At length she sat up, pale, staring, and tearless, gently pushing aside the hand that tried to administer restoratives to her. In this state she remained long; a stupor, fixed and deadly, seemed to have entranced her; the pupils were almost insensible to the light, and fears were whispered of her brain becoming oppressed. The physician, who had been called, uttered distinctly and forcibly into her ears the question: "Fabiola, do you know that your father is dead?" She started, fell back, and a bursting flood of tears relieved her heart and head. She spoke of her father, and called for him amidst her sobs, and said wild and incoherent, but affectionate things about, and to, him. Sometimes she seemed to think him still alive, then she remembered he was dead; and so she wept and moaned, till sleep took the turn of tears, in nursing her shattered mind and frame.

Euphrosyne and Syra alone watched by her. The former had, from time to time, put in the commonplaces of heathen consolation, had reminded her too, how kind a master, how honest a man, how loving a father he had been. But the Christian sat in silence, except to speak gentle and soothing words to her mistress, and served her with an active delicacy, which even then was not unnoticed. What could she do more, unless it was to pray? What hope for else, than that

a new grace was folded up, like a flower, in this tribulation;
that a bright angel was riding in the dark cloud that overshadowed her humbled lady?

As grief receded it left some room for thought. This came to Fabiola in a gloomy and searching form. "What was become of her father? Whither was he gone? Had he melted into unexistence, or had he been crushed into annihilation? Had *his* life been searched through by that unseen eye which sees the invisible? Had he stood the proof of that scrutiny which Sebastian and Syra had described? Impossible! Then what had become of him?" She shuddered as she thought, and put away the reflection from her mind.

Oh, for a ray from some unknown light, that would dart into the grave, and show her what it was! Poetry had pretended to enlighten it, and even glorify it; but had only, in truth, remained at the door, as a genius with drooping head, and torch reversed. Science had stepped in, and come out scared, with tarnished wings and lamp extinguished in the fetid air; for it had only discovered a charnel-house. And philosophy had barely ventured to wander round and round, and peep in with dread, and recoil, and then prate or babble; and, shrugging its shoulders, own that the problem was yet unsolved, the mystery still veiled. Oh, for something, or some one, better than all these, to remove the dismal perplexity!

While these thoughts dwell like gloomy night on the heart of Fabiola, her slave is enjoying the vision of light, clothed in mortal form, translucid and radiant, rising from the grave as from an alembic, in which have remained the grosser qualities of matter, without impairing the essence of its nature. Spiritualized and free, lovely and glorious, it springs from the very hot-bed of corruption. And another and another, from land and sea; from reeking cemetery, and from beneath consecrated altar; from the tangled thicket where solitary murder has been committed on the just, and from fields of ancient battle done by Israel for God; like crystal fountains springing into the air, like brilliant signal-lights, darted from earth to heaven, till a host of millions, side by side, repeoples creation with joyous and undying life. And how knows she this? Because One, greater and better than poet, sage, or sophist, had made the trial; had descended first into the dark couch of death, had blessed it, as He had done the cradle, and made infancy sacred; rendering also death a holy thing, and its place a sanctuary. He went into it in the darkest of evening, and He came forth from it in the brightest of morning; He was laid there wrapped in spices, and he rose again robed in His own fragrant incorruption. And from that day the grave had ceased to be an object of dread to the Christian soul, for it continued what he had made it,—the furrow into which the seed of immortality must needs be cast.

The time was not come for speaking of these things to Fabiola. She mourned still, as they must mourn who have no hope. Day succeeded day in gloomy meditation on the mystery of death, till other cares mercifully roused her. The corpse arrived, and such a funeral followed as Rome then seldom witnessed. Processions by torch-light, in which the waxen effigies of ancestors were borne, and a huge funeral pile, built up of aromatic wood, and scented by the richest spices of Arabia, ended in her gathering up a few handfuls of charred bones, which were deposited in an alabaster urn, and placed in a niche of the family sepulchre, with the name inscribed of their former owner.

Calpurnius spoke the funeral oration; in which, according to the fashionable ideas of the day, he contrasted the virtues of the hospitable and industrious citizen with the false morality of those men called Christians, who fasted and prayed all day, and were stealthily insinuating their dangerous principles into every noble family, and spreading disloyalty and immorality in every class. Fabius, he could have no doubt, if there was any future existence, whereon philosophers differed, was now basking on a green bank in Elysium, and quaffing nectar. "And oh!" concluded the old whining hypocrite, who would have been sorry to exchange one goblet of Falernian for an amphora* of that beverage, "oh! that the gods would hasten the day when I, his humble client, may join him in his shady repose and sober banquets!" This noble sentiment gained immense applause.

To this cure succeeded another. Fabiola had to apply her vigorous mind to examine, and close her father's complicated affairs. How often was she pained at the discovery of what to her seemed injustice, fraud, over-reaching and oppression, in the transactions of one whom the world had applauded as the most honest and liberal of public contractors!

In a few weeks more, in the dark attire of a mourner, Fabiola went forth to visit her friends. The first of these was her cousin Agnes.

* A large earthenware vessel, in which wine was kept in the cellar.

The Peacock, as an Emblem of the Resurrection, found in the Catacombs.

CHAPTER IX.

THE FALSE BROTHER.

E must take our reader back a few steps in the history of Torquatus. On the morning after his fall, he found, on awaking, Fulvius at his bed-side. It was the falconer, who, having got hold of a good hawk, was come to tame him, and train him to strike down the dove for him, in return for a well-fed slavery. With all the coolness of a practised hand, he brought back to his memory every circumstance of the preceding night's debauch, his utter ruin, and only means of escape. With unfeeling precision he strengthened every thread of the last evening's web, and added many more meshes to it.

The position of Torquatus was this: if he made one step towards Christianity, which Fulvius assured him would be fruitless, he would be at once delivered to the judge, and cruelly punished with death. If he remained faithful to his compact of treason, he should want for nothing.

"You are hot and feverish," at last concluded Fulvius; "an early walk, and fresh air, will do you good."

The poor wretch consented; and they had hardly reached the Forum, when Corvinus, as if by accident, met them. After mutual salutations, he said: "I am glad to have fallen in with you; I should like to take you, and show you my father's workshop."

"Workshop?" asked Torquatus with surprise.

"Yes, where he keeps his tools; it has just been beautifully fitted up. Here it is, and that grim old foreman, Catulus, is opening the doors."

They entered into a spacious court with a shed round it, filled with engines of torture of every form. Torquatus shrunk back.

"Come in, masters, don't be afraid," said the old executioner. "There is no fire put on yet, and nobody will hurt you, unless you happen to be a wicked Christian. It's for them we have been polishing up of late."

"Now, Catulus," said Corvinus, "tell this gentleman, who is a stranger, the use of these pretty toys you have here."

Catulus, with good heart, showed them round his museum of horrors, explaining every thing with such hearty good-will, and no end of jokes not quite fit for record, that in his enthusiasm he nearly gave Torquatus practical illustrations of what he described, having once almost caught his ear in a pair of sharp pincers, and another time brought down a mallet within an inch of his teeth.

The rack, a large gridiron, an iron chair with a furnace in it for heating it, large boilers for hot oil or scalding-water baths; ladles for melting lead, and pouring it neatly into the mouth; pincers, hooks and iron combs of varied shapes, for laying bare the ribs; scorpions, or scourges armed with iron or leaden knobs; iron collars, manacles and fetters of the most tormenting make; in fine, swords, knives, and axes in tasteful varieties,* were all commented upon with true relish, and an anticipation of much enjoy-

---

* These instruments of cruelty are mentioned in the *Acts of the Martyrs*, and in ecclesiastical historians.

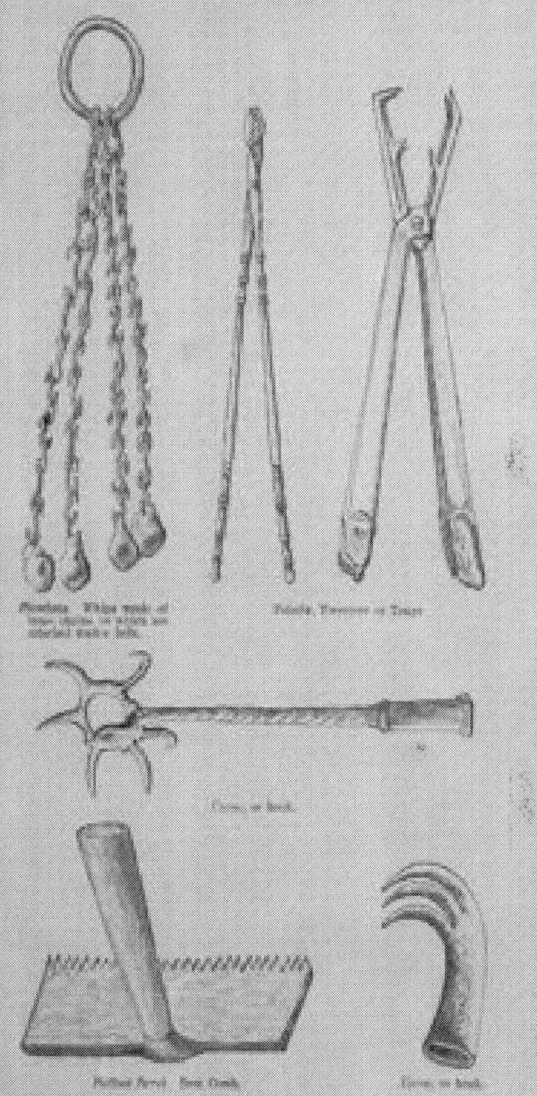

Instruments of Torture used against the Christians. From Hüber's "Circumcisiones de Fiocco."

ment, in seeing them used on those hard-headed and thick-skinned Christians.

Torquatus was thoroughly broken down. He was taken to the baths of Antoninus, where he caught the attention of old Cucumio, the head of the wardrobe department, or capsarius, and his wife Victoria, who had seen him at church. After a good refection, he was led to a gambling-hall in the Thermae, and lost, of course. Fulvius lent him money, but for every farthing, exacted a bond. By these means, he was, in a few days, completely subdued.

Their meetings were early and late; during the day he was left free, lest he should lose his value, through being suspected by Christians. Corvinus had determined to make a tremendous dash at them, so soon as the Edict should have come out. He therefore exacted from Torquatus, as his share of the compact, that the spy should study the principal cemetery where the pontiff intended to officiate. This Torquatus soon ascertained; and his visit to the cemetery of Callistus was in fulfilment of his engagement. When that struggle between grace and sin took place in his soul, which Severus noticed, it was the image of Catulus and his hundred plagues, with that of Fulvius and his hundred bonds, that turned the scale in favor of perdition. Corvinus, after receiving his report, and making from it a rough chart of the cemetery, determined to assail it, early, the very day after the publication of the Decree.

Fulvius took another course. He determined to become acquainted, by sight, with the principal clergy, and leading Christians, of Rome. Once possessed of this knowledge, he was sure no disguise would conceal them from his piercing eyes; and he would easily pick them up, one by one. He therefore insisted upon Torquatus's taking him as his companion, to the first great function that should collect many priests and deacons round the Pope. He overruled every remonstrance, dispelled every fear; and assured Torquatus, that once in, by his password, he should behave perfectly like any Christian. Torquatus soon informed him, that there would be an excellent opportunity at the coming ordination, in that very month of December.

Christ and His Apostles, from a picture in the Catacombs

CHAPTER X.

THE ORDINATION IN DECEMBER.

WHOEVER has read the history of the early Popes, will have become familiar with the fact, recorded almost invariably of each, that he held certain ordinations in the month of December, wherein he created so many priests, and deacons, and so many bishops for different places. The first two orders were conferred to supply clergy for the city; the third was evidently to furnish pastors for other dioceses. In later times, the ember-days in December, regulated by the festival of St. Lucy, were those on which the Supreme Pontiff held his consistories, in which he named his cardinal priests and deacons, and preconized, as it is called, the bishops of all parts of the world. And, though this function is not now coincident with the periods of ordination, still it is continued essentially for the same purpose.

Marcellinus, under whose pontificate our narrative is placed, is stated to have held two ordinations in this month, that is, of course, in different years. It was to one of these that we have alluded, as about to take place.

Where was this solemn function to be performed was Fulvius's first inquiry. And we cannot but think that the answer will be interesting to the Christian antiquary. Nor can our acquaintance with the ancient Roman Church be complete, without our knowing the favored spot where Pontiff after Pontiff preached, and celebrated the divine mysteries, and held his councils, or those glorious ordinations, which sent forth not only bishops but martyrs to govern other churches, and gave to a St. Laurence his diaconate, or to St. Novatus or St. Timotheus his priesthood. There, too, a Polycarp or Irenaeus visited the successor of St. Peter; and thence received their commission the apostles who converted our King Lucius to the faith.

The house which the Roman Pontiffs inhabited, and the church in which they officiated till Constantine installed them in the Lateran palace and basilica, the residence and cathedral of the illustrious line of martyr-popes for 300 years, can be no ignoble spot. And that, in tracing it out, we may not be misguided by national or personal prepossession, we will follow a learned living antiquarian, who, intent upon another research, accidentally has put together all the data requisite for our purpose.*

We have described the house of Agnes's parents as situated in the *Vicus Patricius*, or the Patrician-street. This had another name, for it was also called the street of the Cornelii, *Vicus Corneliorum*, because in it lived the illustrious family of that name. The centurion whom St. Peter converted† belonged to this family; and possibly to him the apostle owed his introduction at Rome to the head of his house, Cornelius Pudens. This senator married Claudia, a noble British lady; and it is singular how the unchaste poet Martial vies with the purest writers when he sings the wedding-song of these two virtuous spouses.

It was in their house that St. Peter lived; and his fellow-apostle St. Paul enumerates them among his familiar friends, as well: "Eubulus and Pudens, and Linus and Claudia,

---

* "Super l'antichissimo altare di legno, rinchiuso nell' altare papale," &c. "On the most ancient wooden altar, enclosed in the papal altar of the most holy Lateran basilica." By Monsig. D. Bartolini. Rome, 1852.

† Acts x.

and all the brethren salute thee."* From that house, then,
went forth the bishops, whom the Prince of the Apostles sent
in every direction, to propagate, and die for, the faith of
Christ. After the death of Pudens, the house became the
property of his children, or grandchildren,† two sons and two

S. Pudentiana, S. Pudentilla, and S. Praxedes.

daughters. The latter are better known, because they have
found a place in the general calendar of the Church, and
because they have given their names to two of the most illustrious churches of Rome, those of St. Praxedes and St. Pudentiana. It is the latter, which Alban Butler calls "the

* 2 Tim. iv. 21.
† A second or younger Pudens is spoken of.

most ancient church in the world," * that marks at once the Vicus Patricius, and the house of Pudens.

As in every other city, so in Rome, the eucharistic sacrifice was offered originally in only one place, by the bishop. And even after more churches were erected, and the faithful met in them, communion was brought to them from the one altar by the deacons, and distributed by the priests. It was Pope Evaristus, the fourth successor of St. Peter, who multiplied the churches of Rome with circumstances peculiarly interesting.

This Pope, then, did two things. First, he enacted that from thenceforward no altars should be erected except of stone, and that they should be consecrated; and secondly, "he distributed the *titles*;" that is, he divided Rome into parishes, to the churches of which he gave the name of "title." The connection of these two acts will be apparent to any one looking at Genesis xxviii.: where, after Jacob had enjoyed an angelic vision, while sleeping with a stone for his pillow, we are told that, "trembling he said, How terrible is this place! *This is no other than the house of God*, and the gate of heaven. And Jacob arising in the morning *took the stone, ... and set it up for a title, pouring oil on the top of it*." †

The church or oratory, where the sacred mysteries were celebrated, was truly, to the Christian, the house of God; and the stone altar, set up in it, was consecrated by the pouring of oil upon it, as is done to this day (for the whole law of Evaristus remains in full force); and thus became a *title*, or monument.‡

Two interesting facts are elicited from this narrative. One is, that to that time there was only one church with an altar in Rome; and no doubt has ever been raised, that this

* May the 19th.
† Verses 17, 18.
‡ It is not necessary to go into the classical uses of the word *titulus*.

was the church afterwards, and yet, known by the name of St. Pudentiana. Another is, that the one altar till then existing was not of stone. It was, in fact, the wooden altar used by St. Peter, and kept in that church, till transferred by St. Sylvester to the Lateran basilica, of which it forms the high altar.* We further conclude, that the law was not retrospective, and that the wooden altar of the Popes was preserved at that church, where it had been first erected, though from time to time it might be carried, and used elsewhere.

The church in the Vicus Patricius, therefore, which existed previous to the creation of *titles*, was not itself a title. It continued to be the episcopal, or rather the pontifical church of Rome. The pontificate of St. Pius I., from 142 to 157, forms an interesting period in its history, for two reasons.

First, that Pope, without altering the character of the church itself, added to it an oratory which he made a *title*;† and having collated to it his brother Pastor, it was called the *titulus Pastoris*, the designation, for a long time, of the cardinalate attached to the church. This shows that the church itself was more than a title.

Secondly, in this pontificate came to Rome, for the second time, and suffered martyrdom, the holy and learned apologist St. Justin. By comparing his writings with his Acts,‡ we come to some interesting conclusions respecting Christian worship in times of persecution.

"In what place do the Christians meet?" he is asked by the judge.

---

* Only the Pope can say Mass on it, or a cardinal, by authority of a special bull. This high altar has been lately magnificently decorated. A plank of the wooden altar has always been preserved in St. Peter's altar, at St. Pudentiana's. It has been lately compared with the wood of the Lateran altar, and found to be identical.

† Its site is now occupied by the Caetani chapel.

‡ Prefixed to the Maurist edition of his works, or in Ruinart, i.

"Do you think," he replies, "that we all meet in one place? It is not so." But when interrogated where he lived, and where he held meetings with his disciples, he answered, "I have lived till now near the house of a certain Martin, at the bath known as the Timotine. I have come to Rome for the second time, nor do I know any other place but the one I have mentioned." The Timotine or Timothean baths were part of the house of the Pudens family, and are those at which we have said that Fulvius and Corvinus met early one morning. Novatus and Timotheus were the brothers of the holy virgins Praxedes and Pudentiana; and hence the baths were called the Novatian and the Timotine, as they passed from one brother to another.

St. Justin, therefore, lived on this spot, and, *as he knew no other in Rome*, attended divine worship there. The very claims of hospitality would suggest it. Now in his apology, describing the Christian liturgy, of course such as he saw it, he speaks of the officiating priest in terms that sufficiently describe the bishop, or supreme pastor of the place; not only by giving him a title applied to bishops in antiquity,[*] but by describing him as the person who has the care of orphans and widows, and succors the sick, the indigent, prisoners, strangers who come as guests, who, "in one word, undertakes to provide for all in want." This could be no other than the bishop or pope himself.

We must further observe, that St. Pius is recorded to have erected a fixed baptismal font in this church, another prerogative of the cathedral, transferred with the papal altar to the Lateran. It is related that the holy Pope

---

[*] Ο προεστως, *præpositus*, see Heb. xiii. 17. Ο των Ρωμαιων προεστως Βικτωρ, "Victor bishop of the Romans." Euseb. H. E. l. v. 24. The Greek word used is the same as in St. Justin.

Stephen (A.D. 257) baptized the tribune Nemesius and his family, with many others, in the *title* of Pastor.* And here it was that the blessed deacon Laurentius distributed the rich vessels of the Church to the poor.

In time this name has given way to another. But the place is the same; and no doubt can exist, that the church of St. Pudentiana was, for the first three centuries, the humble cathedral of Rome.

It was to this spot, therefore, that Torquatus unwillingly consented to lead Fulvius, that he might witness the December ordination.

We find either in sepulchral inscriptions, in martyrologies, or in ecclesiastical history, abundant traces of all the orders, as still conferred in the Catholic Church. Inscriptions perhaps more commonly record those of Lector or reader, and of Exorcist. We will give one interesting example of each. Of a Lector:

CINNAMIVS OPAS LECTOR TITVLI FASCIOLE AMICVS PAVPERVM
QVI VIXIT ANN. XLVI. MENS. VII. D. VIII. DEPOSIT IN PACE
X KAL. MART.†

Of an Exorcist:

MACEDONIVS
EXORCISTA DE KATOLICA.‡

---

* The learned Bianchini plausibly conjectures that the station on Easter Sunday is not at the Lateran (the cathedral), nor at St. Peter's, where the Pope officiates, at one of which it would naturally be expected to be, but at the Liberian basilica, because it used to be held for the administration of baptism at St. Pudentiana's, which is only a stone's throw from it.

† "Cinnamius Opas Lector, of the *title* of Fasciola" (now SS. Nereus and Achilleus), "the friend of the poor, who lived forty-six years, seven months, and eight days. Interred in peace the tenth day before the calends of March." From St. Paul's.

‡ "Macedonius, an exorcist of the Catholic Church." From the cemetery of SS. Thraso and Saturninus, on the Salarian way.

A difference was, however, that one order was not necessarily a passage, or step, to another; but persons remained, often for life, in one of these lesser orders. There was not, therefore, that frequent administration of these, nor probably was it publicly performed with the higher orders.

Torquatus, having the necessary pass-word, entered, accompanied by Fulvius, who soon showed himself expert in acting as others did around him. The assembly was not large. It was held in a hall of the house, converted into a church or oratory, which was mainly occupied by the clergy, and the candidates for orders. Among the latter were Marcus and Marcellianus, the twin brothers, fellow-converts of Torquatus, who received the deaconship, and their father Tranquillinus, who was ordained priest. Of these Fulvius impressed well in his mind the features and figure; and still more did he take note of the clergy, the most eminent of Rome, there assembled. But on one, more than the rest, he fixed his piercing eye, studying his every gesture, look, voice, and lineament.

This was the Pontiff who performed the august rite. Marcellinus had already governed the Church six years, and was of a venerable old age. His countenance, benign and mild, scarcely seemed to betoken the possession of that nerve which martyrdom required, and which he exhibited in his death for Christ. In those days every outward characteristic which could have betrayed the chief shepherd to the wolves was carefully avoided. The ordinary simple garb of respectable men was worn. But there is no doubt that when officiating at the altar, a distinctive robe, the forerunner of the ample chasuble, of spotless white, was cast over the ordinary garment. To this the bishop added a crown, or *infula*, the origin of the later mitre; while in his hand he held the crosier, emblem of his pastoral office and authority.

On him who now stood facing the assembly, before the sacred altar of Peter, which was between him and the people,* the Eastern spy steadied his keenest glance. He scanned him minutely, measured, with his eye, his height, defined the color of his hair and complexion, observed every turn of his head, his walk, his action, his tones, almost his breathing, till he said to himself: "If he stirs abroad, disguised as he may choose, that man is my prize. And I know his worth."

* In the great and old basilicas of Rome the celebrant faces the faithful.

Our Saviour represented as the Good Shepherd, with a Milk-can at his side, as found in the Catacombs.

CHAPTER XI.

THE VIRGINS.

> PRIE IVN PAVSA
> SET PRAETIOSA
> ANNORVM PVLLA
> VIRGO XII TANTVM
> ANCILLA DEI ET XPI
> FL. VINCENTIO ET
> FRAVITO . VC · CONSS.*

IF the learned Thomassinus had known this lately-discovered inscription, when he proved with such abundance of learning, that virginity could be professed in the early Church, at the age of twelve, he would certainly have quoted it.† For can we doubt that "the girl who was a virgin of only twelve years old, a handmaid of God and Christ," was such by consecration to God? Otherwise, the more tender her age, the less wonderful her state of maidenhood.

But although this, the nubile age, according to Roman

---

* "The day before the first of June ceased to live Pretiosa, a girl (*puella*), a virgin of only twelve years of age, the handmaid of God and of Christ. In the consulship of Flavius Vincentius, and Fravitus, a consular man." Found in the cemetery of Callistus.

† *Vetus et Nova Ecclesiæ Disciplina ; circa Beneficia.* Par. I. lib. iii. (Luc. 1737.)

law, was the one at which such dedication to God was permitted by the Church, she reserved to a maturer period that more solemn consecration, when the veil of virginity was given by the bishop; generally on Easter Sunday. That first act probably consisted of nothing more than receiving from the hands of parents a plain dark dress. But when any danger threatened, the Church permitted the anticipation, by many years, of that period, and fortified the spouses of Christ in their holy purpose, by her more solemn blessing.*

A persecution of the most savage character was on the point of breaking out, which would not spare the most tender of the flock; and it was no wonder that they, who in their hearts had betrothed themselves to the Lamb, as His chaste spouses forever, should desire to come to His nuptials before death. They longed naturally to bear the full-grown lily, entwined round the palm, should this be their portion.

Agnes had from her infancy chosen for herself this holiest state. The superhuman wisdom which had ever exhibited itself in her words and actions, blending so gracefully with the simplicity of an innocent and guileless childhood, rendered her ripe, beyond her years, for any measure of indulgence which could be granted, to hearts that panted for their chaste bridal-hour. She eagerly seized on the claim that coming danger gave her, to a more than usual relaxation of that law which prescribed a delay of more than ten years in the fulfilling of her desire. Another postulant joined her in this petition.

We may easily imagine that a holy friendship had been growing between her and Syra, from the first interview which we have described between them. This feeling had been increased by all that Agnes had heard Fabiola say, in praise of her favorite servant. From this, and from the slave's more modest reports, she was satisfied that the work to which she

* Thomas, p. 792.

had devoted herself, of her mistress's conversion, must be entirely left in her hands. It was evidently prospering, owing to the prudence and grace with which it was conducted. In her frequent visits to Fabiola, she contented herself with admiring and approving what her cousin related of Syra's conversations; but she carefully avoided every expression that could raise suspicion of any collusion between them.

Syra as a dependant, and Agnes as a relation, had put on mourning upon Fabius's death; and hence no change of habit would raise suspicion in his daughter's mind, of their having taken some secret, or some joint step. Thus far they could safely ask to be admitted at once to receive the solemn consecration to perpetual virginity. Their petition was granted; but for obvious reasons was kept carefully concealed. It was only a day or two before the happy one of their spiritual nuptials, that Syra told it, as a great secret, to her blind friend.

"And so," said the latter, pretending to be displeased, "you want to keep all the good things to yourself. Do you call that charitable, now?"

"My dear child," said Syra, soothingly, "don't be offended. It was necessary to keep it quite a secret."

"And therefore, I suppose, poor I must not even be present?"

"Oh, yes, Cæcilia, to be sure you may; and see all that you can," replied Syra, laughing.

"Never mind about the seeing. But tell me, how will you be dressed? What have you to get ready?"

Syra gave her an exact description of the habit and veil, their color and form.

"How very interesting!" she said. "And what have you to do?"

The other, amused at her unwonted curiosity, described minutely the short ceremonial.

"Well now, one question more," resumed the blind girl.

"When and where is all this to be? You said I might come, so I must know the time and place."

Syra told her it would be at the *title* of Pastor, at daybreak, on the third day from that. "But what has made you so inquisitive, dearest? I never saw you so before. I am afraid you are becoming quite worldly."

"Never you mind," replied Cæcilia, "if people choose to have secrets from me, I do not see why I should not have some of my own."

Syra laughed at her affected pettishness, for she knew well the humble simplicity of the poor child's heart. They embraced affectionately and parted. Cæcilia went straight to the kind Lucina, for she was a favorite in every house. No sooner was she admitted to that pious matron's presence, than she flew to her, threw herself upon her bosom, and burst into tears. Lucina soothed and caressed her, and soon composed her. In a few minutes she was again bright and joyous, and evidently deep in conspiracy, with the cheerful lady, about something which delighted her. When she left she was all buoyant and blithe, and went to the house of Agnes, in the hospital of which the good priest Dyonisius lived. She found him at home; and casting herself on her knees before him, talked so fervently to him that he was moved to tears, and spoke kindly and consolingly to her. The *Te Deum* had not yet been written; but something very like it rang in the blind girl's heart, as she went to her humble home.

The happy morning at length arrived, and before daybreak the more solemn mysteries had been celebrated, and the body of the faithful had dispersed. Only those remained who had to take part in the more private function, or who were specially asked to witness it. These were Lucina and her son, the aged parents of Agnes, and of course Sebastian. But Syra looked in vain for her blind friend; she had evidently retired with the crowd; and the gentle slave feared she might have hurt her feelings by her reserve, before their last interview.

The hall was still shrouded in the dusk of a winter's twilight, although the glowing east, without, foretold a bright December day. On the altar burned perfumed tapers of large dimensions, and round it were gold and silver lamps

Chair of St. Peter

of great value, throwing an atmosphere of mild radiance upon the sanctuary. In front of the altar was placed the chair no less venerable than itself, now enshrined in the Vatican, the chair of Peter. On this was seated the venerable Pontiff, with staff in hand, and crown on head, and round him stood his ministers, scarcely less worshipful than himself.

From the gloom of the chapel, there came forth first the sound of sweet voices, like those of angels, chanting in soft cadence, a hymn, which anticipated the sentiments soon after embodied in the

"Jesu corona virginum."*

Then there emerged into the light of the sanctuary the procession of already consecrated virgins, led by the priests and deacons who had charge of them. And in the midst of them appeared two, whose dazzling white garments shone the brighter amidst their dark habits. These were the two new postulants, who, as the rest defiled and formed a line on either side, were conducted, each by two professed, to the foot of the altar, where they knelt at the Pontiff's feet. Their bridesmaids, or sponsors, stood near to assist in the function.

Each as she came was asked solemnly what she desired, and expressed her wish to receive the veil, and practise its duties, under the care of those chosen guides. For, although consecrated virgins had begun to live in community before this period, yet many continued to reside at home; and persecution interfered with enclosure. Still there was a place in church, boarded off for the consecrated virgins; and they often met apart, for particular instruction and devotions.

The bishop then addressed the young aspirants, in glowing and affectionate words. He told them how high a call it was to lead on earth the lives of angels, who neither marry nor give in marriage, to tread the same chaste path to heaven which the Incarnate Word chose for His own Mother; and arrived there, to be received into the pure ranks of that picked host, that follows the Lamb whithersoever He goeth. He expatiated on the doctrine of St. Paul, writing to the Corinthians on the superiority of virginity to every other state; and he feelingly described the happiness of having no love on earth but one, which instead of fading, opens out into immortality, in heaven. For bliss, he observed, is but the expanded flower which Divine love bears on earth.

* "Jesu the virgin's crown," the hymn for virgins.

After this brief discourse, and an examination of the candidates for this great honor, the holy Pontiff proceeded to bless the different portions of their religious habits, by prayers probably nearly identical with those now in use; and these were put on them by their respective attendants. The new religious laid their heads upon the altar, in token of their oblation of self. But in the West, the hair was not cut, as it was in the East, but was always left long. A wreath of flowers was then placed upon the head of each; and though it was winter, the well-guarded terrace of Fabiola had been made to furnish bright and fragrant blossoms.

All seemed ended; and Agnes, kneeling at the foot of the altar, was motionless in one of her radiant raptures, gazing fixedly upwards; while Syra, near her, was bowed down, sunk into the depths of her gentle humility, wondering how she should have been found worthy of so much favor. So absorbed were both in their thanksgiving, that they perceived not a slight commotion through the assembly, as if something unexpected was occurring.

They were aroused by the bishop repeating the question: "My daughter, what dost thou seek?" when, before they could look round, each felt a hand seized, and heard the answer returned in a voice dear to both: "Holy father, to receive the veil of consecration to Jesus Christ, my only love on earth, under the care of these two holy virgins, already His happy spouses."

They were overwhelmed with joy and tenderness; for it was the poor blind Cæcilia. When she heard of the happiness that awaited Syra, she had flown, as we have seen, to the kind Lucina, who soon consoled her, by suggesting to her the possibility of obtaining a similar grace. She promised to furnish all that was necessary; only Cæcilia insisted that her dress should be coarse, as became a poor beggar-girl. The priest Dionysius presented to the Pontiff, and obtained the grant of her prayer; and as she wished to have her two friends for sponsors, it was arranged that he should lead her up to the altar after their consecration. Cæcilia, however, kept her secret.

The blessings were spoken, and the habit and veil put on; when they asked her if she had brought no wreath or flowers. Timidly she drew from under her garment the crown she had provided, a bare, thorny branch, twisted into a circle, and presented it, saying:

"I have no flowers to offer to my Bridegroom, neither did He wear flowers for me. I am but a poor girl, and do you think my Lord will be offended, if I ask Him to crown me as He was pleased to be crowned Himself? And then, flowers represent virtues in those that wear them; but my barren heart has produced nothing better than these."

She saw not, with her blind eyes, how her two companions snatched the wreaths from their heads, to put on hers; but a sign from the Pontiff checked them; and amidst moistened eyes, she was led forth, all joyous, in her thorny crown; emblem of what the Church has always taught, that the very queenship of virtue is innocence crowned by penance.

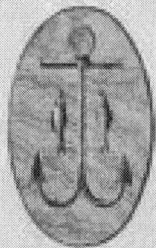

The Anchor and Fishes, an emblem of Christianity, found in the Catacombs.

CHAPTER XII.

THE NOMENTAN VILLA.

THE Nomentan road goes from Rome eastward, and between it and the Salarian is a deep ravine, beyond which on the side of the Nomentan way lies a gracefully undulating ground. Amidst this is situated a picturesque round temple, and near it a truly beautiful basilica, dedicated to St. Agnes. Here was the villa belonging to her, situated about a mile and a half from the city; and thither it had been arranged that the two, now the three, newly consecrated should repair, to spend the day in retirement and tranquil joy. Few more such days, perhaps, would ever be granted them.

We need not describe this rural residence, except to say that everything in it breathed contentment and happiness. It was one of those genial days which a Roman winter supplies. The rugged Apennines were slightly powdered with snow; the ground was barely crisp, the atmosphere transparent, the sunshine glowing, and the heavens cloudless. A few greyish curls of melting smoke from the cottages, and the leafless vines, alone told that it was December. Everything living seemed to know and love the gentle mistress of the place. The doves came and perched upon her shoulder or her hand; the lambs in the paddock frisked, and ran to her the moment she approached, and took the green fragrant herbs which she brought them, with evident pleasure; but none owned her kindly sway so much as old Molossus, the enormous watchdog. Chained beside the gate, so fierce was he, that none but a few favorite domestics durst go near him. But no sooner did Agnes appear than he crouched down, and wagged his bushy tail, and whined, till he was let loose; for now a child might approach him. He never left his mistress's side; he followed her like a lamb; and if she sat down he would lie at her feet, looking into her face, delighted to receive, on his huge head, the caresses of her slender hand.

It was indeed a peaceful day; sometimes calm and quiet, soft and tender, as the three spoke together of the morning's happiness, and of the happier morning of which it was a pledge, above the liquid amber of their present skies; sometimes cheerful and even merry, as the two took Cæcilia to task for the trick she had played them. And she laughed cheerily, as she always did, and told them she had a better trick in store for them yet; which was, that she would cut them out when that next morning came; for she intended to be the first at it, and not the last.

Fabiola had, in the meantime, come to the villa to pay her first visit to Agnes after her calamity, and to thank her for her sympathy. She walked forward, but stopped suddenly on coming near the spot where this happy group were assembled. For when she beheld the two who could see the outward brightness of heaven, hanging over her who seemed to hold all its splendor within her soul, she saw at once, in the scene, the verification of her dream. Yet unwilling to intrude herself unexpectedly upon them, and anxious to find Agnes alone, and not with her own slave and a poor blind girl, she turned away before she was noticed, and walked towards a distant part of the grounds. Still she could not help asking herself, why she could not be cheerful and happy as they? Why was there a gulf between them?

But the day was not destined to finish without its clouds; it would have been too blissful for earth. Besides Fabiola, another person had started from Rome, to pay a less welcome visit to Agnes. This was Fulvius, who had never forgotten the assurances of Fabius, that his fascinating address and brilliant ornaments had turned the weak head of Agnes. He had waited till the first days of mourning were over, and he respected the house in which he had once received such a rude reception, or rather suffered such a summary ejectment. Having ascertained that, for the first time, she had gone without her parents, or any male attendants, to her suburban villa, he considered it a good opportunity for pressing his suit. He rode out of the Nomentan gate, and was soon at Agnes's. He dismounted; said he wished to see her on important business, and, after some importunity, was admitted by the porter. He was directed along a walk, at the end of which she would be found. The sun was declining, and her companions had strolled to a distance, and she was sitting alone in a bright sunny spot, with old Molossus crouching at her feet. The slightest approach to a growl from him, rare when he was with her, made her look up from her work of tying together such winter flowers as the others brought her, while she suppressed, by raising a finger, this expression of instinctive dislike.

Fulvius came near with a respectful, but freer air than usual, as one already assured of his request.

"I have come, Lady Agnes," he said, "to renew to you the expression of my sincere regard; and I could not have chosen a better day, for brighter or fairer scarcely the summer sun could have bestowed."

"Fair, indeed, and bright it has been to me," replied Agnes, borne back in mind to the morning's scene; "and no sun in my life has ever given me fairer,—it can only give me one more fair."

Fulvius was flattered, as if the compliment was to his presence, and answered, "The day, no doubt you mean, of your espousals with one who may have won your heart."

"That is indeed done," she replied, as if unconsciously; "and this is his own precious day."

"And was that wreathed veil upon your head, placed there in anticipation of this happy hour?"

"Yes; it is the sign my beloved has placed upon my countenance, that I recognize no lover but himself."*

"And who is this happy being? I was not without hopes, nor will I renounce them yet, that I have a place in your thoughts, perhaps in your affections."

Agnes seemed scarcely to heed his words. There was no appearance of shyness or timidity in her looks or manner, no embarrassment even:

> "Spotless without, and innocent within,
> She feared no danger, for she knew no sin."

Her childlike countenance remained bright, open, and guileless; her eyes, mildly beaming, looked straight upon Fulvius's face with an earnest simplicity, that made him almost quail before her. She stood up now, with graceful dignity, as she replied:

"Milk and honey exhaled from his lips, as the blood from his stricken cheek impressed itself on mine."†

She is crazed, Fulvius was just beginning to think; when the inspired look of her countenance, and the clear brightness of her eye, as she gazed forwards towards some object seen by herself alone, overawed and subdued him. She recovered in an instant; and again he took heart. He resolved at once to pursue his demand.

---

* "Posuit signum in faciem meam, ut nullum præter eum amatorem admittam." *Office of St. Agnes.*

† "Mel et lac ex ejus ore suscepi, et sanguis ejus ornavit genas meas." *Ibid.*

"Madam," he said, "you are trifling with one who sincerely admires and loves you. I know from the best authority,—yes, the *best* authority,—that of a mutual friend departed, that you have been pleased to think favorably of me, and to express yourself not opposed to my urging my claims to your hand. I now, therefore, seriously and earnestly solicit it. I may seem abrupt and informal, but I am sincere and warm."

"Begone from me, fool of corruption!" she said with calm majesty; "for already a lover has secured my heart, for whom alone I keep my troth, to whom I intrust myself with undivided devotion; one whose love is chaste, whose caress is pure, whose brides never put off their virginal wreaths."*

Fulvius, who had dropped on his knee as he concluded his last sentence, and had thus drawn forth that severe rebuke, rose, filled with spite and fury, at having been so completely deluded. "Is it not enough to be rejected," he said, "after having been encouraged, but must insult be heaped on me too? and must I be told to my face that another has been before me to-day?—Sebastian, I suppose, again——"

"Who are you?" exclaimed an indignant voice behind him, "that dare to utter with disdain, the name of one whose honor is untarnished, and whose virtue is as unchallenged as his courage?"

He turned round, and stood confronted with Fabiola, who, having walked for some time about the garden, thought she would now probably find her cousin disengaged, and by herself. She had come upon him suddenly, and had caught his last words.

* *"Discede a me pabulum mortis, quia jam ab alio amatore præventa sum." "Ipsi soli servo fidem, ipsi me tota devotione committo." "Quem cum amavero casta sum, cum tetigero munda sum, cum accepero virgo sum." Ibid.*

Fulvius was abashed, and remained silent.

Fabiola, with a noble indignation, continued. "And who, too, are you, who, not content with having once thrust yourself into my kinswoman's house, to insult her,

"Haughty Roman dame! thou shalt bitterly rue this day and hour."

presume now to intrude upon the privacy of her rural retreat?"

"And who are you," retorted Fulvius, "who take upon yourself to be imperious mistress in another's house?"

"One," replied the lady, "who, by allowing my cousin to meet you first at her table, and there discovering your designs upon an innocent child, feels herself bound in honor and duty to thwart them, and to shield her from them."

She took Agnes by the hand, and was leading her away; and Molossus required what he never remembered to have received before, but what he took delightedly, a gentle little tap, to keep him from more than growling; when Fulvius, gnashing his teeth, muttered audibly:

"Haughty Roman dame! thou shalt bitterly rue this day and hour. Thou shalt know and feel how Asia can revenge."

A Lamb between Wolves, emblematic of the Church, from a picture in the Cemetery of St. Prætextus.

CHAPTER XIII.

THE EDICT.

THE day being at length arrived for its publication in Rome, Corvinus fully felt the importance of the commission intrusted to him, of affixing in its proper place in the Forum, the edict of extermination against the Christians, or rather the sentence of extirpation of their very name.
News had been received from Nicodemia, that a brave Christian soldier, named George, had torn down a similar imperial decree, and had manfully suffered death for his boldness. Corvinus was determined that nothing of the sort should happen in Rome; for he feared too seriously the consequences of such an occurrence to himself; he therefore took every precaution in his power. The edict had been written in large characters, upon sheets of parchment joined together; and these were nailed to a board, firmly supported by a pillar, against which it was hung, not far from the Puteal Libonis, the magistrate's chair in the Forum. This, however, was not done till the Forum was deserted, and night had well set in. It was thus intended that the edict should meet the eyes of the citizens early in the morning, and strike their minds with more tremendous effect.

To prevent the possibility of any nocturnal attempt to destroy the precious document, Corvinus, with much the same cunning precaution as was taken by the Jewish priests to prevent the Resurrection, obtained for a night-guard to the

Forum, a company of the Pannonian cohort, a body composed of soldiers belonging to the fiercest races of the North, Dacians, Pannonians, Sarmatians, and Germans, whose uncouth features, savage aspect, matted sandy hair, and bushy red moustaches, made them appear absolutely ferocious to Roman eyes. These men could scarcely speak Latin, but were ruled by officers of their own countries, and formed, in the decline of the empire, the most faithful body-guard of the reigning tyrants, often their fellow-countrymen; for there was no excess too monstrous for them to commit, if duly commanded to execute it.

A number of these savages, ever rough and ready, were distributed so as to guard every avenue of the Forum, with strict orders to pierce through, or hew down, any one who should attempt to pass without the watchword, or *symbolum*. This was every night distributed by the general in command through his tribunes and centurions, to all the troops. But to prevent all possibility of any Christian making use of it that night, if he should chance to discover it, the cunning Corvinus had one chosen which he felt sure no Christian would use. It was NUMEN IMPERATORUM, the "Divinity of the Emperors."

The last thing which he did was to make his rounds, giving to each sentinel the strictest injunctions; and most minutely to the one whom he had placed close to the edict. This man had been chosen for his post on account of his rude strength and huge bulk, and the peculiar ferocity of his looks and character. Corvinus gave him the most rigid instructions, how he was to spare nobody, but to prevent any one's interference with the sacred edict. He repeated to him again and again the watchword; and left him, already half-stupid with *sabaia* or beer,* in the merest animal consciousness, that

* "Est autem sabaia ex hordeo vel frumento in liquorem conversis propertius in Illyrico potus." "Sabaia is the drink of the poor in Illyria, made of barley

it was his business, not an unpleasant one, to spear, or sabre, some one or other before morning. The night was raw and gusty, with occasional sharp and slanting showers; and the Dacian wrapped himself in his cloak, and walked up and down, occasionally taking a long pull at a flask concealed about him, containing a liquor said to be distilled from the wild cherries of the Thuringian forests; and in the intervals muddily meditating, not on the wood or river, by which his young barbarians were at play, but how soon it would be time to cut the present emperor's throat, and sack the city.

While all this was going on, old Diogenes and his hearty sons were in their poor house in the Suburra, not far off, making preparations for their frugal meal. They were interrupted by a gentle tap at the door, followed by the lifting of the latch, and the entrance of two young men, whom Diogenes at once recognized and welcomed.

"Come in, my noble young masters; how good of you thus to honor my poor dwelling! I hardly dare offer you our plain fare; but if you will partake of it, you will indeed give us a Christian love-feast."

"Thank you most kindly, father Diogenes," answered the elder of the two, Quadratus, Sebastian's sinewy centurion: "Pancratius and I have come expressly to sup with you. But not as yet; we have some business in this part of the town, and after it we shall be glad to eat something. In the meantime one of your youths can go out and cater for us. Come, we must have something good; and I want you to cheer yourself with a moderate cup of generous wine."

Saying this he gave his purse to one of the sons, with instructions to bring home some better provisions than he knew the simple family usually enjoyed. They sat down;

or wheat, transformed into a liquid." *Ammian. Marcellinus*, lib. xxvi. 8, p. 422, ed. Lips.

and Pancratius, by way of saying something, addressed the old man. "Good Diogenes, I have heard Sebastian say that you remember seeing the glorious Deacon Laurentius die for Christ. Tell me something about him."

"With pleasure," answered the old man. "It is now nearly forty-five years since it happened,* and as I was older then than you are now, you may suppose I remember all quite distinctly. He was indeed a beautiful youth to look at: so mild and sweet, so fair and graceful; and his speech was so gentle, so soft, especially when speaking to the poor. How they all loved him! I followed him everywhere; I stood by as the venerable Pontiff Sixtus was going to death, and Laurentius met him, and so tenderly reproached him, just as a son might a father, for not allowing him to be his companion in the sacrifice of himself, as he had ministered to him in the sacrifice of our Lord's body and blood."

"Those were splendid times, Diogenes, were they not?" interrupted the youth; "how degenerate we are now! What a different race! Are we not, Quadratus?"

The rough soldier smiled at the generous sincerity of his complaint, and bid Diogenes go on.

"I saw him too as he distributed the rich plate of the Church to the poor. We have never had any thing so splendid since. There were golden lamps and candlesticks, censors, chalices, and patens,† besides an immense quantity of silver melted down, and distributed to the blind, the lame, and the indigent."

"But tell me," asked Pancratius, "how did he endure his last dreadful torment? It must have been frightful."

"I saw it all," answered the old fossor, "and it would have been intolerably frightful in another. He had been first placed on the rack, and variously tormented, and he had not

* A. D. 258.
† Prudentius, in his hymn on St. Laurence.

uttered a groan; when the judge ordered that horrid bed, or gridiron, to be prepared and heated. To look at his tender flesh blistering and breaking over the fire, and deeply seared with red burning gashes that cut to the bone where the iron bars went across; to see the steam, thick as from a cauldron, rise from his body, and hear the fire hiss beneath him, as he melted away into it; and every now and then to observe the tremulous quivering that crept over the surface of his skin, the living motion which the agony gave to each separate muscle, and the sharp spasmodic twitches which convulsed, and gradually contracted, his limbs; all this, I own, was the most harrowing spectacle I have ever beheld in all my life. But to look into his countenance was to forget all this. His head was raised up from the burning body, and stretched out, as if fixed on the contemplation of some most celestial vision, like that of his fellow-deacon Stephen. His face glowed indeed with the heat below, and the perspiration flowed down it; but the light from the fire shining upwards, and passing through his golden locks, created a glory round his beautiful head and countenance, which made him look as if already in heaven. And every feature, serene and sweet as ever, was so impressed with an eager, longing look, accompanying the upward glancing of his eye, that you would willingly have changed places with him."

"That I would," again broke in Pancratius, "and, as soon as God pleases! I dare not think that I could stand what he did; for he was indeed a noble and heroic Levite, while I am only a weak imperfect boy. But do you not think, dear Quadratus, that strength is given in that hour, proportionate to our trials, whatever they may be? You, I know, would stand any thing; for you are a fine stout soldier, accustomed to toil and wounds. But as for me, I have only a willing heart to give. Is that enough, think you?"

"Quite, quite, my dear boy," exclaimed the centurion, full

of emotion, and looking tenderly on the youth, who with glistening eyes, having risen from his seat, had placed his hands upon the officer's shoulders. "God will give you strength, as He has already given you courage. But we must not forget our night's work. Wrap yourself well up in your cloak, and bring your toga quite over your head; so! It is a wet and bitter night. Now, good Diogenes, put more wood on the fire, and let us find supper ready on our return. We shall not be long absent; and just leave the door ajar."

"Go, go, my sons," said the old man, "and God speed you! whatever you are about, I am sure it is something praiseworthy."

Quadratus sturdily drew his chlamys, or military cloak, around him, and the two youths plunged into the dark lanes of the Suburra, and took the direction of the Forum. While they were absent, the door was opened, with the well-known salutation of "thanks to God;" and Sebastian entered, and inquired anxiously if Diogenes had seen any thing of the two young men; for he had got a hint of what they were going to do. He was told they were expected in a few moments.

A quarter of an hour had scarcely elapsed, when hasty steps were heard approaching; the door was pushed open, and was as quickly shut, and then fast barred, behind Quadratus and Pancratius.

"Here it is," said the latter, producing, with a hearty laugh, a bundle of crumpled parchment.

"What?" asked all eagerly.

"Why, the grand decree, of course," answered Pancratius, with boyish glee; "look here, 'DOMINI NOSTRI DIOCLETIANUS ET MAXIMIANUS, INVICTI, SENIORES AUGUSTI, PATRES IMPERATORUM ET CÆSARUM,'* and so forth. Here it goes!" And he thrust it into the blazing fire, while the stalwart sons of Diogenes threw

---

* "Our lords Diocletian and Maximian, the unconquered, elder Augusti, fathers of the Emperors and Cæsars."

"Here it goes!" And he thrust it into the blazing fire.

a faggot over it to keep it down, and drown its crackling. There it frizzled, and writhed, and cracked, and shrunk, first one letter or word coming up, then another; first an emperor's praise, and then an anti-Christian blasphemy; till all had subsided into a black ashy mass.

And what else, or more, would those be in a few years who had issued that proud document, when their corpses should have been burnt on a pile of cedar-wood and spices, and their handful of ashes be scraped together, hardly enough to fill a gilded urn? And what also, in very few years more, would that heathenism be, which it was issued to keep alive, but a dead letter at most, and as worthless a heap of extinguished embers as lay on that hearth? And the very empire which these "unconquered" Augusti were bolstering up by cruelty and injustice, how in a few centuries would it resemble that annihilated decree? the monuments of its grandeur lying in ashes, or in ruins, and proclaiming that there is no true Lord but one stronger than Cæsars, the Lord of lords; and that neither counsel nor strength of man shall prevail against Him.

Something like this did Sebastian think, perhaps, as he gazed abstractedly on the expiring embers of the pompous and cruel edict which they had torn down, not for a wanton frolic, but because it contained blasphemies against God and His holiest truths. They knew that if they should be discovered, tenfold tortures would be their lot; but Christians in those days, when they contemplated and prepared for martyrdom, made no calculation on that head. Death for Christ, whether quick and easy, or lingering and painful, was the end for which they looked; and, like brave soldiers going to battle, they did not speculate where a shaft or a sword might strike them, whether a death-blow would at once stun them out of existence, or they should have to writhe for hours upon the ground, mutilated or pierced, to die by inches among the heaps of unheeded slain.

Sebastian soon recovered, and had hardly the heart to reprove the perpetrators of this deed. In truth, it had its ridiculous side, and he was inclined to laugh at the morrow's dismay. This view he gladly took, for he saw Pancratius watched his looks with some trepidation, and his centurion looked a little disconcerted. So, after a hearty laugh, they sat down cheerfully to their meal; for it was not midnight, and the hour for commencing the fast, preparatory to receiving the holy Eucharist, was not arrived. Quadratus's object, besides kindness, in this arrangement, was partly, that if surprised, a reason for their being there might be apparent, partly to keep up the spirits of his younger companion and of Diogenes's household, if alarmed at the bold deed just performed. But there was no appearance of any such feeling. The conversation soon turned upon recollections of Diogenes's youth, and the good old fervent times, as Pancratius would persist in calling them. Sebastian saw his friend home, and then took a round, to avoid the Forum in seeking his own abode. If any one had seen Pancratius that night, when alone in his chamber preparing to retire to rest, he would have seen him every now and then almost laughing at some strange but pleasant adventure.

A Monogram of Christ, found in the Catacombs.

CHAPTER XIV.

THE DISCOVERY.

AT the first dawn of morning, Corvinus was up; and, notwithstanding the gloominess of the day, proceeded straight to the Forum. He found his outposts quite undisturbed, and hastened to the principal object of his care. It would be useless to attempt describing his astonishment, his rage, his fury, when he saw the blank board, with only a few shreds of parchment left, round the nails; and beside it standing, in unconscious stolidity, his Dacian sentinel.

He would have darted at his throat, like a tiger, if he had not seen, in the barbarian's twinkling eye, a sort of hyena squint, which told him he had better not. But he broke out at once into a passionate exclamation:

"Sirrah! how has the edict disappeared? Tell me directly!"

"Softly, softly, Herr Kornweiner," answered the imperturbable Northern. "There it is as you left it in my charge."

"Where, you fool? Come and look at it."

The Dacian went to his side, and for the first time confronted the board; and after looking at it for some moments, exclaimed: "Well, is not that the board you hung up last night?"

"Yes, you blockhead, but there was writing on it, which is gone. That is what you had to guard."

"Why, look you, captain, as to writing, you see I know nothing, having never been a scholar; but as it was raining all night, it may have been washed out."

"And as it was blowing, I suppose the parchment on which it was written was blown off?"

"No doubt, Herr Kornweiner; you are quite right."

"Come, sir, this is no joking matter. Tell me, at once, who came here last night."

"Why, two of them came."

"Two of what?"

"Two wizards, or goblins, or worse."

"None of that nonsense for me." The Dacian's eye flashed drunkenly again. "Well, tell me, Arminius, what sort of people they were, and what they did."

"Why, one of them was but a stripling, a boy, tall and thin; who went round the pillar, and I suppose must have taken away what you miss, while I was busy with the other."

"And what of him? What was *he* like?"

The soldier opened his mouth and eyes, and stared at Corvinus for some moments, then said, with a sort of stupid solemnity, "What was he like? Why, if he was not Thor himself, he wasn't far from it. I never felt such strength."

"What did he do to show it?"

"He came up first, and began to chat quite friendly, asked me if it was not very cold, and that sort of thing. At last I remembered that I had to run through any one that came near me——"

"Exactly," interrupted Corvinus; "and why did you not do it?"

"Only because he wouldn't let me. I told him to be off, or I should spear him, and drew back and stretched out my javelin; when in the quietest manner, but I don't know how, he twisted it out of my hand, broke it over his knee, as if it had been a mountebank's wooden sword, and dashed the iron-headed piece fast into the ground, where you see it, fifty yards off."

"Then why did you not rush on him with your sword, and despatch him at once? But where is your sword? it is not in your scabbard."

The Dacian, with a stupid grin, pointed to the roof of the neighboring basilica, and said: "There, don't you see it shining on the tiles, in the morning light?" Corvinus looked, and there indeed he saw what appeared like such an object, but he could hardly believe his own eyes.

"How did it get there, you stupid booby?" he asked.

The soldier twisted his moustache in an ominous way, which made Corvinus ask again more civilly, and then he was answered:

"He, or it, whatever it was, without any apparent effort, by a sort of conjuring, whisked it out of my hand, and up where you see it, as easily as I could cast a quoit a dozen yards."

"And then?"

"And then, he and the boy, who came from round the pillar, walked off in the dark."

"What a strange story!" muttered Corvinus to himself; "yet there are proofs of the fellow's tale. It is not every one who could have performed that feat. But pray, sirrah, why did you not give the alarm, and rouse the other guards to pursuit?"

"First, Master Kornweiner, because, in my country, we will fight any living men, but we do not choose to pursue hobgoblins. And, secondly, what was the use? I saw the board that you gave into my care all safe and sound."

"Stupid barbarian!" growled Corvinus, but well within his teeth; then added: "This business will go hard with you; you know it is a capital offence."

"What is?"

"Why, to let a man come up and speak to you, without giving the watchword."

"Gently, captain; who says he did not give it? I never said so."

"But did he, though? Then it could be no Christian."

"Oh yes, he came up, and said quite plainly, *Nomen Imperatorum*."*

"What?" roared out Corvinus.

"*Nomen Imperatorum*."

"'*Nomen Imperatorum*' was the watchword," shrieked the enraged Roman.

"*Nomen* or *Nomen*, it's all the same, I suppose. A letter can't make any difference. You call me Arminius, and I call myself Hermann, and they mean the same. How should *I* know your nice points of language?"

Corvinus was enraged at himself; for he saw how much better he would have gained his ends, by putting a sharp, intelligent prætorian on duty, instead of a sottish, savage foreigner. "Well," he said, in the worst of humors, "you will have to answer to the emperor for all this; and you know he is not accustomed to pass over offences."

"Look you now, Herr Krumnbeiner," returned the soldier, with a look of sly stolidity; "as to that, we are pretty well in the same boat." (Corvinus turned pale, for he knew this was true.) "And you must contrive something to save me, if you want to save yourself. It was you the emperor made responsible, for the what-d'ye-call-it?—that board."

"You are right, my friend; I must make it out that a strong body attacked you, and killed you at your post. So shut yourself up in quarters for a few days, and you shall have plenty of beer, till the thing blows over."

The soldier went off, and concealed himself. A few days

* The name of the Emperor.

after, the dead body of a Dacian, evidently murdered, was washed on the banks of the Tiber. It was supposed he had fallen in some drunken row; and no further trouble was taken about it. The fact was indeed so; but Corvinus could have given the best account of the transaction. Before, however, leaving the ill-omened spot in the Forum, he had carefully examined the ground, for any trace of the daring act; when he picked up, close under the place of the edict, a knife, which he was sure he had seen at school, in possession of one of his companions. He treasured it up, as an implement of future vengeance, and hastened to provide another copy of the decree

An Emblem of Paradise, found in the Catacombs.

CHAPTER XV.

EXPLANATIONS.

HEN morning had fairly broken, crowds streamed, from every side, into the Forum, curious to read the tremendous edict so long menaced. But when they found only a bare board, there was a universal uproar. Some admired the spirit of the Christians, so generally reckoned cowardly; others were indignant at the audacity of such an act; some ridiculed the officials concerned in the proclamation; others were angry that the expected sport of the day might be delayed.

At an early hour the places of public fashionable resort were all occupied with the same theme. In the great Antonian Thermæ a group of regular frequenters were talking it over. There were Scaurus the lawyer, and Proculus, and Fulvius, and the philosopher Calpurnius, who seemed very busy with some musty volumes, and several others.

"What a strange affair this is, about the edict!" said one.

"Say rather, what a treasonable outrage against the divine emperors!" answered Fulvius.

"How was it done?" asked a third.

"Have you not heard," said Proculus, "that the Dacian guard stationed at the Puteal was found dead, with twenty-seven poniard-wounds on him, nineteen of which would have sufficed each by itself to cause death?"

"No, that is quite a false report," interrupted Scaurus; "it was not done by violence, but entirely by witchcraft. Two women came up to the soldier, who drove his lance at one, and it passed clean through her, and stuck in the ground on the other side, without making any wound in her. He then hacked at the other with his sword, but he might as well have struck at marble. She then threw a pinch of powder upon him, and he flew into the air, and was found, asleep and unhurt, this morning, on the roof of the Æmilian basilica. A friend of mine, who was out early, saw the ladder up, by which he had been brought down."

"Wonderful!" many exclaimed. "What extraordinary people these Christians must be!"

"I don't believe a word of it," observed Proculus. "There is no such power in magic; and certainly I don't see why these wretched men should possess it more than their betters. Come, Calpurnius," he continued, "put by that old book, and answer these questions. I learnt more, one day after dinner, about these Christians from you, than I had heard in all my life before. What a wonderful memory you must have, to remember so accurately the genealogy and history of that barbarous people! Is what Scaurus has just told us possible, or not?"

Calpurnius delivered himself, with great pompousness, as follows:

"There is no reason to suppose such a thing impossible; for the power of magic has no bounds. To prepare a powder that would make a man fly in the air, it would be only necessary to find some herbs in which air predominates more than the other three elements. Such for instance are pulse, or lentils, according to Pythagoras. These, being gathered when the sun is in Libra, the nature of which is to balance even heavy things in the air, at the moment of conjunction with Mercury, a winged power as you know, and properly energized by certain mysterious words, by a skilful magician, then reduced to powder in a mortar made out of an aerolite, or stone that had flown up into the sky, and come down again, would no doubt, when rightly used, enable, or force a person to fly up into the air. It is well known, indeed, that the Thessalian witches go at pleasure through the clouds, from place to place, which must be done by means of some such charm.

"Then, as to the Christians; you will remember, excellent Proculus, that in the account to which you have done me the honor to allude, which was at the deified Fabius's table, if I remember right, I mentioned that the sect came originally from Chaldæa, a country always famous for its occult arts. But we have a most important evidence bearing on this matter, recorded in history. It is quite certain, that here in Rome, a certain Simon, who was sometimes called Simon Peter, and at other times Simon Magus, actually in public flew up high into the air; but his charm having slipped out of his belt, he fell and broke both his legs; for which reason he was obliged to be crucified with his head downwards."

"Then are all Christians necessarily sorcerers?" asked Scaurus.

"Necessarily; it is part of their superstition. They believe their priests to have most extraordinary power over nature. Thus, for example, they think they can bathe the bodies of people in water, and their souls acquire thereby wonderful gifts and superiority, should they be slaves, over their masters, and the divine emperors themselves."

"Dreadful!" all cried out.

"Then, again," resumed Calpurnius, "we all know what a frightful crime some of them committed last night, in tearing down a supreme edict of the imperial deities; and even suppose (which the gods avert) that they carried their treasons still further, and attempted their sacred lives, they believe that they have only to go to one of those priests, own the crime, and ask for pardon; and, if he gives it, they consider themselves as perfectly guiltless."

"Fearful!" joined in the chorus.

"Such a doctrine," said Scaurus, "is incompatible with the safety of the state. A man who thinks he can be pardoned by another man of every crime, is capable of committing any."

"And that, no doubt," observed Fulvius, "is the cause of this new and terrible edict against them. After what Calpurnius has told us about these desperate men, nothing can be too severe against them."

Fulvius had been keenly eyeing Sebastian, who had entered during the conversation; and now pointedly addressed him.

"And you, no doubt, think so too, Sebastian; do you not?"

"I think," he calmly replied, "that if the Christians be such as Calpurnius describes them, infamous sorcerers, they deserve to be exterminated from the face of the earth. But even so, I would gladly give them one chance of escape."

"And what is that?" sneeringly asked Fulvius.

"That no one should be allowed to join in destroying them, who could not prove himself freer from crime than they. I would have no one raise his hand against them, who cannot show that he has never been an adulterer, an extortioner, a deceiver, a drunkard, a bad husband, father, or child, a profligate, or a thief. For with being any of these, no one charges the poor Christians."*

Fulvius winced under the catalogue of vices, and still more under the indignant, but serene, glance of Sebastian. But at the word "thief," he fairly leapt. Had the soldier seen him pick up the scarf in Fabiola's house? Be it so or not, the dislike he had taken to Sebastian, at their first meeting, had ripened into hatred at their second; and hatred in that heart was only written in blood. He had only intensity now to add to that feeling.

* See Lucian's address to the judge, upon Ptolemaeus's condemnation, in the beginning of St. Justin's Second Apology, or Ruinart, vol. i. p. 100.

Sebastian went out; and his thoughts got vent in familiar words of prayer. "How long, O Lord! how long? What hopes can we entertain of the conversion of many to the truth, still less of the conversion of this great empire, so long as we find even honest and learned men believing at once every calumny spoken against us; treasuring up, from age to age, every fable and fiction about us; and refusing even to inquire into our doctrines, because they have made up their minds that they are false and contemptible?"

He spoke aloud, believing himself alone, when a sweet voice answered him at his side: "Good youth, whoever thou art that speakest thus, and methinks I know thy voice, remember that the Son of God gave light to the dark eye of the body, by spreading thereon clay; which, in man's hands, would have only blinded the seeing. Let us be as dust beneath His feet, if we wish to become His means of enlightening the eyes of men's souls. Let us be trampled on a little longer in patience; perhaps even from our ashes may come out the spark to blaze."

"Thank you, thank you, Cecilia," said Sebastian, "for your just and kind rebuke. Whither tripping on so gaily on this first day of danger?"

"Do you not know that I have been named guide of the cemetery of Callistus? I am going to take possession. Pray, that I may be the first flower of this coming spring."

And she passed on, singing blithely. But Sebastian begged her to stay one moment.

CHAPTER XVI.

THE WOLF IN THE FOLD.

AFTER the adventures of the night, our youths had not much time for rest. Long before daybreak the Christians had to be up, and assemble at their several titles, so as to disperse before day. It was to be their last meeting there. The oratories were to be closed, and divine worship had to begin, from that day, in the subterranean churches of the cemeteries. It could not, indeed, be expected that all would be able to travel with safety, even on the Sunday, some miles beyond the gate.* A great privilege was, consequently, granted to the faithful, at such times of trouble, that of preserving the blessed Eucharist in their houses, and communicating themselves privately in the morning, "before taking other food," as Tertullian expresses it.†

The faithful felt, not as sheep going to the slaughter, not as criminals preparing for execution, but as soldiers arming for fight. Their weapons, their food, their strength, their courage, were all to be found in their Lord's table. Even the lukewarm and the timid gathered fresh spirit from the bread of life. In churches, as yet may be seen in the cemeteries,

---

* There was one cemetery called *ad sextum Philippi*, which is supposed to have been situated six miles from Rome; but many were three miles from the heart of the city.

† *Ad Uxorem*, lib. ii. c. 5.

were chairs placed for the penitentiaries, before whom the sinner knelt, and confessed his sins, and received absolution. In moments like this the penitential code was relaxed, and the terms of public expiation shortened; and the whole night had been occupied by the zealous clergy in preparing their flocks for, to many, their last public communion on earth.

We need not remind our readers that the office then performed was essentially, and in many details, the same as they daily witness at the Catholic altar. Not only was it considered, as now, to be the Sacrifice of Our Lord's Body and Blood, not only were the oblation, the consecration, the communion alike, but many of the prayers were identical; so that the Catholic hearing them recited, and still more the priest reciting them, in the same language as the Roman Church of the Catacombs spoke, may feel himself in active and living communion with the martyrs who celebrated, and the martyrs who assisted at those sublime mysteries.

On the occasion which we are describing, when the time came for giving the kiss of peace—a genuine embrace of brotherly love—sobs could be heard and bursts of tears; for it was to many a parting salutation. Many a youth clung to his father's neck, scarcely knowing whether that day might not sever them, till they waved their palm-branches together in heaven. And how would mothers press their daughters to their bosom, in the fervor of that new love which fear of long separation enkindled! Then came the communion, more solemn than usual, more devout, more hushed to stillness. "The Body of Our Lord Jesus Christ," said the priest to each, as he offered him the sacred food. "Amen," replied the receiver, with thrilling accents of faith and love. Then extending in his hand an *ozarium*, or white linen cloth, he received in it a provision of the Bread of Life, sufficient to last him till some future feast. This was most carefully and rev-

The Blessed Eucharist, in the Early Ages of the Church.

crently folded, and laid in the bosom, wrapped up often in another and more precious covering, or even placed in a gold locket.* It was now that, for the first time, poor Syra regretted the loss of her rich embroidered scarf, which would long before have been given to the poor, had she not studiously reserved it for such an occasion, and such a use. Nor had her mistress been able to prevail upon her to accept any objects of value, without a stipulation that she might dispose of them as she liked, that was in charitable gifts.

The various assemblies had broken up before the discovery of the violated edict. But they may rather be said to have adjourned to the cemeteries. The frequent meetings of Torquatus with his two heathen confederates in the baths of Caracalla had been narrowly watched by the capsarius and his wife, as we have already remarked; and Victoria had overheard the plot to make an inroad into the cemetery of Callistus on the day after publication. The Christians, therefore, considered themselves safer the first day, and took advantage of the circumstance to inaugurate, by solemn offices, the churches of the catacombs, which, after some years' disuse, had been put into good repair and order by the *fossores*, had been in some places repainted, and furnished with all requisites for divine worship.

But Corvinus, after getting over his first dismay, and having as speedily as possible another, though not so grand, a copy of the edict affixed, began better to see the dismal probabilities of serious consequences from the wrath of his imperial master. The Dacian was right: *he* would have to answer for the loss. He felt it necessary to do something that very day, which might wipe off the disgrace he had incurred, before

---

* When the Vatican cemetery was explored, in 1871, there were found in tombs two small square golden boxes, with a ring at the top of the lid. These very ancient sacred vessels are considered by Bottari to have been used for carrying the Blessed Eucharist round the neck (*Roma Subterranea*, tom. i. fig. 11); and Pellicia confirms this by many arguments (*Christianæ Eccl. Politia*, tom. iii. p. 26).

again meeting the emperor's look. He determined to anticipate the attack on the cemetery, intended for the following day.

He repaired, therefore, while it was still early, to the baths, where Fulvius, ever jealously watchful over Torquatus, kept him in expectation of Corvinus's coming to hold council with them. The worthy trio concerted their plans. Corvinus, guided by the reluctant apostate, at the head of a chosen band of soldiers who were at his disposal, had to make an incursion into the cemetery of Callistus, and drive, or drag thence the clergy and principal Christians; while Fulvius, remaining outside with another company, would intercept them and cut off all retreat, securing the most important prizes, and especially the Pontiff and superior clergy, whom his visit to the ordination would enable him to recognize. This was his plan. "Let fools," he said to himself, "act the part of ferrets in the warren; I will be the sportsman outside."

In the meantime Victoria overheard sufficient to make her very busy dusting and cleaning, in the retired room where they were consulting, without appearing to listen. She told all to Cucumio; and he, after much scratching of his head, hit upon a notable plan for conveying the discovered information to the proper quarter.

Sebastian, after his early attendance on divine worship, unable, from his duties at the palace to do more, had proceeded, according to almost universal custom, to the baths, to invigorate his limbs by their healthy refreshment, and also to remove from himself the suspicion, which his absence on that morning might have excited. While he was thus engaged, the old *copiosarius*, as he had had himself rattlingly called in his ante-posthumous inscription, wrote on a slip of parchment all that his wife had heard about the intention of an immediate assault, and of getting possession of the holy Pontiff's person. This he fastened with a pin or needle to the inside of Sebastian's tunic, of which he had charge, as he durst not speak to him in the presence of others.

The officer, after his bath, went into the hall where the events of the morning were being discussed, and where Fulvius was waiting, till Corvinus should tell him that all was ready. Upon going out, disgusted, he felt himself, as he walked, pricked by something on his chest: he examined his garments, and found the paper. It was written in about as elegant a latinity as Cucumio's epitaph, but he made it out sufficiently to consider it necessary for him to turn his steps towards the Via Appia, instead of the Palatine, and convey the important information to the Christians assembled in the cemetery.

Having, however, found a fleeter and surer messenger than himself, in the poor blind girl, who would not attract the same attention, he stopped her, gave her the note, after adding a few words to it, with the pen and ink which he carried, and bade her bear it, as speedily as possible, to its destination. But, in fact, he had hardly left the baths, when Fulvius received information that Corvinus and his troop were by that time hastening across the fields, so as to avoid suspicion, towards the appointed spot. He mounted his horse immediately, and went along the high-road; while the Christian soldier, in a by-way, was instructing his blind messenger.

When we accompanied Diogenes and his party through the catacombs, we stopped short of the subterranean church, because Severus would not let it be betrayed to Torquatus. In this the Christian congregation was now assembled, under its chief pastor. It was constructed on the principle common to all such excavations, for we can hardly call them edifices.

The reader may imagine two of the *cubicula* or chambers, which we have before described, placed one on each side of a gallery or passage, so that their doors, or rather wide entrances, are opposite one another. At the end of one will be found an *arcosolium* or altar-tomb: and the probable conjecture is, that in this division the men, under charge of the *ostiarii*,* and in the other the women, under the care of the deaconesses, were

Ruins of the basilica of St. Alexander, on the Nomentan Way. From Reber's "Catacombes de Rome."

assembled. This division of the sexes at divine worship was a matter of jealous discipline in the early Church.

Often these subterranean churches were not devoid of architectural decoration. The walls, especially near the altar, were plastered and painted, and half columns, with their bases and capitals, not ungracefully cut out of the sandstone, divided

* Door-keepers,—an office constituting a lower order in the Church.

Confirmation, in the Early Ages of the Church.

the different parts or ornamented the entrances. In one instance, indeed in the chief basilica yet discovered in the cemetery of Callistus, there is a chamber without any altar, communicating with the church by means of a funnel-shaped opening, piercing the earthen wall, here some twelve feet thick, and entering the chamber, which is at a lower level, at the height of five or six feet, in a slanting direction; so that all that was spoken in the church could be heard, yet nothing that was done there could be seen, by those assembled in the chamber. This is very naturally supposed to have been the place reserved for the class of public penitents called *audientes* or hearers, and for the catechumens, not yet initiated by baptism.

The basilica, in which the Christians were assembled, when Sebastian sent his message, was like the one discovered in the cemetery of St. Agnes. Each of the two divisions was double, that is, consisted of two large chambers, slightly separated by half-columns, in what we may call the women's church, and by flat pilasters in the men's, one of these surfaces having in it a small niche for an image or lamp. But the most remarkable feature of this basilica is a further prolongation of the structure, so as to give it a chancel or presbytery. This is about the size of half each other division, from which it is separated by two columns against the wall, as well as by its lesser height, after the manner of modern chancels. For while each portion of each division has first a lofty-arched tomb in its wall, and four or five tiers of graves above it, the elevation of the chancel is not much greater than that of those *arcosolia* or altar-tombs. At the end of the chancel, against the middle of the wall, is a chair with back and arms cut out of the solid stone, and from each side proceeds a stone bench, which thus

A Cathedra or Reserved Chair in the Catacomb of Saint Agnes.

occupies the end and two sides of the chancel. As the table of the arched-tomb behind the chair is higher than the back of the throne, and as this is immovable, it is clear that the divine mysteries could not have been celebrated upon it. A portable altar must, therefore, have been placed before the throne, in an isolated position in the middle of the sanctuary; and this, tradition tell us, was the wooden altar of St. Peter.

We have thus the exact arrangements to be found in the

churches built after the peace, and yet to be seen in all the ancient basilicas in Rome—the episcopal chair in the centre of the apse, the presbytery or seat for the clergy on either hand, and the altar between the throne and the people. The early Christians thus anticipated underground, or rather gave the principles which directed, the forms of ecclesiastical architecture.

It was in such a basilica, then, that we are to imagine the faithful assembled, when Corvinus and his satellites arrived at the entrance of the cemetery. This was the way which Torquatus knew, leading down by steps from a half-ruinous building, choked up with faggots. They found the coast clear, and immediately made their arrangements. Fulvius, with one body of ten or twelve men, lurked to guard the entrance, and seize all who attempted to come out or go in. Corvinus, with Torquatus and a smaller body of eight, prepared to descend.

"I don't like this underground work," said an old, grey-bearded legionary. "I am a soldier, and not a rat-catcher. Bring me my man into the light of day, and I will fight him hand to hand, and foot to foot; but I have no love for being stifled or poisoned, like vermin in a drain."

This speech found favor with the soldiers. One said, "There may be hundreds of these skulking Christians down there, and we are little more than half a dozen."

"This is not the sort of work we receive our pay for," added another.

"It's their sorceries I care for," continued a third, "and not their valor."

It required all the eloquence of Fulvius to screw up their resolution. He assured them there was nothing to fear; that the cowardly Christians would run before them like hares, and that they would find more gold and silver in the church than a year's pay would give them. Thus encouraged, they went groping down to the bottom of the stairs. They could distinguish lamps at intervals, stretching into the gloomy length before them.

"Hush!" said one, "listen to that voice!"

An Altar with its Episcopal Chair, in the Cemetery of Saint Agnes

From far away its accents came, softened by distance, but they were the notes of a fresh youthful voice, that quailed not with fear; so clear, that the very words could be caught, as it intoned the following verses:

"Dominus illuminatio mea, et salus mea; quem timebo?

"Dominus protector vitae meae; a quo trepidabo?"*

Then came a full chorus of voices, singing, like the sound of many waters:

"Dum appropriant super me nocentes, ut edant carnes meas; qui tribulant me, inimici mei, ipsi infirmati sunt et ceciderunt."†

A mixture of shame and anger seized on the assailants as they heard these words of calm confidence and defiance. The single voice again sang forth, but in apparently fainter accents:

"Si consistant adversum me castra, non timebit cor meum."‡

"I thought I knew that voice," muttered Corvinus. "I ought to know it out of a thousand. It is that of my bane, the cause of all last night's curse and this day's trouble. It is that of Pancratius, who pulled down the edict. On, on, my men; any reward for him, dead or alive!"

"But, stop," said one, "let us light our torches."

"Hark!" said a second, while they were engaged in this operation; "what is that strange noise, as if of scratching and hammering at a distance? I have heard it for some time."

"And, look!" added a third; "the distant lights have disappeared, and the music has ceased. We are certainly discovered."

"No danger," said Torquatus, putting on a boldness which he did not feel. "That noise only comes from those old moles, Diogenes and his sons, busy preparing graves for the Christians we shall seize."

---

* "The Lord is my light and my salvation: whom shall I fear? The Lord is the protector of my life: of whom shall I be afraid?"

† "While the wicked draw nigh me, to eat my flesh, my enemies that trouble me have themselves been weakened and have fallen."

‡ "If armies in camp shall stand together against me, my heart shall not fear."—Ps. xxvi.

Torquatus had in vain advised the troop not to bring torches, but to provide themselves with such lamps as we see Diogenes represented carrying, in his picture, or waxen tapers, which he had brought for himself; but the men swore they would not go down without plenty of light, and such means for it as could not be put out by a draught of wind, or a stroke

An Altar in the Cemetery of SS. Nereo

on the arm. The effects were soon obvious. As they advanced, silently and cautiously, along the low narrow gallery, the resinous torches crackled and hissed with a fierce glare, which heated and annoyed them; while a volume of thick pitchy smoke from each rolled downwards on to the bearers from the roof, half stifled them, and made a dense atmosphere of cloud around themselves, which effectually dimmed their light. Torquatus kept at the head of the party, counting every turning right and left, as he had noted them; though he found

every mark which he had made carefully removed. He was
staggered and baulked, when, after having counted little more
than half the proper number, he found the road completely
blocked up.

The fact was, that keener eyes than he was aware of had
been on the look-out. Severus had never relaxed his watchfulness, determined not to be surprised. He was near the
entrance to the cemetery below, when the soldiers reached it
above; and he ran forward at once to the place where the
sand had been prepared for closing the road; near which his
brother and several other stout workmen were stationed, in
case of danger. In a moment, with that silence and rapidity
to which they were trained, they set to work lustily, shovelling
the sand across the narrow and low corridor from each side,
while well-directed blows of the pick brought from the low
roof behind, huge flakes of sandstone, which closed up the
opening. Behind this barrier they stood, hardly suppressing
a laugh as they heard their enemies through its hoarse
separation. Their work it was which had been heard,
and which had screened off the lights, and deadened the
song.

Torquatus's perplexity was not diminished by the volley
of oaths and imprecations, and the threats of violence which
were showered upon him, for a fool or a traitor. "Stay one
moment, I entreat you," he said. "It is possible I have mistaken my reckoning. I know the right turn by a remarkable
tomb a few yards within it; I will just step into one or two
of the last corridors, and see."

With these words, he ran back to the next gallery on the
left, advanced a few paces, and totally disappeared.

Though his companions had followed him to the very
mouth of the gallery, they could not see how this happened.
It appeared like witchcraft, in which they were quite ready to
believe. His light and himself seemed to have vanished at

once. "We will have no more of this work," they said; "either Torquatus is a traitor, or he has been carried off by magic." Worried, heated in the close atmosphere, almost inflamed by their lights, begrimed, blinded, and choked by the pitchy smoke, crest-fallen and disheartened, they turned back; and since their road led straight to the entrance, they flung away their blazing torches into the side galleries, one here and one there, as they passed by, to get rid of them. When they looked back, it seemed as if a triumphal illumination was kindling up the very atmosphere of the gloomy corridor. From the mouths of the various caverns came forth a fiery light which turned the dull sandstone into a bright crimson; while the volumes of smoke above, hung like amber clouds along the whole gallery. The sealed tombs, receiving the unusual reflection on their yellow tiles, or marble slabs, appeared covered with golden or silver plates, set in the red damask of the walls. It looked like a homage paid to martyrdom, by the very furies of heathenism, on the first day of persecution. The torches which they had kindled to destroy, only served to shed brightness on monuments of that virtue which had never failed to save the Church.

But before these foiled hounds with drooping heads had reached the entrance, they recoiled before the sight of a singular apparition. At first they thought they had caught a glimpse of daylight; but they soon perceived it was the glimmering of a lamp. This was held steadily by an upright, immovable figure, which thus received its light upon itself. It was clothed in a dark dress, so as to resemble one of those bronze statues, which have the head and extremities of white marble, and startle one, when first seen; so like are they to living forms.

"Who can it be? What is it?" the men whispered to one another.

"A sorceress," replied one.

"The *genius loci*,"* observed another.

"A spirit," suggested a third.

Still, as they approached stealthily towards it, it did not appear conscious of their presence; "there was no speculation in its eyes;" it remained unmoved and unscared. At length, two got sufficiently near to seize the figure by its arms.

"Who are you?" asked Corvinus, in a rage.

"A Christian," answered Cecilia, with her usual cheerful gentleness.

"Bring her along," he commanded; "some one at least shall pay for our disappointment."

* The guardian genius of the place.

The Case of the Man born Blind, from a picture in the Catacombs.

CHAPTER XVII.

THE FIRST FLOWER.

CECILIA, already forewarned, had approached the cemetery by a different, but neighboring entrance. No sooner had she descended than she snuffed the strong odor of the torches. "This is none of our incense, I know," she said to herself; "the enemy is already within."

She hastened therefore to the place of assembly and delivered Sebastian's note; adding also what she had observed. It warned them to disperse and seek the shelter of the inner and lower galleries; and begged of the Pontiff not to leave till he should send for him, as his person was particularly sought for.

Pancratius urged the blind messenger to save herself too. "No," she replied, "my office is to watch the door, and guide the faithful safe."

"But the enemy may seize you."

"No matter," she answered, laughing; "my being taken may save much worthier lives. Give me a lamp, Pancratius."

"Why, you cannot see by it," observed he, smiling.

"True, but others can."

"They may be your enemies."

"Even so," she answered, "I do not wish to be taken in the dark. If my Bridegroom come to me in the night of this cemetery, must He not find me with my lamp trimmed?"

Off she started, reached her post, and hearing no noise except that of quiet footsteps, she thought they were those of friends, and held up her lamp to guide them.

When the party came forth, with their only captive, Fulvius was perfectly furious. It was worse than a total failure; it was ridiculous—a poor mouse come out of the bowels of the earth. He railed Corvinus till the wretch winced and foamed; then suddenly he asked, "And where is Torquatus?" He heard the account of his sudden disappearance, told in as many ways as the Dacian guard's adventure; but it annoyed him greatly. He had no doubt whatever, in his own mind, that he had been duped by his supposed victim, who had escaped into the unsearchable mazes of the cemetery. If so, this captive would know, and he determined to question her. He stood before her, therefore, put on his most searching and awful look, and said to her sternly, "Look at me, woman, and tell me the truth."

"I must tell you the truth without looking at you, sir," answered the poor girl, with her cheerfullest smile and softest voice; "do you not see that I am blind?"

"Blind!" all exclaimed at once, as they crowded to look at her. But over the features of Fulvius there passed the slightest possible emotion, just as much as the wave that runs, pursued by a playful breeze, over the ripe meadow. A knowledge had flashed into his mind, a clue had fallen into his hand.

"It will be ridiculous," he said, "for twenty soldiers to march through the city, guarding a blind girl. Return to your quarters, and I will see you are well rewarded. You, Corvinus, take my horse, and go before to your father, and tell him all. I will follow in a carriage with the captive."

"No treachery, Fulvius," he said, vexed and mortified.

"Mind you bring her. The day must not pass without a sacrifice."

"Do not fear," was the reply.

Fulvius, indeed, was pondering whether, having lost one spy, he should not try to make another. But the placid gentleness of the poor beggar perplexed him more than the boisterous zeal of the gamester, and her sightless orbs defied him more than the restless roll of the toper's. Still, the first thought that had struck him he could yet pursue. When alone in a carriage with her, he assumed a soothing tone, and addressed her. He knew she had not overheard the last dialogue.

"My poor girl," he said, "how long have you been blind?"

"All my life," she replied.

"What is your history? Whence do you come?"

"I have no history. My parents were poor, and brought me to Rome when I was four years old, as they came to pray, in discharge of a vow made for my life in early sickness, to the blessed martyrs Chrysanthus and Daria. They left me in charge of a pious lame woman, at the door of the title of Fasciola, while they went to their devotions. It was on that memorable day, when many Christians were buried at their tomb, by earth and stones cast down upon them. My parents had the happiness to be of the number."

"And how have you lived since?"

"God became my only Father then, and His Catholic Church my mother. The one feeds the birds of the air, the other nurses the weaklings of the flock. I have never wanted for any thing since."

"But you can walk about the streets freely, and without fear, as well as if you saw."

"How do you know that?"

"I have seen you. Do you remember very early one

morning in the autumn, leading a poor lame man along the Vicus Patricius?"

She blushed and remained silent. Could he have seen her put into the poor old man's purse her own share of the alms?

"You have owned yourself a Christian?" he asked negligently.

"Oh, yes! how could I deny it?"

"Then that meeting was a Christian meeting?"

"Certainly; what else could it be?"

He wanted no more; his suspicions were verified. Agnes, about whom Torquatus had been able or willing to tell him nothing, was certainly a Christian. His game was made. She must yield, or he would be avenged.

After a pause, looking at her steadfastly, he said, "Do you know whither you are going?"

"Before the judge of earth, I suppose, who will send me to my Spouse in heaven."

"And so calmly?" he asked in surprise; for he could see no token from the soul to the countenance, but a smile.

"So joyfully rather," was her brief reply.

Having got all that he desired, he consigned his prisoner to Corvinus at the gates of the Æmilian basilica, and left her to her fate. It had been a cold and drizzling day like the preceding evening. The weather, and the incident of the night, had kept down all enthusiasm; and while the prefect had been compelled to sit in-doors, where no great crowd could collect, as hours had passed away without any arrest, trial, or tidings, most of the curious had left, and only a few more persevering remained, past the hour of afternoon recreation in the public gardens. But just before the captive arrived, a fresh knot of spectators came in, and stood near one of the side-doors, from which they could see all.

As Corvinus had prepared his father for what he was to expect, Tertullus, moved with some compassion, and imagining there could be little difficulty in overcoming the obstinacy of a poor, ignorant, blind beggar, requested the spectators to remain perfectly still, that he might try his persuasion on her, alone, as she would imagine, with him; and he threatened heavy penalties on any one who should presume to break the silence.

It was as he had calculated. Cæcilia knew not that any one else was there, as the prefect thus kindly addressed her:

"What is thy name, child?"

"Cæcilia."

"It is a noble name; hast thou it from thy family?"

"No; I am not noble; except because my parents, though poor, died for Christ. As I am blind, those who took care of me called me *Cæca*,[*] and then, out of kindness, softened it into Cæcilia."

"But now, give up all this folly of the Christians, who have kept thee only poor and blind. Honor the decrees of the divine emperors, and offer sacrifice to the gods; and thou shalt have riches, and fine clothes, and good fare; and the best physicians shall try to restore thee thy sight."

"You must have better motives to propose to me than those; for the very things for which I most thank God and His Divine Son, are those which you would have me put away."

"How dost thou mean?"

"I thank God that I am poor and meanly clad, and fare not daintily; because by all these things I am the more like Jesus Christ, my only Spouse."

"Foolish girl!" interrupted the judge, losing patience a little; "hast thou learnt all these silly delusions already? at least thou canst not thank thy God that He has made thee sightless."

[*] Blind.

"For that, more than all the rest, I thank Him daily and hourly with all my heart."

"How so? dost thou think it a blessing never to have seen the face of a human being, or the sun, or the earth? What strange fancies are these?"

"They are not so, most noble sir. For in the midst of what you call darkness, I see a spot of what I must call light, it contrasts so strongly with all around. It is to me what the sun is to you, which I know to be local from the varying direction of its rays. And this object looks upon me as with a countenance of intensest beauty, and smiles upon me ever. And I know it to be that of Him whom I love with undivided affection. I would not for the world have its splendor dimmed by a brighter sun, nor its wondrous loveliness confounded with the diversities of others' features, nor my gaze on it drawn aside by earthly visions. I love Him too much not to wish to see Him always alone."

"Come, come! let me have no more of this silly prattle. Obey the emperors at once, or I must try what a little pain will do. That will soon tame thee."

"Pain?" she echoed innocently.

"Yes, pain. Hast thou never felt it? hast thou never been hurt by any one in thy life?"

"Oh, no! Christians never hurt one another."

The rack was standing, as usual, before him; and he made a sign to Catulus to place her upon it. The executioner pushed her back on it by her arms; and as she made no resistance, she was easily laid extended on its wooden couch. The loops of the ever-ready ropes were in a moment passed round her ankles, and arms drawn over the head. The poor sightless girl saw not who did all this; she knew not but it might be the same person who had been conversing with her. If there had been silence hitherto, men now held their very breath; while Cæcilia's lips moved in earnest prayer.

"Once more, before proceeding further, I call on thee to sacrifice to the gods, and escape cruel torments," said the judge, with a sterner voice.

"Neither torments nor death," firmly replied the victim tied to the altar, "shall separate me from the love of Christ. I can offer up no sacrifice but to the one living God; and its ready oblation is myself."

The prefect made a signal to the executioner, and he gave one rapid whirl to the two wheels of the rack, round the windlasses of which the ropes were wound; and the limbs of the maiden were stretched with a sudden jerk, which, though not enough to wrench them from their sockets, as a further turn would have done, sufficed to inflict an excruciating, or more truly, a *racking* pain, through all her frame. Far more grievous was this, from the preparation and the cause of it being unseen, and from that additional suffering which darkness inflicts. A quivering of her features and a sudden paleness alone gave evidence of her torture.

"Ha! ha!" the judge exclaimed, "thou feelest that? Come, let it suffice; obey, and thou shalt be freed."

She seemed to take no heed of his words, but gave vent to her feelings in prayer: "I thank Thee, O Lord Jesus Christ, that Thou hast made me suffer pain the first time for Thy sake. I have loved Thee in peace; I have loved Thee in comfort; I have loved Thee in joy,—and now in pain I love Thee still more. How much sweeter it is to be like Thee, stretched upon Thy Cross, even than resting upon the hard couch at the poor man's table!"

"Thou triflest with me," exclaimed the judge, thoroughly vexed, "and makest light of my lenity. We will try something stronger. Here, Catulus, apply a lighted torch to her sides."*

---

* The rack was used for a double purpose; as a direct torment, and to keep the body distended for the application of other tortures. This of fire was one of the most common.

A thrill of disgust and horror ran through the assembly, which could not help sympathizing with the poor blind creature. A murmur of suppressed indignation broke out from all sides of the hall.

Cæcilia, for the first time, learnt that she was in the midst of a crowd. A crimson glow of modesty rushed into her brow, her face, and neck, just before white as marble. The angry judge checked the rising gush of feeling; and all listened in silence, as she spoke again, with warmer earnestness than before:

"O my dear Lord and Spouse! I have been ever true and faithful to Thee! Let me suffer pain and torture for Thee; but spare me confusion from human eyes. Let me come to Thee at once; not covering my face with my hands in shame when I stand before Thee."

Another muttering of compassion was heard.

"Catulus!" shouted the baffled judge in fury; "do your duty, sirrah! what are you about, fumbling all day with that torch?"

The executioner advanced, and stretched forth his hand to her robe, to withdraw it for the torture; but he drew back, and, turning to the prefect, exclaimed in softened accents:

"It is too late. She is dead!"

"Dead!" cried out Tertullus; "dead with one turn of the wheel? impossible!"

Catulus gave the rack a turn backwards, and the body remained motionless. It was true; she had passed from the rack to the throne, from the scowl of the judge's countenance to her Spouse's welcoming embrace. Had she breathed out her pure soul, as a sweet perfume, in the incense of her prayer? or had her heart been unable to get back its blood, from the intensity of that first virginal blush?*

* There are many instances in the lives of martyrs of their deaths being the fruit of prayer, as in St. Praxedes, St. Cæcilia, St. Agatha, &c.

In the stillness of awe and wonder, a clear bold voice cried out, from the group near the door: "Impious tyrant, dost thou not see, that a poor blind Christian hath more power over life and death, than thou or thy cruel masters?"

"What! a third time in twenty-four hours wilt thou dare to cross my path? This time thou shalt not escape."

These were Corvinus's words, garnished with a furious imprecation, as he rushed from his father's side round the enclosure before the tribunal, towards the group. But as he ran blindly on, he struck against an officer of herculean build, who, no doubt quite accidentally, was advancing from it. He reeled, and the soldier caught hold of him, saying:

"You are not hurt, I hope, Corvinus?"

"No, no; let me go, Quadratus, let me go."

"Where are you running to in such a hurry? can I help you?" asked his captor, still holding him fast.

"Let me loose, I say, or he will be gone."

"Who will be gone?"

"Pancratius," answered Corvinus, "who just now insulted my father."

"Pancratius!" said Quadratus, looking round, and seeing that he had got clear off; "I do not see him." And he let him go; but it was too late. The youth was safe at Diogenes's, in the Suburra.

While this scene was going on, the prefect, mortified, ordered Catulus to see the body thrown into the Tiber. But another officer, muffled in his cloak, stepped aside and beckoned to Catulus, who understood the sign, and stretched out his hand to receive a purse held out to him.

"Out of the Porta Capena, at Lucina's villa, an hour after sunset," said Sebastian.

"It shall be delivered there safe," said the executioner.

"Of what do you think did that poor girl die?" asked a spectator from his companion, as they went out.

"Of fright, I fancy," he replied.

"Of Christian modesty," interposed a stranger who passed them.

The Woman of Samaria, from a picture in the Cemetery of St. Domitilla.

CHAPTER XVIII.

RETRIBUTION.

THE prefect of the city went to give his report on the untoward events of the day, and do what was possible to screen his worthless son. He found the emperor in the worst of moods. Had Corvinus come in his way early in the day, nobody could have answered for his head. And now the result of the inroad into the cemetery had revived his anger, when Tertullus entered into the audience-chamber. Sebastian contrived to be on guard.

"Where is your booby of a son?" was the first salutation which the prefect received.

"Humbly waiting your divinity's pleasure outside, and anxious to propitiate your godlike anger, for the tricks which fortune has played upon his zeal."

"Fortune!" exclaimed the tyrant; "fortune indeed! His own stupidity and cowardice: a pretty beginning, forsooth; but he shall smart for it. Bring him in."

The wretch, whining and trembling, was introduced; and cast himself at the emperor's feet, from which he was spurned, and sent rolling, like a lashed hound, into the midst of the hall. This set the imperial divinity a-laughing, and helped to mollify its wrath.

"Come, sirrah! stand up," he said, "and let me hear an account of yourself. How did the edict disappear?"

Corvinus told a rambling tale, which occasionally amused the emperor; for he was rather taken with the trick. This was a good symptom.

"Well," he said at last, "I will be merciful to you. Lictors, bind your fasces." They drew their axes forth, and felt their edges. Corvinus again threw himself down, and exclaimed:

"Spare my life; I have important information to furnish, if I live."

"Who wants your worthless life?" responded the gentle Maximian. "Lictors, put aside your axes; the rods are good enough for him."

In a moment his hands were seized and bound, his tunic was stripped off his shoulders, and a shower of blows fell upon them, delivered with well-regulated skill, till he roared and writhed, to the great enjoyment of his imperial master.

Smarting and humbled, he had to stand again before him.

"Now, sir," said the latter, "what is the wonderful information you have to give?"

"That I know who perpetrated the outrage of last night, on your imperial edict."

"Who was it?"

"A youth named Pancratius, whose knife I found under where the edict had been cut away."

"And why have you not seized him and brought him to justice?"

"Twice this day he has been almost within my grasp, for I have heard his voice; but he has escaped me."

"Then let him not escape a third time, or you may have to take his place. But how do you know him, or his knife?"

"He was my school-fellow at the school of Cassianus, who turned out to be a Christian."

"A Christian presume to teach my subjects, to make them enemies of their country, disloyal to their sovereigns, and contemners of the gods! I suppose it was he who taught that young viper Pancratius to pull down our imperial edict. Do you know where he is?"

"Yes, sire; Torquatus, who has abandoned the Christian superstition, has told me."

"And pray who is this Torquatus?"

"He is one who has been staying some time with Chromatius and a party of Christians in the country."

"Why, this is worse and worse. Is the ex-prefect then, too, become a Christian?"

"Yes, and lives with many others of that sect in Campania."

"What perfidy! what treachery! I shall not know whom to trust next. Prefect, send some one immediately to arrest all these men, and the school-master, and Torquatus."

"He is no longer a Christian," interposed the judge.

"Well, what do I care?" replied the emperor peevishly; "arrest as many as you can, and spare no one, and make them smart well; do you understand me? Now begone, all; it is time for my supper."

Corvinus went home; and, in spite of medicinal applications, was feverish, sore, and spiteful all night; and next morning begged his father to let him go on the expedition into Campania, that so he might retrieve his honor, gratify his revenge, and escape the disgrace and sarcasm that was sure to be heaped on him by Roman society.

When Fulvius had deposited his prisoner at the tribunal, he hastened home to recount his adventures, as usual, to Eurotas. The old man listened with imperturbable sternness to the barren recital, and at last said, coldly:

"Very little profit from all this, Fulvius."

"No immediate profit, indeed; but a good prospect in view, at least."

"How so?"

"Why, the Lady Agnes is in my power. I have made

sure, at last, that she is a Christian. I can now necessarily either win her or destroy her. In either case her property is mine."

"Take the second alternative," said the old man, with a keen glow in his eye, but no change of face; "it is the shorter, and less troublesome, way."

"But my honor is engaged; I cannot allow myself to be spurned in the manner I told you."

"You *have* been spurned, however; and that calls for vengeance. You have no time to lose, remember, in fodery. Your funds are nearly exhausted, and nothing is coming in. You *must* strike a blow."

"Surely, Eurotas, you would prefer my trying to get this wealth by honorable," (Eurotas smiled at the idea coming into either of their minds) "rather than by foul, means."

"Get it, get it any way, provided it be the surest and the speediest. You know our compact. Either the family is restored to wealth and splendor, or it ends in and with you. It shall never linger on in disgrace, that is, in poverty."

"I know, I know, without your every day reminding me of the bitter condition," said Fulvius, wringing his hands, and writhing in all his body. "Give me time enough, and all will be well."

"I give you time, till all is hopeless. Things do not look bright at present. But, Fulvius, it is time that I tell you who I am."

"Why, were you not my father's faithful dependant, to whose care he intrusted me?"

"I was your father's elder brother, Fulvius, and am the head of the family. I have had but one thought, but one aim in life, the restoring of our house to that greatness and splendor, from which my father's negligence and prodigality had brought it down. Thinking that your father, my brother, had greater ability than myself for this work, I resigned my rights and gains to him upon certain terms; one of which was your guardianship, and the exclusive forming of your mind. You know how I have trained you, to care nothing about the means, so that our great ends be carried."

Fulvius, who had been riveted with amazement and deep attention on the speaker, shrunk into himself with shame, at this baring of both their hearts. The dark old man fixed his eyes more intently than ever, and went on:

"You remember the black and complicated crime by which we concentrated in your hands the divided remnant of family wealth."

Fulvius covered his face with his hands and shuddered, then said entreatingly, "Oh, spare me that, Eurotas; for heaven's sake spare me!"

"Well, then," resumed the other, unmoved as ever, "I will be brief. Remember, nephew, that he who does not recoil from a brilliant future, to be gained by guilt, must not shrink from a past that prepared it by crime. For the future will one day be the past. Let our compact, therefore, be straight-forward and honest, for there is an honesty even in sin. Nature has given you abundance of selfishness and cunning, and she has given me boldness and remorselessness in directing and applying them. Our lot is cast by the same throw, — we become rich, or die, together."

Fulvius, in his heart, cursed the day that he came to Rome, or bound himself to his stern master, whose mysterious tie was so much stronger than he had known before. But he felt himself spell-bound to him, and powerless as the kid in the lion's jaws. He retired to his couch with a heavier heart than ever; for a dark, impending fate never failed to weigh upon his soul every returning night.

The reader will perhaps be curious to know what has become of the third member of our worthy trio, the apostate Torquatus. When, confused and bewildered, he ran to look for the tomb which was to guide him, it so happened, that, just within the gallery which he entered, was a neglected staircase, cut in the sandstone, down to a lower story of the cemetery. The steps had been worn round and smooth, and the descent was precipitous. Torquatus, carrying his light before him, and running heedlessly, fell headlong down the opening, and remained stunned and insensible at the bottom, till long after his companions had retired. He then revived, and for some time was so confused that he knew not where he was. He arose and groped about, till, consciousness completely returning, he remembered that he was in a catacomb, but could not make out how he was alone and in the dark. It then struck him that he had a supply of tapers about him, and means of lighting them. He employed these, and was cheered by finding himself again in light. But he had wandered from the staircase, of which, indeed, he recollected nothing, and went on, and on, entangling himself more inextricably in the subterranean labyrinth.

He felt sure that, before he had exhausted his strength or his tapers, he should come to some outlet. But by degrees he began to feel serious alarm. One after the other his lights were burnt out, and his vigor began to fail, for he had been fasting from early morning; and he found himself coming back to the same spot, after he had wandered about apparently for hours. At first he had looked negligently around him, and had carelessly read the inscriptions on the tombs. But as he grew fainter, and his hope of relief weaker, these solemn monuments of death began to speak to his soul, in a language that it could not refuse to hear, nor pretend to misunderstand. "Deposited in peace," was the inmate of one; "resting in Christ" was another; and even the thousand nameless ones around them reposed in silent calm, each with the seal of the Church's motherly care stamped upon his place of rest. And within, the embalmed remains awaited the sound of angelic trumpet-notes, to awaken them to a happy resurrection. And he, in a few more hours, would be dead like them; he was lighting his last taper, and had sunk down upon a heap of mould; but would he be laid in peace, by pious hands, as they? On the cold ground, alone, he should die, unpitied, unmourned, unknown. There he should rot, and drop to pieces; and if, in after years, his bones, cast out from Christian sepulture, should be found, tradition might conjecture that they were the accursed remains of an apostate lost in the cemetery. And even they might be cast out, as he was, from the communion of that hallowed ground.

It was coming on fast; he could feel it; his head reeled, his heart fluttered. The taper was getting too short for his fingers, and he placed it on a stone beside him. It might burn three minutes longer; but a drop filtering through the ceiling, fell upon it, and extinguished it. So covetous did he feel of those three minutes more of light, so jealous was he of that little taper-end, as his last link with earth's joys, so anxious was he to have one more look at things without, lest he should be forced to look at those within, that he drew forth his flint and steel, and labored for a quarter of an hour to get a light from tinder, damped by the cold perspiration on his body. And when he had lighted his remnant of candle, instead of profiting by its flame to look around him, he fixed his eyes upon it with an idiotic stare, watching it burn down, as though it were the charm which bound his life, and this must expire with it. And soon the last spark gleamed smouldering like a glow-worm, on the red earth, and died.

Was he dead too? he thought. Why not? Darkness, complete and perpetual, had come upon him. He was cut off for ever from consort with the living, his mouth would no more taste food, his ears never again hear a sound, his eyes behold no light, or thing, again. He was associated with the dead, only his grave was much larger than theirs; but, for all that, it was as dark and lonely, and closed for ever. What else is death?

No, it could not be death as yet. Death had to be followed by something else. But even this was coming. The worm was beginning to gnaw his conscience, and it grew apace to a viper's length, and twisted itself round his heart. He tried to think of pleasant things, and they came before him; the quiet hours in the villa with Chromatius and Polycarp, their kind words, and last embrace. But from the beautiful vision darted a withering flash; he had betrayed them; he had told of them; to whom? To Fulvius and Corvinus. The fatal chord was touched, like the tingling nerve of a tooth, that darts its agony straight to the centre of the brain. The drunken debauch, the dishonest play, the base hypocrisy, the vile treachery, the insincere apostasy, the remorseful sacrileges of the last days, and the murderous attempt of that morning, now came dancing, like demons hand in hand, in the dark before him, shouting, laughing, jibing, weeping, moaning, gnashing their teeth; and sparks of fire flying before his eyes, from his enfeebled brain, seemed to dart from glaring torches in their hands. He sank down and covered his eyes.

"I may be dead, after all," he said to himself; "for the infernal pit can have nothing worse than this."

His heart was too weak for rage; it sunk within him in the impotence of despair. His strength was ebbing fast, when he fancied he heard a distant sound. He put away the thought; but the wave of a remote harmony beat again upon his ear. He raised himself up; it was becoming distinct. So sweet it sounded, so like a chorus of angelic voices, but in another sphere, that he said to himself: "Who would have thought that Heaven was so near to hell! Or are they accompanying the fearful Judge to try me?"

And now a faint glimmer of light appeared at the same

distance as the sounds; and the words of the strain were clearly heard:

"In pace, in idipsum, dormiam et requiescam."*

"Those words are not for me. They might do at a martyr's entombment; they cannot at a reprobate's burial."

The light increased; it was like a dawn glowing into day; it entered the gallery and passed across it, bearing in it, as in a mirror, a vision too distinct to be unreal. First, there came virgins robed and holding lamps; then four who carried between them a form wrapped up in a white linen cloth, with a crown of thorns upon the head; after them the youthful acolyte Tarcisius bearing a censer steaming with perfumed smoke; and, after others of the clergy, the venerable Pontiff himself, attended by Reparatus, and another deacon. Diogenes and his sons, with sorrowful countenances, and many others, among whom he could distinguish Sebastian, closed the procession. As many bore lamps or tapers, the figures seemed to move in an unchanging atmosphere of mildest light.

And as they passed before him, they chanted the next verse of the psalm:

"Quoniam Tu Domine singulariter in spe constituisti me."†

"*That*," he exclaimed, rousing himself up, "*that* is for me."

With this thought he had sprung upon his knees; and by an instinct of grace words which he had before heard came back to him like an echo; words suited to the moment; words which he felt that he *must* speak. He crept forward, faint and feeble, turned along the gallery through which the funeral procession was passing, and followed it, unobserved, at a distance. It entered a chamber and lighted it up, so that a pict-

---

* "In peace, in the selfsame, I will sleep and I will rest." *Ps.* iv. 9.
† For Thou, O Lord, singularly hast placed me in hope. *Ps.* v. 10.

The Marriage Feast.

ure of the Good Shepherd looked brightly down on him. But he would not pass the threshold, where he stood striking his breast and praying for mercy.

The body had been laid upon the ground, and other psalms and hymns were sung, and prayers recited, all in that cheerful tone and joyous mood of hopefulness, with which the Church has always treated of death. At length it was placed in the tomb prepared for it, under an arch. While this was being done, Torquatus drew nigh to one of the spectators, and whispered to him the question:

"Whose funeral is this?"

"It is the *deposition*," he answered, "of the blessed Cæcilia, a blind virgin, who this morning fell into the hands of the soldiers, in this cemetery, and whose soul God took to Himself."

"Then I am her murderer," he exclaimed, with a hollow moan; and staggering forward to the holy bishop's feet, fell prostrate before him. It was some time before his feelings could find vent in words; when these came, they were the ones he had resolved to utter:

"Father, I have sinned before heaven, and against Thee, and I am not worthy to be called Thy child."

The Pontiff raised him up kindly, and pressed him to his bosom, saying, "Welcome back, my son, whoever thou art, to thy Father's house. But thou art weak and faint, and needest rest."

Some refreshment was immediately procured. But Torquatus would not rest till he had publicly avowed the whole of his guilt, including the day's crimes; for it was still the evening of the same day. All rejoiced at the prodigal's return, at the lost sheep's recovery. Agnes looked up to heaven from her last affectionate glance on the blind virgin's shroud, and thought that she could almost see her seated at the feet of her Spouse, smiling, with her eyes wide open, as she cast down a handful of flowers on the head of the penitent, the first-fruits of her intercession in heaven.

Diogenes and his sons took charge of him. An humble lodging was procured for him, in a Christian cottage near, that he might not be within the reach of temptation, or of vengeance, and he was enrolled in the class of penitents, where years of expiation, shortened by the intercession of confessors—that is, future martyrs—would prepare him for full re-admission to the privileges he had forfeited.*

* The penitentiary system of the early Church will be better described in any volume that embodies the antiquity of the second period of ecclesiastical history, that of *The Church of the Basilicas*. It is well known, especially from the writings of St. Cyprian, that those who proved weak in persecution, and were subjected to public penance, obtained a shortening of its term,—that is, an indulgence,—through the intercession of confessors, or of persons imprisoned for the faith.

Jesus cures the Blind Man, from a picture in the Cemetery of St. Domitilla.

CHAPTER XIX.

TWOFOLD REVENGE.

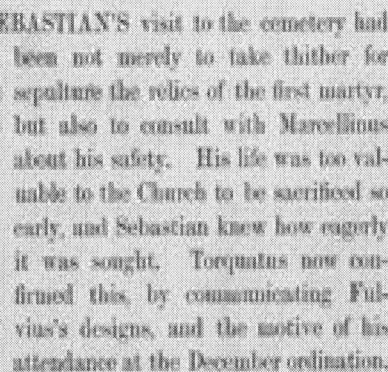
SEBASTIAN'S visit to the cemetery had been not merely to take thither for sepulture the relics of the first martyr, but also to consult with Marcellinus about his safety. His life was too valuable to the Church to be sacrificed so early, and Sebastian knew how eagerly it was sought. Torquatus now confirmed this, by communicating Fulvius's designs, and the motive of his attendance at the December ordination. The usual papal residence was no longer safe; and a bold idea had been adopted by the courageous soldier,—the "Protector of the Christians," as his acts tell us he had been authoritatively called. It was to lodge the Pontiff where no one could suspect him to be, and where no search would be dreamt of, in the very palace of the Cæsars.* Efficiently disguised, the holy Bishop left the cemetery, and, escorted by Sebastian and Quadratus, was safely housed in the apartments of Irene, a Christian lady of rank, who lived in a remote part of the Palatine, in which her husband held a household office.

Early next morning Sebastian was with Pancratius. "My dear boy," he said, "you must leave Rome instantly, and go

* This is related in the Acts just referred to.

into Campania. I have horses ready for you and Quadratus; and there is no time to be lost."

"And why, Sebastian?" replied the youth, with sorrowful face and tearful eye. "Have I done something wrong, or are you doubtful of my fortitude?"

"Neither, I assure you. But you have promised to be guided by me in all things, and I never considered your obedience more necessary than now."

"Tell me why, good Sebastian, I pray."

"It must be a secret as yet."

"What, *another* secret?"

"Call it the same, to be revealed at the same time. But I can tell you what I want you to do, and that I think will satisfy you. Corvinus has got orders to seize on Chromatius and all his community, yet young in the faith, as the wretched example of Torquatus has shown us; and, what is worse, to put your old master Cassianus, at Fundi, to a cruel death. I want you to hasten before his messenger (perhaps he may go himself), and put them on their guard."

Pancratius looked up brightly again; he saw that Sebastian trusted him. "Your wish is enough reason for me," said he, smiling; "but I would go the world's end to save my good Cassianus, or any other fellow-Christians."

He was soon ready, took an affectionate leave of his mother; and before Rome had fully shaken off sleep, he and Quadratus, each with well-furnished saddle-bags on their powerful steeds, were trotting across the campagna of Rome, to reach the less-frequented, and safer, track of the Latin way.

Corvinus having resolved to keep the hostile expedition in his own hands, as honorable, lucrative, and pleasant, it was delayed a couple of days, both that he might feel more comfortable about his shoulders, and that he might make proper preparations. He had a chariot hired, and engaged a body of

Numidian runners, who could keep up with a carriage at full speed. But he was thus two days behind our Christians, though he, of course, travelled by the shorter and more beaten Appian road.

When Pancratius arrived at the Villa of Statues, he found the little community already excited, by the rumors, which had reached it, of the edict's publication. He was welcomed most warmly by all; and Sebastian's letter of advice was received with deep respect. Prayer and deliberation succeeded its perusal, and various resolutions were taken. Marcus and Marcellianus, with their father Tranquillinus, had already gone to Rome for the ordination. Nicostratus, Zoë, and others followed them now. Chromatius, who was not destined for the crown of martyrdom, though commemorated, by the Church, with his son, on the 11th of August, found shelter for a time in Fabiola's villa, for which letters had been procured from its mistress, without her knowing the reason why; for he wished to remain in the neighborhood a little while longer. In fine, the villa *ad Statuos* was left in charge of a few faithful servants, fully to be depended upon.

When the two messengers had given themselves and their horses a good rest, they travelled, by the same road as Torquatus had lately trodden, to Fundi, where they put up at an obscure inn out of the town, on the Roman road. Pancratius soon found out his old master, who embraced him most affectionately. He told him his errand, and entreated him to fly, or at least conceal himself.

"No," said the good man, "it must not be. I am already old, and I am weary of my unprofitable profession. I and my servant are the only two Christians in the town. The best families have, indeed, sent their children to my school, because they knew it would be kept as moral as paganism will permit; but I have not a friend among my scholars, by reason of this very strictness. And they want even the natural retirement of Roman heathens. They are rude provincials; and I believe there are some among the elder ones who would not scruple to take my life, if they could do so with impunity."

"What a wretched existence indeed, Cassianus, you must be leading! Have you made no impression on them?"

"Little or none, dear Pancratius. And how can I, while I am obliged to make them read those dangerous books, full of fables, which Roman and Greek literature contain? No, I have done little by my words; perhaps my death may do more for them."

Pancratius found all expostulation vain, and would have almost joined him in his resolution to die; only he had promised Sebastian not to expose his life during the journey. He, however, determined to remain about the town till he saw the end.

Corvinus arrived with his men at the villa of Chromatius; and early in the morning rushed suddenly through the gates, and to the house. He found it empty. He searched it through and through, but discovered neither a person, a book, nor a symbol of Christianity. He was confounded and annoyed. He looked about; and having found a servant working in the garden, asked him where his master was.

"Master no tell slave where he go," was the reply, in a latinity corresponding to such a rude phraseology.

"You are trifling with me. Which way did he and his companions go?"

"Through yonder gate."

"And then?"

"Look that way," answered the servant. "You see gate? very well; you see no more. Me work here, me see gate, me see no more."

"When did they go? at least you can answer that."

"After the two come from Rome."

"What two? Always two, it seems."

"One good youth, very handsome, sing so sweet. The other very big, very strong, oh, very. See that young tree pulled up by the roots? He do that as easy as me pull my spade out of the ground."

"The very two," exclaimed Corvinus, thoroughly enraged. "Again that dastardly boy has marred my plans and destroyed my hopes. He shall suffer well for it."

As soon as he was a little rested, he resumed his journey, and determined to vent all his fury on his old master; unless, indeed, he whom he considered his evil genius should have been there before him. He was engaged during his journey, in plotting vengeance upon master and fellow-student; and he was delighted to find, that one at least was at Fundi, when he arrived. He showed the governor his order for the arrest and punishment of Cassianus, as a most dangerous Christian; but that officer, a humane man, remarked that the commission superseded ordinary jurisdiction in the matter, and gave Corvinus full power to act. He offered him the assistance of an executioner, and other requisites; but they were declined. Corvinus had brought an abundant supply of strength and cruelty, in his own body-guard. He took, however, a public officer with him.

He proceeded to the school-house when filled with scholars; shut the doors, and reproached Cassianus, who advanced with open hand and countenance to greet him, as a conspirator against the state and a perfidious Christian. A shout arose from the boyish mob; and by its tone, and by the look which he cast around, Corvinus learnt there were many present like himself—young bears' cubs, with full-grown hyenas' hearts within them.

"Boys!" he shouted out, "do you love your master Cassianus? He was once mine too, and I owe him many a grudge."

A yell of execration broke out from the benches.

"Then I have good news for you; here is permission from the divine emperor Maximian for you to do what you like to him."

A shower of books, writing tablets, and other school missiles, was directed against the master, who stood unmoved, with his arms folded, before his persecutor. Then came a rush from all sides, with menacing attitudes of a brutal onslaught.

"Stop, stop," cried out Corvinus, "we must go more systematically to work than this."

He had reverted in thought to the recollection of his own sweet school-boy days; that time which most look back on from hearts teeming with softer feelings than the contemplation of present things can suggest. He indulged in the reminiscence of that early season in which others find but the picture of unselfish, joyous, happy hours; and he sought in the recollection what would most have gratified him then, that he might bestow it as a boon on the hopeful youths around him. But he could think of nothing that would have been such a treat to him, as to pay back to his master every stroke of correction, and write in blood upon him every word of reproach that he had received. Delightful thought, now to be fulfilled!

It is far from our intention to harrow the feelings of our gentle readers by descriptions of the cruel and fiendish torments inflicted by the heathen persecutors on our Christian forefathers. Few are more horrible, yet few better authenticated, than the torture practised on the martyr Cassianus. Placed, bound, in the midst of his ferocious young tigers, he was left to be the lingering victim of their feeble cruelty. Some, as the Christian poet Prudentius tells us, cut their tasks upon him with the steel points used in engraving writing on wax-covered tablets; others exercised the ingenuity of a precocious brutality, by inflicting every possible torment on his lacerated body. Loss of blood, and acute pain, at length exhausted him, and he fell on the floor without power to rise. A shout of exultation followed, new insults were inflicted, and the troop of youthful demons broke loose, to tell the story of their sport at their respective homes. To give Christians decent burial never entered into the minds of their persecutors; and Corvinus, who had glutted his eyes with the spectacle of his vengeance, and had urged on the first efforts at cruelty of his ready instruments, left the expiring man where he lay, to die unnoticed. His faithful servant, however, raised him up, and laid him on his bed, and sent a token, as he had preconcerted, to Pancratius, who was soon at his side, while his companion looked after preparations for their departure. The youth was horrified at what he beheld, and at the recital of his old master's exquisite torture, as he was edified by the account of his patience. For not a word of reproach had escaped him, and prayer alone had occupied his thoughts and tongue.

Cassianus recognized his dear pupil, smiled upon him, pressed his hand in his own, but could not speak. After lingering till morning he placidly expired. The last rites of Christian sepulture were modestly paid to him on the spot, for the house was his; and Pancratius hurried from the scene, with a heavy heart and a no slight rising of its indignation, against the heartless savage who had devised and witnessed, without remorse, such a tragedy.

He was mistaken, however. No sooner was his revenge fulfilled than Corvinus felt all the disgrace and shame of what he had done; he feared it should be known to his father, who had always esteemed Cassianus; he feared the anger of the parents, whose children he had that day effectually demoralized, and fleshed to little less than parricide. He ordered his horses to be harnessed, but was told they must have some more hours' rest. This increased his displeasure;

remorse tormented him, and he sat down to drink, and so drown care and pass time. At length he started on his journey, and after baiting for an hour or two, pushed on through the night. The road was heavy from continued rain, and ran along the side of the great canal which drains the Pontine marshes, and between two rows of trees.

Corvinus had drunk again at his halt, and was heated with wine, vexation, and remorse. The dragging pace of his jaded steeds provoked him, and he kept lashing them furiously on. While they were thus excited they heard the tramp of horses coming fast on behind, and dashed forward at an uncontrollable speed. The attendants were soon left at a distance, and the frightened horses passed between the trees on to the narrow path by the canal, and galloped forward, rocking the chariot from side to side at a reckless rate. The horsemen behind hearing the violent rush of hoofs and wheels, and the shout of the followers, clapped spurs to their horses, and pushed gallantly forward. They had passed the runners some way when they heard a crash and a plunge. The wheel had struck the trunk of a tree, the chariot had turned over, and its half-drunken driver had been tossed head over heels into the water. In a moment Pancratius was off his horse and by the side of the canal, together with his companion.

By the faint light of the rising moon, and by the sound of his voice, the youth recognized Corvinus struggling in the muddy stream. The side was not deep, but the high clayey bank was wet and slimy, and every time he attempted to climb it his foot slipped, and he fell back into the deep water in the middle. He was, in fact, already becoming benumbed and exhausted by his wintry bath.

"It would serve him right to leave him there," muttered the rough centurion.

"Hush, Quadratus! how can you say so? give me hold of your hand. So!" said the youth, leaning over the bank and seizing his enemy by his arm, just as he was relaxing his hold on a withered shrub, and falling back fainting into the stream. It would have been his last plunge. They pulled him out and laid him on the road, a pitiable figure for his greatest foe. They chafed his temples and hands, and he had begun to revive when his attendants came up. To their care they consigned him, together with his purse, which had fallen from his belt as they drew him from the canal. But Pancratius took possession of his own pen-knife, which dropped out with it, and which Corvinus carried about him, as evidence to convict him of having cut down the edict. The servants pretended to Corvinus, when he had regained consciousness, that they had drawn him out of the water, but that his purse must have been lost in it, and lay still buried in the deep mud. They bore him to a neighboring cottage, while the carriage was being repaired, and had a good carouse with his money while he slept.

Two acts of revenge had been thus accomplished in one day,—the pagan and the Christian.

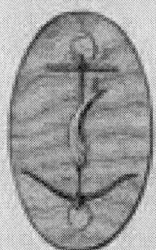

The Anchor and Fish, emblems of Christianity, found in the Catacombs.

CHAPTER XX.

THE PUBLIC WORKS.

IF, before the edict, the Thermæ of Dioclesian were being erected by the labor and sweat of Christian prisoners, it will not appear surprising, that their number and their sufferings should have greatly increased, with the growing intensity of a most savage persecution. That emperor himself was expected for the inauguration of his favorite building, and hands were doubled on the work to expedite its completion. Chains of supposed culprits arrived each day from the port of Luna, from Sardinia, and even from the Crimea, or Chersonesus, where they had been engaged in quarries or mines; and were put to labor in the harder departments of the building art. To transport materials, to saw and cut stone and marble, to mix the mortar, and to build up the walls, were the duties allotted to the religious culprits, many of whom were men little accustomed to such menial toil. The only recompense which they received for their labor, was that of the mules and oxen which shared their occupation. Little better, if better, than a stable to sleep in, food sufficient in quantity to keep up their strength, clothing enough to guard them from the inclemency of the season, this was all they had to expect. Fetters on their ankles, heavy chains to prevent their escape, increased their sufferings; and task-masters, acceptable in proportion as they were unreasonable, watched every gang with lash or stick in hand, ever ready to add pain to toil, whether it were to vent their own wanton cruelty upon unresisting objects, or to please their crueller masters.

But the Christians of Rome took peculiar care of these blessed confessors, who were particularly venerated by them. Their deacons visited them, by bribing their guards; and young men would boldly venture among them, and distribute more nourishing food, or warmer clothing to them, or give them the means of conciliating their keepers, so as to obtain better treatment at their hands. They would then also recommend themselves to their prayers, as they kissed the chains and the bruises, which these holy confessors bore for Christ.

This assemblage of men, convicted of serving faithfully their divine Master, was useful for another purpose. Like the stew in which the luxurious Lucullus kept his lampreys ready fattened for a banquet; like the cages in which rare birds, the pens in which well-fed cattle, were preserved for the sacrifice, or the feast of an imperial anniversary; like the dens near the amphitheatre, in which ferocious beasts were fed for exhibition at the public games; just so were the public works the preserves, from which at any time could be drawn the materials for a sanguinary hecatomb, or a gratification of the popular appetite for cruel spectacles, on any occasion of festivity; public stores of food for those fierce animals, whenever the Roman people wished to share in their savage propensities.

Such an occasion was now approaching. The persecution had lingered. No person of note had been yet captured; the failures of the first day had not been fully repaired; and something more wholesale was expected. The people demanded more sport; and an approaching imperial birthday justified their gratification. The wild beasts, which Sebastian and Pancratius had heard, yet roared for their lawful prey. "*Christianos ad leones*" might seem to have been interpreted by them, as meaning "that the Christians of right belonged to them."

One afternoon, towards the end of December, Corvinus proceeded to the Baths of Diocletian, accompanied by Catulus, who had an eye for proper combatants in the amphitheatre, such as a good dealer would have for cattle at a fair. He called for Rabirius, the superintendent of the convict department, and said to him:

"Rabirius, I am come by order of the emperor, to select a sufficient number of the wicked Christians under your charge, for the honor of fighting in the amphitheatre, on occasion of the coming festival."

"Really," answered the officer, "I have none to spare. I am obliged to finish the work in a given time, and I cannot do so, if I am left short of hands."

"I cannot help that; others will be got to replace those that are taken from you. You must walk Catulus and myself through your works, and let us choose those that will suit us."

Rabirius, grumbling at this unreasonable demand, submitted nevertheless to it, and took them into a vast area, just vaulted over. It was entered by a circular vestibule lighted from above, like the Pantheon. This led into one of the shorter arms of a cruciform hall of noble dimensions, into which opened a number of lesser, though still handsome, chambers. At each angle of the hall, where the arms intersected one another, a huge granite pillar of one block had to be erected. Two were already in their places, one was girt with ropes delivered round capstans, ready to be raised on the morrow. A number of men were actively employed in making final preparations. Catulus nudged Corvinus, and pointed, with his thumb, to two fine youths, who, stripped slave-fashion to their waists, were specimens of manly athletic forms.

"I must have those two, Rabirius," said the willing purveyor to wild beasts; "they will do charmingly. I am sure they are Christians, they work so cheerfully."

"I cannot possibly spare them at present. They are worth six men, or a pair of horses, at least, to me. Wait till the heavy work is over, and then they are at your service."

"What are their names, that I may take a note of them? And mind, keep them up in good condition."

"They are called Largus and Smaragdus; they are young men of excellent family, but work like plebeians, and will go with you nothing loth."

"They shall have their wish," said Corvinus, with great glee. And so they had later.

As they went through the works, however, they picked out a number of captives, for many of whom Rabirius made resistance, but generally in vain. At length they came near one of those chambers which flanked the eastern side of the longer arm of the hall. In one of them they saw a number of convicts (if we must use the term) resting after their labor. The centre of the group was an old man, most venerable in appearance, with a long white beard streaming on his breast, mild in aspect, gentle in word, cheerful in his feeble action. It was the confessor Saturninus, now in his eightieth year, yet loaded with two heavy chains. At each side were the more youthful laborers, Cyriacus and Sisinnius, of whom it is recorded, that, in addition to their own task-work, one on each side, they bore up his bonds. Indeed, we are told that their particular delight was, over and above their own assigned portion of toil, to help their weaker brethren, and perform their work for them.* But their time was not yet come; for both of them, before they received their crowns, were ordained deacons in the next pontificate.

Several other captives lay on the ground, about the old man's feet, as he, seated on a block of marble, was talking to them, with a sweet gravity, which riveted their attention, and seemed to make them forget their sufferings. What was he saying to them? Was he requiting Cyriacus for his extraordinary charity, by telling him that, in commemoration of it, a portion of the immense pile which they were toiling to raise, would be dedicated to God, under his invocation, become a title, and close its line of titulars by an illustrious name?† Or was he recounting another more glorious vision, how this smaller oratory was to be superseded and absorbed by a glorious temple in honor of the Queen of Angels, which should comprise the entire of that superb hall, with its vestibule, under the directing skill of the mightiest artistic genius that the world should ever see?‡ What more consoling thought could have been vouchsafed to those poor oppressed captives, than that they were not so much erecting baths for the luxury of a heathen people, or the prodigality of a wicked emperor, as in truth building up one of the stateliest churches in which the true God is worshipped, and the Virgin Mother, who bore Him incarnate, is affectionately honored?

From a distance Corvinus saw the group; and passing, asked the superintendent the names of those who composed it. He enumerated them readily; then added, "You may as well

---

* See Piazza, on the church of *Santa Maria degli Angeli*, in his work on the Stations of Rome.

† The last cardinal of the extinct title of St. Cyriacus's, formed out of a part of these Baths, was Cardinal Bembo.

‡ Michelangelo. The noble and beautiful church of Sta. Maria degli Angeli was made by him out of the central hall and circular vestibule, described in the text. The floor was afterwards raised, and thus the pillars were shortened, and the height of the building diminished by several feet.

take that old man, if you like; for he is not worth his keep, as far as work goes."

"Thank you," replied Corvinus, "a pretty figure he would cut in the amphitheatre. The people are not to be put off with decrepit old creatures, whom a single stroke of a bear's or tiger's paw kills outright. They like to see young blood flowing, and plenty of life struggling against wounds and blows, before death comes to decide the contest. But there is one there whom you have not named. His face is turned from us; he has not the prisoner's garb, nor any kind of fetter. Who can it be?"

"I do not know his name," answered Rabirius; "but he is a fine youth, who spends much of his time among the convicts, relieves them, and even at times helps them in their work. He pays, of course, well for being allowed all this; so it is not our business to ask questions."

"But it is mine, though," said Corvinus, sharply; and he advanced for this purpose. The voice caught the stranger's ear, and he turned round to look.

Corvinus sprung upon him with the eye and action of a wild beast, seized him, and called out, with exultation, "Fetter him instantly. This time at least, Pancratius, thou shalt not escape."

A Monogram of Christ, found in the Catacombs.

CHAPTER XXI.

THE PRISON.

IF a modern Christian wishes really to know what his forefathers underwent for the faith, during three centuries of persecution, we would not have him content himself with visiting the catacombs, as we have tried to make him do, and thus learning what sort of life they were compelled to lead; but we would advise him to peruse those imperishable records, the *Acts of the Martyrs*, which will show him how they were made to die. We know of no writings so moving, so tender, so consoling, and so ministering of strength to faith and to hope, after God's inspired words, as these venerable monuments. And if our reader, so advised, have not leisure sufficient to read much upon this subject, we would limit him willingly to one specimen, the genuine Acts of SS. Perpetua and Felicitas. It is true that they will be best read by the scholar in their plain African latinity; but we trust that some one will soon give us a worthy English version of these, and some other similar, early Christian documents. The ones which we have singled out are the same as were known to St. Augustine, and cannot be read by any one without emotion. If the reader would compare the morbid sensibility, and the overstrained excitement, endeavored to be produced by a modern French writer, in the imaginary journal of a culprit condemned to death, down to the immediate approach of execution, with the unaffected pathos, and charming truthfulness, which pervades the corresponding narrative of Vivia Perpetua, a delicate lady of twenty-one years of age, he would not hesitate in concluding, how much more natural, graceful, and interesting are the simple recitals of Christianity, than the boldest fictions of romance. And when our minds are sad, or the petty persecutions of our times incline our feeble hearts to murmur, we cannot do better than turn to that really golden, because truthful legend, or to the history of the noble martyrs of Vienne, or Lyons, or to the many similar, still extant records, to nerve our courage, by the contemplation of what children and women, catechumens and slaves, suffered, unmurmuring, for Christ.

But we are wandering from our narrative. Pancratius, with some twenty more, fettered, and chained together, were led through the streets to prison. As they were thus dragged along, staggering and stumbling helplessly, they were unmercifully struck by the guards who conducted them; and any persons near enough to reach them, dealt them blows and kicks without remorse. Those further off pelted them with stones or offal, and assailed them with insulting ribaldry.* They reached the Mamertine prison at last, and were thrust down into it, and found there already other victims, of both sexes, awaiting their time of sacrifice. The youth had just time, while he was being handcuffed, to request one of the captors to inform his mother and Sebastian of what had happened, and he slipped his purse into his hand.

A prison in ancient Rome was not the place to which a poor man might court committal, hoping there to enjoy better fare and lodging than he did at home. Two or three of these dungeons, for they are nothing better, still remain; and a brief description of the one which we have mentioned will give our

* See the account of St. Pothinus, *Ruinart*, i. p. 148.

readers some idea of what confessorship cost, independent of martyrdom.

The Mamertine prison is composed of two square subterranean chambers, one below the other, with only one round aperture in the centre of each vault, through which alone light, air, food, furniture, and men could pass. When the upper story was full, we may imagine how much of the two first could reach the lower. No other means of ventilation,

The Mamertine Prison.

drainage, or access could exist. The walls, of large stone blocks, had, or rather have, rings fastened into them for securing the prisoners; but many used to be laid on the floor, with their feet fastened in the stocks; and the ingenious cruelty of the persecutors often increased the discomfort of the damp stone floor, by strewing with broken potsherds this only bed allowed to the mangled limbs and welted backs of the tortured Christians. Hence we have in Africa a company of martyrs, headed by SS. Saturninus and Dativus, who all perished through their sufferings in prison. And the acts of the

Lyonese martyrs inform us that many new-comers expired in the jail, killed by severities, before their bodies had endured any torments; while, on the contrary, some who returned to it so cruelly tortured that their recovery appeared hopeless, without any medical or other assistance, there regained their health.* At the same time the Christians bought access to these abodes of pain, but not of sorrow, and furnished whatever could, under such circumstances, relieve the sufferings and increase the comforts, temporal and spiritual, of these most cherished and venerated of their brethren.

Roman justice required at least the outward forms of trial, and hence the Christian captives were led from their dungeons before the tribunal; where they were subjected to an interrogatory, of which most precious examples have been preserved in the proconsular Acts of Martyrs, just as they were entered by the secretary or registrar of the court.

When the Bishop of Lyons, Pothinus, now in his ninetieth year, was asked, "Who is the God of the Christians?" he replied, with simple dignity, "If thou shalt be worthy, thou shalt know."† Sometimes the judge would enter into a discussion with his prisoner, and necessarily get the worst of it; though the latter would seldom go further with him than simply reiterating his plain profession of the Christian faith. Often, as in the case of one Ptolomæus, beautifully recited by St. Justin, and in that of St. Perpetua, he was content to ask the simple question, Art thou a Christian? and upon an affirmative reply, proceeded to pronounce capital sentence.

Pancratius and his companion stood before the judge; for it wanted only three days to the *munus*, or games, at which they were to "fight with wild beasts."

"What art thou?" he asked of one.

"I am a Christian, by the help of God," was the rejoinder.

---

* *Ruinart*, p. 145.
† "Si dignus fueris, cognosces." *Ib.*

"And who art thou?" said the prefect to Rusticus.

"I am, indeed, a slave of Cæsar's," answered the prisoner; "but becoming a Christian, I have been freed by Christ Himself; and by His grace and mercy I have been made partaker of the same hope as those whom you see."

Then turning to a holy priest, Lucianus, venerable for his years and his virtues, the judge thus addressed him: "Come, be obedient to the gods themselves, and to the imperial edicts."

"No one," answered the old man, "can be reprehended or condemned who obeys the precepts of Jesus Christ our Saviour."

"What sort of learning and studies dost thou pursue?"

"I have endeavored to master every science, and have tried every variety of learning. But finally I adhered to the doctrines of Christianity, although they do not please those who follow the wanderings of false opinions."

"Wretch! dost thou find delight in *that* learning?"

"The greatest; because I follow the Christians in right doctrine."

"And what is that doctrine?"

"The right doctrine, which we Christians piously hold, is to believe in one God, the Maker and Creator of all things visible and invisible; and to confess the Lord Jesus Christ the Son of God, anciently foretold by the prophets, who will come to judge mankind, and is the preacher and master of salvation, to those who will learn well under Him. I indeed, as a mere man, am too weak and insignificant to be able to utter any thing great *of His infinite Deity*: this office belongs to the prophets."*

"Thou art, methinks, a master of error to others, and deservest to be more severely punished than the rest. Let this Lucianus be kept in the nerve (stocks) with his feet

* Acts of St. Justin. *Ruinart*, p. 123.

stretched to the fifth hole."—And you two women, what are your names and condition?"

"I am a Christian, who have no spouse but Christ. My name is Secunda," replied the one.

"And I am a widow, named Rufina, professing the same saving faith," continued the other.

At length, after having put similar questions, and receiving similar answers from all the others, except from one wretched man, who, to the grief of the rest, wavered and agreed to offer sacrifice, the prefect turned to Pancratius, and thus addressed him: "And now, insolent youth, who hadst the audacity to tear down the edict of the divine emperors, even for thee there shall be mercy, if yet thou wilt sacrifice to the gods. Show thus at once thy piety and thy wisdom, for thou art yet but a stripling."

Pancratius signed himself with the sign of the saving cross, and calmly replied, "I am the servant of Christ. Him I acknowledge by my mouth, hold firm in my heart, *incessantly adore*. This youth which you behold in me has the wisdom of grey hairs if it worship but one God. But your gods, with those who adore them, are destined to eternal destruction." †

"Strike him on the mouth for his blasphemy, and beat him with rods," exclaimed the angry judge.

"I thank thee," replied meekly the noble youth, "that thus I suffer some of the same punishment as was inflicted on my Lord." ‡

The prefect then pronounced sentence in the usual form. "Lucianus, Pancratius, Rusticus, and others, and the women Secunda and Rufina, who have all owned themselves Christians, and refuse to obey the sacred emperor, or worship the

---

* This is mentioned as the extreme possible extension.
† Ib. p. 56, Acts of St. Felicitas and her sons.
‡ p. 236, Acts of St. Perpetua, &c.

gods of Rome, we order to be exposed to wild beasts, in the Flavian amphitheatre."

The mob howled with delight and hatred, and accompanied the confessors back to their prison with this rough music; but they were gradually overawed by the dignity of their gait, and the shining calmness of their countenances. Some men asserted that they must have perfumed themselves, for they could perceive a fragrant atmosphere surrounding their persons.*

* pp. 219 and 146, Acts of Lyonese Martyrs.

The Blessed Virgin, from a fresco found in the Cemetery of St. Agnes.

CHAPTER XXII.

THE VIATICUM.

A TRUE contrast to the fury and discord without, was the scene within the prison. Peace, serenity, cheerfulness, and joy reigned there; and the rough stone walls and vaults re-echoed to the chant of psalmody, in which Pancratius was precentor, and in which depth called out to depth; for the prisoners in the lower dungeon responded to those above, and kept up the alternation of verses, in those psalms which the circumstances naturally suggested.

The eve of "fighting with," that is being torn to pieces by wild beasts, was always a day of greater liberty. The friends of the intended victims were admitted to see them; and the Christians boldly took full advantage of the permission to flock to the prison, and commend themselves to the prayers of the blessed confessors of Christ. At evening they were led forth to enjoy what was called the free supper, that is, an abundant, and even luxurious, public feast. The table was surrounded by pagans, curious to watch the conduct and looks of the morrow's combatants. But they could discern neither the bravado and boisterousness, nor the dejection and bitterness of ordinary culprits. To the guests it was truly an *agape*, or love-feast; for they supped with calm joyfulness amidst cheerful conversation. Pancratius, however, once or twice reproved the unfeeling curiosity, and rude remarks of the crowd, saying, "To-morrow is not sufficient for you, because you love to look upon the objects of your future hatred. To-day you are our friends; to-morrow our foes. But mark well our countenances, that you may know them again in the day of judgment." Many retired at this rebuke, and not a few were led by it to conversion.*

But while the persecutors thus prepared a feast for the bodies of their victims, the Church, their mother, had been preparing a much more dainty banquet for the souls of her children. They had been constantly attended on by the deacons, particularly Reparatus, who would gladly have joined their company. But his duty forbade this at present. After, therefore, having provided as well as possible for their temporal wants, he had arranged with the pious priest Dionysius, who still dwelt in the house of Agnes, to send, towards evening, sufficient portions of the Bread of Life, to feed, early in the morning of their battle, the champions of Christ. Although the deacons bore the consecrated elements from the principal church to others, where they were only distributed by the titulars, the office of conveying them to the martyrs in prison, and even to the dying, was committed to inferior ministers. On this day, that the hostile passions of heathen Rome were unusually excited by the coming slaughter of so many Christian victims, it was a work of more than common danger to discharge this duty. For the revelations of Torquatus had made it known that Fulvius had carefully noted all the ministers of the sanctuary, and given a description of them to his numerous active spies. Hence they could scarcely venture out by day, unless thoroughly disguised.

The sacred Bread was prepared, and the priest turned round from the altar on which it was placed, to see who would be its safest bearer. Before any other could step for-

* Acts of Llorens Martyrs, p. 119.

ward, the young acolyte Tarcisius knelt at his feet. With his hands extended before him, ready to receive the sacred deposit, with a countenance beautiful in its lovely innocence as an angel's, he seemed to entreat for preference, and even to claim it.

"Thou art too young, my child," said the kind priest, filled with admiration of the picture before him.

"My youth, holy father, will be my best protection. Oh! do not refuse me this great honor." The tears stood in the boy's eyes, and his cheeks glowed with a modest emotion as he spoke these words. He stretched forth his hands eagerly, and his entreaty was so full of fervor and courage that the plea was irresistible. The priest took the Divine Mysteries wrapped up carefully in a linen cloth, then in an outer covering, and put them on his palms, saying:

"Remember, Tarcisius, what a treasure is intrusted to thy feeble care. Avoid public places as thou goest along; and remember that holy things must not be delivered to dogs, nor pearls be cast before swine. Thou wilt keep safely God's sacred gifts?"

"I will die rather than betray them," answered the holy youth, as he folded the heavenly trust in the bosom of his tunic, and with cheerful reverence started on his journey. There was a gravity beyond the usual expression of his years stamped upon his countenance, as he tripped lightly along the streets, avoiding equally the more public, and the too low, thoroughfares.

As he was approaching the door of a large mansion, its mistress, a rich lady without children, saw him coming, and was struck with his beauty and sweetness, as, with arms folded on his breast, he was hastening on. "Stay, one moment, dear child," she said, putting herself in his way; "tell me thy name, and where do thy parents live?"

"I am Tarcisius, an orphan boy," he replied, looking up,

smilingly; "and I have no home, save one which it might be displeasing to thee to hear."

"Then come into my house and rest; I wish to speak to thee. Oh, that I had a child like thee!"

"Not now, noble lady, not now. I have intrusted to me a most solemn and sacred duty, and I must not tarry a moment in its performance."

"Then promise to come to me to-morrow; this is my house."

"If I am alive, I will," answered the boy with a kindled look, which made him appear to her as a messenger from a higher sphere. She watched him a long time, and after some deliberation determined to follow him. Soon, however, she heard a tumult with horrid cries, which made her pause on her way, until they had ceased, when she went on again.

In the meantime, Tarcisius, with his thoughts fixed on better things than her inheritance, hastened on, and shortly came into an open space, where boys, just escaped from school, were beginning to play.

"We just want one to make up the game; where shall we get him?" said their leader.

"Capital!" exclaimed another, "here comes Tarcisius, whom I have not seen for an age. He used to be an excellent hand at all sports. Come, Tarcisius," he added, stopping him by seizing his arm, "whither so fast? take a part in our game, that's a good fellow."

"I can't, Petilius, now; I really can't. I am going on business of great importance."

"But you shall," exclaimed the first speaker, a strong and bullying youth, laying hold of him. "I will have no sulking, when I want any thing done. So come, join us at once."

"I entreat you," said the poor boy feelingly, "do let me go."

"No such thing," replied the other. "What is that you seem to be carrying so carefully in your bosom? A letter, I suppose; well, it will not addle by being for half an hour out of its nest. Give it to me, and I will put it by safe while we play." And he snatched at the sacred deposit in his breast.

"Never, never," answered the child, looking up towards heaven.

"I *will* see it," insisted the other rudely; "I will know what is this wonderful secret." And he commenced pulling him roughly about. A crowd of men from the neighborhood soon got round; and all asked eagerly what was the matter. They saw a boy, who, with folded arms, seemed endowed with a supernatural strength, as he resisted every effort of one much bigger and stronger, to make him reveal what he was bearing. Cuffs, pulls, blows, kicks seemed to have no effect. He bore them all without a murmur, or an attempt to retaliate; but he unflinchingly kept his purpose.

"What is it? what can it be?" one began to ask the other; when Fulvius chanced to pass by, and joined the circle round the combatants. He at once recognized Tarcisius, having seen him at the Ordination; and being asked, as a better-dressed man, the same question, he replied contemptuously, as he turned on his heel, "What is it? Why, only a Christian ass, bearing the mysteries."*

This was enough. Fulvius, while he scorned such unprofitable prey, knew well the effect of his word. Heathen curiosity, to see the mysteries of the Christians revealed, and to insult them, was aroused, and a general demand was made to Tarcisius, to yield up his charge. "Never with life," was his only reply. A heavy blow from a smith's fist nearly stunned him, while the blood flowed from the wound. Another and another followed, till, covered with bruises, but with his arms crossed fast upon his breast, he fell heavily on the ground. The mob closed upon him, and were just seizing him, to tear open his thrice-holy trust, when they felt themselves pushed

* *Asinus portans mysteria*, a Latin proverb.

aside, right and left, by some giant strength. Some went reeling to the further side of the square, others were spun round and round, they knew not how, till they fell where they were, and the rest retired before a tall, athletic officer, who was the author of this overthrow. He had no sooner cleared the ground, than he was on his knees, and with tears in his eyes, raised up the bruised and fainting boy, as tenderly as a mother could have done, and in most gentle tones asked him, "Are you much hurt, Tarcisius?"

"Never mind me, Quadratus," answered he, opening his eyes with a smile; "but I am carrying the divine mysteries; take care of them."

The soldier raised the boy in his arms with tenfold reverence, as if bearing not only the sweet victim of a youthful sacrifice, a martyr's relics, but the very King and Lord of Martyrs, and the divine Victim of eternal salvation. The child's head leaned in confidence on the stout soldier's neck, but his arms and hands never left their watchful custody of the confided gift; and his gallant bearer felt no weight in the hallowed double burden which he carried. No one stopped him, till a lady met him and stared amazedly at him. She drew nearer, and looked closer at what he carried. "Is it possible?" she exclaimed with terror, "is that Tarcisius, whom I met a few moments ago, so fair and lovely? Who can have done this?"

"Madam," replied Quadratus, "they have murdered him because he was a Christian."

The lady looked for an instant on the child's countenance. He opened his eyes upon her, smiled, and expired. From that look came the light of faith: she hastened to be a Christian likewise.

The venerable Dionysius could hardly see for weeping, as he removed the child's hands, and took from his bosom, unviolated, the Body of holies; and he thought he looked more like

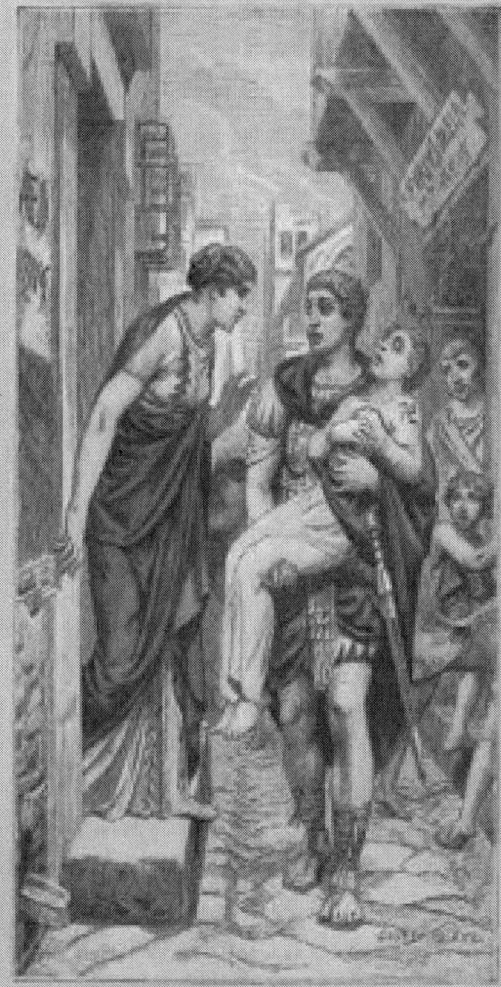

"Is it possible?" she exclaimed with tears, "is that Terentius, whom I met a few moments ago, so fair and lovely!"

an angel now, sleeping the martyr's slumber, than he did when living scarcely an hour before. Quadratus himself bore him to the cemetery of Callistus, where he was buried amidst the admiration of older believers; and later the holy Pope Damasus composed for him an epitaph, which no one can read, without concluding that the belief in the real presence of Our Lord's Body in the Blessed Eucharist was the same then as now:

> "Tarcisium sanctum Christi sacramenta gerentem,
> Cum male sana manus peteret vulgare profanis;
> Ipse animam potius voluit dimittere vacuam
> Prodere quam canibus rabidis coelestia membra."*

He is mentioned in the Roman martyrology, on the 15th of August, as commemorated in the cemetery of Callistus; whence his relics were, in due time, translated to the church of St. Sylvester in Campo, as an old inscription declares.

News of this occurrence did not reach the prisoners till after their feast; and perhaps the alarm that they were to be deprived of the spiritual food to which they looked forward for strength, was the only one that could have overcast, even slightly, the serenity of their souls. At this moment Sebastian entered, and perceived at once that some unpleasant news had arrived, and as quickly divined what it was; for Quadratus had already informed him of all. He cheered up, therefore, the confessors of Christ; assured them that they should not be deprived of their coveted food; then whispered

> * "Christ's secret gifts, by good Tarcisius borne,
> The mob profanely bade him to display;
> He rather gave his own limbs to be torn,
> Than Christ's celestial to mad dogs betray."
>
> Carmen, xviii.

See also Baronius's notes to the *Martyrology*. The words "(Christi) coelestia membra," applied to the Blessed Eucharist, supply one of those casual, but most striking, arguments that result from identity of habitual thought in antiquity, more than from the use of studied or conventional phrases.

a few words to Reparatus the deacon, who flew out immediately with a look of bright intelligence.

Sebastian, being known to the guards, had passed freely in, and out of, the prison daily; and had been indefatigable in his care of its inmates. But now he was come to take his last farewell of his dearest friend, Pancratius, who had longed for this interview. They drew to one side, when the youth began:

"Well, Sebastian, do you remember when we heard the wild beasts roar, from your window, and looked at the many gaping arches of the amphitheatre, as open for the Christian's triumph?"

"Yes, my dear boy; I remember that evening well, and it seemed to me as if your heart anticipated then, the scenes that await you to-morrow."

"It did, in truth. I felt an inward assurance that I should be one of the first to appease the roaring fury of those deputies of human cruelty. But now that the time is come, I can hardly believe myself worthy of so immense an honor. What can I have done, Sebastian, not indeed to deserve it, but to be chosen out as the object of so great a grace?"

"You know, Pancratius, that it is not he who willeth, nor he that runneth, but God who hath mercy, that maketh the election. But tell me rather, how do you now feel about to-morrow's glorious destiny?"

"To tell the truth, it seems to me so magnificent, so far beyond my right to claim, that sometimes it appears more like a vision than a certainty. Does it not sound almost incredible to you, that I who this night am in a cold, dark, and dismal prison, shall be, before another sun has set, listening to the harping of angelic lyres, walking in the procession of white-robed Saints, inhaling the perfume of celestial incense, and drinking from the crystal waters of the stream of life? Is it not too like what one may read or hear about another, but hardly dares to think is to be, in a few hours, real of himself?"

"And nothing more than you have described, Pancratius?"

"Oh, yes, far more; far more than one can name without presumption. That I, a boy just come out of school, who have done nothing for Christ as yet, should be able to say, 'Sometime to-morrow, I shall see Him face to face, and adore Him, and shall receive from Him a palm and a crown, yea, and an affectionate embrace,'—I feel is so like a beautiful hope, that it startles me to think it will soon be *that* no longer. And yet, Sebastian," he continued fervently, seizing both his friend's hands, "it is true; it is true!"

"And more still, Pancratius."

"Yes, Sebastian, more still, and more. To close one's eyes upon the faces of men, and open them in full gaze on the face of God; to shut them upon ten thousand countenances scowling on you with hatred, contempt, and fury, from every step of the amphitheatre, and unclose them instantly upon that one sunlike intelligence, whose splendor would dazzle or scorch, did not its beams surround, and embrace, and welcome us; to dart them at once into the furnace of God's heart, and plunge into its burning ocean of mercy and love without fear of destruction: surely, Sebastian, it sounds like presumption in me to say, that to-morrow—nay, hush! the watchman from the capitol is proclaiming midnight—that to-day, to-day, I shall enjoy all this!"

"Happy Pancratius!" exclaimed the soldier, "you anticipate already by some hours the raptures to come."

"And do you know, dear Sebastian," continued the youth, as if unconscious of the interruption, "it looks to me so good and merciful in God, to grant me such a death. How much more willingly must one at my age face it, when it puts an end to all that is hateful on earth, when it extinguishes but the sight of hideous beasts and sinning men, scarcely less frightful than they, and hushes only the fiend-like yells of both! How much more trying would it be to part with the last tender look of a mother like mine, and shut one's ears to the sweet plaint of her patient voice! True, I shall see her and hear her, for the last time, as we have arranged, to-day before my fight; but I know she will not unnerve me."

A tear had made its way into the affectionate boy's eye; but he suppressed it, and said with a gay tone:

"But, Sebastian, you have not fulfilled your promise,—your double promise to me,—to tell me the secrets you concealed from me. This is your last opportunity; so, come, let me know all."

"Do you remember well what the secrets were?"

"Right well, indeed, for they have much perplexed me. First on that night of the meeting in your apartments, you said there was one motive strong enough to check your ardent desire to die for Christ; and lately you refused to give me your reason for despatching me hastily to Campania, and joined this secret to the other: how, I cannot conceive."

"Yet they form but one. I had promised to watch over your true welfare, Pancratius: it was a duty of friendship and love that I had assumed. I saw your eagerness after martyrdom; I knew the ardent temperament of your youthful heart; I dreaded lest you should commit yourself by some over-daring action which might tarnish, even as lightly as a breath does finely-tempered steel, the purity of your desire, or tip with a passing blight one single leaf of your palm. I determined, therefore, to restrain my own earnest longings, till I had seen you safe through danger. Was this right?"

"Oh, it was too kind of you, dear Sebastian; it was nobly kind. But how is this connected with my journey?"

"If I had not sent you away, you would have been seized for your boldly tearing down the edict, or your rebuke of the judge in his court. You would have been certainly condemned, and

Each one, approaching devoutly, and with tears of gratitude, received from his consecrated hand his share,—that is, the whole of the impaired food.

would have suffered for Christ; but your sentence would have proclaimed a different, and a civil, offence; that of rebellion against the emperors. And moreover, my dear boy, you would have been singled out for a triumph. You would have been pointed at by the very heathens with honor, as a gallant and daring youth; you might have been disturbed, even in your conflict, by a transient cloud of pride; at any rate, you would have been spared that ignominy which forms the distinctive merit and the special glory of dying for simply being a Christian."

"Quite true, Sebastian," said Pancratius with a blush.

"But when I saw you," continued the soldier, "taken in the performance of a generous act of charity towards the confessors of Christ; when I saw you dragged through the streets, chained to a galley-slave, as a common culprit; when I saw you pelted and hooted, like other believers; when I heard sentence pronounced on you in common with the rest, because you are a Christian, and for nothing else, I felt that my task was ended; I would not have raised a finger to save you."

"How like God's love has yours been to me,—so wise, so generous, and so unsparing!" sobbed out Pancratius, as he threw himself on the soldier's neck; then continued: "Promise me one thing more: that this day you will keep near me to the end, and will secure my last legacy to my mother."

"Even if it cost my life, I will not fail. We shall not be parted long, Pancratius."

The deacon now gave notice that all was ready for offering up the holy oblation in the dungeon itself. The two youths looked round, and Pancratius was indeed amazed. The holy priest Lucianus was laid stretched on the floor, with his limbs painfully distended in the *colusto* or stocks, so that he could not rise. Upon his breast Reparatus had spread the three linen cloths requisite for the altar; on them was laid

the unleavened bread, and the mingled chalice, which the
deacon steadied with his hand. The head of the aged priest
was held up as he read the accustomed prayers, and performed the prescribed ceremonies of the oblation and consecration. And then each one, approaching devoutly, and with
tears of gratitude, received from his consecrated hand his
share,—that is, the whole of the Mystical Food.*

Marvellous and beautiful instance of the power of adapta-
tion in God's Church! Fixed as are her laws, her ingenious
love finds means, through their very relaxation, to demonstrate their principles; nay, the very exception presents only
a sublimer application of them. Here was a minister of God,
and a dispenser of His mysteries, who for once was privileged
to be, more than others, like Him whom he represented—at
once the Priest and the Altar. The Church prescribed that
the Holy Sacrifice should be offered only over the relics of
martyrs; here was a martyr, by a singular prerogative, permitted to offer it over his own body. Yet living, he "lay
beneath the feet of God." The bosom still heaved, and the
heart panted under the Divine Mysteries, it is true; but that
was only part of the action of the minister; while self was
already dead, and the sacrifice of life was, in all but act, completed in him. There was only Christ's life within and without the sanctuary of the breast.† Was ever viaticum for martyrs more worthily prepared?

---

* Such a celebration of the Divine Mysteries, by a priest of this name at
Antioch, is recorded in his Acts. (See *Ruinart*, tom. iii. p. 182, note.)

† "I live now, not I, but Christ liveth in me." Gal. ii. 20.

CHAPTER XXIII.

THE FIGHT.

THE morning broke light and frosty; and the sun, glittering on the gilded ornaments of the temples and other public buildings, seemed to array them in holiday splendor. And the people, too, soon came forth into the streets in their gayest attire, decked out with unusual richness. The various streams converge towards the Flavian amphitheatre, now better known by the name of the Coliseum. Each one directs his steps to the arch indicated by the number of his ticket, and thus the huge monster keeps sucking in by degrees that stream of life, which soon animates and enlivens its oval tiers over tiers of steps, till its interior is tapestried all round with human faces, and its walls seem to rock and wave to and fro, by the swaying of the living mass. And, after this shall have been gorged with blood, and inflamed with fury, it will melt once more, and rush out in a thick continuous flow through the many avenues by which it entered, now bearing their fitting name of *Vomitoria*; for never did a more polluted stream of the dregs and pests of humanity issue from an unbecoming reservoir, through ill-assorted channels, than the Roman mob, drunk with the blood of martyrs, gushing forth from the pores of the splendid amphitheatre.

The emperor came to the games surrounded by his court,

with all the pomp and circumstance which befitted an imperial festival, keen as any of his subjects to witness the cruel games, and to feed his eyes with a feast of carnage. His throne was on the eastern side of the amphitheatre, where a large space, called the *pulvinar*, was reserved, and richly decorated for the imperial court.

The Coliseum.

Various sports succeeded one another; and many a gladiator killed, or wounded, had sprinkled the bright sand with blood, when the people, eager for fiercer combats, began to call, or roar for the Christians and the wild beasts. It is time, therefore, for us to think of our captives.

Before the citizens were astir, they had been removed from the prison to a strong chamber called the *spoliatorium*, the press-room, where their fetters and chains were removed. An attempt was made to dress them gaudily as heathen priests and priestesses; but they resisted, urging that as they had come spontaneously to the fight, it was unfair to make them appear in a disguise which they abhorred. During the early part of the day they remained thus together encouraging one another, and singing the Divine praises, in spite of the shouts which drowned their voices from time to time.

While they were thus engaged, Corvinus entered, and,

with a look of insolent triumph, thus accosted Pancratius:

"Thanks to the gods, the day is come which I have long desired. It has been a tiresome and tough struggle between us who should fall uppermost. I have won it."

"How sayest thou, Corvinus? when and how have I contended with thee?"

"Always; every where. Thou hast haunted me in my dreams; thou hast danced before me like a meteor, and I have tried in vain to grasp thee. Thou hast been my tormentor, my evil genius. I have hated thee; devoted thee to the infernal gods; cursed thee and loathed thee; and now my day of vengeance is come."

"Methinks," replied Pancratius, smiling, "this does not look like a combat. It has been all on one side; for *I* have done none of these things towards thee."

"No? thinkest thou that I believe thee, when thou hast lain ever as a viper on my path, to bite my heel and overthrow me?"

"Where, I again ask?"

"Every where, I repeat. At school; in the Lady Agnes's house; in the Forum; in the cemetery; in my father's own court; at Chromatius's villa. Yes, every where."

"And nowhere else but where thou hast named? when thy chariot was dashed furiously along the Appian way, didst thou not hear the tramp of horses' hoofs trying to overtake thee?"

"Wretch!" exclaimed the prefect's son in a fury; "and was it thy accursed steed which, purposely urged forward, frightened mine, and nearly caused my death?"

"No, Corvinus, hear me calmly. It is the last time we shall speak together. I was travelling quietly with a companion towards Rome, after having paid the last rites to our master Cassianus" (Corvinus winced, for he knew not this before), "when I heard the clatter of a runaway chariot; and then, indeed, I put spurs to my horse; and it is well for thee that I did."

"How so?"

"Because I reached thee just in time; when thy strength was nearly exhausted, and thy blood almost frozen by repeated plunges in the cold canal; and when thy arm, already benumbed, had let go its last stay, and thou wast falling backwards for the last time into the water. I saw thee; I knew thee, as I took hold of thee, insensible. I had in my grasp the murderer of one most dear to me. Divine justice seemed to have overtaken him; there was only my will between him and his doom. It was my day of vengeance, and I fully gratified it."

"Ha! and how, pray?"

"By drawing thee out, and laying thee on the bank, and chafing thee till thy heart resumed its functions; and then consigning thee to thy servants, rescued from death."

"Thou liest!" screamed Corvinus; "my servants told me that *they* drew me out."

"And did they give thee my knife, together with thy leopard-skin purse, which I found on the ground, after I had dragged thee forth?"

"No; they said the purse was lost in the canal. It *was* a leopard-skin purse, the gift of an African sorceress. What sayest thou of the knife?"

"That it is here, see it, still rusty with the water; thy purse I gave to thy slaves; my own knife I retained for myself; look at it again. Dost thou believe me now? Have I been always a viper on thy path?"

Too ungenerous to acknowledge that he had been conquered in the struggle between them, Corvinus only felt himself withered, degraded, before his late school-fellow, crumbled like a clot of dust in his hands. His very heart seemed to him to blush. He felt sick, and staggered, hung down his head, and sneaked away. He cursed the games, the emperor, the yelling rabble, the roaring beasts, his horses and chariot, his slaves,

his father, himself,—every thing and every body except one—
he could not, for his life, curse Pancratius.

He had reached the door, when the youth called him
back. He turned and looked at him with a glance of respect,
almost approaching to love. Pancratius put his hand on
his arm, and said, "Corvinus, *I* have freely forgiven thee.
There is One above, who cannot forgive without repentance.
Seek pardon from Him. If not, I foretell to thee this day,
that by whatsoever death I die, thou too shalt one day perish."

Corvinus slunk away, and appeared no more that day.
He lost the sight on which his coarse imagination had
gloated for days, which he had longed for during months. When
the holiday was over he was found by his father completely
intoxicated: it was the only way he knew of drowning remorse.

As he was leaving the prisoners, the *lanista*, or master of
the gladiators, entered the room and summoned them to the
combat. They hastily embraced one another, and took leave
on earth. They entered the arena, or pit of the ampitheatre,
opposite the imperial seat, and had to pass between two files
of *venatores*, or huntsmen, who had the care of the wild beasts,
each armed with a heavy whip, wherewith he inflicted a blow on
every one as he went by him. They were then brought forward, singly or in groups, as the people desired, or the directors
of the spectacle chose. Sometimes the intended prey was placed
on an elevated platform to be more conspicuous; at another
time he was tied up to posts to be more helpless. A favorite
sport was to bundle up a female victim in a net, and expose
her to be rolled, tossed, or gored by wild cattle.* One
encounter with a single wild beast often finished the martyr's
course; while occasionally three or four were successively let
loose, without their inflicting a mortal wound. The confessor

---

* See the Acts of the Martyrs of Lyons, Ruinart, vol. i. p. 152 (where will be
found the account of the martyrdom of a youth of fifteen), and those of St. Perpetua and Felicitas, p. 221.

was then either remanded to prison for further torments, or taken back to the *spoliatorium*, where the gladiator's apprentices amused themselves with despatching him.

But we must content ourselves with following the last steps of our youthful hero, Pancratius. As he was passing through the corridor that led to the amphitheatre, he saw Sebastian standing on one side, with a lady closely enwrapped in her mantle, and veiled. He at once recognized her, stopped before her, knelt, and taking her hand, affectionately kissed it.

"Bless me, dear mother," he said, "in this your promised hour."

"See, my child, the heavens," she replied, "and look up thither, where Christ with His saints expecteth thee. Fight the good fight for thy soul's sake, and show thyself faithful and steadfast in thy Saviour's love.* Remember him too whose precious relic thou bearest round thy neck."

"Its price shall be doubled in thine eyes, my sweet mother, ere many hours are over."

"On, on, and let us have none of this fooling," exclaimed the *lanista*, adding a stroke of his cane.

Lucina retreated; while Sebastian pressed the hand of her son, and whispered in his ear, "Courage, dearest boy; may God bless you! I shall be close behind the emperor; give me a last look there, and—your blessing."

"Ha! ha! ha!" broke out a fiendish tone close behind him. Was it a demon's laugh? He looked behind, and caught only a glimpse of a fluttering cloak rounding a pillar. Who could it be? He guessed not. It was Fulvius, who in those words had got the last link in a chain of evidence that he had long been weaving—that Sebastian was certainly a Christian.

Pancratius soon stood in the midst of the arena, the last

* See the Acts of St. Felicitas and her seven sons, *Ruinart*, vol. i. p. 35.

of the faithful band. He had been reserved, in hopes that the sight of others' sufferings might shake his constancy; but the effect had been the reverse. He took his stand where he was placed, and his yet delicate frame contrasted with the swarthy and brawny limbs of the executioners who surrounded him. They now left him alone; and we cannot better describe him than Eusebius, an eye-witness, does a youth a few years older:

"You might have seen a tender youth, who had not yet entered his twentieth year, standing without fetters, with his hands stretched forth in the form of a cross, and praying to God most attentively, with a fixed and untrembling heart; not retiring from the place where he first stood, nor swerving the least, while bears and leopards, breathing fury and death in their very snort, were just rushing on to tear his limbs in pieces. And yet, I know not how, their jaws seemed seized and closed by some divine and mysterious power, and they drew altogether back."*

Such was the attitude, and such the privilege of our heroic youth. The mob were frantic, as they saw one wild beast after another careering madly round him, roaring, and lashing its sides with its tail, while he seemed placed in a charmed circle which they could not approach. A furious bull, let loose upon him, dashed madly forward, with his neck bent down, then stopped suddenly, as though he had struck his head against a wall, pawed the ground, and scattered the dust around him, bellowing fiercely.

"Provoke him, thou coward!" roared out, still louder, the enraged emperor.

Pancratius awoke as from a trance, and waving his arms ran towards his enemy;† but the savage brute, as if a lion had

---

* *Hist. Eccles.* lib. viii. c. 7.

† Euseb. ibid. See also St. Ignatius's letter to the Romans, in his Acts, ap. *Ruinart*, vol. i. p. 48.

been rushing on him, turned round and ran away towards the entrance, where, meeting his keeper, he tossed him high into the air. All were disconcerted except the brave youth, who had resumed his attitude of prayer; when one of the crowd shouted out: "He has a charm round his neck; he is a sorcerer!" The whole multitude re-echoed the cry, till the emperor, having commanded silence, called out to him, "Take that amulet from thy neck, and cast it from thee, or it shall be done more roughly for thee."

"Sire," replied the youth, with a musical voice, that rang sweetly through the hushed amphitheatre, "it is no charm that I wear, but a memorial of my father, who in this very place made gloriously the same confession which I now humbly make; I am a Christian; and for love of Jesus Christ, God and man, I gladly give my life. Do not take from me this only legacy, which I have bequeathed, richer than I received it, to another. Try once more; it was a panther which gave him his crown; perhaps it will bestow the same on me."

For an instant there was dead silence; the multitude seemed softened, won. The graceful form of the gallant youth, his now inspired countenance, the thrilling music of his voice, the intrepidity of his speech, and his generous self-devotion to his cause, had wrought upon that cowardly herd. Pancratius felt it, and his heart quailed before their mercy more than before their rage; he had promised himself heaven that day; was he to be disappointed? Tears started into his eyes, as stretching forth his arms once more in the form of a cross, he called aloud, in a tone that again vibrated through every heart:

"To-day; oh yes, to-day, most blessed Lord, is the appointed day of Thy coming. Tarry not longer; enough has Thy power been shown in me to them that believe not in Thee; show now Thy mercy to me who in Thee believe!"

Pancratius was still standing in the same place, facing the concourse, apparently as absorbed in higher thoughts, as not to heed the movements of his enemy.

"The panther!" shouted out a voice. "The panther!" responded twenty. "The panther!" thundered forth a hundred thousand, in a chorus like the roaring of an avalanche.* A cage started up, as if by magic, from the midst of the sand, and as it rose its side fell down, and freed the captive of the desert.† With one graceful bound the elegant savage gained its liberty; and, though enraged by darkness, confinement, and hunger, it seemed almost playful, as it leaped and turned about, frisked and gambolled noiselessly on the sand. At last it caught sight of its prey. All its feline cunning and cruelty seemed to return, and to conspire together in animating the cautious and treacherous movements of its velvet-clothed frame. The whole amphitheatre was as silent as if it had been a hermit's dell, while every eye was intent, watching the stealthy approaches of the sleek brute to its victim. Pancratius was still standing in the same place, facing the emperor, apparently so absorbed in higher thoughts as not to heed the movements of his enemy. The panther had stolen round him, as if disdaining to attack him except in front. Crouching upon its breast, slowly advancing one paw before another, it had gained its measured distance, and there it lay for some moments of breathless suspense. A deep snarling growl, an elastic spring through the air, and it was seen gathered up like a leech, with its hind feet on the chest, and its fangs and fore claws on the throat of the martyr.

He stood erect for a moment, brought his right hand to his mouth, and looking up at Sebastian with a smile, directed to him, by a graceful wave of his arm, the last salutation of his lips—and fell. The arteries of the neck had been severed, and the slumber of martyrdom at once settled on

* The amphitheatre could contain 150,000.
† This was an ordinary device. The underground constructions for its practice have been found in the Coliseum.

his eyelids. His blood softened, brightened, enriched, and blended inseparably with that of his father, which Lucina had hung about his neck. The mother's sacrifice had been accepted.*

* The martyr Saturus, torn by a leopard, and about to die, addressed the soldier Pudens, not yet a Christian, in words of exhortation; then asked him for the ring on his finger, dipped it in his own blood, and gave it back, "leaving him the inheritance of the pledge, and the memorial of his blood." *Ap. Bunsen*, vol. i. p. 225.

A Lamp bearing a Monogram of Christ, found in the Catacombs.

CHAPTER XXIV.

THE CHRISTIAN SOLDIER.

THE body of the young martyr was deposited in peace on the Aurelian way, in the cemetery which soon bore his name, and gave it, as we have before observed, to the neighboring gate. In times of peace a basilica was raised over his tomb, and yet stands to perpetuate his honor.

The persecution now increased its fury, and multiplied its daily victims. Many whose names have appeared in our pages, especially the community of Chromatius's villa, rapidly fell. The first was Zoë, whose dumbness Sebastian had cured. She was surprised by a heathen rabble praying at St. Peter's tomb, and was hurried to trial, and hung with her head over a smoky fire, till she died. Her husband, with three others of the same party, was taken, repeatedly tortured, and beheaded. Tranquillinus, the father of Marcus and Marcellianus, jealous of Zoë's crown, prayed openly at St. Paul's tomb; he was taken and summarily stoned to death. His twin sons suffered also a cruel death. The treachery of Torquatus, by his describing his former companions, especially the gallant Tiburtius, who was now beheaded,[*] greatly facilitated this wholesale destruction.

[*] He is commemorated on the 11th of August, with his father Chromatius, as has been already observed.

Sebastian moved in the midst of this slaughter, not like a builder who saw his work destroyed by a tempest, nor a shepherd who beheld his flock borne off by marauders. He felt as a general on the battle-field, who looked only to the victory; counting every one as glorious who gave his life in its purchase, and as ready to give his own should it prove to be the required price. Every friend that fell before him was a bond less to earth, and a link more to heaven; a care less below, a claim more above. He sometimes sat lonely, or paused silently, on the spots where he had conversed with Pancratius, recalling to mind the buoyant cheerfulness, the graceful thoughts, and the unconscious virtue of the amiable and comely youth. But he never felt as if they were more separated than when he sent him on his expedition to Campania. He had redeemed his pledge to him, and now it was soon to be his own turn. He knew it well; he felt the grace of martyrdom swelling in his breast, and in tranquil certainty he awaited its hour. His preparation was simple: whatever he had of value he distributed to the poor, and he settled his property, by sale, beyond the reach of confiscation.

Fulvius had picked up his fair share of Christian spoils; but, on the whole, he had been disappointed. He had not been obliged to ask for assistance from the emperor, whose presence he avoided; but he had put nothing by; he was not getting rich. Every evening he had to bear the reproachful and scornful interrogatory of Eurotas on the day's success. Now, however, he told his stern master—for such he had become—that he was going to strike at higher game, the emperor's favorite officer, who must have made a large fortune in the service.

He had not long to wait for his opportunity. On the 9th of January a court was held, attended, of course, by all aspirants for favors, or fearers of imperial wrath. Fulvius was there, and, as usual, met with a cold reception. But after bearing silently the muttered curses of the royal brute, he boldly advanced, dropped on one knee, and thus addressed him:

"Sire, your divinity has often reproached me with having made, by my discoveries, but a poor return for your gracious countenance and liberal subsidies. But now I have found out the foulest of plots, and the basest of ingratitudes, in immediate contact with your divine person."

"What dost thou mean, booby?" asked impatiently the tyrant. "Speak at once, or I'll have the words pulled out of thy throat by an iron hook."

Fulvius rose, and directing his hand, in accompaniment to his words, said with a bitter blandness of tone: "Sebastian is a Christian."

The emperor started from his throne in fury.

"Thou liest, villain! Thou shalt prove thy words, or thou shalt die such a piecemeal death, as no Christian dog ever endured."

"I have sufficient proof recorded here," he replied, producing a parchment, and offering it, kneeling.

The emperor was about to make an angry answer, when, to his utter amazement, Sebastian, with unruffled looks and noble mien, stood before him, and in the calmest accents said:

"My liege, I spare you all trouble of proof. I am a Christian, and I glory in the name."

As Maximian, a rude though clever soldier, without education, could hardly when calm express himself in decent Latin, when he was in a passion his language was composed of broken sentences, mingled with every vulgar and coarse epithet. In this state he was now; and he poured out on Sebastian a torrent of abuse, in which he reproached him with every crime, and called him by every opprobrious name, within his well-stocked repertory of vituperation. The two crimes, however, on which he rung his loudest changes were, ingratitude and treachery. He had nursed, he said, a viper in his bosom, a scorpion, an evil demon; and he only wondered he was still alive.

The Christian officer stood the volley, as intrepidly as ever he had borne the enemy's assault, on the field of battle.

"Listen to me, my royal master," he replied, "perhaps for the last time. I have said I am a Christian; and in this you have had the best pledge of your security."

"How do you mean, ungrateful man?"

"Thus, noble emperor: that if you want a body-guard around you of men who will spill their last drop of life's blood for you, go to the prison and take the Christians from the stocks on the floor, and from the fetter-rings on the walls; send to the courts and bear away the mutilated confessors from the rack and the gridiron; issue orders to the amphitheatres, and snatch the mangled half that lives from the jaws of tigers; restore them to such shape as yet they are capable of, put weapons into their hands, and place them around you; and in this maimed and ill-favored host there will be more fidelity, more loyalty, more daring for you, than in all your Dacian and Pannonian legions. You have taken half their blood from them, and they will give you willingly the other half."

"Folly and madness!" returned the sneering savage. "I would sooner surround myself with wolves than with Christians. Your treachery proves enough for me."

"And what would have prevented me at any time from acting the traitor, if I had been one? Have I not had access to your royal person by night as by day; and have I proved a traitor? No, emperor, none has ever been more faithful than I to you. But I have another, and a higher Lord to serve; one who will judge us both; and His laws I must obey rather than yours."

"And why have you, like a coward, concealed your religion? To escape, perhaps, the bitter death you have deserved!"

"No, sire; no more coward than traitor. No one better than yourself knows that I am neither. So long as I could do any good to my brethren, I refused not to live amidst their carnage and my afflictions. But hope had at last died within me; and I thank Fulvius with all my heart, for having, by his accusation, spared me the embarrassment of choice between seeking death or enduring life."

"I will decide that point for you. Death is your award; and a slow lingering one it shall be. But," he added, in a lower tone, as if speaking to himself, "this must not get out. All must be done quietly at home, or treachery will spread. Here, Quadratus, take your Christian tribune under arrest. Do you hear, dolt? Why do you not move?"

"Because I too am a Christian!"

Another burst of fury, another storm of vile language, which ended in the stout centurion's being ordered at once to execution. But Sebastian was to be differently dealt with.

"Order Hyphax to come hither," roared the tyrant. In a few minutes, a tall, half-naked Numidian made his appearance. A bow of immense length, a gaily-painted quiver full of arrows, and a short broad-sword, were at once the ornaments and the weapons of the captain of the African archers. He stood erect before the emperor, like a handsome bronze statue, with bright enamelled eyes.

"Hyphax, I have a job for you to-morrow morning. It must be well done," said the emperor.

"Perfectly, sire," replied the dusky chief, with a grin which showed another set of enamels in his face.

"You see the captain Sebastian?" The negro bowed assent. "He turns out to be a Christian!"

If Hyphax had been on his native soil, and had trodden

suddenly on a hooded asp or a scorpion's nest, he could not have started more. The thought of being so near a Christian, —to him who worshipped every abomination, believed every absurdity, practised every lewdness, committed any atrocity!

Maximian proceeded, and Hyphax kept time to every member of his sentences by a nod, and what *he* meant to be a smile;—it was hardly an earthly one.

"You will take Sebastian to your quarters; and early to-morrow morning,—not this evening, mind, for I know that by this time of day you are all drunk,—but to-morrow morning, when your hands are steady, you will tie him to a tree in the grove of Adonis, and you will slowly shoot him to death. Slowly, mind; none of your fine shots straight through the heart or the brain, but plenty of arrows, till he die exhausted by pain and loss of blood. Do you understand me? Then take him off at once. And mind, silence; or else——"

A Monogram of Christ, found in the Catacombs.

CHAPTER XXV.

THE RESCUE.

IN spite of every attempt at concealment, the news was soon spread among all connected with the court, that Sebastian had been discovered to be a Christian, and was to be shot to death on the morrow. But on none did the double intelligence make such an impression as on Fabiola.

Sebastian a Christian! she said to herself; the noblest, purest, wisest of Rome's nobility a member of that vile, stupid sect? Impossible! Yet, the fact seems certain. Have I, then, been deceived? Was he not that which he seemed? Was he a mean impostor, who affected virtue, but was secretly a libertine? Impossible, too! Yes, this was indeed impossible! She had certain proofs of it. He knew that he might have had her hand and fortune for the asking, and he had acted most generously and most delicately towards her. He was what he seemed, that she was sure—not gilded, but gold.

Then how account for this phenomenon, of a Christian being all that was good, virtuous, amiable?

One solution never occurred to Fabiola's mind, that he

was all this *because* he was a Christian. She only saw the problem in another form; how could he be all that he was *in spite* of being a Christian?

She turned it variously in her mind, in vain. Then it came to her thought thus. Perhaps, after all, good old Chromatius was right, and Christianity may not be what I have fancied; and I ought to have inquired more about it. I am sure Sebastian never did the horrible things imputed to Christians. Yet every body charges them with them.

Might there not be a more refined form of this religion, and a more grovelling one; just as she knew there was in her own sect, Epicureanism? one coarse, material, wallowing in the very mire of sensualism; the other refined, sceptical and reflective. Sebastian would belong to the higher class, and despise and loathe the superstitions and vices of the commoner Christians. Such a hypothesis might be tenable; but it was hard to reconcile to her intellect, how a man like that noble soldier could, any way, have belonged to that hated race. And yet he was ready to die for their faith! As to Zoë and the others, she had heard nothing, for she had only returned the day before from a journey made into Campania, to arrange her father's affairs.

What a pity, she thought, that she had not talked more to Sebastian on such subjects! But it was now too late; to-morrow morning he would be no more. This second thought came with the sharp pang of a shaft shot into her heart. She felt as if she personally were about to suffer a loss, as if Sebastian's fate were going to fall on some one closely bound to her, by some secret and mysterious tie.

Her thoughts grew darker and sadder, as she dwelt on these ideas amidst the deepening gloom. She was suddenly disturbed by the entrance of a slave with a light. It was Afra, the black servant, who came to prepare her mistress's evening repast, which she wished to take alone. While busy with her arrangements, she said, "Have you heard the news, madam?"

"What news?"

"Only that Sebastian is going to be shot with arrows to-morrow morning. What a pity; he was such a handsome youth!"

"Be silent, Afra; unless you have some information to give me on the subject."

"Oh, of course, my mistress; and my information is indeed very astonishing. Do you know that he turns out to be one of those wretched Christians?"

"Hold your peace, I pray you, and do not prate any more about what you do not understand."

"Certainly not, if you so wish it; I suppose his fate is quite a matter of indifference to you, madam. It certainly is to me. He won't be the first officer that my countrymen have shot. Many they have killed, and some they have saved. But of course that was all chance."

There was a significance in her words and tones, which did not escape the quick ear and mind of Fabiola. She looked up, for the first time, and fixed her eyes searchingly on her maid's swarthy face. There was no emotion in it; she was placing a flagon of wine upon the table, just as if she had not spoken. At length the lady said to her:

"Afra, what do you mean?"

"Oh, nothing, nothing. What can a poor slave know? Still more, what can she do?"

"Come, come, you meant by your words something that I must know."

The slave came round the table, close to the couch on which Fabiola rested, looked behind her, and around her, then whispered, "Do you want Sebastian's life preserved?"

Fabiola almost leaped up, as she replied, "Certainly."

The servant put her finger to her lip, to enforce silence, and said, "It will cost dear."

"Name your price."

"A hundred *sestertia*,* and my liberty."

"I accept your terms; but what is my security for them?"

"They shall be binding only if, twenty-four hours after the execution, he is still alive."

"Agreed; and what is yours?"

"Your word, lady."

"Go, Afra, lose not a moment."

"There is no hurry," quietly replied the slave, as she completed, unhurried, the preparations for supper.

She then proceeded at once to the palace, and to the Mauritanian quarters, and went in directly to the commander.

"What dost thou want, Jubala," he said, "at this hour? There is no festival to-night."

"I know, Hyphax; but I have important business with thee."

"What is it about?"

"About thee, about myself, and about thy prisoner."

"Look at *him* there," said the barbarian, pointing across the court, which his door commanded. "You would not think that *he* is going to be shot to-morrow. See how soundly he sleeps. He could not do so better, if he were going to be married instead."

"As thou and I, Hyphax, intend to be the next day."

"Come, not quite so fast; there are certain conditions to be fulfilled first."

"Well, what are they?"

"First, thy manumission. I cannot marry a slave."

"That is secured."

* About 880l.

"Secondly, a dowry, a *good* dowry, mind; for I never wanted money more than now."

"That is safe too. How much dost thou expect?"

"Certainly not less than three hundred pounds."*

"I bring thee six hundred."

"Excellent! where didst thou get all this cash? Whom hast thou robbed? whom hast thou poisoned, my admirable priestess? Why wait till *after* to-morrow? Let it be to-morrow, to-night, if it please thee."

"Be quiet now, Hyphax; the money is all lawful gain; but it has its conditions, too. I said I came to speak about the prisoner also."

"Well, what has he to do with our approaching nuptials?"

"A great deal."

"What now?"

"He must not die."

The captain looked at her with a mixture of fury and stupidity. He seemed on the point of laying violent hands on her; but she stood intrepid and unmoved before him, and seemed to command him by the strong fascination of her eye, as one of the serpents of their native land might do a vulture.

"Art mad?" he at last exclaimed; "thou mightest as well at once ask for my head. If thou hadst seen the emperor's face, when he issued his orders, thou wouldst have known he will have no trifling with him here."

"Pshaw! pshaw! man; of course the prisoner will appear dead, and will be reported as dead."

"And if he finally recover?"

"His fellow-Christians will take care to keep him out of the way."

"Didst thou say twenty-four hours alive? I wish thou hadst made it twelve."

* We give equivalents in English money, as more intelligible.

"Well, but I know that thou canst calculate close. Let him die in the twenty-fifth hour, for what I care."

"It is impossible, Jubala, impossible; he is too important a person."

"Very well, then; there is an end to our bargain. The money is given only on this condition. Six hundred pounds thrown away!" And she turned off to go.

"Stay, stay," said Hyphax, eagerly; the demon of covetousness coming uppermost. "Let us see. Why, my fellows will consume half the money, in bribes and feasting."

"Well, I have two hundred more in reserve for that."

"Sayest thou so, my princess, my sorceress, my charming demon? But that will be too much for my scoundrels. We will give them half, and add the other half—to our marriage-settlements, shan't we?"

"As it pleases thee, provided the thing is done according to my proposal."

"It is a bargain, then. He shall live twenty-four hours; and after that, we will have a glorious wedding."

Sebastian, in the meantime, was unconscious of these amiable negotiations for his safety; for, like Peter between two guards, he was slumbering soundly by the wall of the court. Fatigued with his day's work, he had enjoyed the rare advantage of retiring early to rest; and the marble pavement was a good enough soldier's bed. But, after a few hours' repose, he awoke refreshed; and now that all was hushed, he silently rose, and with outstretched arms, gave himself up to prayer.

The martyr's prayer is not a preparation for death; for his is a death that needs no preparation. The soldier who suddenly declares himself a Christian, bends down his head, and mingles his blood with that of the confessor, whom he had come to execute; or the friend, of unknown name, who salutes the martyr going to death, is seized, and made to bear him willing company,"* is as prepared for martyrdom, as he who has passed months in prison engaged in prayer. It is not a cry, therefore, for the forgiveness of past sin; for there is a consciousness of that perfect love, which sendeth out fear, an inward assurance of that highest grace, which is incompatible with sin.

Nor in Sebastian was it a prayer for courage or strength; for the opposite feeling, which could suggest it, was unknown to him. It never entered into his mind to doubt, that as he had faced death intrepidly for his earthly sovereign on the battle-field, so he should meet it joyfully for his heavenly Lord, in any place.

His prayer, then, till morning, was a gladsome hymn of glory and honor to the King of kings, a joining with the seraph's glowing eyes, and ever-shaking wings, in restless homage.

Then when the stars in the bright heavens caught his eyes, he challenged them as wakeful sentinels like himself, to exchange the watchword of Divine praises; and as the night-wind rustled in the leafless trees of the neighboring court of Adonis, he bade its wayward music compose itself, and its rude harping upon the vibrating boughs form softer hymns,—the only ones that earth could utter in its winter night-hours.

Now burst on him the thrilling thought that the morning hour approached, for the cock had crowed; and he would soon hear those branches murmuring over him to the sharp whistle of flying arrows, unerring in their aim. And he offered himself gladly to their sharp tongues, hissing as the serpent's, to drink his blood. He offered himself as an oblation for God's honor, and for the appeasing of his wrath. He offered himself particularly for the afflicted Church, and prayed that his death might mitigate her sufferings.

* Called thence St. Adauctus.

And then his thoughts rose higher, from the earthly to the celestial Church; soaring like the eagle from the highest pinnacle of the mountain-peak, towards the sun. Clouds have rolled away, and the blue embroidered veil of morning is rent in twain, like the sanctuary's, and he sees quite into its revealed depths; far, far inwards, beyond senates of saints and legions of angels, to what Stephen saw of inmost and intensest glory. And now his hymn was silent; harmonies came to him, too sweet and perfect to brook the jarring of a terrestrial voice; they came to him, requiring no return; for they brought heaven into his soul; and what could he give back? It was as a fountain of purest refreshment, more like gushing light than water, flowing from the foot of the Lamb, and poured into his heart, which could only be passive, and receive the gift. Yet in its sparkling bounds, as it rippled along towards him, he could see the countenance now of one, and then of another of the happy friends who had gone before him; as if they were drinking, and bathing, and disporting, and plunging, and dissolving themselves in those living waters.

His countenance was glowing as with the very reflection of the vision, and the morning dawn just brightening (oh, what a dawn that is!), caught his face as he stood up, with his arms in a cross, opposite the east; so that when Hyphax opened his door and saw him, he could have crept across the court and worshipped him on his face.

Sebastian awoke as from a trance; and the chink of sesterces sounded in the mental ears of Hyphax; so he set scientifically about earning them. He picked out of his troop of a hundred, five marksmen, who could split a flying arrow with a fleeter one, called them into his room, told them their reward, concealing his own share, and arranged how the execution was to be managed. As to the body, Christians had already secretly offered a large additional sum for its delivery, and two slaves were to wait outside to receive it. Among his own followers he could fully depend on secrecy.

Sebastian was conducted into the neighboring court of the palace, which separated the quarters of these African archers from his own dwelling. It was planted with rows of trees, and consecrated to Adonis. He walked cheerfully in the midst of his executioners, followed by the whole band, who were alone allowed to be spectators, as they would have been of an ordinary exhibition of good archery. The officer was stripped and bound to a tree, while the chosen five took their stand opposite, cool and collected. It was at best a desolate sort of death. Not a friend, not a sympathizer near; not one fellow-Christian to bear his farewell to the faithful, or to record for them his last accents, and the constancy of his end. To stand in the middle of the crowded amphitheatre, with a hundred thousand witnesses of Christian constancy, to see the encouraging looks of many, and hear the whispered blessings of a few loving acquaintances, had something cheering, and almost inspiring in it; it lent at least the feeble aid of human emotions, to the more powerful sustainment of grace. The very shout of an insulting multitude put a strain upon natural courage, as the hunter's cry only nerves the stag at bay. But this dead and silent scene, at dawn of day, shut up in the court of a house; this being, with most unfeeling indifference tied up, like a truss of hay, or a stuffed figure, to be coolly aimed at, according to the tyrant's orders; this being alone in the midst of a horde of swarthy savages, whose very language was strange, uncouth, and unintelligible; but who were no doubt uttering their rude jokes, and laughing, as men do before a match or a game, which they are going to enjoy; all this had more the appearance of a piece of cruelty, about to be acted in a gloomy forest by banditti, than open and glorious confession of Christ's name; it looked and felt more like assassination than martyrdom.

But Sebastian cared not for all this. Angels looked over the wall upon him; and the rising sun, which dazzled his eyes, but made him a clearer mark for his bowmen, shone not more brightly on him, than did the countenance of the only Witness he cared to have of suffering endured for His sake.

The first Moor drew his bow-string to his ear, and an arrow trembled in the flesh of Sebastian. Each chosen marksman followed in turn; and shouts of applause accompanied each hit, so cleverly approaching, yet avoiding, according to the imperial order, every vital part. And so the game went on; every body laughing, and brawling, and jeering, and enjoying it without a particle of feeling for the now drooping frame, painted with blood;* all in sport, except the martyr, to whom all was sober earnest—each sharp pang, the enduring smart, the exhaustion, the weariness, the knotty bonds, the constrained attitude! Oh! but earnest too was the steadfast heart, the untiring spirit, the unwavering faith, the unruffled patience, the unsated love of suffering for his Lord. Earnest was the prayer, earnest the gaze of the eye on heaven, earnest the listening of the ear for the welcoming strain of the heavenly porters, as they should open the gate.

It was indeed a dreary death; yet this was not the worst. After all, death came not; the golden gates remained unbarred; the martyr in heart, still reserved for greater glory even upon earth, found himself not suddenly translated from death to life, but sunk into unconsciousness in the lap of angels. His tormentors saw when they had reached their intended measure; they cut the cords that bound him; and Sebastian fell exhausted, and to all appearance dead, upon the carpet of blood which he had spread for himself on the pavement. Did he lie, like a noble warrior, as he now appears in marble under his altar, in his own dear church?

* "Membraque picta cruore novo." *Prud. περὶ στεϕ.* ii. 39.

We at least cannot imagine him as more beautiful. And not only that church do we love, but that ancient chapel which stands in the midst of the ruined Palatine, to mark the spot on which he fell."

* The reader, when visiting the Crystal Palace, will find in the Roman Court an excellent model of the Roman Forum. On the raised mound of the Palatine hill, between the arches of Titus and Constantine, he will see a chapel of fair dimensions standing alone. It is the one to which we allude. It has been lately repaired by the Barberini family.

Elias carried up to Heaven, from a picture found in the Catacombs.

CHAPTER XXVI.

THE REVIVAL.

NIGHT was far advanced, when the black slave, having completed her marriage settlement quite to her own satisfaction, was returning to her mistress's house. It was, indeed, a cold wintry night, so she was well wrapped up, and in no humor to be disturbed. But it was a lovely night, and the moon seemed to be stroking, with a silvery hand, the downy robe of the .* She paused beside it; and, after a silence of some moments, broke out into a loud laugh, as if some ridiculous recollection connected itself in her mind with that beautiful object. She was turning round to proceed on her way, when she felt herself roughly seized by the arm.

"If you had not laughed," said her captor, bitterly, "I should not have recognized you. But that hyena laugh of yours is unmistakable. Listen, the wild beasts, your African cousins, are answering it from the amphitheatre. What was it about, pray?"

"About you."

"How about me?"

"I was thinking of our last interview in this place, and what a fool you made of yourself."

* The fountain before described.

"How kind of you, Afra, to be thinking of me, especially as I was not just then thinking of you, but of your countrymen in those cells."

"Cease your impertinence, and call people by their proper names. I am not Afra the slave any longer; at least I shall not be so in a few hours; but Jubala, the wife of Hyphax, commander of the Mauritanian archers."

"A very respectable man, no doubt, if he could speak any language besides his gibberish; but these few hours of interval may suffice for the transaction of our business. You made a mistake, methinks, in what you said just now. It was you, was it not, that made a fool of me at our last meeting? What has become of your fair promises, and of my fairer gold, which were exchanged on that occasion? Mine, I know, proved sterling; yours, I fear, turned out but dust."

"No doubt; for so says a proverb in my language: 'the dust on a wise man's skirts is better than the gold in the fool's girdle.' But let us come to the point; did you really ever believe in the power of my charms and philters?"

"To be sure I did; do you mean they were all imposture?"

"Not quite all; you see we have got rid of Fabius, and the daughter is in possession of the fortune. That was a preliminary step of absolute necessity."

"What! do you mean that your incantations removed the father?" asked Corvinus, amazed, and shrinking from her. It was only a sudden bright thought of Afra's, so she pushed her advantage, saying:

"To be sure; what else? It is easy thus to get rid of any one that is too much in the way."

"Good night, good night," he replied in great fear.

"Stay a moment," she answered, somewhat propitiated; "Corvinus, I gave you two pieces of advice worth all your gold that night. One you have acted against; the other you have not followed."

"How?"

"Did I not tell you not to hunt the Christians, but to catch them in your toils? Fulvius has done the second, and has gained something. You have done the first, and what have you earned?"

"Nothing but rage, confusion, and stripes."

"Then I was a good counsellor in the one advice; follow me in the second."

"What was it?"

"When you had become rich enough by Christian spoil, to offer yourself, with your wealth, to Fabiola. She has till now coldly rejected every offer; but I have observed one thing carefully. Not a single suit has been accompanied by riches. Every spendthrift has sought her fortune to repair his own; depend upon it, he that wins the prize must come on the principle that two and two make four. Do you understand me?"

"Too well, for where are my two to come from?"

"Listen to me, Corvinus, for this is our last interview; and I rather like you, as a hearty, unscrupulous, relentless, and unfeeling good hater." She drew him nearer and whispered: "I know from Eurotas, out of whom I can wheedle anything, that Fulvius has some splendid Christian prizes in view, one especially. Come this way into the shadow, and I will tell you how surely you may intercept his treasure. Leave to him the cool murder that will be necessary, for it may be troublesome; but step in between him and the spoil. He would do it to you any day."

She spoke to him for some minutes in a low and earnest tone; and at the end, he broke out into the loud exclamation, "Excellent!" What a word in such a mouth!

She checked him by a pull, and pointing to the building opposite, exclaimed: "Hush! look there!"

How are the tables turned; or, rather, how has the world

gone round in a brief space! The last time these two wicked beings were on the same spot, plotting bane to others, the window above was occupied by two virtuous youths, who, like two spirits of good, were intent on unravelling their web of mischief, and countermining their dark approaches. They are gone thence, the one sleeping in his tomb, the other slumbering on the eve of execution. Death looks to us like a holy power, seeing how much he prefers taking to his society the good, rather than the evil. He snatches away the flower, and leaves the weed its poisonous life, till it drops into mature decay.

But at the moment that they looked up, the window was occupied by two other persons.

"That is Fulvius," said Corvinus, "who just came to the window."

"And the other is his evil demon, Eurotas," added the slave. They both watched and listened from their dark nook.

Fulvius came again, at that moment, to the window, with a sword in his hand, carefully turning and examining the hilt in the bright moonlight. He flung it down at last, exclaiming with an oath, "It is only brass, after all."

Eurotas came with, to all appearance, a rich officer's belt, and examined it carefully. "All false stones! Why, I declare the whole of the effects are not worth fifty pounds. You have made but a poor job of this, Fulvius."

"Always reproaching me, Eurotas. And yet this miserable gain has cost me the life of one of the emperor's most favorite officers."

"And no thanks probably from your master for it." Eurotas was right.

Next morning, the slaves who received the body of Sebastian were surprised by a swarthy female figure passing by them, and whispering to them, "He is still alive."

Instead, therefore, of carrying him out for burial, they bore him to the apartment of Irene. The early hour of the morning, and the emperor's having gone, the evening before, to his favorite Lateran palace, facilitated this movement. Instantly Dionysius was sent for, and he pronounced every wound curable; not one arrow having touched a vital organ. But loss of blood had taken place to such a fearful extent, that he considered weeks must elapse before the patient would be fit to move.

For four-and-twenty hours Afra assiduously called, almost every hour, to ask how Sebastian was. When the probationary term was finished, she conducted Fabiola to Irene's apartment, to receive herself assurance that he breathed, though scarcely more. The deed of her liberation from servitude was executed, her dowry was paid, and the whole Palatine and Forum rang with the mad carouse and hideous rites of her nuptials.

Fabiola inquired after Sebastian with such tender solicitude that Irene doubted not that she was a Christian. The first few times she contented herself with receiving intelligence at the door, and putting into the hands of Sebastian's hostess a large sum towards the expenses of his recovery; but after two days, when he was improving, she was courteously invited to enter; and, for the first time in her life, she found herself consciously in the bosom of a Christian family.

Irene, we are told, was the widow of Castulus, one of the Chromatian band of converts. Her husband had just suffered death; but she remained still, unnoticed, in the apartments held by him in the palace. Two daughters lived with her; and a marked difference in their behavior soon struck Fabiola, as she became familiar with them. One evidently thought Sebastian's presence an intrusion, and seldom or never approached him. Her behavior to her mother was rude and haughty, her ideas all belonged to the common

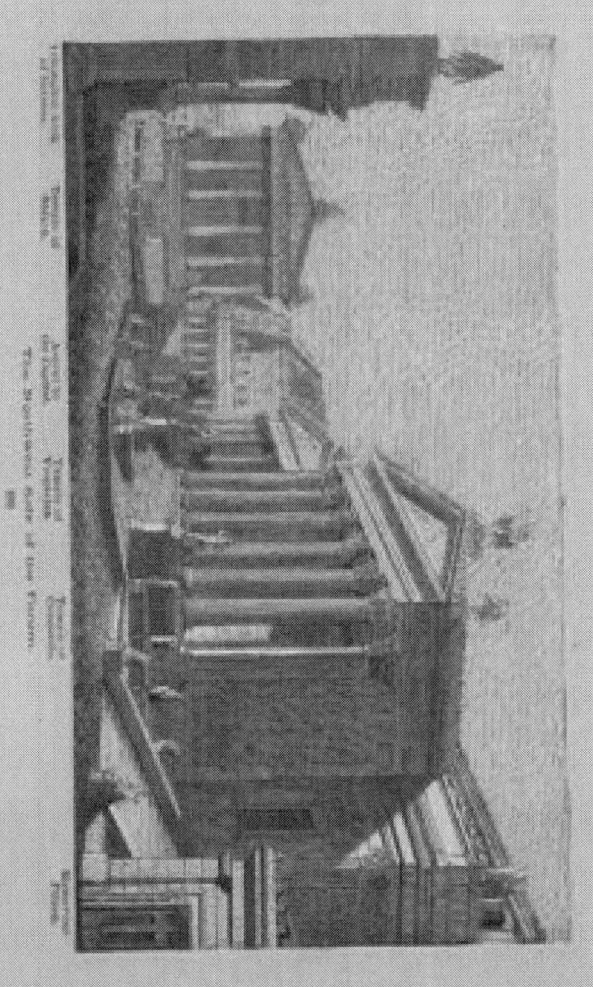

world,—she was selfish, light, and forward. The other, who was the younger, was a perfect contrast to her,—so gentle, docile and affectionate; so considerate about others; so devoted to her mother; so kind and attentive to the poor patient. Irene herself was a type of the Christian matron, in the middle class of life. Fabiola did not find her intelligent, or learned, or witty, or highly polished; but she saw her always calm, active, sensible, and honest. Then she was clearly warm-hearted, generous, deeply affectionate, and sweetly patient. The pagan lady had never seen such a household,—so simple, frugal, and orderly. Nothing disturbed it, except the character of the elder sister. In a few days it was ascertained that the daily visitor was not a Christian; but this caused no change in their treatment of her. Then she in her turn made a discovery which mortified her—that the elder daughter was still heathen. All that she saw made a favorable impression on her, and softened the hard crust of prejudice on her mind. For the present, however, her thoughts were all absorbed in Sebastian, whose recovery was slow. She formed plans with Irene for carrying him off to her Campanian villa, where she would have leisure to confer with him on religion. An insuperable obstacle, however, rose to this project.

We will not attempt to lead our reader into the feelings of Sebastian. To have yearned after martyrdom, to have prayed for it, to have suffered all its pangs, to have died in it as far as human consciousness went, to have lost sight of this world, and now to awaken in it again, no martyr, but an ordinary wayfaring man on probation, who might yet lose salvation,—was surely a greater trial than martyrdom itself. It was to be like a man who, in the midst of a stormy night, should try to cross an angry river, or tempestuous arm of the sea, and, after struggling for hours, and having his skiff twirled round and round and all but upset, should find himself relanded on the same side as he started from. Or, it was like St. Paul sent back to earth and to Satan's buffets, after having heard the mysterious words which only one Intelligence can utter. Yet no murmur escaped him, no regret. He adored in silence the Divine Will, hoping that its purpose was only to give him the merit of a double martyrdom. For this second crown he so earnestly longed, that he rejected every proposal for flight and concealment.

"I have now," he generously said, "earned one privilege of a martyr, that of speaking boldly to the persecutors. This I will use the first day that I can leave my bed. Nurse me, therefore, well, that it may be the sooner."

Moses receiving the Law, from a picture in the Cemetery of "Sant' Ponziano."

CHAPTER XXVII.

THE SECOND CROWN.

THE memorable plot which the black slave betrayed to Corvinus, was one to which allusion has already been made, in the conversation between Fulvius and his guardian. He was convinced from the blind martyr's unsuspecting admissions, that Agnes was a Christian, and he believed he had now two strings to his bow; either he could terrify her into marriage with himself, or he could destroy her, and obtain a good share of her wealth by confiscation. He was nerved for this second alternative by the taunts and exhortations of Eurotas; but, despairing of obtaining another interview, he wrote her a respectful, but pressing letter, descriptive of his disinterested attachment to her, and entreating her to accept his suit. There was but the faintest hint at the end, that duty might compel him to take another course, if humble petition did not prevail.

To this application he received a calm, well-bred, but unmistakable refusal; a stern, final, and hopeless rejection. But more, the letter stated in clear terms, that the writer was already espoused to the spotless Lamb, and could admit from no perishable being expressions of personal attachment. This rebuff steeled his heart against pity; but he determined to act prudently.

In the meantime, Fabiola, seeing the determination of

Sebastian not to fly, conceived the romantic idea of saving him, in spite of himself, by extorting his pardon from the emperor. She did not know the depth of wickedness in man's heart. She thought the tyrant might fume for a moment, but that he would never condemn a man twice to death. Some pity and mercy, she thought, must linger in his breast; and her earnest pleading and tears would extract them, as heat does the hidden balsam from the hard wood. She accordingly sent a petition for an audience; and knowing the covetousness of the man, presumed, as she said, to offer him a slight token of her own and her late father's loyal attachment. This was a ring with jewels of rare beauty, and immense value. The present was accepted; but she was merely told to attend with her memorial at the Palatine on the 20th, in common with other petitioners, and wait for the emperor's descent by the great staircase, on his way to sacrifice. Unencouraging as was this answer, she resolved to risk any thing, and do her best.

The appointed day came; and Fabiola, in her mourning habits, worn both as a suppliant, and for her father's death, took her stand in a row of far more wretched creatures than herself, mothers, children, sisters, who held petitions for mercy, for those dearest to them, now in dungeons or mines. She felt the little hope she had entertained die within her at the sight of so much wretchedness, too much for it all to expect favor. But fainter grew its last spark, at every step that the tyrant took down the marble stairs, though she saw her brilliant ring sparkling on his coarse hand. For on each step he snatched a paper from some sorrowful suppliant, looked at it scornfully, and either tore it up, or dashed it on the ground. Only here and there, he handed one to his secretary, a man scarcely less imperious than himself.

It was now nearly Fabiola's turn: the emperor was only

two steps above her, and her heart beat violently, not from fear of man, but from anxiety about Sebastian's fate. She would have prayed, had she known how, or to whom. Maximian was stretching out his hand to take a paper offered to him, when he drew back, and turned round, on hearing his name most unceremoniously and peremptorily called out. Fabiola looked up too; for she knew the voice.

Opposite to her, high in the white marble wall, she had observed an open window, corniced in yellow marble, which gave light to a back corridor leading to where Irene's apartments were. She now looked up, guided by the voice, and in the dark panel of the window, a beautiful but awful picture was seen. It was Sebastian, wan and thin, who, with features almost etherealized, calm and stern, as if no longer capable of passion, or strong emotion, stood there before them; his lacerated breast and arms appearing amidst the loose drapery he had thrown around him. For he had heard the familiar trumpet-notes, which told him of the emperor's approach, and he had risen, and crept thus far, to greet him.*

"Maximian!" he cried out, in a hollow but distinct voice.

"Who art thou, sirrah! that makest so free with thine emperor's name?" asked the tyrant, turning upon him.

"I am come as from the dead, to warn thee that the day of wrath and vengeance is fast approaching. Thou hast spilt the blood of God's Saints upon the pavement of this city; thou hast cast their holy bodies into the river, or flung them away upon the dunghills at the gates. Thou hast pulled down God's temples, and profaned His altars, and rifled the inheritance of His poor. For these, and thine own foul crimes and lewdnesses, thine injustices and oppressions, thy covet-

* See the Acts of St. Sebastian.

ousness and thy pride, God hath judged thee, and His wrath shall soon overtake thee; and thou shalt die the death of the violent; and God will give His Church an emperor after His own heart. And thy memory shall be accursed through the whole world, till the end of time. Repent thee, while thou hast time, impious man; and ask forgiveness of God, in the name of Him, the Crucified, whom thou hast persecuted till now."

Deep silence was held while these words were fully uttered. The emperor seemed under the influence of a paralyzing awe; for soon recognizing Sebastian, he felt as if standing in the presence of the dead. But quickly recovering himself and his passion, he exclaimed: "Ho! some of you, go round instantly and bring him before me" (he did not like to pronounce his name). "Hyphax here! Where is Hyphax? I saw him just now."

But the Moor had at once recognized Sebastian, and run off to his quarters. "Ha! he is gone, I see; then here, you dolt, what's your name?" (addressing Corvinus, who was attending his father,) "go to the Numidian court, and summon Hyphax here directly."

With a heavy heart Corvinus went on his errand. Hyphax had told his tale, and put his men in order of defence. Only one entrance at the end of the court was left open; and when the messenger had reached it, he durst not advance. Fifty men stood along each side of the space, with Hyphax and Jubala at the opposite end. Silent and immovable, with their dark chests and arms bare, each with his arrow fixed, and pointed to the door, and the string ready drawn, they looked like an avenue of basalt statues, leading to an Egyptian temple.

"Hyphax," said Corvinus, in a tremulous voice, "the emperor sends for you."

"Tell his majesty, respectfully, from me," replied the

African, "that my men have sworn, that no man passes that threshold, coming in, or going out, without receiving, through his breast or his back, a hundred shafts into his heart; until the emperor shall have sent us a token of forgiveness for every offence."

Corvinus hastened back with this message, and the emperor received it with a laugh. They were men with whom he could not afford to quarrel; for he relied on them in battle, or insurrection, for picking out the leaders. "The cunning rascals!" he exclaimed. "There, take that trinket to Hyphax's black spouse." And he gave him Fabiola's splendid ring. He hastened back, delivered his gracious embassy, and threw the ring across. In an instant every bow dropt, and every string relaxed. Jubala, delighted, sprang forward and caught the ring. A heavy blow from her husband's fist felled her to the ground, and was greeted with a shout of applause. The savage seized the jewel; and the woman rose, to fear that she had only exchanged one slavery for a worse.

Hyphax screened himself behind the imperial command. "If," he said, "you had allowed us to send an arrow through his head or heart, all would have been straight. As it was, we are not responsible."

"At any rate, I will myself see my work done properly this time," said Maximian. "Two of you fellows with clubs come here."

Two of his attendant executioners came from behind; Sebastian, scarcely able to stand, was also there; mild and intrepid. "Now, my men," said the barbarian, "I must not have any blood spilt on these stairs; so you knock the life out of him with your cudgels; make clean work of it. Madam, what is your petition?"—stretching out his hand to Fabiola, whom he recognized, and so addressed more respectfully. She was horrified and disgusted, and almost fainting at the sight before her; so she said, "Sire, I fear it is too late!"

"Why too late?" looking at the paper. A flash came from his eye, as he said to her: "What! You knew that Sebastian was alive? Are you a Christian?"

"No, sire," she replied. Why did the denial almost dry up in her throat? She could not for her life have said she was any thing else. Ah! Fabiola, thy day is not far off.

"But, as you said just now," replied the emperor, more serene, returning her petition, "I fear it is too late; I think that blow must have been the *ictus gratiosus*."*

"I feel faint, sire," said she, respectfully; "may I retire?"

"By all means. But, by the bye, I have to thank you for the beautiful ring which you sent, and which I have given to Hyphax's wife" (lately her own slave!). "It will look more brilliant on a black hand than even on mine. Adieu!" and he kissed his hand with a wicked smile, as if there were no martyr's body near to witness against him. He was right; a heavy blow on the head had proved fatal; and Sebastian was safe where he had so longed to be. He bore with him a double palm, and received a twofold crown. Yet still, an ignominious end before the world; beaten to death without ceremony, while the emperor conversed. How much of martyrdom is in its disgrace! Woe to us when we know that our *sufferings* earn us honor!

The tyrant, seeing his work completed, ordered that Sebastian at least should not be cast into the Tiber nor on a dunghill. "Put plenty of weights to his body," he added, "and throw it into the Cloaca,† to rot there, and

---

* The *coup de grace*, the blow by which culprits were "put out of their pain." Breaking the legs of the crucified was considered an *ictus gratiosus*.

† The great sewer of Rome.

be the food of vermin. The Christians at least shall not have it." This was done; and the Saint's Acts inform us, that in the night he appeared to the holy matron Lucina, and directed her where to find his sacred remains. She obeyed his summons, and they were buried with honor, where now stands his basilica.

Christ blessing a Child, from a picture in the Cemetery of the Latin Way.

CHAPTER XXVIII.

THE CRITICAL DAY: ITS FIRST PART.

THERE are critical days in the life of man and of mankind. Not merely the days of Marathon, of Cannæ, or of Lepanto, in which a different result might have influenced the social or political fate of mankind. But it is probable that Columbus could look back upon not only the day, but the precise hour, the decision of which secured to the world all that he taught and gave it, and to himself the singular place which he holds among its worthies. And each of us, little and insignificant as he may be, has had his critical day; his day of choice, which has decided his fate through life; his day of Providence, which altered his position or his relations to others; his day of grace, when the spiritual conquered the material. In whatever way it has been, every soul, like Jerusalem,* has had its day.

And so with Fabiola, has not all been working up towards a crisis? Emperor and slave, father and guest, the good and the wicked, Christian and heathen, rich and poor; then life and death, joy and sorrow, learning and simplicity, silence and conversation, have they not all come as agents, pulling at her mind in opposite ways, yet all directing her noble and generous, though haughty and impetuous, soul one way, as the breeze and the rudder struggle against one another, only to determine the ship's single path? By what shall the resolution of these contending forces be determined? That rests

* "If thou hadst known, and in this thy day," etc. *St. Luke*, xix. 42.

not with man; wisdom, not philosophy, can decide. We have been engaged with events commemorated on the 20th of January; let the reader look, and see what comes on the following day in his calendar, and he will agree it must be an important day in our little narrative.

From the audience Fabiola retired to the apartments of Irene, where she found nothing but desolation and sorrow. She sympathized fully with the grief around her, but she saw and felt that there was a difference between her affliction and theirs. There was a buoyancy about them; there was almost an exultation breaking out through their distress; their clouds were sun-lit and brightened at times. Hers was a dead and sullen, a dull and heavy gloom, as if she had sustained a hopeless loss. Her search after Christianity, as associated with anything amiable or intelligent, seemed at an end. Her desired teacher, or informant, was gone. When the crowd had moved away from the palace, she took affectionate leave of the widow and her daughters; but, some way or other, she could not like the heathen one as she loved her sister.

She sat alone at home, and tried to read; she took up volume after volume of favorite works on Death, on Fortitude, on Friendship, on Virtue; and every one of them seemed insipid, unsound, and insincere. She plunged into a deeper and a deeper melancholy, which lasted till towards evening, when she was disturbed by a letter being put into her hand. The Greek slave, Graja, who brought it in, retired to the other end of the room, alarmed and perplexed by what she witnessed. For her mistress had scarcely glanced over the note, than she leaped up wildly from her seat, threw her hair into disorder with her hands, which she pressed, as in agony, on her temples, stood thus for a moment, looking up with an unnatural stare in her eyes, and then sank heavily down again on her chair with a deep groan. Thus she remained for some minutes, holding the letter in both her hands, with her arms relaxed, apparently unconscious.

"Who brought this letter?" she then asked, quite collected.

"A soldier, madam," answered the maid.

"Ask him to come here."

While her errand was being delivered, she composed herself, and gathered up her hair. As soon as the soldier appeared she held this brief dialogue:

"Whence do you come?"

"I am on guard at the Tullian prison."

"Who gave you the letter?"

"The Lady Agnes herself."

"On what cause is the poor child there?"

"On the accusation of a man named Fulvius, for being a Christian."

"For nothing else?"

"For nothing, I am sure."

"Then we shall soon set that matter right. I can give witness to the contrary. Tell her I will come presently; and take this for your trouble."

The soldier retired, and Fabiola was left alone. When there was something to do her mind was at once energetic and concentrated, though afterwards the tenderness of womanhood might display itself the more painfully. She wrapped herself close up, proceeded alone to the prison, and was at once conducted to the separate cell, which Agnes had obtained in consideration of her rank, backed by her parents' handsome largitions.

"What is the meaning of this, Agnes?" eagerly inquired Fabiola, after a warm embrace.

"I was arrested a few hours ago, and brought hither."

"And is Fulvius fool enough, as well as scoundrel, to trump up an accusation against you, which five minutes will confute? I will go to Tertullus myself, and contradict his absurd charge at once."

"What charge, dearest?"

"Why, that you are a Christian."

"And so I am, thank God!" replied Agnes, making on herself the sign of the cross.

The announcement did not strike Fabiola like a thunderbolt, nor rouse her, nor stagger her, nor perplex her. Sebastian's death had taken all edge or heaviness from it. She had found that faith existing in what she had considered the type of every manly virtue; she was not surprised to find it in her, whom she had loved as the very model of womanly perfection. The simple grandeur of that child's excellence, her guileless innocence, and unexcepting kindness, she had almost worshipped. It made Fabiola's difficulties less, it brought her problem nearer to a solution, to find two such peerless beings to be not mere chance-grown plants, but springing from the same seed. She bowed her head in a kind of reverence for the child, and asked her, "How long have you been so?"

"All my life, dear Fabiola; I sucked the faith, as we say, with my mother's milk."

"And why did you conceal it from me?"

"Because I saw your violent prejudices against us; how you abhorred us as practisers of the most ridiculous superstitions, as perpetrators of the most odious abominations. I perceived how you contemned us as unintellectual, uneducated, unphilosophical, and unreasonable. You would not hear a word about us; and the only object of hatred to your generous mind was the Christian name."

"True, dearest Agnes; yet I think that had I known that you, or Sebastian, was a Christian, I could not have hated it. I could have loved any thing in you."

"You think so now, Fabiola; but you know not the force

of universal prejudice, the weight of falsehood daily repeated. How many noble minds, fine intellects, and loving hearts have they enslaved, and induced to believe us to be all that we are not, something even worse than the worst of others!"

"Well, Agnes, it is selfish in me to argue thus with you in your present position. You will of course compel Fulvius to *prove* that you are a Christian."

"Oh, no! dear Fabiola; I have already confessed it, and intend to do so again publicly in the morning."

"In the morning!—what, to-morrow?" asked Fabiola, shocked at the idea of any thing so immediate.

"Yes, to-morrow. To prevent any clamor or disturbance about me (though I suspect few people will care much), I am to be interrogated early, and summary proceedings will be taken. Is not that good news, dear?" asked Agnes eagerly, seizing her cousin's hands. And then putting on one of her ecstatic looks, she exclaimed, "Behold, what I have long coveted, I already see; what I have hoped for, I hold safe; to Him alone I feel already associated in heaven, whom here on earth I have loved with all devotedness.* Oh! is He not beautiful, Fabiola, lovelier far than the angels who surround Him! How sweet His smile! how mild His eye! how bland the whole expression of His face! And that sweetest and most gracious Lady, who ever accompanies Him, our Queen and Mistress, who loves Him alone, how winningly doth she beckon me forward to join her train! I come! I come!—They are departed, Fabiola; but they return early for me to-morrow; early, mind, and we part no more."

Fabiola felt her own heart swell and heave, as if a new element were entering in. She knew not what it was, but it seemed something better than a mere human emotion. She

* "Ecce quod concupivi jam video, quod speravi jam teneo; ipsi sum juncta in cœlis quem in terris posita tota devotione dilexi." *Office of St. Agnes.*

had not yet heard the name of Grace. Agnes, however, saw the favorable change in her spirit, and inwardly thanked God for it. She begged her cousin to return before dawn to her, for their final farewell.

At this same time a consultation was being held at the house of the prefect, between that worthy functionary and his worthier son. The reader had better listen to it, to learn its purport.

"Certainly," said the magistrate, "if the old sorceress was right in one thing, she ought to be in the other. I will answer, from experience, how powerful is wealth in conquering any resistance."

"And you will allow, too," rejoined Corvinus, "from the enumeration we have made, that among the competitors for Fabiola's hand, there has not been one who could not justly be rather called an aspirant after her fortune."

"Yourself included, my dear Corvinus."

"Yes, so far; but not if I succeed in offering her, with myself, the lady Agnes's great wealth."

"And in a manner too, methinks, that will more easily gain upon what I hear of her generous and lofty disposition. Giving her that wealth independent of conditions, and then offering yourself to her, will put her under one of two obligations, either to accept you as her husband, or throw you back the fortune."

"Admirable, father! I never saw the second alternative before. Do you think there is no possibility of securing it except through her?"

"None whatever. Fulvius, of course, will apply for his share; and the probability is, that the emperor will declare he intends to take it all for himself. For he hates Fulvius. But if I propose a more popular and palpably reasonable plan, of giving the property to the nearest relation, who worships the gods—this Fabiola does, don't she?"

"Certainly, father."

"I think he will embrace it; while I am sure there is no chance of his making a free gift to me. The proposal from a judge would enrage him."

"Then how will you manage it, father?"

"I will have an imperial rescript prepared during the night, ready for signature; and I will proceed immediately after the execution to the palace, magnify the unpopularity which is sure to follow it, lay it all on Fulvius, and show the emperor how his granting the property to the next in the settlement of it, will redound greatly to his credit and glory. He is as vain as he is cruel and rapacious; and one vice must be made to fight another."

"Nothing could be better, my dear father; I shall retire to rest with an easy mind. To-morrow will be the critical day of my life. All my future depends upon whether I am accepted or rejected."

"I only wish," added Tertullus, rising, "that I could have seen this peerless lady, and sounded the depths of her philosophy, before your final bargain was struck."

"Fear not, father; she is well worthy of being your daughter-in-law. Yes, to-morrow is indeed the turning-point of my fortunes."

Even Corvinus can have his critical day. Why not Fabiola?

While this domestic interview was going on, a conference was taking place between Fulvius and his amiable uncle. The latter, entering late, found his nephew sitting sullen and alone in the house, and thus accosted him:

"Well, Fulvius, is she secured?"

"She is, uncle, as fast as bars and walls can make her; but her spirit is free and independent as ever."

"Never mind that; sharp steel makes short work of spirit. Is her fate certain? and are its consequences sure?"

"Why, if nothing else happens, the first is safe; the second have still to encounter imperial caprice. But I own I feel pain and remorse at sacrificing so young a life, and for an insecure result."

"Come, Fulvius," said the old man sternly, looking as cold as a grey rock in the morning mist; "no softness, I hope, in this matter. Do you remember what day is to-morrow?"

"Yes; the twelfth before the calends of February."*

"The critical day always for you. It was on this day that to gain another's wealth, you committed——"

"Peace, peace!" interrupted Fulvius in agony. "Why will you always remind me of every thing I most wish to forget?"

"Because of this: you wish to forget yourself, and that must not be. I must take from you every pretence to be guided by conscience, virtue, or even honor. It is folly to affect compassion for any one's life, who stands in the way of your fortune, after what you did to *her*."

Fulvius bit his lip in silent rage, and covered his crimson face with his hands. Eurotas roused him by saying: "Well, then, to-morrow is another, and probably a final critical day for you. Let us calmly weigh its prospects. You will go to the emperor, and ask for your rightful share in the confiscated property. Suppose it is granted?"

"I will sell it as quick as possible, pay my debts, and retire to some country where my name has never been heard."

"Suppose your claims are rejected?"

"Impossible, impossible!" exclaimed Fulvius, racked by the very idea; "it is my right, hardly earned. It cannot be denied me."

"Quietly, my young friend; let us discuss the matter coolly. Remember our proverb: 'From the stirrup to the

* Jan. 21.

saddle there has been many a fall.' *Suppose* only that your rights are refused you."

"Then I am a ruined man. I have no other prospect before me, of retrieving my fortunes here. Still I must fly hence."

"Good; and what do you owe at Janus's arch?"*

"A good couple of hundred sestertia,† between principal and compound interest at fifty per cent, to that unconscionable Jew Ephraim."

"On what security?"

"On my sure expectation of this lady's estates."

"And if you are disappointed, do you think he will let you fly?"

"Not if he knows it, most assuredly. But we must be prepared from this moment for any emergency; and that with the utmost secrecy."

"Leave that to me, Fulvius; you see how eventful the issue of to-morrow may be to you, or rather of to-day; for morning is approaching. Life or death to you hang upon it; it is the great day of your existence. Courage then, or rather an inflexible determination, steel you to work out its destiny!"

* In or near the forum stood several arches dedicated to Janus, and called simply by his name, near which usurers or money-lenders kept their posts.
† 1000*l.*

A Monogram of Christ, found in the Catacombs.

CHAPTER XXIX.

THE SAME DAY: ITS SECOND PART.

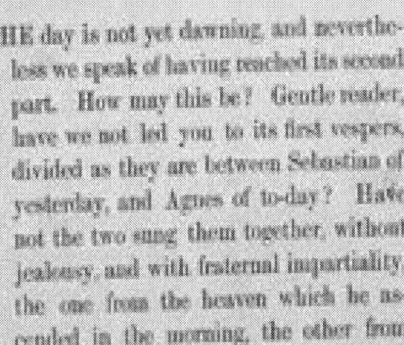HE day is not yet dawning, and nevertheless we speak of having reached its second part. How may this be? Gentle reader, have we not led you to its first vespers, divided as they are between Sebastian of yesterday, and Agnes of to-day? Have not the two sung them together, without jealousy, and with fraternal impartiality, the one from the heaven which he ascended in the morning, the other from the dungeon into which she descended in the evening? Glorious Church of Christ! great in the unclashing combination of thy unity, stretching from heaven to beneath the earth, wherever exists a prison-house of the just.

From his lodgings Fulvius went out into the night-air, which was crisp and sharp, to cool his blood, and still his throbbing brows. He wandered about, almost without any purpose; but found himself imperceptibly drawing nearer and nearer to the Tullian prison. As he was literally without affection, what could be his attraction thither? It was a strangely compounded feeling, made up of as bitter ingredients as ever filled the poisoner's cup. There was gnawing remorse; there was baffled pride; there was goading avarice; there was humbling shame; there was a terrible sense of the approaching consummation of his villany. It was true, he had been rejected, scorned, baffled by a mere child, while her fortune was necessary for his rescue from beggary and death,—so at least he reasoned; yet he would still rather have her hand than her head. Her murder appeared revoltingly atrocious to him, unless absolutely inevitable. So he would give her another chance.

He was now at the prison gate, of which he possessed the watchword. He pronounced it, entered, and, at his desire, was conducted to his victim's cell. She did not flutter, nor run into a corner, like a bird into whose cage the hawk has found entrance; calm and intrepid, she stood before him.

"Respect me here, Fulvius, at least," she gently said; "I have but a few hours to live: let them be spent in peace."

"Madam," he replied, "I have come to lengthen them, if you please, to years; and, instead of peace, I offer happiness."

"Surely, sir, if I understand you, the time is past for this sad vanity. Thus to address one whom you have delivered over to death, is at best a mockery."

"It is not so, gentle lady; your fate is in your own hands; only your own obstinacy will give you over to death. I have come to renew, once more, my offer, and with it that of life. It is your last chance."

"Have I not before told you that I am a Christian; and that I would forfeit a thousand lives rather than betray my faith?"

"But now I ask you no longer to do this. The gates of the prison are yet open to me. Fly with me; and, in spite of the imperial decrees, you shall be a Christian, and yet live."

"Then have I not clearly told you that I am already espoused to my Lord and Saviour Jesus Christ, and that to Him alone I keep eternal faith?"

"Folly and madness! Persevere in it till to-morrow, and

that may be awarded to you which you fear more than death, and which will drive this illusion forever from your mind."

"I fear nothing for Christ. For know, that I have an angel ever guarding me, who will not suffer his Master's handmaid to suffer scorn.* But now, cease this unworthy importunity, and leave me the last privilege of the condemned—solitude."

Fulvius had been gradually losing patience, and could no longer restrain his passion. Rejected again, baffled once more by a child, this time with the sword hanging over her neck! A flame irrepressible broke out from the smouldering heat within him; and, in an instant, the venomous ingredients that we have described as mingled in his heart, were distilled into one black, solitary drop,—HATRED. With flashing look, and furious gesture, he broke forth:

"Wretched woman, I give thee one more opportunity of rescuing thyself from destruction. Which wilt thou have, life with me, or death?"

"Death even I will choose for her, rather than life with a monster like thee!" exclaimed a voice just within the door.

"She shall have it," he rejoined, clenching his fist, and darting a mad look at the new speaker; "and thou too, if again thou darest to fling thy baneful shadow across my path."

Fabiola was alone for the last time with Agnes. She had been for some minutes unobserved watching the contest, between what would have appeared to her, had she been a Christian, an angel of light and a spirit of darkness; and truly Agnes looked like the first, if human creature ever did. In preparation for her coming festival of full espousals to the Lamb, when she should sign her contract of everlasting love,

* "Marem enim habeo custodem corporis mei, Angelum Domini." *The Breviary.*

as He had done, in blood, she had thrown over the dark garments of her mourning a white and spotless bridal robe. In the midst of that dark prison, lighted by a solitary lamp, she looked radiant and almost dazzling; while her tempter, wrapped up in his dark cloak, crouching down to rush out of the low door of the dungeon, looked like a black and vanquished demon, plunging into an abyss beneath.

Then Fabiola looked into her countenance, and thought she had never seen it half so sweet. No trace of anger, of fear, of flurry, or agitation was there; no paleness, no flush, no alternations of hectic excitement and pallid depression. Her eyes beamed with more than their usual mild intelligence; her smile was as placid and cheerful as it ever was, when they discoursed together. Then there was a noble air about her, a greatness of look and manner, which Fabiola would have compared to that mien and stateliness, and that ambrosial atmosphere by which, in poetical mythology, a being of a higher sphere was recognized on earth.* It was not inspiration, for it was passionless; but it was such expression and manner, as her highest conceptions of virtue and intellect, combined in the soul, might be supposed to stamp upon the outward form. Hence her feelings passed beyond love into a higher range; they were more akin to reverence.

Agnes took one of her hands in each of her own, crossed them upon her own calm bosom, and looking into her face with a gaze of blandest earnestness, said:

"Fabiola, I have one dying request to make you. You have never refused me any; I am sure you will not this."

"Speak not thus to me, dearest Agnes; you must not request; you command me now."

"Then promise me, that you will immediately apply your mind to master the doctrines of Christianity. I know you

* "Incessu patuit Dea.

will embrace them; and then you will no longer be to me what you are now."

"And what is that?"

"Dark, dark, dearest Fabiola. When I look upon you thus, I see in you a noble intellect, a generous disposition, an affectionate heart, a cultivated mind, a fine moral feeling, and a virtuous life. What can be desired more in woman? and yet over all these splendid gifts there hangs a cloud, to my eyes, of gloomy shadow, the shade of death. Drive it away, and all will be lightsome and bright."

"I feel it, dear Agnes,—I feel it. Standing before you, I seem to be as a black spot compared to your brightness. And how, embracing Christianity, shall I become light like you?"

"You must pass, Fabiola, through the torrent that sunders us." (Fabiola started, recollecting her dream). "Waters of refreshment shall flow over your body, and oil of gladness shall embalm your flesh; and the soul shall be washed clean as driven snow, and the heart be softened as the babe's. From that bath you will come forth a new creature, born again to a new and immortal life."

"And shall I lose all that you have but just now prized in me?" asked Fabiola, somewhat downcast.

"As the gardener," answered the martyr, "selects some hardy and robust, but unprofitable plant, and on it engrafts but a small shoot of one that is sweet and tender, and the flowers and fruits of this belong to the first, and yet deprive it of no grace, no grandeur, no strength that it had before, so will the new life you shall receive ennoble, elevate, and sanctify (you can scarcely understand this word), the valuable gifts of nature and education which you already possess. What a glorious being Christianity will make you, Fabiola!"

"What a new world you are leading me to, dear Agnes! Oh, that you were not leaving me outside its very threshold!"

"Hark!" exclaimed Agnes, in an ecstasy of joy. "They come, they come! You hear the measured tramp of the soldiers in the gallery. They are the bridesmen coming to summon me. But I see on high the white-robed bridesmaids borne on the bright clouds of morning, and beckoning me forward. Yes, my lamp is trimmed, and I go forth to meet the Bridegroom. Farewell, Fabiola; weep not for me. Oh, that I could make you feel, as I do, the happiness of dying for Christ! And now I will speak a word to you which I never have addressed to you before,—God bless you!" And she made the sign of the Cross on Fabiola's forehead. An embrace, convulsive on Fabiola's part, calm and tender on Agnes's, was their last earthly greeting. The one hastened home, filled with a new and generous purpose; the other resigned herself to the shame-stricken guard.

Over the first part of the martyr's trials we cast a veil of silence, though ancient Fathers, and the Church in her offices, dwell upon it, as doubling her crown.* Suffice it to say, that her angel protected her from harm;† and that the purity of her presence converted a den of infamy into a holy and lovely sanctuary.‡ It was still early in the morning when she stood again before the tribunal of the prefect, in the Roman Forum; unchanged and unscathed, without a blush upon her smiling countenance, or a pang of sorrow in her innocent heart. Only her unshorn hair, the symbol of virginity, which had been let

* "Duplex corona est pudicæ martyri." *Prudentius.*
† "Ingressu Agnes turpitudinis locum, Angelum Domini præparatum invenit." *The Breviary.*
‡ The Church of St. Agnes in the Piazza Navona, one of the most beautiful in Rome.

"Cui posse soli Omnipotens dedit
Castum vel ipsum reddere lenonem.
*   *   *   *   *
Nil non pudicum est, quod pia visere
Dignaris, almo vel pede tangere."
Prudentius.

loose, flowed down, in golden waves, upon her snow-white dress."*

It was a lovely morning. Many will remember it to have been a beautiful day on its anniversary, as they have walked out of the Nomentan gate, now the Porta Pia, towards the church which bears our virgin-martyr's name, to see blessed upon her altar the two lambs, from whose wool are made the palliums sent by the Pope to the archbishops of his communion. Already the almond-trees are hoary, not with frost, but with blossoms; the earth is being loosened round the vines, and spring seems latent in the swelling buds, which are watching for the signal from the southern breeze, to burst and expand.† The atmosphere, rising into a cloudless sky, has just that temperature that one loves, of a sun, already vigorous, not heating, but softening, the slightly frosty air. Such we have frequently experienced St. Agnes's day, together with joyful thousands, hastening to her shrine.

The judge was sitting in the open Forum, and a sufficient crowd formed a circle round the charmed space, which few, save Christians, loved to enter. Among the spectators were two whose appearance attracted general attention; they stood opposite each other, at the ends of the semicircle formed by the multitude. One was a youth, enveloped in his toga, with a slouching hat over his eyes, so that his features could not be distinguished. The other was a lady of aristocratic mien, tall and erect, such as one does not expect to meet on such an occasion. Wrapped close about her, and so ample as to veil her from head to foot, like the beautiful ancient statue, known among artists by the name of Modesty,‡ she had a scarf or mantle of Indian workmanship, woven in richest pattern of

---

* "Non intorto crine capnt comptum." Her head not dressed with braided hair. *St. Ambrose*, lib. I. de Virgin. c. 2. See Prudentius's description of St. Eulalia, περὶ στεφ. hymn. iii. 31.
† "Solvitur acris hyems, grata vice veris et Favoni." *Horace.*
‡ Pudicitia.

crimson, purple, and gold, a garment truly imperial, and less suitable, than even female presence, to this place of doom and blood. A slave, or servant, of superior class attended her, carefully veiled also, like her mistress. The lady's mind seemed intent on one only object, as she stood immovable, leaning with her elbow on a marble post.

Agnes was introduced by her guards into the open space, and stood intrepid facing the tribunal. Her thoughts seemed

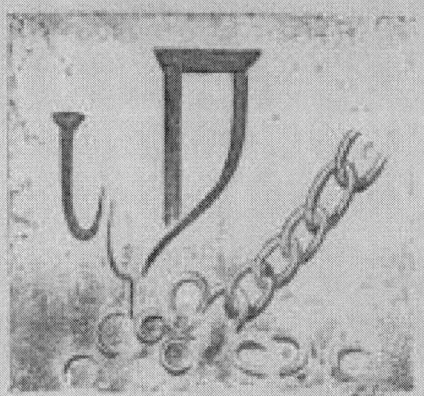

Chains for the Martyrs, after a picture found in 1845, in a crypt at Milan.

to be far away; and she took no notice even of those two who, till she appeared, had been objects of universal observation.

"Why is she unfettered?" asked the prefect angrily.

"She does not need it: she walks so readily," answered Catulus; "and she is so young."

"But she is obstinate as the oldest. Put manacles on her hands at once."

The executioner turned over a quantity of such prison ornaments,—to Christian eyes really such,—and at length selected a pair as light and small as he could find, and placed them round her wrists. Agnes playfully, and with a smile,

The judge angrily reproved the executioner for his hesitation, and bid him at once do his duty.

shook her hands, and they fell, like St. Paul's viper, clattering at her feet."

"They are the smallest we have, sir," said the softened executioner; "one so young ought to wear other bracelets."

"Silence, man!" rejoined the exasperated judge, who, turning to the prisoner, said, in a blander tone:

"Agnes, I pity thy youth, thy station, and the bad education thou hast received. I desire, if possible, to save thee. Think better while thou hast time. Renounce the false and pernicious maxims of Christianity, obey the imperial edicts, and sacrifice to the gods."

"It is useless," she replied, "to tempt me longer. My resolution is unalterable. I despise thy false divinities, and can only love and serve the one living God. Eternal Ruler, open wide the heavenly gates, until lately closed to man. Blessed Christ, call to Thee the soul that cleaveth unto Thee: victim first to Thee by virginal consecration; now to Thy Father by martyrdom's immolation."†

"I waste time, I see," said the impatient prefect, who saw symptoms of compassion rising in the multitude. "Secretary, write the sentence. We condemn Agnes, for contempt of the imperial edicts, to be punished by the sword."

"On what road, and at what mile-stone, shall the judgment be executed?"‡ asked the headsman.

"Let it be carried into effect at once," was the reply.

Agnes raised for one moment her hands and eyes to heaven, then calmly knelt down. With her own hands she

---

* St. Ambrose, *ubi supra*.

† "Æterne Rector, divide januas,
Cœli, observatas terrigenis prius,
Ac te sequentem, Christe, animam voca,
Cum virginalem, tum Patris hostiam."
Prudentius, περὶ στεφ. 14.

‡ This was the usual practice, to behead out of the gate, at the second, third, or fourth mile-stone; but it is clear from Prudentius and other writers that St. Agnes suffered at the place of trial, of which we have other instances.

drew forward her silken hair over her head, and exposed her neck to the blow.* A pause ensued, for the executioner was trembling with emotion, and could not wield his sword.† As the child knelt alone, in her white robe, with her head inclined, her arms modestly crossed upon her bosom, and her amber locks hanging almost to the ground, and veiling her features, she might not unaptly have been compared to some rare plant, of which the slender stalk, white as the lily, bent with the luxuriancy of its golden blossom.

The judge angrily reproved the executioner for his hesitation, and bid him at once do his duty. The man passed the back of his rough left hand across his eyes, as he raised his sword. It was seen to flash for an instant in the air; and the next moment, flower and stem were lying scarcely displaced on the ground. It might have been taken for the prostration of prayer, had not the white robe been in that minute dyed into a rich crimson—washed in the blood of the Lamb.

The man on the judge's right hand had looked with unflinching eye upon the stroke, and his lip curled in a wicked triumph over the fallen. The lady opposite had turned away her head, till the murmur, that follows a suppressed breath in a crowd, told her all was over. She then boldly advanced forward, unwound from round her person her splendid brocaded mantle, and stretched it as a pall, over the mangled body. A burst of applause followed this graceful act of womanly feeling,‡ as the lady stood, now in the garb of deepest mourning, before the tribunal.

"Sir," she said in a tone clear and distinct, but full of emotion, "grant me one petition. Let not the rude hands of

---

* Prudentius.

† St. Ambrose.

‡ Prudentius mentions that a sudden fall of snow shrouded thus the body of St. Eulalia lying in the Forum. *Ubi sup.*

The Christian Martyr

your servants again touch and profane the hallowed remains of her, whom I have loved more than any thing on earth; but let me bear them hence to the sepulchre of her fathers; for she was noble as she was good."

Tertullus was manifestly irritated, as he replied: "Madam, whoever you may be, your request cannot be granted. Catulus, see that the body be cast, as usual, into the river, or burnt."

"I entreat you, sir," the lady earnestly insisted, "by every claim which female virtue has upon you, by any tear which a mother has shed over you, by every soothing word which a sister has ever spoken to you, in illness or sorrow; by every ministration of their gentle hands, I implore you to grant my humble prayer. And if, when you return home this evening, you will be met at the threshold by daughters, who will kiss your hand, though stained with the blood of one, whom you may feel proud if they resemble, be able to say to them, at least, that this slightest tribute to the maidenly delicacy which they prize has not been refused."

Such common sympathy was manifested that Tertullus, anxious to check it, asked her sharply:

"Pray, are you, too, a Christian?"

She hesitated for one instant, then replied, "No, sir, I am not; but I own that if anything could make me one, it would be what I have seen this day."

"What do you mean?"

"Why, that to preserve the religion of the empire such beings as she whom you have slain" (her tears interrupted her for a moment) "should have to die; while monsters who disgrace the shape and name of man should have to live and flourish. Oh, sir, you know not what you have blotted out from earth this day! She was the purest, sweetest, holiest thing I ever knew upon it, the very flower of womanhood, though yet a child. And she might have lived yet, had she not scorned the proffered hand of a vile adventurer, who pursued her with his loathsome offers into the seclusion of her villa, into the sanctuary of her home, and even into the last retreat of her dungeon. For this she died, that she would not endow with her wealth, and ennoble by her alliance, that Asiatic spy."

She pointed with calm scorn at Fulvius, who bounded forward, and exclaimed with fury: "She lies, foully and calumniously, sir. Agnes openly confessed herself a Christian."

"Bear with me, sir," replied the lady, with noble dignity, "while I convict him; and look on his face for proof of what I say. Didst thou not, Fulvius, early this morning, seek that gentle child in her cell, and deliberately tell her (for unseen, I heard you) that if she would but accept thy hand, not only wouldst thou save her life, but, despising the imperial commands, secure her still remaining a Christian?"

Fulvius stood, pale as death: stood, as one does for a moment who is shot through the heart, or struck by lightning. He looked like a man on whom sentence is going to be pronounced,—not of death, but of eternal pillory, as the judge addressed him, saying:

"Fulvius, thy very look confirms this grievous charge. I could arraign thee on it, for thy head, at once. But take my counsel, begone hence forever. Flee, and hide thyself, after such villany, from the indignation of all just men, and from the vengeance of the gods. Show not thy face again here, nor in the Forum, nor in any public place of Rome. If this lady pleases, even now I will take her deposition against thee. Pray, madam," he asked most respectfully, "may I have the honor of knowing your name?"

"Fabiola," she replied.

The judge was now all complacency, for he saw before him, he hoped, his future daughter-in-law. "I have often heard of you, madam," he said, "and of your high accomplishments and exalted virtues. You are, moreover, nearly allied to this victim of treachery, and have a right to claim her body. It is at your disposal." This speech was interrupted at its beginning by a loud hiss and yell that accompanied Fulvius's departure. He was pale with shame, terror, and rage.

Fabiola gracefully thanked the prefect, and beckoned to Syra, who attended her. The servant again made a signal to some one else; and presently four slaves appeared bearing a lady's litter. Fabiola would allow no one but herself and

A Stand Tile, used as a mark for a martyr's grave.

Syra to raise the relics from the ground, place them on the litter, and cover them with their precious pall. "Bear this treasure to its own home," she said, and followed as mourner with her maid. A little girl, all in tears, timidly asked if she might join them.

"Who art thou?" asked Fabiola.

"I am poor Emerentiana, *her* foster-sister," replied the child; and Fabiola led her kindly by the hand.

The moment the body was removed, a crowd of Christians, children, men, and women, threw themselves forward, with sponges and linen cloths, to gather up the blood. In vain did the guards fall on them, with whips, cudgels, and even with sharper weapons, so that many mingled their own blood with that of the martyr. When a sovereign, at his coronation, or on first entering his capital, throws, according to ancient custom, handfuls of gold and silver coins among the crowd, he does not create a more eager competition for his scattered treasures, than there was among those primitive Christians, for what they valued more than gold or precious stones, the ruby drops which a martyr had poured from his heart for his Lord. But all respected the prior claim of one; and here it was the deacon Reparatus, who, at risk of life, was present, phial in hand, to gather the blood of Agnes's testimony; that it might be appended, as a faithful seal, to the record of martyrdom on her tomb.

The Resurrection of Lazarus, from the Cemetery of St. Domitilla.

CHAPTER XXX.

THE SAME DAY: ITS THIRD PART.

TERTULLUS hastened at once to the palace; fortunately, or unfortunately, for these candidates for martyrdom. There he met Corvinus, with the prepared rescript, elegantly engrossed in *uncial*, that is, large capital letters. He had the privilege of immediate admission into the imperial presence; and, as a matter of business, reported the death of Agnes, exaggerated the public feeling likely to be caused by it, attributed it all to the folly and mismanagement of Fulvius, whose worst guilt he did not disclose for fear of having to try him, and thus bringing out what he was now doing; depreciated the value of Agnes's property, and ended by saying that it would be a gracious act of clemency, and one sure to counteract unpopular feelings, to bestow it upon her relative, who by settlement was her next heir. He described Fabiola as a young lady of extraordinary intellect and wonderful learning, who was most zealously devoted to the worship of the gods, and daily offered sacrifice to the genius of the emperors.

"I know her," said Maximian, laughing, as if at the recollection of something very droll. "Poor thing! she sent me a splendid ring, and yesterday asked me for that wretched Sebastian's life, just as they had finished cudgelling him to death." And he laughed immoderately, then continued: "Yes, yes, by all means; a little inheritance will console her, no doubt, for the loss of that fellow. Let a rescript be made out, and I will sign it."

Tertullus produced the one prepared, saying he had fully relied on the emperor's magnanimous clemency; and the imperial barbarian put a signature to it which would have disgraced a schoolboy. The prefect at once consigned it to his son.

Scarcely had he left the palace, when Fulvius entered. He had been home to put on a proper court attire, and remove from his features, by the bath and the perfumer's art, the traces of his morning's passion. He felt a keen presentiment that he should be disappointed. Eurotas's cool discussion of the preceding evening had prepared him; the cross of all his designs, and his multiplied disappointments that day, had strengthened this instinctive conviction. One woman, indeed, seemed born to meet and baffle him whichever way he turned; but, "thank the gods," he thought, "she cannot be in my way here. She has this morning blasted my character for ever; she cannot claim my rightful reward; she has made me an outcast; it is not in her power to make me a beggar." This seemed his only ground of hope. Despair, indeed, urged him forward; and he determined to argue out his claims to the confiscated property of Agnes, with the only competitor he could fear, the rapacious emperor himself. He might as well risk his life over it, for if he failed, he was utterly ruined. After waiting some time, he entered the audience-hall, and advanced with the blandest smile that he could muster to the imperial feet.

"What want you here?" was his first greeting.

"Sire," he replied, "I have come humbly to pray your royal justice, to order my being put into immediate possession of my share of the Lady Agnes's property. She has been convicted of being a Christian upon my accusation, and she has just suffered the merited penalty of all who disobey the imperial edicts."

"That is all quite right; but we have heard how stupidly you mismanaged the whole business as usual, and have raised murmurings and discontent in the people against us. So, now, the sooner you quit our presence, palace, and city, the better for yourself. Do you understand? We don't usually give such warnings twice."

"I will obey instantly every intimation of the supreme will. But I am almost destitute. Command what of right is mine to be delivered over to me, and I part immediately."

"No more words," replied the tyrant, "but go at once. As to the property which you demand with so much pertinacity, you cannot have it. We have made over the whole of it, by an irrevocable rescript, to an excellent and deserving person, the Lady Fabiola."

Fulvius did not speak another word; but kissed the emperor's hand and slowly retired. He looked a ruined, broken man. He was only heard to say, as he passed out of the gate: "Then, after all, she *has* made me a beggar too." When he reached home, Eurotas, who read his answer in his nephew's eye, was amazed at his calmness.

"I see," he drily remarked, "it is all over."

"Yes; are your preparations made, Eurotas?"

"Nearly so. I have sold the jewels, furniture, and slaves, at some loss; but, with the trifle I had in hand, we have enough to take us safe to Asia. I have retained Stabio, as the most trusty of our servants; he will carry our small travelling requisites on his horse. Two others are preparing for you and me. I have only one thing more to get for our journey, and then I am ready to start."

"Pray what is that?"

"The poison. I ordered it last night, but it will only be ready at noon."

"What is that for?" asked Fulvius, with some alarm.

"Surely you know," rejoined the other, unmoved. "I am willing to make one more trial any where else; but our bargain is clear; my father's family must not end in beggary. It must be extinguished in honor."

Fulvius bit his lip, and said, "Well, be it as you like, I am weary of life. Leave the house as soon as possible, for fear of Ephraim, and be with your horses at the third mile on the Latin gate soon after dusk. I will join you there. For I, too, have an important matter to transact before I start."

"And what is that?" asked Eurotas, with a rather keen curiosity.

"I cannot tell even you. But if I am not with you by two hours after sunset, give me up, and save yourself without me."

Eurotas fixed upon him his cold dark eye, with one of those looks which ever read Fulvius through; to see if he could detect any lurking idea of escape from his gripe. But his look was cool and unusually open, and the old man asked no more. While this dialogue was going on, Fulvius had been divesting himself of his court garments, and attiring himself in a travelling suit. So completely did he evidently prepare himself for his journey, without necessity of returning home, that he even took his weapons with him; besides his sword, securing in his girdle, but concealed under his cloak, one of those curved daggers, of highest temper and most fatal form, which were only known in the East.

Eurotas proceeded at once to the Numidian quarters in the palace, and asked for Jubala; who entered with two small flasks of different sizes, and was just going to give some explanations, when her husband, half-drunk, half-furious, was seen approaching. Eurotas had just time to conceal the flasks in his belt, and slip a coin into her hand, when Hyphax came up. His wife had mentioned to him the offers which Eurotas had made to her before marriage, and had excited in his hot African blood a jealousy that amounted to hatred. The savage rudely thrust his wife out of the apartment, and would have picked a quarrel with the Syrian; had not the latter, his purpose being accomplished, acted with forbearance, assured the archer-chief that he should never more see him, and retired.

It is time, however, that we return to Fabiola. The reader is probably prepared to hear us say, that she returned home a Christian; and yet it was not so. For what as yet did she know of Christianity, to be said to profess it? In Sebastian and Agnes she had indeed willingly admired the virtue, unselfish, generous, and more than earthly, which now she was ready to attribute to that faith. She saw that it gave motives of actions, principles of life, elevation of mind, courage of conscience, and determination of virtuous will, such as no other system of belief ever bestowed. And even if, as she now shrewdly suspected, and intended in calmer moments to ascertain, the sublime revelations of Syra, concerning an unseen sphere of virtue, and its all-seeing Ruler, came from the same source, to what did it all amount more than to a grand moral and intellectual system, partly practical, partly speculative, as all codes of philosophic teaching were? This was a very different thing from Christianity. She had as yet heard nothing of its real and essential doctrines, its fathomless, yet accessible, depths of mystery; the awful, vast, and heaven-high structure of faith, which the simplest soul may contain; as a child's eye will take in the perfect reflection and counterpart of a mountain, though a giant cannot scale it. She had never heard of a God, One in Trinity; of the co-equal Son incarnate for man. She had never been told of the marvellous history, of Redemption by God's sufferings and death. She had not heard of Nazareth, or Bethlehem, or Calvary.

How could she call herself a Christian, or be one, in ignorance of all this?

How many names had to become familiar and sweet to her which as yet were unknown, or barbarous—Mary, Joseph, Peter, Paul, and John? Not to mention the sweetest of all, His, whose name is balm to the wounded heart, or as honey dropping from the broken honeycomb. And how much had she yet to learn about the provision for salvation on earth, in the Church, in grace, in sacraments, in prayer, in love, in charity to others! What unexplored regions lay beyond the small tract which she had explored!

No; Fabiola returned home, exhausted almost by the preceding day and night, and the sad scenes of the morning, and retired to her own apartment, no longer perhaps even a philosopher, yet not a Christian. She desired all her servants to keep away from the court which she occupied, that she might not be disturbed by the smallest noise; and she forbade any one to have access to her. There she sat in loneliness and silence, for several hours, too excited to obtain rest from slumber. She mourned long over Agnes, as a mother might over a child suddenly carried off. Yet, was there not a tinge of light upon the cloud that overshadowed her, more than when it hung over her father's bier? Did it not seem to her an insult to reason, an outrage to humanity, to think that *she* had perished; that she had been permitted to walk forward in her bright robe, and with her smiling countenance, and with her joyous, simple heart, straight on—into nothing; that she had been allured by conscience, and justice, and purity, and truth, on, on, till with arms outstretched to embrace them, she stepped over a precipice, beneath which yawned annihilation? No. Agnes, she felt sure, was happy somehow, somewhere; or justice was a senseless word.

"How strange," she further thought, "that every one whom I have known endowed with superior excellence, men like Sebastian, women like Agnes, should turn out to have belonged to the scorned race of Christians! One only remains, and to-morrow I will interrogate her."

When she turned from these, and looked round upon the heathen world, Fulvius, Tertullus, the Emperor, Calpurnius,— nay, she shuddered as she surprised herself on the point of mentioning her own father's name—it sickened her to see the contrast of baseness with nobleness, vice with virtue, stupidity with wisdom, and the sensual with the spiritual. Her mind was thus being shaped into a mould, which some form of practical excellence must be found to fill, or it must be broken; her soul was craving as a parched soil, which heaven must send its waters to refresh, or it must become an eternal desert.

Agnes, surely, well deserved the glory of gaining, by her death, her kinswoman's conversion; but was there not one, more humble, who had established a prior claim? One who had given up freedom, and offered life, for this unselfish gain?

While Fabiola was alone and desolate, she was disturbed by the entrance of a stranger, introduced under the ominous title of "A messenger from the emperor." The porter had at first denied him admittance; but upon being assured that he bore an important embassy from the sovereign, he felt obliged to inquire from the steward what to do; when he was informed that no one with such a claim could be refused entrance.

Fabiola was amazed, and her displeasure was somewhat mitigated, by the ridiculous appearance of the person deputed in such a solemn character. It was Corvinus, who with clownish grace approached her, and in a studied speech, evidently got up very floridly, and intrusted to a bad memory, laid at her feet an imperial rescript, and his own sincere affection, the Lady Agnes's estates, and his clumsy hand. Fabiola could not at all comprehend the connection between the two combined presents, and never imagined that the one was a bribe for the other. So she desired him to return her humble thanks to the emperor for his gracious act; adding, "Say that I am too ill to-day to present myself, and do him homage."

"But these estates, you are aware, were forfeited and confiscated," he gasped out in great confusion, "and my father has obtained them for you."

"That was unnecessary," said Fabiola, "for they were settled on me long ago, and became mine the moment"—she faltered, and after a strong effort at self-mastery, she continued—"the moment they ceased to be another's; they did not fall under confiscation."

Corvinus was dumb-foundered; at last he stumbled into something, meant for an humble petition to be admitted as an aspirant after her hand, but understood by Fabiola to be a demand of recompense, for procuring or bringing so important a document. She assured him that every claim he might have on her should be fully and honorably considered at a more favorable moment; but as she was exceedingly wearied and unwell, she must beg him to leave her at present. He did so quite elated, fancying that he had secured his prize.

After he was gone she hardly looked at the parchment, which he had left open on a small table by her couch, but sat musing on the sorrowful scenes she had witnessed, till it wanted about an hour to sunset. Sometimes her reveries turned to one point, sometimes to another of the late events; and, at last, she was dwelling on her being confronted with Fulvius, that morning, in the Forum. Her memory vividly replaced the entire scene before her, and her mind gradually worked itself into a state of painful excitement, which she at length checked by saying aloud to herself: "Thank heaven! I shall never behold that villain's face again."

The words were scarcely out of her mouth, when she

shaded her eyes with her hand, as she raised herself up on her couch, and looked towards the door. Was it her overheated fancy which beguiled her, or did her wakeful eyes show her a reality? Her ears decided the question, by these words which they heard:

"Pray, madam, who is the man whom you honor by that gracious speech?"

"You, Fulvius," she said, rising with dignity. "A further intruder still; not only into the house, the villa, and the dungeon, but into the most secret apartments of a lady's residence; and what is worse, into the house of sorrow of one whom you have bereaved. Begone at once, or I will have you ignominiously expelled hence."

"Sit down and compose yourself, lady," rejoined the intruder; "this is my last visit to you; but we have a reckoning to make together of some weight. As to crying out, or bringing in help, you need not trouble yourself; your orders to your servants to keep aloof, have been too well obeyed. There is no one within call."

It was true. Fulvius found the way prepared unwittingly for him by Corvinus; for upon presenting himself at the door the porter, who had seen him twice dine at the house, told him of the strict orders given, and assured him that he could not be admitted unless he came from the emperor, for such were his instructions. That, Fulvius said, was exactly his case; and the porter, wondering that so many imperial messengers should come in one day, let him pass. He begged that the door might be left unfastened, in case the porter should not be at his post when he retired; for he was in a hurry, and should not like to disturb the house in such a state of grief. He added that he required no guide, for he knew the way to Fabiola's apartment.

Fulvius seated himself opposite to the lady, and continued:

"You ought not to be offended, madam, with my unexpectedly coming upon you, and overhearing your amiable soliloquies about myself; it is a lesson I learned from yourself in the Tullian prison. But I must begin my scores from an earlier date. When, for the first time, I was invited by your worthy father to his table, I met one whose looks and words at once gained my affections,—I need not now mention her name,—and whose heart, with instinctive sympathy, returned them."

"Insolent man!" Fabiola exclaimed, "to allude to such a topic here; it is false that any such affection ever existed on either side."

"As to the Lady Agnes," resumed Fulvius, "I have the best authority, that of your lamented parent, who more than once encouraged me to persevere in my suit, by assuring me that his cousin had confided to him her reciprocating love."

Fabiola was mortified; for she now remembered that this was too true, from the hints which Fabius had given her, of his stupid misunderstanding.

"I know well, that my dear father was under a delusion upon this subject; but I, from whom that dear child concealed nothing——"

"Except her religion," interrupted Fulvius, with bitter irony.

"Peace!" Fabiola went on; "that word sounds like a blasphemy on your lips—I knew that you were but an object of loathing and abhorrence to her."

"Yes, after you had made me such. From that hour of our first meeting you became my bitter and unrelenting foe, in conspiracy with that treacherous officer, who has received his reward, and whom you had destined for the place I courted. Repress your indignation, lady, for I *will* be heard out,—you undermined my character, you poisoned her feelings, and you turned my love into necessary enmity."

"Your love!" now broke in the indignant lady; "even if all that you have said were not basely false, what love could you have for *her?* How could *you* appreciate her artless simplicity, her genuine honesty, her rare understanding, her candid innocence, any more than the wolf can value the lamb's gentleness, or the vulture the dove's mildness? No, it was her wealth, her family connection, her nobility, that you grasped at, and nothing more; I read it in the very flash of your eye, when first it fixed itself, as a basilisk's, upon her."

"It is false!" he rejoined; "had I obtained my request, had I been thus worthily mated, I should have been found equal to my position, domestic, contented, and affectionate; as worthy of possessing her as——"

"As any one can be," struck in Fabiola, "who, in offering his hand, expresses himself equally ready, in three hours, to espouse or to murder the object of his affection. And she prefers the latter, and he keeps his word. Begone from my presence; you taint the very atmosphere in which you move."

"I will leave when I have accomplished my task, and you will have little reason to rejoice when I do. You have then purposely, and unprovoked, blighted and destroyed in me every honorable purpose of life, withered my only hope, cut me off from rank, society, respectable ease, and domestic happiness.

"That was not enough. After acting in that character, with which you summed up my condemnation, of a spy, and listened to my conversation, you this morning threw off all sense of female propriety, and stood forward prominently in the Forum, to complete in public what you had begun in private, excite against me the supreme tribunal, and through it the emperor, and arouse an unjust popular outcry and vengeance; such as, but for a feeling stronger than fear, which brings me hither, would make me now skulk, like a hunted wolf, till I could steal out of the nearest gate."

"And, Fulvius, I tell you," interposed Fabiola, "that the moment you cross its threshold, the average of virtue will be raised in this wicked city. Again I bid you depart from my house, at least; or at any rate I will withdraw from this offensive intrusion."

"We part not yet, lady," said Fulvius, whose countenance had been growing every moment more flushed, as his lips had been becoming more deadly pale. He rudely grasped her arm, and pushed her back to her seat; "and beware," he added, "how you attempt again either to escape or to bring aid; your first cry will be your last, cost me what it may.

"You have made me, then, an outcast, not only from society but from Rome, an exile, a houseless wanderer on a friendless earth; was not that enough to satisfy your vengeance? No: you must needs rob me of my gold, of my rightfully, though painfully earned wealth; peace, reputation, my means of subsistence, all *you* have stolen from me, a youthful stranger."

"Wicked and insolent man!" exclaimed now the indignant Roman lady, reckless of consequences, "you shall answer heavily for your temerity. Dare you, in my own house, call me a thief?"

"I dare; and I tell you this is your day of reckoning, and not mine. I have earned, even if by crime, it is nothing to you, my full share of your cousin's confiscated property. I have earned it hardly, by pangs and rendings of the heart and soul, by sleepless nights of struggles with fiends that have conquered; ay, and with one at home that is sterner than they; by days and days of restless search for evidence, amidst the desolation of a proud, but degraded spirit. Have I not a right to enjoy it?

"Ay, call it what you will, call it my blood-money; the

more infamous it is, the more base in you to step in and snatch it from me. It is like a rich man tearing the carrion from the hound's jaws, after he has swollen his feet and rent his skin in hunting it down."

"I will not seek for further epithets by which to call you; your mind is deluded by some vain dream," said Fabiola, with an earnestness not untinged with alarm. She felt she was in the presence of a madman, one in whom violent passion, carried off by an unchecked, deeply-moved fancy, was lashing itself up to that intensity of wicked excitement, which constitutes a moral frenzy,—when the very murderer thinks himself a virtuous avenger. "Fulvius," she continued, with studied calmness, and looking fully into his eyes, "I now entreat you to go. If you want money, you shall have it; but go, in heaven's name go, before you destroy your reason by your anger."

"What vain fancy do you mean?" asked Fulvius.

"Why, that I should have ever dreamt about Agnes's wealth or property on such a day, or should have taken any advantage of her cruel death."

"And yet it is so; I have it from the emperor's mouth that he has made it over to you. Will you pretend to make me believe, that this most generous and liberal prince ever parted with a penny unsolicited, ay, or unbribed?"

"Of this I know nothing. But I know, that I would rather have died of want than petitioned for a farthing of such property!"

"Then would you make me rather believe, that in this city there is any one so disinterested as, undesired, to have petitioned for you? No, no, Lady Fabiola, all this is too incredible. But what is that?" And he pounced with eagerness on the imperial rescript, which had remained unlooked at, since Corvinus had left it. The sensation to him was like that of Æneas when he saw Pallas's belt upon the body of Turnus. The fury, which seemed to have been subdued by his subtlety, as he had been reasoning to prove Fabiola guilty, flashed up anew at the sight of this fatal document. He eyed it for a minute, then broke out, gnashing his teeth with rage:

"Now, madam, I convict you of baseness, rapacity, and unnatural cruelty, far beyond any thing you have dared to charge on me! Look at this rescript, beautifully engrossed, with its golden letters and emblazoned margins; and presume to say that it was prepared in the one hour that elapsed between your cousin's death and the emperor's telling me that he had signed it? Nor do you pretend to know the generous friend who procured you the gift. Bah! while Agnes was in prison at latest; while you were whining and moaning over her; while you were reproaching me for cruelty and treachery towards her,—me, a stranger and alien to her! you, the gentle lady, the virtuous philosopher, the loving, fondling kinswoman, you, my stern reprover, were coolly plotting to take advantage of my crime, for securing her property, and seeking out the elegant scribe, who should gild your covetousness with his pencil, and paint over your treason to your own flesh and blood, with his blushing *minium*."*

"Cease, madman, cease!" exclaimed Fabiola, endeavoring in vain to master his glaring eye. But he went on in still wilder tone:

"And then, forsooth, when you have thus basely robbed me, you offer me money. You have out-plotted me, and you pity me! You have made me a beggar, and then you offer me alms,—alms out of my own wages, the wages which even hell allows its fated victims while on earth!"

Fabiola rose again, but he seized her with a maniac's gripe, and this time did not let her go. He went on:

"Now listen to the last words that I will speak, or they

* Red paint.

may be the last that you will hear. Give back to me that unjustly obtained property; it is not fair that I should have the guilt, and you its reward. Transfer it by your sign manual to me as a free and loving gift, and I will depart. If not, you have signed your own doom." A stern and menacing glance accompanied these words.

Fabiola's haughty self rose again erect within her; her Roman heart, unsubdued, stood firm. Danger only made her fearless. She gathered her robe with matronly dignity around her, and replied:

"Fulvius, listen to my words, though they should be the last that I may speak; as certainly they shall be the last that you shall hear from me.

"Surrender this property to you? I would give it willingly to the first leper that I might meet in the street, but to you, never. Never shall you touch thing that belonged to that holy maiden, be it a gem or be it a straw! That touch would be pollution. Take gold of mine, if it please you; but any thing that ever belonged to her, from me no treasures can ransom. And one legacy I prize more than all her inheritance. You have now offered me two alternatives, as last night you did her, to yield to your demands, or die. Agnes taught me which to choose. Once again, I say, depart."

"And leave you to possess what is mine? leave you to triumph over me, as one whom you have outwitted—you honored, and I disgraced—you rich, and I penniless—you happy, and I wretched? No, never! I cannot save myself from what you have made me; but I can prevent your being what you have no right to be. For this I have come here; this is my day of Nemesis.* Now die!" While he was speaking these reproaches, he was slowly pushing her backwards with his left hand towards the couch from which she

* Revenge.

had risen; while his right was tremblingly feeling for something in the folds of his bosom.

As he finished his last word, he thrust her violently down upon the couch, and seized her by the hair. She made no resistance, she uttered no cry; partly a fainting and sickening sensation came over her; partly a noble feeling of self-respect checked any unseemly exhibition of fear, before a scornful enemy. Just as she closed her eyes, she saw something like lightning above her; she could not tell whether it was his glaring eye or flashing steel.

In another moment she felt oppressed and suffocated, as if a great weight had fallen upon her; and a hot stream was flowing over her bosom.

A sweet voice full of earnestness sounded in her ears:

"Cease, Orontius; I am thy sister Miriam!"

Fulvius, in accents choked by passion, replied:

"It is false; give me up my prey!"

A few words more were faintly spoken in a tongue unknown to Fabiola; when she felt her hair released, heard the dagger dashed to the ground, and Fulvius cry out bitterly, as he rushed out of the room:

"O Christ! this is Thy Nemesis!"

Fabiola's strength was returning; but she felt the weight upon her increase. She struggled, and released herself. Another body was lying in her place, apparently dead, and covered with blood.

It was the faithful Syra, who had thrown herself between her mistress's life and her brother's dagger.

CHAPTER XXXI.

DIONYSIUS.

ΔΙΟΝΥΣΙΟΥ
ΙΑΤΡΟΥ
ΠΡΕΣΒΥΤΕΡΟΥ*

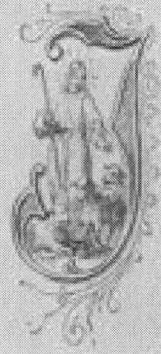

HE great thoughts, which this occurrence would naturally have suggested to the noble heart of Fabiola, were suppressed for a time, by the exigencies of the moment. Her first care was to stanch the flowing blood with whatever was nearest at hand. While she was engaged in this work, there was a general rush of servants towards her apartment. The stupid porter had begun to be uneasy at Fulvius's long stay (the reader has now heard his real name), when he saw him dash out of the door like a maniac, and thought he perceived stains of blood upon his garment. He immediately gave the alarm to the entire household.

Fabiola by a gesture stopped the crowd at the door of her room, and desired only Euphrosyne and her Greek maid to enter. The latter, since the influence of the black slave had been removed, had attached herself most affectionately to Syra, as we must still call her, and had, with great docility,

---

* "[The tomb] of Dionysius, physician [and] priest," lately found at the entrance to the crypt of St. Cornelius, in the cemetery of Callistus.

listened to her moral instructions. A slave was instantly despatched for the physician who had always been sent for by Syra in illness, Dionysius, who, as we have already observed, lived in the house of Agnes.

In the meantime Fabiola had been overjoyed at finding the blood cease to flow so rapidly, and still more at seeing her

Cemetery of Callixtus.

servant open her eyes upon her, though only for a moment. She would not have exchanged for any wealth the sweet smile which accompanied that look.

In a few minutes the kind physician arrived. He carefully examined the wound, and pronounced favorably on it for the present. The blow, as aimed, would have gone straight to Fabiola's heart. But her loving servant, in spite of prohibition, had been hovering near her mistress during the whole day; never intruding, but anxious for any opportunity which might offer, of seconding those good impressions of grace, which the morning's scenes could not fail to have produced. While in a neighboring room she heard violent tones which were too familiar to her ears; and hastened noiselessly round, and within the curtain which covered the door of Fabiola's own apartment. She stood concealed in the dusk, on the very spot where Agnes had, a few months before, consoled her.

She had not been there long when the last struggle commenced. While the man was pushing her mistress backwards, she followed him close behind; and as he was lifting his arm, passed him, and threw her body over that of his victim. The blow descended, but misdirected, through the shock she gave his arm; and it fell upon her neck, where it inflicted a deep wound, checked, however, by encountering the collar-bone. We need not say what it cost her to make this sacrifice. Not the dread of pain, nor the fear of death could for a moment have deterred her; it was the horror of imprinting on her brother's brow the mark of Cain, the making him doubly a fratricide, which deeply anguished her. But she had offered her life for her mistress. To have fought with the assassin, whose strength and agility she knew, would have been useless; to try to alarm the house before one fatal blow was struck was hopeless; and nothing remained but to accomplish her immolation, by substituting herself for the intended victim. Still she wished to spare her brother the consummation of his crime, and in doing so manifested to Fabiola their relationship and their real names.

In his blind fury he refused her credit; but the words, in their native tongue, which said, "Remember my scarf which you picked up here," brought back to his memory so terrible a domestic tale, that had the earth opened a cavern in that moment before his feet, he would have leaped into it, to bury his remorse and shame.

Strange, too, it proved, that he should not have ever allowed Eurotas to get possession of that family relic, but should, ever since he regained it, have kept it apart as a sacred thing; and when all else was being packed up, should have folded it up and put it in his breast. And now, in the act of drawing out his eastern dagger, he had plucked this out too, and both were found upon the floor.

Dionysius, immediately after dressing the wound, and administering proper restoratives, which brought back consciousness, desired the patient to be left perfectly quiet, to see as few persons as possible, so as to prevent excitement, and to go on with the treatment which he prescribed until midnight. "I will call" he added, "very early in the morning, when I must see my patient alone." He whispered a few words in her ear, which seemed to do her more good than all his medicines; for her countenance brightened into an angelic smile.

Fabiola had her placed in her own bed, and, allotting to her attendants the outward room, reserved to herself exclusively the privilege, as she deemed it, of nursing the servant, to whom a few months before she could hardly feel grateful for having tended her in fever. She had informed the others how the wound had been inflicted, concealing the relationship between her assailant and her deliverer.

Although herself exhausted and feverish, she would not leave the bedside of the patient; and when midnight was past, and no more remedies had to be administered, she sank to rest upon a low couch close to the bed. And now what were her thoughts, when, in the dim light of a sick room, she opened her mind and heart to them? They were simple and earnest. She saw at once the reality and truth of all that her servant had ever spoken to her. When she last conversed with her, the principles which she heard with delight, had appeared to her wholly beyond practice, beautiful theories, which could not be brought to action. When Miriam had described a sphere of virtue, wherein no approbation or reward of man was to be expected, but only the approving eye of God, she had admired the idea, which powerfully seized her generous mind; but she had rebelled against its becoming the constraining rule of hourly conduct. Yet, if the stroke under which she cast herself had proved fatal, as it might easily have done, where would have been her reward? What, then, could have been her motive but that very theory, as it seemed, of responsibility to an unseen power?

And when Miriam had discoursed of heroism in virtue as being its ordinary standard, how chimerical the principle had seemed! Yet here, without preparation, without forethought, without excitement, without glory,—nay, with marked desire of concealment, this slave had performed a deed of self-sacrifice, heroic in every way. From what could that result but from habitual heroism of virtue, ready at any hour to do what would ennoble forever a soldier's name? She was no dreamer, then, no theorist, but a serious, real practiser of all that she taught. Could this be a philosophy? Oh, no, it must be a religion! the religion of Agnes and of Sebastian, to whom she considered Miriam every way equal. How she longed to converse with her again!

Early in the morning, according to his promise, the physician returned, and found his patient much improved. He desired to be left alone with her; when, having spread a linen cloth upon the table, and placed lighted tapers upon it, he drew from his bosom an embroidered scarf, and uncovered a golden box, the sacred contents of which she well knew. Approaching her he said:

"My dear child, as I promised you, I have now brought you not merely the truest remedy of every ailment, bodily and spiritual, but the very Physician Himself, who by His word alone restoreth all things,* whose touch opens the eyes of the

* "Qui verbo suo sanavit universa." *The Breviary.*

blind and the ears of the deaf, whose will cleanses lepers, the hem of whose garment sends forth virtue to cure all. Are you ready to receive Him?"

"With all my heart," she replied, clasping her hands; "I long to possess Him whom alone I have loved, in whom I have believed, to whom my heart belongs."

"Does no anger or indignation exist in your soul against him who has injured you? does any pride or vanity arise in your mind at the thought of what you have done? or are you conscious of any other fault requiring humble confession and absolution before receiving the sacred gift into your breast?"

"Full of imperfection and sin I know myself to be, venerable father; but I am not conscious of any knowing offence. I have had no need to forgive him to whom you allude; I love him too much for that, and would willingly give my life to save him. And of what have I to be proud, a poor servant, who have only obeyed my Lord's commands?"

"Invite then, my child, this Lord into your house, that coming He may heal you, and fill you with His grace."

Approaching the table, he took from it a particle of the Blessed Eucharist, in the form of unleavened bread, which, being dry, he moistened in water, and placed within her lips.[*] She closed them upon it, and remained for some time absorbed in contemplation.

And thus did the holy Dionysius discharge his twofold office of physician and priest, attributed to him on his tomb.

[*] Eusebius, in his account of Serapion, teaches us that this was the manner of administering Holy Communion to the sick, without the cup, or under only one kind.

CHAPTER XXXII.

THE SACRIFICE ACCEPTED.

THROUGH the whole of that day the patient seemed occupied with deep, but most pleasing thoughts. Fabiola, who never left her, except for moments to give necessary directions, watched her countenance with a mixture of awe and delight. It appeared as if her servant's mind were removed from surrounding objects, and conversing in a totally different sphere. Now a smile passed like a sunbeam across her features, now a tear trembled in her eye, or flowed down her cheeks; sometimes her pupils were raised and kept fixed on heaven for a considerable time, while a blissful look of perfect and calm enjoyment sat unvarying upon her; and then she would turn round with an expression of infinite tenderness towards her mistress, and hold out her hand to be clasped in hers. And Fabiola could sit thus for hours in silence, which was as yet prescribed; feeling it an honor, and thinking it did her good, to be in contact with such a rare type of virtue.

At length, in the course of the day, after giving her patient some nourishment, she said to her, smiling: "I think you are much better, Miriam, already. Your physician must have given you some wonderful medicine."

"Indeed he has, my dearest mistress."

Fabiola was evidently pained; and leaning over her, said softly: "Oh, do not, I entreat you, call me by such a title. If it has to be used, it should be by me towards you. But, in fact, it is no longer true; for what I long intended has now been done; and the instrument of your liberation has been ordered to be made out, not as a freedwoman, but as an *ingenua*;* for such I know you are."

Miriam looked her thanks, for fear of further hurting Fabiola's feelings; and they continued to be happy together in silence.

Towards evening Dionysius returned, and found so great an improvement, that, ordering more nourishing food, he permitted a little quiet conversation.

"I must now," said Fabiola, so soon as they were alone, "fulfill the first duty, which my heart has been burning to discharge, that of thanking you,—I wish I knew a stronger word,—not for the life which you have saved me, but for the magnanimous sacrifice which you made for it—and, let me add, the unequalled example of heroic virtue, which alone inspired it."

"After all, what have I done, but simple duty? You had a right to my life, for a much less cause than to save yours," answered Miriam.

"No doubt," responded Fabiola, "it appears so to you, who have been trained to the doctrine which overpowered me, that the most heroic acts ought to be considered by men as performances of ordinary duties."

"And thereby," rejoined Miriam, "they cease to be what you have called them."

"No, no," exclaimed Fabiola, with enthusiasm; "do not

---

* Persons freed from slavery retained the title of *freedmen* or *freedwomen* (*liberti*, *libertæ*) of the person to whom they had belonged, as "of Augustus." If they had belonged originally to a free class, they were liberated as *ingenui* or *ingenuæ* (well-born) and restored by emancipation to that class.

try to make me mean and vile to my own heart, by teaching me to undervalue what I cannot but prize as an unrivalled act of virtue. I have been reflecting on it, night and day, since I witnessed it; and my heart has been yearning to speak to you of it, and even yet I dare not, or I should oppress your weakness with my overcharged feelings. It was noble, it was grand, it was beyond all reach of praise; though I know you do not want it. I cannot see any way in which the sublimeness of the act could have been enhanced, or human virtue rise one step higher."

Miriam, who was now raised to a reclining position, took Fabiola's hand between both hers; and turning round towards her, in a soft and mild, but most earnest tone, thus addressed her:

"Good and gentle lady, for one moment listen to me. Not to depreciate what you are good enough to value, since it pains you to hear it, but to teach you how far we still are from what might have been done, let me trace for you a parallel scene, but where all shall be reversed. Let it be a slave—pardon me, dear Fabiola, for another pang—I see it in your face, but it shall be the last—yes, a slave brutish, ungrateful, rebellious to the most benign and generous of masters. And let the stroke, not of an assassin, but of the minister of justice, impend over his head. What would you call the act, how would you characterize the virtue, of that master, if out of pure love, and that he might reclaim that wretched man, he should rush beneath the axe's blow, ay, and its preceding ignominious stripes, and have written in his will, that he made that slave heir to his titles and his wealth, and desired him to be considered as his brother?"

"O Miriam, Miriam, you have drawn a picture too sublime to be believed of man. You have not eclipsed your own deed, for I spoke of *human* virtue. To act as you have now described would require, if possible, that of a God!"

Miriam pressed the folded hand to her bosom, fixed on Fabiola's wondering eyes a look of heavenly inspiration, as she sweetly and solemnly replied: "AND JESUS CHRIST, WHO DID ALL THIS FOR MAN, WAS TRULY GOD."

Fabiola covered her face with both her hands, and for a long time was silent. Miriam prayed earnestly in her own tranquil heart.

"Miriam, I thank you from my soul," at length Fabiola said; "you have fulfilled your promise of guiding me. For some time I have only been fearing that you might not be a Christian; but it could not be.

"Now tell me, are those awful, but sweet words, which you just now uttered, which have sunk into my heart as deeply, as silently, and as irrevocably as a piece of gold dropped upon the surface of the still ocean, goes down into its depths,—are those words a mere part of the Christian system, or are they its essential principle?"

"From a simple allegory, dear lady, your powerful mind has, in one bound, reached and grasped the master-key of our whole teaching: the alembic of your fine understanding has extracted, and condensed into one thought, the most vital and prominent doctrines of Christianity. You have distilled them into their very essence.

"That man, God's creature and bondsman, rebelled against his Lord; that justice irresistible had doomed and pursued him; that this very Lord 'took the form of a servant, and in habit was found like a man;'* that in this form he suffered stripes, buffets, mockery, and shameful death, became the 'Crucified One,' as men here call Him, and thereby rescued man from his fate, and gave him part in His own riches and kingdom: all this is comprised in the words that I have spoken.

"And you had reached the right conclusion. Only God

* Phil. ii. 7.

could have performed so godlike an action, or have offered so sublime an expiation."

Fabiola was again wrapped up in silent thought, till she timidly asked:

"And was it to this that you referred in Campania, when you spoke of God alone being a victim worthy of God?"

"Yes; but I further alluded to the continuation of that sacrifice, even in our own days, by a marvellous dispensation of an all-powerful love. However, on this I must not yet speak."

Fabiola resumed: "I every moment see how all that you have ever spoken to me coheres and fits together, like the parts of one plant; all springing one from another. I thought it bore only the lovely flowers of an elegant theory; you have shown me in your conduct how these can ripen into sweet and solid fruit. In the doctrine which you have just explained, I seem to myself to find the noble stem from which all the others branch forth—even to that very fruit. For who would refuse to do for another, what is much less than God has done for him? But, Miriam, there is a deep and unseen root whence springs all this, possibly dark beyond contemplation, deep beyond reach, complex beyond man's power to unravel; yet perhaps simple to a confiding mind. If, in my present ignorance, I can venture to speak, it should be vast enough to occupy all nature, rich enough to fill creation with all that is good and perfect in it, strong enough to bear the growth of your noble tree, till its summit reach above the stars, and its branches to the ends of earth.

"I mean, your idea of that God, whom you made me fear, when you spoke to me as a philosopher of Him, and taught me to know as the ever-present watchman and judge; but whom I am sure you will make me love when, as a Christian, you exhibit Him to me as the root and origin of such boundless tenderness and mercy.

"Without some deep mystery in His nature, as yet unknown to me, I cannot fully apprehend that wonderful doctrine of man's purchase."

"Fabiola," responded Miriam, "more learned teachers than I should undertake the instruction of one so gifted and so acute. But will you believe me if I attempt to give you some explanation?"

"Miriam," replied Fabiola, with strong emphasis, "ONE WHO IS READY TO DIE FOR ANOTHER, WILL CERTAINLY NOT DECEIVE ME."

"And now," rejoined the patient, smiling, "you have again seized a great principle—that of FAITH. I will, therefore, be only the simple narrator of what Jesus Christ, who truly died for us, has taught us. You will believe my word only as that of a faithful witness; you will accept His, as that of an unerring God."

Fabiola bowed her head, and listened with reverential mind to her, in whom she had long honored a teacher of marvellous wisdom, which she drew from some unknown school; but whom now she almost worshipped as an angel, who could open to her the flood-gates of the eternal ocean, whose waters are the unfathomable Wisdom, overflowing on earth.

Miriam expounded, in the simple terms of Catholic teaching, the sublime doctrine of the Trinity; then after relating the fall of man, unfolded the mystery of the Incarnation, giving, in the very words of St. John, the history of the Eternal Word, till He was made flesh, and dwelt among men. Often was she interrupted by the expressions of admiration or assent which her pupil uttered; never by cavil or doubt. Philosophy had given place to religion, captiousness to docility, incredulity to faith.

But now a sadness seemed to have come over Fabiola's heart: Miriam read it in her looks, and asked her its cause.

"I hardly dare tell you," she replied. "But all that you have related to me is so beautiful, so divine, that it seems to me necessarily to end here.

"The Word (what a noble name!), that is, the expression of God's love, the externation of His wisdom, the evidence of His power, the very breath of His life-giving life, which is Himself, becometh flesh. Who shall furnish it to Him? Shall He take up the cast-off slough of a tainted humanity, or shall a new manhood be created expressly for *Him?* Shall He take His place in a double genealogy, receiving thus into Himself a twofold tide of corruption; and shall there be any one on earth daring and high enough to call himself His father?"

"No," softly whispered Miriam; "but there shall be one holy enough, and humble enough, to be worthy to call herself His mother!

"Almost 800 years before the Son of God came into the world, a prophet spoke, and recorded his words, and deposited the record of them in the hands of the Jews, Christ's inveterate enemies; and his words were these: 'Behold, a Virgin shall conceive and bear a Son, and His name shall be called Emanuel,'* which in the Hebrew language signifies 'God with us,' that is with men.

"This prophecy was of course fulfilled in the conception and birth of God's Son on earth."

"And who was *she?*" asked Fabiola, with great reverence.

"One whose very name is blessed by every one that truly loves her Son. Mary is the name by which you will know her: Miriam, its original in her own tongue, is the one by which I honor her. Well, you may suppose, was she prepared for such high destiny by holiness and virtue; not as cleansed, but as ever clean; not as purified, but as always pure; not

* Isaias vii. 14.

freed, but exempted, from sin. The tide of which you spoke, found before her the dam of an eternal decree, which could not brook that the holiness of God should mingle with what it could only redeem, by keeping extraneous to itself. Bright as the blood of Adam, when the breath of God sent it sparkling through his veins, pure as the flesh of Eve, while standing yet in the mould of the Almighty hands, as they drew it from the side of the slumbering man, were the blood and the flesh, which the Spirit of God formed into the glorious humanity, that Mary gave to Jesus.

"And after this glorious privilege granted to our sex, are you surprised that many, like your sweet Agnes, should have chosen this peerless Virgin as the pattern of their lives; should find in her, whom God so elected, the model of every virtue; and should, in preference to allowing themselves to be yoked, even by the tenderest of ties, to the chariot-wheels of this world, seek to fly upwards on wings of undivided love like hers?"

After a pause and some reflection, Miriam proceeded briefly to detail the history of our Saviour's birth, His laborious youth, His active but suffering public life, and then His ignominious Passion. Often was the narrative interrupted by the tears and sobs of the willing listener and ready learner. At last the time for rest had come, when Fabiola humbly asked:

"Are you too fatigued to answer one question more?"

"No," was the cheerful reply.

"What hope," said Fabiola, "can there be for one who cannot say she was ignorant, for she pretended to know every thing; nor that she neglected to learn, for she affected eagerness after every sort of knowledge; but can only confess that she scorned the true wisdom, and blasphemed its Giver;—for one who has scoffed at the very torments which proved the love, and sneered at the death which was the ran-sensing, of Him whom she has mocked at, as the 'Crucified?'"

A flood of tears stopped her speech.

Miriam waited till their relieving flow had subsided into that gentler dew which softens the heart; then in soothing tones addressed her as follows:

"In the days of our Lord there lived a woman who bore the same name as His spotless Mother; but she had sinned publicly, degradingly, as you, Fabiola, would abhor to sin. She became acquainted, we know not how, with her Redeemer; in the secrecy of her own heart, she contemplated earnestly, till she came to love intensely, His gracious and condescending familiarity with sinners, and His singular indulgence and forgivingness to the fallen. She loved and loved still more; and, forgetting herself, she only thought how she might manifest her love, so that it might bring honor, however slight, to Him, and shame, however great, on herself.

"She went into the house of a rich man, where the usual courtesies of hospitality had been withheld from its Divine guest, into the house of a haughty man who spurned, in the presumption of his heart, the public sinner; she supplied the attentions which had been neglected to Him whom she loved; and she was scorned, as she expected, for her obtrusive sorrow."

"How did she do this, Miriam?"

"She knelt at His feet as He sat at table; she poured out upon them a flood of tears; she wiped them with her luxurious hair, she kissed them fervently, and she anointed them with rich perfume."

"And what was the result?"

"She was defended by Jesus against the carping gibes of His host; she was told that she was forgiven on account of her love, and was dismissed with kindest comfort."

"And what became of her?"

"When on Calvary He was crucified, two women were privileged to stand close to Him; Mary the sinless, and Mary the penitent: to show how unsullied and repentant love may walk hand in hand, beside Him who said that He had 'come to call not the just, but sinners to repentance.'"

No more was said that night. Miriam, fatigued with her exertion, sank into a placid slumber. Fabiola sat by her side, filled to her heart's brim with this tale of love. She pondered over it again and again; and she still saw more and more how every part of this wonderful system was consistent. For if Miriam had been ready to die for her, in imitation of her Saviour's love, so had she been as ready to forgive her, when she had thoughtlessly injured her. Every Christian, she now felt, ought to be a copy, a representative of his Master; but the one that slumbered so tranquilly beside her was surely true to her model, and might well represent Him to her.

When, after some time, Miriam awoke, she found her mistress (for her patent of freedom was not yet completed) lying at her feet, over which she had sobbed herself to sleep. She understood at once the full meaning and merit of this self-humiliation; she did not stir, but thanked God with a full heart that her sacrifice had been accepted.

Fabiola, on awaking, crept back to her own couch, as she thought, unobserved. A secret, sharp pang it had cost her to perform this act of self-abasement; but she had thoroughly humbled the pride of her heart. She felt for the first time that her heart was Christian.

CHAPTER XXXIII.

MIRIAM'S HISTORY.

THE next morning, when Dionysius came, he found both patient and nurse so radiant and so happy, that he congratulated them both on having had a good night's rest. Both laughed at the idea; but concurred in saying that it had been the happiest night of their lives. Dionysius was surprised, till Miriam, taking the hand of Fabiola, said:

"Venerable priest of God, I confide to your fatherly care this catechumen, who desires to be fully instructed in the mysteries of our holy faith, and to be regenerated by the waters of eternal salvation."

"What!" asked Fabiola, amazed, "are you more than a physician?"

"I am, my child," the old man replied; "unworthily I hold likewise the higher office of a priest in God's Church."

Fabiola unhesitatingly knelt before him, and kissed his hand. The priest placed his right hand upon her head, and said to her:

"Be of good courage, daughter; you are not the first of your house whom God has brought into His holy Church. It is now many years since I was called in here, under the guise of a physician, by a former servant, now no more; but in reality it was to baptize, a few hours before her death, the wife of Fabius."

"My mother!" exclaimed Fabiola. "She died immediately after giving me birth. And did she die a Christian?"

"Yes; and I doubt not that her spirit has been hovering about you through life by the side of the angel who guards you, guiding you unseen to this blessed hour. And, before the throne of God, she has been unceasing in her supplications on your behalf."

Joy tenfold filled the breasts of the two friends; and after arrangements had been made with Dionysius for the necessary instructions and preparations for Fabiola's admission to baptism, she went up to the side of Miriam, and taking her hand, said to her in a low, soft voice:

"Miriam, may I from henceforth call you sister?" A pressure of the hand was the only reply which she could give.

With their mistress, the old nurse, Euphrosyne, and the Greek slave, placed themselves, as we now say, under instruction, to receive baptism on Easter-eve. Nor must we forget one who was already enrolled in the list of catechumens, and whom Fabiola had taken home with her and kept, Emerentiana, the foster-sister of Agnes. It was her delight to make herself useful, by being the ready messenger between the sick-room and the rest of the house.

During her illness, as her strength improved, Miriam imparted many particulars of her previous life to Fabiola; and as they will throw some light on our preceding narrative, we will give her history in a continuous form.

Some years before our story commenced, there lived in Antioch a man who, though not of ancient family, was rich, and moved in the highest circles of that most luxurious city. To keep his position, he was obliged to indulge in great expense; and from want of strict economy, he had gradually become oppressed with debt. He was married to a lady of great virtue, who became a Christian, at first secretly, and afterwards continued so, with her husband's reluctant consent. In the meantime their two children, a son and daughter, had received their domestic education under her care. The former, Orontius, so called from the favorite stream which watered the city, was fifteen when his father first discovered his wife's religion. He had learnt much from his mother of the doctrines of Christianity, and had been with her an attendant on Christian worship; and hence he possessed a dangerous knowledge, of which he afterwards made so fatal a use.

But he had not the least inclination to embrace the doctrines, or adopt the practices of Christianity; nor would he hear of preparing for baptism. He was wilful and artful, with no love for any restraint upon his passions, or for any strict morality. He looked forward to distinction in the world, and to his full share in all its enjoyments. He had been, and continued to be, highly educated; and besides the Greek language, then generally spoken at Antioch, he was acquainted with Latin, which he spoke readily and gracefully, as we have seen, though with a slight foreign accent. In the family, the vernacular idiom was used with servants, and often in familiar conversation. Orontius was not sorry when his father removed him from his mother's control, and insisted that he should continue to follow the dominant and favored religion of the state.

As to the daughter, who was three years younger, he did not so much care. He deemed it foolish and unmanly to take much trouble about religion; to change it especially, or abandon that of the empire, was, he thought, a sign of weakness. But women being more imaginative, and more under the sway of the feelings, might be indulged in any fancies of this sort. Accordingly he permitted his daughter Miriam, whose name was Syrian, as the mother belonged to a rich family from Edessa, to continue in the free exercise of her new faith. She became, in addition to her high mental cultivation, a model of virtue, simple and unpretending. It was a period, we may observe, in which the city of Antioch was renowned for the learning of its philosophers, some of whom were eminent as Christians.

A few years later, when the son had reached manhood, and had abundantly unfolded his character, the mother died. Before her end, she had seen symptoms of her husband's impending ruin; and, determined that her daughter should not be dependent on his careless administration, nor on her son's ominous selfishness and ambition, she secured effectually from the covetousness of both, her own large fortune, which was settled on her daughter. She resisted every influence, and every art, employed to induce her to release this property, or allow it to merge in the family resources, and be made available towards relieving their embarrassments. And on her death-bed, among other solemn parental injunctions, she laid this on her daughter's filial sense of duty, that she never would allow, after coming of age, any alteration in this arrangement.

Matters grew worse and worse; creditors pressed; property had been injudiciously disposed of; when a mysterious person, called Eurotas, made his appearance in the family. No one but its head seemed to know him; and he evidently looked upon him as at once a blessing and a curse, the bearer both of salvation and of ruin.

The reader is in possession of Eurotas's own revelations; it is sufficient to add, that being the elder brother, but conscious that his rough, morose, and sinister character did not fit him for sustaining the position of head of the family and administering quietly a settled property, and having a haughty ambition to raise his house into a nobler rank, and increase even its riches, he took but a moderate sum of money as capital, vanished for years, embarked in the desperate traffic of interior Asia, penetrated into China and India, and came back home with a large fortune, and a collection of rare gems, which helped his nephew's brief career, but misguided him to ruin in Rome.

Eurotas, instead of a rich family, into which to pour superfluous wealth, found only a bankrupt house to save from ruin. But his family pride prevailed; and after many reproaches, and bitter quarrels with his brother, but concealed from all else, he paid off his debts by the extinction of his own capital, and thus virtually became master of all the wreck of his brother's property, and of the entire family.

After a few years of weary life, the father sickened and died. On his death-bed, he told Orontius that he had nothing to leave him, that all he had lived on for some years, the very house over his head, belonged to his friend Eurotas, whose relationship he did not further explain, whom he must look up to entirely for support and guidance. The youth thus found himself, while full of pride, ambition, and voluptuousness, in the hands of a cold-hearted, remorseless, and no less ambitious man, who soon prescribed as the basis of mutual confidence, absolute submission to his will, while he should act in the capacity of an inferior, and the understood principle, that nothing was too great or too little, nothing too good or too wicked to be done, to restore family position and wealth.

To stay at Antioch was impossible after the ruin which had overtaken the house. With a good capital in hand, much might be done elsewhere. But now, even the sale of all left would scarcely cover the liabilities discovered after the father's death. There was still untouched the sister's fortune; and both agreed that this *must* be got from her. Every artifice was tried, every persuasion employed, but she simply and firmly resisted; both in obedience to her mother's dying orders, and because she had in view the establishment of a house for consecrated virgins, in which she intended to pass her days. She was now just of legal age to dispose of her

own property. She offered them every advantage that she
could give them; proposed that for a time they should all live
together upon her means. But this did not answer their purpose; and when every other course had failed, Eurotas began
to hint, that one who stood so much in their way should be got
rid of at any cost.

Orontius shuddered at the first proposal of the thought.
Eurotas familiarized him gradually with it, till—shrinking yet
from the actual commission of fratricide—he thought he had
almost done something virtuous, as the brothers of Joseph
imagined they did, by adopting a slower and less sanguinary
method of dealing with an obnoxious brother. Stratagem and
unseen violence, of which no law could take cognizance, and
which no one would dare reveal, offered him the best chance
of success.

Among the privileges of Christians in the first ages, we
have already mentioned that of reserving the Blessed Eucharist at home for domestic communion. We have described the
way in which it was enfolded in an *ocarium*, or linen cloth,
again often preserved in a richer cover. This precious gift
was kept in a chest (*arca*) with a lid, as St. Cyprian has
informed us.* Orontius well knew this; and he was moreover aware that its contents were more prized than silver or
gold; that, as the Fathers tell us, to drop negligently a crumb
of the consecrated bread was considered a crime;† and that
the name of "pearl," which was given to the smallest fragment,‡ showed that it was so precious in a Christian's eye,

---

* "Cum arcam suam, in qua Domini sanctum fuit, manibus indignis tentasset aperire, igne inde surgente deterrita est, ne auderet attingere." "When she attempted to open, with unworthy hands, her chest, in which was the holy (body) of our Lord, she was deterred from daring to touch it, by fire rising up from it." *De Lapsis*.

† See Martenne, *De antiquis Ecclesiæ Ritibus*.

‡ So in the eastern liturgies. Portunatus calls the Blessed Eucharist, "Corporis Agni margaritum ingens." "The huge pearl of the Body of the Lamb." Lib. iii. car. 25.

that he would part with all he possessed to rescue it from sacrilegious profanation.

The scarf richly embroidered with pearls, which has more than once affected our narrative, was the outer covering in which Miriam's mother had preserved this treasure; and her daughter valued it both as a dear inheritance, and as a consecrated object, for she continued its use.

One day, early in the morning, she knelt before her ark; and after fervent preparation by prayer, proceeded to open it. To her dismay she found it already unlocked, and her treasure gone! Like Mary Magdalen at the sepulchre, she wept bitterly, because they had taken her Lord, and she knew not where they had laid Him. Like her, too, "as she was weeping she stooped down and looked" again into her ark, and found a paper, which in the confusion of the first glance she had overlooked.

It informed her that what she sought was safe in her brother's hands, and might be ransomed. She ran at once to him, where he was closeted with the dark man, in whose presence she always trembled; threw herself on her knees before him, and entreated him to restore what she valued more than all her wealth. He was on the point of yielding to her tears and supplications, when Eurotas fixed his stern eye upon him, overawed him, then himself addressed her, saying:

"Miriam, we take you at your word. We wish to put the earnestness and reality of your faith to a sufficient test. Are you truly sincere in what you offer?"

"I will surrender any thing, all I have, to rescue from profanation the Holy of Holies."

"Then sign that paper," said Eurotas, with a sneer.

She took the pen in her hand, and after running her eye over the document, signed it. It was a surrender of her entire property to Eurotas. Orontius was furious when he saw himself overreached by the man to whom he had suggested the snare for his sister. But it was too late; he was only the faster in his unsparing gripe. A more formal renunciation of her rights was exacted from Miriam, with the formalities required by the Roman law.

For a short time she was treated soothingly; then hints began to be given to her of the necessity of moving, as Orontius and his friend intended to proceed to Nicomedia, the imperial residence. She asked to be sent to Jerusalem, where she would obtain admission into some community of holy women. She was accordingly embarked on board a vessel, the captain of which bore a suspicious character, and was very sparingly supplied with means. But she bore round her neck what she had given proof of valuing more than any wealth. For, as St. Ambrose relates of his brother Satyrus, yet a catechumen, Christians carried round their necks the Holy Eucharist, when embarking for a voyage.* We need not say that Miriam bore it securely folded in the only thing of price she cared to take from her father's house.

When the vessel was out at sea, instead of coasting towards Joppe or any port on the coast, the captain stood straight out, as if making for some distant shore. What his purpose was, it was difficult to conjecture; but his few passengers became alarmed, and a serious altercation ensued. This was cut short by a sudden storm; the vessel was carried forward at the mercy of the winds for some days, and then dashed to pieces on a rocky island near Cyprus. Like Satyrus, Miriam attributed her reaching the shore in safety to the precious burden which she bore. She was almost the only survivor; at least she saw no other person saved. Those, therefore, that did live besides, on returning to Antioch, reported her death, together with that of the remaining passengers and crew.

She was picked up on the shore by men who lived on such

* De morte Satyri.

spoil. Destitute and friendless, she was sold to a trader in slaves, taken to Tarsus, on the mainland, and again sold to a person of high rank, who treated her with kindness.

After a short time, Fabius instructed one of his agents in Asia to procure a slave of polished manners and virtuous character, if possible, at any price, to attend on his daughter; and Miriam, under the name of Syra, came to bring salvation to the house of Fabiola.

Ordination. From a picture in the Catacombs.

CHAPTER XXXIV

BRIGHT DEATH.

T was a few days after the occurrences related in our last chapter but one, that Fabiola was told, that an old man in great anguish, real or pretended, desired to speak with her. On going down to him and asking him his name and business, he replied:

"My name, noble lady, is Ephraim; and I have a large debt secured on the property of the late Lady Agnes, which I understand has now passed into your hands; and I am come, therefore, to claim it from you, for otherwise I am a ruined man!"

"How is that possible?" asked Fabiola in amazement. "I cannot believe that my cousin ever contracted debts."

"No, not she," rejoined the usurer, a little abashed; "but a gentleman called Fulvius, to whom the property was to come by confiscation; so I advanced him large sums upon it."

Her first impulse was to turn the man out of the house; but the thought of the sister came to her mind, and she civilly said to him:

"Whatever debts Fulvius has contracted I will discharge; but with only legal interest, and without regard to usurious contracts."

"But think of the risks I run, madam. I have been most moderate in my rates, I assure you."

"Well," she answered, "call on my steward, and he shall settle all. You are running no risks now at least."

She gave instructions, accordingly, to the freed-man who managed her affairs, to pay this sum on those conditions, which reduced it to one half the demand. But she soon engaged him in a more laborious task, that of going through the whole of her late father's accounts, and ascertaining every case of injury or oppression, that restitution might be made. And further, having ascertained that Corvinus had really obtained the imperial rescript, through his father, by which her own lawful property was saved from confiscation, though she refused ever to see him, she bestowed upon him such a remuneration as would ensure him comfort through life.

These temporal matters being soon disposed of, she divided her attention between the care of the patient and preparation for her Christian initiation. To promote Miriam's recovery, she removed her, with a small portion of her household, to a spot dear to both, the Nomentan villa. The spring had set in, and Miriam could have her couch brought to the window, or, in the warmest part of the day, could even be carried down into the garden before the house, where, with Fabiola on one side and Emerentiana on the other, and poor Molossus, who had lost all his spirit, at her feet, they would talk of friends lost, and especially of her with whom every object around was associated in their memories. And no sooner was the name of Agnes mentioned, than her old faithful guard would prick up his ears and wag his tail, and look around him. They would also frequently discourse on Christian subjects, when Miriam would follow up, humbly and unpretendingly, but with the warm glow which had first charmed Fabiola, the instructions given by the holy Dionysius.

Thus, for instance, when he had been treating of the virtue and meaning of the sign of the cross to be used in baptism, "whether on the forehead of believers, or over the water, by which they were to be regenerated, or the oil with which, as well as the chrism, they were anointed, or the sacrifice by which they are fed;"* Miriam explained to the catechumens its more domestic and practical use, and exhorted them to practise faithfully what all good Christians did, that is, to make this holy sign upon themselves already, "in the course and at the beginning of every work, on coming in and going out, when putting on their clothes, or sandals, when they washed, sat down to table, lighted their lamp, lay down in bed, or sat on a chair, in whatever conversation they should be engaged."†

But it was observed with pain, by all but Fabiola, that the patient, though the wound had healed, did not gain strength. It is often the mother or sister that is last to see the slow waste of illness, in child or sister. Love is so hopeful, and so blind! There was a hectic flush on her cheek, she was emaciated and weak, and a slight cough was heard from time to time. She lay long awake, and she desired to have her bed so placed that from early dawn she could look out upon one spot more fair to them all than the richest parterre.

There had long been in the villa an entrance to the cemetery on this road; but from this time it had already received the name of Agnes; for near its entrance had this holy martyr been buried. Her body rested in a *cubiculum* or chamber, under an arched tomb. Just above the entrance into this chamber, and in the middle of the grounds, was an opening, surrounded above by a low parapet, concealed by shrubs,

---

* St. Aug. Tract. cxviii. in Joan.

† Tertullian (who lived earlier than two hundred years after Christ, and is the oldest Latin ecclesiastical writer) *de Corona Milit.* c. 3.

Calpira threw down herself, with a low scream, and what was her distress at finding poor Rasmondona lying weltering in her blood, and perfectly dead.

which gave light and air to the room below. Towards this point Miriam loved to look, as the nearest approach she could make, in her infirm health, to the sepulchre of one whom she so much venerated and loved.

Early one morning, beautiful and calm, for it wanted but a few weeks to Easter, she was looking in that direction, when she observed half-a-dozen young men, who on their way to angle in the neighboring Anio, were taking a short cut across the villa, and so committing a trespass. They passed by this opening; and one of them, having looked down, called the others.

"This is one of those underground lurking-places of the Christians."

"One of their rabbit-holes into the burrow."

"Let us go in," said one.

"Yes, and how shall we get up again?" asked a second.

This dialogue she could not hear, but she saw what followed it. One who had looked down more carefully, shading his eyes from the light, called the others to do the same, but with gestures which enjoined silence. In a moment they pulled down large stones from the rock-work of a fountain close at hand, and threw down a volley of them at something below. They laughed very heartily as they went away; and Miriam supposed that they had seen some serpent or other noxious animal below, and had amused themselves with pelting it.

When others were stirring she mentioned the occurrence, that the stones might be removed. Fabiola went down herself with a few servants, for she was jealous of the custody of Agnes's tomb. What was her distress at finding poor Emerentiana gone down to pray at her foster-sister's tomb, lying weltering in her blood, and perfectly dead. It was discovered that, the evening before, passing by some Pagan orgies near the river, and being invited to join in them, she had not only refused, but had reproached the partakers in them with their wickedness, and with their cruelties to Christians. They assailed her with stones, and grievously wounded her; but she escaped from their fury into the villa. Feeling herself faint and wounded, she crept unnoticed to the tomb of Agnes, there to pray. She had been unable to move away when some of her former assailants discovered her. Those brutal Pagans had anticipated the ministry of the Church, and had conferred upon her the baptism of blood. She was buried near Agnes, and the modest peasant child received the honor of annual commemoration among the Saints.

Fabiola and her companions went through the usual course of preparation, though abridged on account of the persecution. By living at the very entrance into a cemetery, and one furnished with such large churches, they were enabled to pass through the three stages of catechumenship. First they were *hearers*,* admitted to be present, while the lessons were read; then *kneelers*,† who assisted at a portion of the liturgical prayers; and lastly *elect*, or *petitioners*‡ for baptism.

Once in this last class, they had to attend frequently in church, but more particularly on the three Wednesdays following the first, the fourth, and the last Sundays in Lent, on which days the Roman Missal yet retains a second collect and lesson, derived from this custom. Any one perusing the present rite of baptism in the Catholic Church, especially that of adults, will see condensed into one office what used to be anciently distributed through a variety of functions. On one day the renunciation of Satan was made, previous to its repetition just before baptism; on another the touching of the ears and nostrils, or the *Epipheta*, as it was called. Then were

* Auditores. ‡ Electi and competentes.
† Genuflectentes.

Baptism in the Early Ages of the Church.

repeated exorcisms, and genuflections, and signings of crosses on the forehead and body,* breathings upon the candidate, and other mysterious rites. More solemn still was the unction, which was not confined to the head, but extended to the whole body.

The Creed was also faithfully learnt, and committed to memory. But the doctrine of the Blessed Eucharist was not imparted till after baptism.

In these multiplied preparatory exercises the penitential time of Lent passed quickly and solemnly, till at last Easter-eve arrived.

It does not fall to our lot to describe the ceremonial of the Church in the administration of the Sacraments. The liturgical system received its great developments after peace had been gained; and much that belongs to outward forms and splendor was incompatible with the bitter persecution which the Church was undergoing.

It is enough for us to have shown, how not only doctrines and great sacred rites, but how even ceremonies and accessories were the same in the three first centuries as now. If our example is thought worth following, some one will perhaps illustrate a brighter period than we have chosen.

The baptism of Fabiola and her household had nothing to cheer it but purely spiritual joy. The titles in the city were all closed, and among them that of St. Pastor with its papal baptistery.

Early, therefore, on the morning of the auspicious day, the party crept round the walls to the opposite side of the city, and following the Via Portuensis, or road that led to the port at the mouth of the Tiber, turned into a vineyard near Cæsar's gardens, and descended into the cemetery of Pontianus, cele-

* These will be found, particularly in the baptism of adults, joined with repetitions of the *Our Father*.

brated as the resting-place of the Persian martyrs, SS. Abdon and Sennen.

The morning was spent in prayer and preparation, when towards evening the solemn office, which was to be protracted through the night, commenced.

When the time for the administration of baptism arrived, it was indeed but a dreary celebration that it introduced. Deep in the bowels of the earth the waters of a subterranean stream had been gathered into a square well or cistern, from four to five feet deep. They were clear, indeed, but cold and bleak, if we may use the expression, in their subterranean bath, formed out of the *tufa*, or volcanic rock. A long flight of steps led down to this rude baptistery, a small ledge at the side sufficed for the minister and the candidate, who was thrice immersed in the purifying waters.

The whole remains to this day, just as it was then, except that over the water is now to be seen a painting of St. John baptizing our Lord, added probably a century or two later.

Immediately after Baptism followed Confirmation, and then the neophyte, or new-born child of the Church, after due instruction, was admitted for the first time to the table of his Lord, and nourished with the Bread of angels.

It was not till late on Easter-day that Fabiola returned to her villa; and a long and silent embrace was her first greeting of Miriam. Both were so happy, so blissful, so fully repaid for all that they had been to one another for months, that no words could give expression to their feelings. Fabiola's grand idea and absorbing pride, that day was, that now she had risen to the level of her former slave; not in virtue, not in beauty of character, not in greatness of mind, not in heavenly wisdom, not in merit before God; oh! no; in all this she felt herself infinitely her inferior. But as a child of God, as heiress to an eternal kingdom, as a living member of the body of

Christ, as admitted to a share in all His mercies, to all the price of His redemption, as a new creature in Him, she felt that she was equal to Miriam, and with happy glee she told her so.

Never had she been so proud of splendid garment as she was of the white robe, which she had received as she came out of the font, and which she had to wear for eight days.

But a merciful Father knows how to blend our joys and sorrows, and sends us the latter when He has best prepared us for them. In that warm embrace which we have mentioned, she for the first time noticed the shortened breath, and heaving chest of her dear sister. She would not dwell upon it in her thoughts, but sent to beg Dionysius to come on the morrow. That evening they all kept their Easter banquet together; and Fabiola felt happy to preside at Miriam's side over a table, at which reclined or sat her own converted slaves, and those of Agnes's household, all of whom she had retained. She never remembered having enjoyed so delightful a supper.

Early next morning, Miriam called Fabiola to her side, and with a fond, caressing manner, which she had never before displayed, said to her:

"My dear sister, what will you do, when I have left you?"

Poor Fabiola was overpowered with grief. "Are you then going to leave me? I had hoped we should live for ever as sisters together. But if you wish to leave Rome, may I not accompany you, at least to nurse you, to serve you?"

Miriam smiled, but a tear was in her eye, as taking her sister's hand, she pointed up towards heaven. Fabiola understood her, and said: "O, no, no, dearest sister. Pray to God, who will refuse you nothing, that I may not lose you. It is selfish, I know; but what can I do without you? And now too, that I have learnt how much they who reign with Christ can do for us by intercession, I will pray to Agnes* and Sebastian, to interpose for me, and avert so great a calamity.

"Do get well; I am sure there is nothing serious in the matter; the warm weather, and the genial climate of Campania, will soon restore you. We will sit again together by the spring, and talk over better things than philosophy."

Miriam shook her head, not mournfully, but cheerfully, as she replied:

"Do not flatter yourself, dearest; God has spared me till I should see this happy day. But His hand is on me now for death, as it has been hitherto for life; and I hail it with joy. I know too well the number of my days."

"Oh! let it not be so soon!" sobbed out Fabiola.

"Not while you have on your white garment, dear sister," answered Miriam. "I know you would wish to mourn for me; but I would not rob you of one hour of your mystic whiteness."

Dionysius came, and saw a great change in his patient, whom he had not visited for some time. It was as he had feared it might be. The insidious point of the dagger had curled round the bone, and injured the pleura; and phthisis

---

* * Agnæ sepulchrum est Romulea in domo,
Fortis puellæ, martyris inclitæ.
Conspectu in ipso condita turrium
Servat salutem virgo Quiritum :
Necnon et ipsos protegit advenas,
Puro ac fideli pectore supplices."
                             Prudentius.

"The tomb of Agnes graces Rome,
A maiden brave, a martyr great.
Resting in sight of bastioned gate,
From harm the virgin shields her home;
Nor to the stranger help denies,
If sought with pure and faithful sighs."

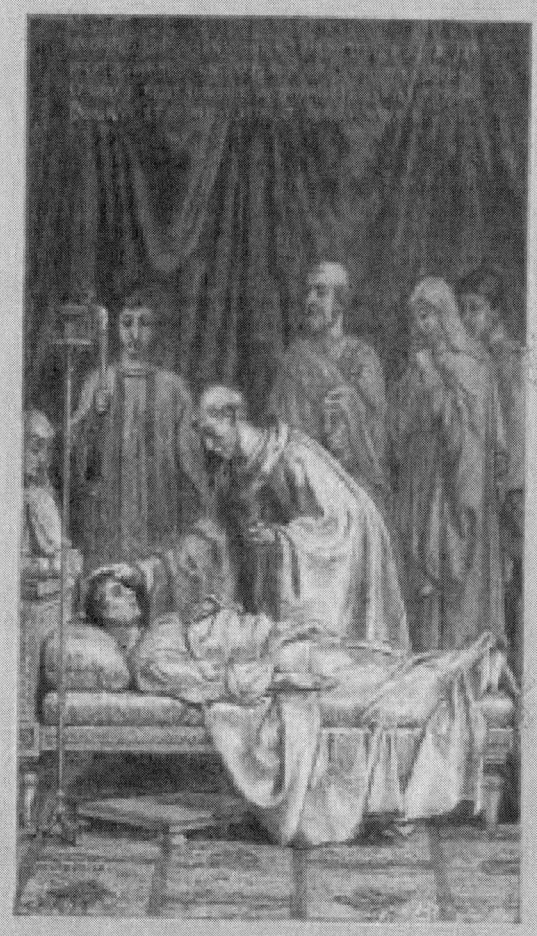

Administering the Sacrament of Extreme Unction, in the Early Ages of the Church.

had rapidly set in. He confirmed Miriam's most serious anticipations.

Fabiola went to pray for resignation at the sepulchre of Agnes; she prayed long and fervently, and with many tears, then returned.

"Sister," she said with firmness, "God's will be done, I am ready to resign even you to Him. Now, tell me, I entreat you, what would you have me do, after you are taken from me?"

Miriam looked up to heaven, and answered, "Lay my body at the feet of Agnes, and remain to watch over us, to pray to her, and for me; until a stranger shall arrive from the East, the bearer of good tidings."

On the Sunday following, "Sunday of the white garments," Dionysius celebrated, by special permission, the sacred mysteries in Miriam's room, and administered to her the most holy Communion, as her viaticum. This private celebration, as we know from St. Augustine and others was not a rare privilege.[*] Afterwards, he anointed her with oil, accompanied by prayer, the last Sacrament which the Church bestows.

Fabiola and the household who had attended these solemn rites, with tears and prayers, now descended into the crypt, and after the divine offices returned to Miriam in their darker raiment.

"The hour is come," said she, taking Fabiola's hand. "Forgive me, if I have been wanting in duty to you, and in good example."

This was more than Fabiola could stand, and she burst into tears. Miriam soothed her, and said, "Put to my lips the sign of salvation when I can speak no more; and, good Dionysius, remember me at God's altar when I am departed."

---

[*] St. Ambrose said Mass in the house of a lady beyond the Tiber. (Paulinus, in his Life, tom. ii. Oper. ed. Bened.) St. Augustine mentions a priest's saying Mass in a house supposed to be infested with evil spirits. De Civ. D. lib. xxii. c. 8.

He prayed at her side, and she replied, till at length her voice failed her. But her lips moved, and she pressed them on the cross presented to her. She looked serene and joyful, till at length raising her hand to her forehead, then bringing it to her breast, it fell dead there, in making the saving sign. A smile passed over her face, and she expired, as thousands of Christ's children have expired since.

Fabiola mourned much over her; but this time she mourned as they do who have hope.

Portrait of Our Saviour, from the Catacomb of St. Calixtus.

Constantine, the first Christian Emperor, after a medal of the time.

Part Third.—Victory.

CHAPTER I.

THE STRANGER FROM THE EAST.

WE appear to ourselves to be walking in solitude. One by one, those whose words and actions, and even thoughts, have hitherto accompanied and sustained us, have dropped off, and the prospect around looks very dreary. But is all this unnatural? We have been describing not an ordinary period of peace and every-day life, but one of warfare, strife, and battle. Is it unnatural that the bravest, the most heroic, should have fallen thick around us? We have been reviving the memory of the cruellest persecution which the Church ever suffered, when it was proposed to erect a column bearing the inscription that the Christian name had been extinguished. Is it strange that the holiest and purest should have been the earliest to be crowned?

And yet the Church of Christ has still to sustain many

years of sharper persecution than we have described. A succession of tyrants and oppressors kept up the fearful war upon her, without intermission, in one part of the world or another for twenty years, even after Constantine had checked it

Diocletian.
After a medal in the Cabinet of France.

wherever his power reached. Diocletian, Galerius, Maximinus, and Licinius in the East, Maximian and Maxentius in the West, allowed no rest to the Christians under their several dominions. Like one of those rolling storms which go over half the world, visiting various countries with their ravaging energy, while their gloomy foreboding or sullen wake simultaneously overshadow them all, so did this persecution wreak its fury first on one country, then on another, destroying every thing Christian, passing from Italy to Africa, from Upper Asia to

Licinius.
From a Gold Medal in the French Collection.

Maxentius.
From a Silver Medal in the French Collection.

Galerius Maximinus.
From a Silver Medal in the French Collection.

Palestine, Egypt, and then back to Armenia, while it left no place in actual peace, but hung like a blighting storm-cloud over the entire empire.

And yet the Church increased, prospered, and defied this world of sin. Pontiff stepped after Pontiff at once upon the footstool of the papal throne and upon the scaffold; councils were held in the dark halls of the catacombs; bishops came to Rome, at risk of their lives, to consult the successor of St. Peter; letters were exchanged between Churches far distant and the supreme Ruler of Christendom, and between different Churches, full of sympathy, encouragement and affection; bishop succeeded bishop in his see, and ordained priests and other ministers to take the place of the fallen, and be a mark set upon the bulwarks of the city for the enemy's aim; and the work of Christ's imperishable kingdom went on without interruption, and without fear of extinction.

Indeed it was in the midst of all these alarms and conflicts, that the foundations were being laid of a mighty system, destined to produce stupendous effects in after ages. The persecution drove many from the cities, into the deserts of Egypt, where the monastic state grew up, so as to make "the wilderness rejoice and flourish like the lily bud forth and blossom, and rejoice with joy and praise."* And so, when Diocletian had been degraded from the purple, and had died a peevish destitute old man, and Galerius had been eaten up alive by ulcers and worms, and had acknowledged, by public edict, the failure of his attempts, and Maximian Herculeus had strangled himself, and Maxentius had perished in the Tiber, and Maximinus had expired amidst tortures inflicted by Divine justice equal to any he had inflicted on Christians, his very eyes having started from their sockets, and Licinius had been put to death by Constantine; the spouse of Christ, whom they had all conspired to destroy, stood young and blooming as ever, about to enter into her great career of universal diffusion and rule.

It was in the year 313 that Constantine, having defeated Maxentius, gave full liberty to the Church. Even if ancient writers had not described it, we may imagine the joy and gratitude of the poor Christians on this great change. It was like the coming forth, and tearful though happy greeting, of the inhabitants of a city decimated by plague, when proclamation has gone forth that the infection has ceased. For here, after ten years of separation and concealment, when families could scarcely meet in the cemeteries nearest to them, many

* Isaias xxxv. 1, 2.

did not know who among friends or kinsfolk had fallen victims, or who might yet survive. Timid at first, and then more courageous, they ventured forth; soon the places of old assembly, which children born in the last ten years had not seen, were cleansed, or repaired, refitted and reconciled,* and opened to public, and now fearless, worship.

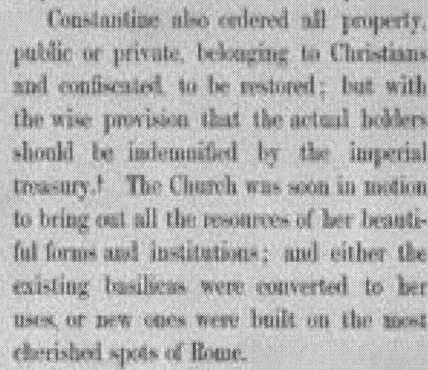

Constantine also ordered all property, public or private, belonging to Christians and confiscated, to be restored; but with the wise provision that the actual holders should be indemnified by the imperial treasury.† The Church was soon in motion to bring out all the resources of her beautiful forms and institutions; and either the existing basilicas were converted to her uses, or new ones were built on the most cherished spots of Rome.

Let not the reader fear that we are going to lead him forward into a long history. This will belong to some one better qualified, for the task of unfolding the grandeur and charms of free and unfettered Christianity. We have only to show the land of promise from above, spread like an inviting paradise before our feet; we are not the Josue that must lead others in. The little that we have to add in this brief third part of our humble book, is barely what is necessary for its completion.

We will then suppose ourselves arrived at the year 318, fifteen years after our last scene of death. Time and permanent laws have given security to the Christian religion, and the Church is likewise more fully establishing her organization.

---

* The ceremony employed after desecration.
† Euseb. H. E. lib. x. c. 5.

A Marriage in the Early Ages of the Church.

Many who on the return of peace had hung down their heads, having by some act of weak condescension escaped death, had by this time expiated their fall by penance; and now and then an aged stranger would be saluted reverently by the passers-by, when they saw that his right eye had been burned out, or his hand mutilated; or when his halting gait showed that the tendons of the knee had been severed, in the late persecution, for Christ's sake.*

If at this period our friendly reader will follow us out of the Nomentan gate, to the valley with which he is already acquainted, he will find sad havoc among the beautiful trees and flower-beds of Fabiola's villa. Scaffold-poles are standing up in place of the first; bricks, marbles, and columns lie upon the latter. Constantia, the daughter of Constantine, had prayed at St. Agnes's tomb, when not yet a Christian, to beg the cure of a virulent ulcer, had been refreshed by a vision, and completely cured. Being now baptized, she was repaying her debt of gratitude, by building over her tomb her beautiful basilica. Still the faithful had access to the crypt in which she was buried; and great was the concourse of pilgrims, that came from all parts of the world.

One afternoon, when Fabiola returned from the city to her villa, after spending the day in attending to the sick, in an hospital established in her own house, the *fossor*, who had charge of the cemetery, met her with an air of great interest, and no small excitement, and said:

"Madam, I sincerely believe that the stranger from the East, whom you have so long expected, is arrived."

Fabiola, who had ever treasured up the dying words of Miriam, eagerly asked, "Where is he?"

"He is gone again," was the reply.

---

* In the East, some governors, wearied with wholesale murders, adopted this more merciful way of treating Christians towards the end of the persecution. See Eusebius.

The lady's countenance fell. "But how," she asked again, "do you know it was he?" The excavator replied:

"In the course of the morning I noticed, among the crowd, a man not yet fifty, but worn by mortification and sorrow, to premature old age. His hair was nearly grey, as was his long beard. His dress was eastern, and he wore the cloak which the monks from that country usually do. When he came before the tomb of Agnes, he flung himself upon the pavement with such a passion of tears, such groans, such sobs, as moved all around to compassion. Many approached him, and whispered, 'Brother, thou art in great distress; weep not so, the saint is merciful.' Others said to him, 'We will all pray for thee, fear not.'* But he seemed to be beyond comfort. I thought to myself, surely in the presence of so gentle and kind a saint, none ought to be thus disconsolate or heart-broken, except only one man."

"Go on, go on," broke in Fabiola; "what did he next?"

"After a long time," continued the fossor, "he arose, and drawing from his bosom a most beautiful and sparkling ring, he laid it on her tomb. I thought I had seen it before, many years ago."

"And then?"

"Turning round he saw me, and recognized my dress. He approached me, and I could feel him trembling, as, without looking in my face, he timidly asked me: 'Brother, knowest thou if there lie buried any where here about a maiden from Syria, called Miriam?' I pointed silently to the tomb. After a pause of great pain to himself, so agitated now that his voice faltered, he asked me again: 'Knowest thou, brother, of what she died?' 'Of consumption,' I replied. 'Thank God!' he ejaculated, with the sigh of relieved anguish, and fell prostrate on the ground. Here too he moaned and cried

* This scene is described from reality.

for more than an hour, then, approaching the tomb, affectionately kissed its cover, and retired."

"It is he, Torquatus, it is he!" warmly exclaimed Fabiola; "why did you not detain him?"

"I durst not, lady; after I had once seen his face, I had not courage to meet his eye. But I am sure he will return again; for he went towards the city."

"He must be found," concluded Fabiola. "Dear Miriam, thou hadst, then, this consoling foresight in death!"

Noe and the Ark, as a symbol of the Church, from a picture in the Catacombs.

CHAPTER II.

THE STRANGER IN ROME.

EARLY next morning, the pilgrim was passing through the Forum, when he saw a group of persons gathered round one whom they were evidently teasing. He would have paid but little attention to such a scene in a public thoroughfare, had not his ear caught a name familiar to it. He therefore drew nigh. In the centre was a man, younger than himself; but if *he* looked older than he was, from being wan and attenuated, the other did so much more from being the very contrary. He was bald and bloated, with a face swelled, and red, and covered with blotches and boils. A drunken cunning swam in his eye, and his gait and tone were those of a man habitually intoxicated. His clothes were dirty, and his whole person neglected.

"Ay, ay, Corvinus," one youth was saying to him, "won't you get your deserts, now? Have you not heard that Constantine is coming this year to Rome, and don't you think the Christians will have their turn about now?"

"Not they," answered the man we have described, "they have not the pluck for it. I remember we feared it, when Constantine published his first edict, after the death of Maxentius, about liberty for the Christians, but next year he put us out of fear, by declaring all religions to be equally permitted."*

"That is all very well, as a general rule," interposed another, determined farther to plague him; "but is it not supposed that he is going to look up those who took an active part in the late persecution, and have the *lex talionis*† executed on them; stripe for stripe, burning for burning, and wild beast for wild beast?"

"Who says so?" asked Corvinus turning pale.

"Why, it would surely be very natural," said one.

"And very just," added another.

"Oh, never mind," said Corvinus, "they will always let one off for turning Christian. And, I am sure, I would turn any thing, rather than stand—"

"Where Pancratius stood," interposed a third, more malicious.

"Hold your tongue," broke out the drunkard, with a tone of positive rage. "Mention his name again, if you dare!" And he raised his fist, and looked furiously at the speaker.

"Ay, because he told you how you were to die," shouted the youngster, running away. "Heigh! Heigh! a panther here for Corvinus!"

All ran away before the human beast, now lashed into fury, more than they would have done from the wild one of the desert. He cursed them, and threw stones after them.

The pilgrim, from a short distance, watched the close of the scene, then went on. Corvinus moved slowly along the same road, that which led towards the Lateran basilica, now the Cathedral of Rome. Suddenly a sharp growl was heard,

---

* Eusebius, *ubi sup.*

† The law of retaliation, such as was prescribed also in the Mosaic law, "an eye for an eye, a tooth for a tooth," &c.

and with it a piercing shriek. As they were passing by the Coliseum, near the dens of the wild beasts, which were prepared for combats among themselves, on occasion of the emperor's visit, Corvinus, impelled by the morbid curiosity natural to persons who consider themselves victims of some fatality, connected with a particular object, approached the cage in which a splendid panther was kept. He went close to the bars, and provoked the animal, by gestures and words; saying: "Very likely, indeed, that you are to be the death of me! You are very safe in your den." In that instant, the enraged animal made a spring at him, and through the wide bars of the den, caught his neck and throat in its fangs, and inflicted a frightful lacerated wound.

The wretched man was picked up, and carried to his lodgings, not far off. The stranger followed him, and found them mean, dirty, and uncomfortable in the extreme; with only an old and decrepit slave, apparently as sottish as his master, to attend him. The stranger sent him out to procure a surgeon, who was long in coming; and, in the meantime, did his best to stanch the blood.

While he was so occupied, Corvinus fixed his eyes upon him with a look of one delirious, or demented.

"Do you know me?" asked the pilgrim, soothingly.

"Know you? No—yes. Let me see—Ha! the fox! my fox! Do you remember our hunting together those hateful Christians. Where have you been all this time? How many of them have you caught?" And he laughed outrageously.

"Peace, peace, Corvinus," replied the other. "You must be very quiet, or there is no hope for you. Besides, I do not wish you to allude to those times; for I am myself now a Christian."

"You a Christian?" broke out Corvinus savagely. "You who have shed more of their best blood than any man? Have you been forgiven for all this? Or have you slept quietly upon it? Have no furies lashed you at night? no phantoms haunted you? no viper sucked your heart? If so, tell me how you have got rid of them all, that I may do the same. If not, they will come, they will come! Vengeance and fury! why should they not have tormented you as much as me?"

"Silence, Corvinus; I have suffered as you have. But I have found the remedy, and will make it known to you, as soon as the physician has seen you, for he is approaching."

The doctor saw him, dressed the wound, but gave little hope of recovery, especially in a patient whose very blood was tainted by intemperance.

The stranger now resumed his seat beside him, and spoke of the mercy of God, and His readiness to forgive the worst of sinners; whereof he himself was a living proof. The unhappy man seemed to be in a sort of stupor; if he listened, not comprehending what was said. At length his kind instructor, having expounded to him the fundamental mysteries of Christianity, in hope, rather than certainty, of being attended to, went on to say:

"And now, Corvinus, you will ask me, how is forgiveness to be applied to one who believes all this? It is by Baptism, by being born again of water and the Holy Ghost."

"What?" exclaimed the sick man loathingly.

"By being washed in the laver of regenerating water."

He was interrupted by a convulsive growl rather than a moan. "Water! water! no water for me! Take it away!" And a strong spasm seized the patient's throat.

His attendant was alarmed, but sought to calm him. "Think not," he said, "that you are to be taken hence in your present fever, and to be plunged into *water*" (the sick man shuddered, and moaned); "in clinical baptism,* a few drops suffice, not more than is in this pitcher." And he showed him the water in a small vessel. At the sight of it, the patient writhed and foamed at the mouth, and was shaken by a violent convulsion. The sounds that proceeded from him, resembled a howl from a wild beast, more than any utterance of human lips.

The pilgrim saw at once that hydrophobia, with all its horrible symptoms, had come upon the patient, from the bite of the enraged animal. It was with difficulty that he and the servant could hold him down at times. Occasionally he broke out into frightful paroxysms of blasphemous violence against God and man. And then, when this subsided, he would go on moaning thus;

"Water they want to give me! water! water! none for me! It is fire! fire! that I have, and that is my portion. I am already on fire, within, without! Look how it comes creeping up, all round me, it advances every moment nearer and nearer!" And he beat off the fancied flame with his hands on either side of his bed, and he blew at it round his head. Then turning towards his sorrowful attendants, he would say, "why don't you put it out? you see it is already burning me."

Thus passed the dreary day, and thus came the dismal night, when the fever increased, and with it the delirium, and the violent accesses of fury, though the body was sinking. At length he raised himself up in bed, and looking with half-glazed eyes straight before him, he exclaimed in a voice choked with bitter rage:

"Away, Pancratius, begone! Thou hast glared on me long enough. Keep back thy panther! Hold it fast; it

* Clinical baptism, or that of persons confined to their beds was administered by pouring or sprinkling the water on the head. See Bingham, book xi. c. 11.

is going to fly at my throat. It comes! Oh!" And with a convulsive grasp, as if pulling the beast from off his throat, he plucked away the bandage from his wound. A gush of blood poured over him, and he fell back, a hideous corpse, upon the bed.

His friend saw how unrepenting persecutors died.

The Sacrifice of Abraham, from a picture in the Catacombs.

CHAPTER III.

AND LAST.

THE next morning, the pilgrim proceeded to discharge the business which had been interfered with by the circumstances related in the preceding chapter. He might have been first seen busily employed inquiring after some one about the Januses in the Forum. At length, the person was found; and the two walked towards a dirty little office under the Capitol, on the ascent called the *Clivus Asyli*. Old musty books were brought out, and searched column after column, till they came to the date of the "Consuls Dioclesian Augustus, the eighth time, and Maximian Herculeus Augustus, the seventh time."* Here they found sundry entries, with reference to certain documents. A roll of mouldy parchments of that date was produced, docketed as referred to, and the number corresponding to the entries was drawn out, and examined. The result of the investigation seemed perfectly satisfactory to both parties.

"It is the first time in my life," said the owner of the den, "that I ever knew a person who had got clear off, come back, after fifteen years, to inquire after his debts. A Christian, I presume, sir?"

* A. D. 305.

"Certainly, by God's mercy."

"I thought as much; good morning, sir. I shall be happy to accommodate you at any time, at as reasonable rates as my father Ephraim, now with Abraham. A great fool that for his pains, I must say, begging his pardon," he added, when the stranger was out of hearing.

With a decided step and a brighter countenance than he had yet displayed, he went straight to the villa on the Nomentan way; and after again paying his devotions in the crypt, but with a lighter heart, he at once addressed the fossor, as if they had never been parted: "Torquatus, can I speak with the Lady Fabiola?"

"Certainly," answered the other; "come this way."

Neither alluded, as they went along, to old times, nor to the intermediate history of either. There seemed to be an understanding, instinctive to both, that all the past was to be obliterated before men, as they hoped it was before God. Fabiola had remained at home that and the preceding day, in hopes of the stranger's return. She was seated in the garden close to a fountain, when Torquatus, pointing to her, retired.

She rose, as she saw the long-expected visitor approach, and an indescribable emotion thrilled through her, when she found herself standing in his presence.

"Madam," he said, in a tone of deep humility and earnest simplicity. "I should never have presumed to present myself before you, had not an obligation of justice, as well as many of gratitude, obliged me."

"Orontius," she replied,—"is this the name by which I must address you?" (he signified his assent) "you can have no obligations towards me, except that which our great Apostle charges on us, that we love one another."

"I know you feel so. And therefore I would not have pretended, unworthy as I am, to intrude upon you for any lower motive than one of strict duty. I know what gratitude I owe you for the kindness and affection lavished upon one now dearer to me than any sister can be on earth, and how you discharged towards her the offices of love which I had neglected."

"And thereby sent her to me," interposed Fabiola, "to be my angel of life. Remember, Orontius, that Joseph was sold by his brethren, only that he might save his race."

"You are too good, indeed, towards one so worthless," resumed the pilgrim; "but I will not thank you for your kindness to another who has repaid you so richly. Only this morning I have learnt your mercy to one who could have no claim upon you."

"I do not understand you," observed Fabiola.

"Then I will tell you all plainly," rejoined Orontius. "I have now been for many years a member of one of those communities in Palestine, of men who live separated from the world in desert places, dividing their day, and even their night, between singing the Divine praises, contemplation, and the labor of their hands. Severe penance for our past transgressions, fasting, mourning, and prayer form the great duty of our penitential state. Have you heard of such men here?"

"The fame of holy Paul and Anthony is as great in the West as in the East," replied the lady.

"It is with the greatest disciple of the latter that I have lived, supported by his great example, and the consolation he has given me. But one thought troubled me, and prevented my feeling complete assurance of safety even after years of expiation. Before I left Rome I had contracted a heavy debt, which must have been accumulating at a frightful rate of interest, till it had reached an overwhelming amount. Yet it was an obligation deliberately contracted, and not to be justly evaded. I was a poor cenobite,* barely living on the produce of the few palm-leaf mats that I could weave, and the scanty herbs that would grow in the sand. How could I discharge my obligations?

"Only one means remained. I could give myself up to my creditor as a slave, to labor for him and endure his blows and scornful reproaches in patience, or to be sold by him for my value, for I am yet strong. In either case, I should have had my Saviour's example to cheer and support me. At any rate, I should have given up all that I had—myself.

"I went this morning to the Forum, found my creditor's son, examined his accounts, and found that you had discharged my debt in full. I am, therefore, your bondsman, Lady Fabiola, instead of the Jew's." And he knelt humbly at her feet.

"Rise, rise," said Fabiola, turning away her weeping eyes. "You are no bondsman of mine, but a dear brother in our common Lord."

Then sitting down with him, she said: "Orontius, I have a great favor to ask from you. Give me some account of how you were brought to that life, which you have so generously embraced."

"I will obey you as briefly as possible. I fled, as you know, one sorrowful night from Rome, accompanied by a man"—his voice choked him.

"I know, I know whom you mean,—Eurotas," interrupted Fabiola.

"The same, the curse of our house, the author of all mine, and my dear sister's sufferings. We had to charter a vessel at great expense from Brundusium, whence we sailed for Cyprus. We attempted commerce and various speculations, but all failed. There was manifestly a curse on all that we undertook. Our means melted away, and we were obliged to

* The religious who lived in community, or common life, were so called.

seek some other country. We crossed over to Palestine, and settled for a while at Gaza. Very soon we were reduced to distress; every body shunned us, we knew not why; but my conscience told me that the mark of Cain was on my brow."

Orontius paused and wept for a time, then went on:

"At length, when all was exhausted, and nothing remained but a few jewels, of considerable price indeed, but with which, I knew not why, Eurotas would not part, he urged me to take up the odious office of denouncing Christians; for a furious persecution was breaking out. For the first time in my life I rebelled against his commands, and refused to obey. One day he asked me to walk out of the gates; we wandered far, till we came to a delightful spot in the midst of the desert. It was a narrow dell, covered with verdure, and shaded by palm-trees; a little clear stream ran down, issuing from a spring in a rock at the head of the valley. In this rock we saw grottoes and caverns; but the place seemed uninhabited. Not a sound could be heard but the bubbling of the water.

"We sat down to rest, when Eurotas addressed me in a fearful speech. The time was come, he told me, when we must both fulfil the dreadful resolution he had taken, that we must not survive the ruin of our family. Here we must both die; the wild beasts would consume our bodies, and no one would know the end of its last representatives.

"So saying, he drew forth two small flasks of unequal sizes, handed me the larger one, and swallowed the contents of the smaller.

"I refused to take it, and even reproached him for the difference of our doses; but he replied that he was old, and I young; and that they were proportioned to our respective strengths. I still refused, having no wish to die. But a sort of demoniacal fury seemed to come over him; he seized me with a giant's grasp, as I sat on the ground, threw me on my back, and exclaiming, 'We must both perish together,' forcibly poured the contents of the phial, without sparing me a drop, down my throat.

"In an instant, I was unconscious; and remained so, till I awoke in a cavern, and faintly called for drink. A venerable old man, with a white beard, put a wooden bowl of water to my lips. 'Where is Eurotas?' I asked. 'Is that your companion?' inquired the old monk. 'Yes,' I answered. 'He is dead,' was the reply. I know not by what fatality this had happened; but I bless God with all my heart, for having spared me.

"That old man was Hilarion, a native of Gaza, who, having spent many years with the holy Anthony in Egypt, had that year* returned to establish the cenobitic and eremitical life in his own country, and had already collected several disciples. They lived in the caves hard by, and took their refection under the shade of those palms, and softened their dry food in the water of that fountain.

"Their kindness to me, their cheerful piety, their holy lives, won on me as I recovered. I saw the religion which I had persecuted in a sublime form; and rapidly recalled to mind the instructions of my dear mother, and the example of my sister; so that yielding to grace, I bewailed my sins at the feet of God's minister,† and received baptism on Easter-eve."

"Then we are doubly brethren, nay twin children of the Church; for I was born to eternal life, also, on that day. But what do you intend to do now?"

"Set out this evening on my return. I have accomplished the two objects of my journey. The first was to cancel my debt; my second was to lay an offering on the shrine of Agnes. You will remember," he added, smiling, "that your good

---

* A. D. 303.

† Confession of sins in private was made before baptism. See Bingham, *Origines*, b. xi. ch. viii. § 14.

father unintentionally deceived me into the idea, that she coveted the jewels I displayed. Fool that I was! But I resolved, after my conversion, that she should possess the best that remained in Eurotas's keeping; so I brought it to her."

"But have you means for your journey?" asked the lady, timidly.

"Abundant," he replied, "in the charity of the faithful. I have letters from the Bishop of Gaza, which procure me every where sustenance and lodging; but I will accept from you a cup of water and a morsel of bread, in the name of a disciple."

They rose, and were advancing towards the house, when a woman rushed madly through the shrubs, and fell at their feet, exclaiming: "Oh, save me! dear mistress, save me! He is pursuing me, to kill me!"

Fabiola recognized, in the poor creature, her former slave Jubala; but her hair was grizzly and dishevelled, and her whole aspect bespoke abject misery. She asked whom she meant.

"My husband," she replied; "long has he been harsh and cruel, but to-day he is more brutal than usual. Oh, save me from him!"

"There is no danger here," replied the lady; "but I fear, Jubala, you are far from happy. I have not seen you for a long, long time."

"No, dear lady, why should I come to tell you of all my woes? Oh! why did I ever leave you and your house, where I ought to have been so happy? I might then with you, and Graja, and good old departed Euphrosyne, have learnt to be good myself, and have embraced Christianity!"

"What, have you really been thinking of this, Jubala?"

"For a long time, lady, in my sorrows and remorse. For

I have seen how happy Christians are, even those who have been as wicked as myself. And because I hinted this to my husband this morning, he has beaten me, and threatened to take my life. But, thank God, I have been making myself acquainted with Christian doctrines, through the teaching of a friend."

"How long has this bad treatment gone on, Jubala?" asked Orontius, who had heard of it from his uncle.

"Ever," she replied, "since soon after marriage, I told him of an offer made to me previously, by a dark foreigner, named Eurotas. Oh! he was indeed a wicked man, a man of black passions and remorseless villany. Connected with him, is my most racking recollection."

"How was that?" asked Orontius, with eager curiosity.

"Why, when he was leaving Rome, he asked me to prepare for him two narcotic potions; one for any enemy, he said, should he be taken prisoner. This was to be certainly fatal; another had to suspend consciousness for a few hours only, should he require it for himself.

"When he came for them, I was just going to explain to him, that, contrary to appearances, the small phial contained a fatally concentrated poison, and the large one a more diluted and weaker dose. But my husband came in at the moment, and in a fit of jealousy thrust me from the room. I fear some mistake may have been committed, and that unintentional death may have ensued."

Fabiola and Orontius looked at one another in silence, wondering at the just dispensations of Providence; when they were aroused by a shriek from the woman. They were horrified at seeing an arrow quivering in her bosom. As Fabiola supported her, Orontius, looking behind him, caught a glimpse of a black face grinning hideously through the fence. In the next moment a Numidian was seen flying away on his horse, with his bow bent, Parthian-wise over his shoulder, ready for any pursuer. The arrow had passed, unobserved, between Orontius and the lady.

"Jubala," asked Fabiola, "dost thou wish to die a Christian?"

"Most earnestly," she replied.

"Dost thou believe in One God in Three Persons?"

"I firmly believe in all the Christian Church teaches."

"And in Jesus Christ, who was born and died for our sins?"

"Yes, in all that you believe." The reply was more faint.

"Make haste, make haste, Orontius," cried Fabiola, pointing to the fountain.

He was already at its basin, filling full his two hands, and coming instantly, poured their contents on the head of the poor African, pronouncing the words of baptism; and, as she expired, the water of regeneration mingled with her blood of expiation.

After this distressing, yet consoling, scene, they entered the house, and instructed Torquatus about the burial to be given to this doubly-baptized convert.

Orontius was struck with the simple neatness of the house, so strongly contrasting with the luxurious splendor of Fabiola's former dwelling. But suddenly his attention was arrested, in a small inner room, by a splendid shrine or casket, set with jewels, but with an embroidered curtain before it, so as to allow only the frame of it to be seen. Approaching nearer, he read inscribed on it:

"THE BLOOD OF THE BLESSED MIRIAM, SHED BY CRUEL HANDS!"

Orontius turned deadly pale; then changed to a deep crimson; and almost staggered.

Fabiola saw this, and going up to him kindly and frankly, placed her hand upon his arm, and mildly said to him:

"Orontius, there is that within, which may well make us both blush deeply, but not therefore despond."

So saying she drew aside the curtain, and Orontius saw within a crystal plate, the embroidered scarf so much connected with his own, and his sister's history. Upon it were lying two sharp weapons, the points of both which were rusted with blood. In one he recognized his own dagger; the other appeared to him like one of those instruments of female vengeance, with which he knew heathen ladies punished their attendant slaves.

"We have both," said Fabiola, "unintentionally inflicted a wound, and shed the blood of her, whom now we honor as a sister in heaven. But for my part, from the day when I did so, and gave her occasion to display her virtue, I date the dawn of grace upon my soul. What say you, Orontius?"

"That I, likewise, from the instant that I so misused her, and led to her exhibition of such Christian heroism, began to feel the hand of God upon me, that has led me to repentance and forgiveness."

"It is thus ever," concluded Fabiola. "The example of our Lord has made the martyrs; and the example of the martyrs leads us upwards to Him. Their blood softens our hearts; His alone cleanses our souls. Theirs pleads for mercy; His bestows it.

"May the Church, in her days of peace and of victories, never forget what she owes to the age of her martyrs. As for us two, we are indebted to it for our spiritual lives. May many, who will only read of it, draw from it the same mercy and grace!"

They knelt down, and prayed long together silently before the shrine.

They then parted, to meet no more.

After a few years, spent by Orontius in penitential

fervor, a green mound by the palms, in the little dell near Gaza, marked the spot where he slept the sleep of the just.

And after many years of charity and holiness, Fabiola withdrew to rest in peace, in company with Agnes and Miriam.

Made in the USA
Middletown, DE
15 July 2025